Author: Dr. Lloyd W. Benjamin III, Indiana State University

Additional Contributors: Kevin L. Runion and Bryan S. Duncan

Design & Editorial Direction: Emerge Marketing Solutions, LLC

Copyright © 2020 by Indiana State University

All rights reserved including the right of reproduction in whole or in part in any form or format except as otherwise permitted under sections 107 or 109 of the 1976 United States Copyright Act without either the prior permission of the Publisher, or authorization through payment of the appropriate per-copy fee to the Copyright Clearance Center, 222 Rosewood Drive, Danvers, MA 09123 (978) 750-8400, fax (878) 750-4744. Requests to the Publisher should be submitted to University Marketing, Indiana State University, Terre Haute, IN 47809, (812) 237-3773.

Photographs: Wabash Valley Visions & Voices
Indiana State University
Special Collections: University Archives
University Marketing (Indiana State University)
Vigo County Historical Society and Museum
Vigo County Public Library

Library of Congress-in-Publication Data

(Author) Lloyd W. Benjamin III

(Title) Indiana State University: Building a Legacy

Published in the United States by Indiana State University, Terre Haute, Indiana 47809

First Edition
ISBN: 978-0-578-64286-4

INDIANA STATE UNIVERSITY
BUILDING A LEGACY
1865-2019

DR. LLOYD W. BENJAMIN III

Indiana State University Building a Legacy

TABLE OF CONTENTS

Foreword – President Deborah J. Curtis, Ph.D.	3
Acknowledgments – Dr. Lloyd W. Benjamin III, Ph.D.	5
Introduction	7
The Beginning	8
Chapter 1 – William A. Jones *(1869-1879)*	12
Chapter 2 – George P. Brown *(1879-1885)*	20
Chapter 3 – William W. Parsons *(1885-1921)*	26
Chapter 4 – Linnaeus N. Hines *(1921-1933)*	48
Chapter 5 – Ralph N. Tirey *(1934-1953)*	70
Chapter 6 – Raleigh W. Holmstedt *(1953-1965)*	92
Chapter 7 – Alan C. Rankin *(1965-1975)*	142
Chapter 8 – Richard G. Landini *(1975-1992)*	178
Chapter 9 – John W. Moore *(1992-2000)*	208
Chapter 10 – Lloyd W. Benjamin III *(2000-2008)*	218
Chapter 11 – Daniel J. Bradley *(2008-2018)*	240
Designing a Legacy: Campus Master Planning	248
Indiana State University Timeline	264
Glossary	286
Index	288
Art Index	291
Photo Credits	292

FOREWORD

In the nearly 150 years since its opening in 1870, the physical growth of campus has mirrored that of Indiana State Normal School (ISNS) into the Indiana State Teachers College, Indiana State College, and finally, Indiana State University (ISU). What started as a single building on a parcel of land donated by the City of Terre Haute has grown into a campus with 72 buildings spread across 250 acres, and seven remote properties, including University Apartments and the Sycamore Outdoor Center (formerly known as the Brazil Field Campus).

As our institution added other educational offerings to its original mission of educating teachers for the common schools of Indiana, it expanded its footprint and built the facilities necessary to accommodate this growth.

As a graduate of ISU, I was thrilled to see the campus' transformation when I returned as a candidate for the twelfth presidency. A great deal of innovative thinking went into beautifying what had been an urban campus with streets running through its interior into a park-like setting with the high-tech facilities necessary for preparing students for today's world.

That work continues with the dedication of the renovated Fine Arts and Commerce Building, a $15 million project, and the reopening of the former Arena Building (the second phase of the $64 million Health and Human Services Building addition and renovation project), both in the fall of 2019. A $50 million upgrade to Hulman Center will be completed in late 2020. Next will be an $18.4 million renovation of Dreiser Hall, which was approved by the Indiana General Assembly for the 2019-21 biennium. In addition to the jobs and economic impact generated by these projects, the $400 million in construction on our campus during the last decade signals a progressive, dynamic university that is well-positioned for the future.

Support for our facilities has come from a variety of sources. Most notably, the Indiana General Assembly has been tremendously supportive of our capital requests. We are so appreciative of the state's support and the strong advocacy for Indiana State that our local legislators have always displayed.

The City of Terre Haute has been a partner throughout our history, beginning with its pledge of $50,000 and land, as stipulated in the 1865 legislation, requiring this of any community vying to become the home of ISNS. When the Normal School's building was

destroyed by fire in 1888, the city again came to our aid, providing funding to rebuild. In addition to multiple examples of financial support, the City of Terre Haute also helped Indiana State develop into a true campus through the approval of various street closings, allowing for our continued growth and creation of such iconic spots as Dede Plaza and Fountain. The city also gifted Fairbanks Library, now Fairbanks Hall, to the university in 1979.

The Federal Government, through the Works Progress Administration, has supported the construction of numerous facilities on campus including Tirey Hall, Fine Arts and Commerce Building, Laboratory School and the original Parsons Hall. Federal funds have also contributed to the Science Building renovation, Myers Technology Center, the Cherry Street Transportation Facility and Federal Hall (the original building and recent renovation.)

Of course, our alumni and friends have left their mark on our campus facilities. Their names are evident across campus – the Hulmans, the Roots, the Dedes, the Scotts, the Gibsons, the Oakley Foundation, and others. We deeply appreciate their support to help transform our campus to better serve our students.

This book provides a wealth of information on our facilities throughout our 150-year history and includes issues, challenges, and opportunities faced by each of the first 11 presidents.

This volume is a great addition to our Sesquicentennial Celebration, marking the 150th anniversary of our founding in 1865 through the 150th anniversary of opening as Indiana State Normal School in 1870. I know you will enjoy reading this thoughtful look at this aspect of our history.

Deborah J. Curtis, Ph.D.
President

ACKNOWLEDGMENTS

I wish to express my gratitude to Indiana State University and its leadership for the support I have received while researching and writing. I had the benefit of a semester-long sabbatical and financial support, allowing me to research and prepare the manuscript. Many have been patient. A project I thought might take three years extended beyond eight.

I am especially appreciative of the support provided by President Curtis, Dianne McKee, Vice President for Finance, and Provost Emeritus, Jack Maynard. I would be remiss if I did not mention additional members of my cabinet when I served as President who contributed to this legacy: Kevin Snyder, Gregg Floyd, and Tom Ramey.

I would like to express my appreciation to my colleagues in the Department of Art and Design, Dr. Alden Cavanaugh, (Chairperson) and Dr. Christopher Olsen (Dean of the College of Arts and Sciences), who have enabled me to commit time to this work. Respectful thanks to Mr. Ewing Miller, architect, whose legacy we experience daily on campus.

I want to express my appreciation to Kevin Runion (Associate Vice President for University Facilities Management emeritus) who has served as collaborator, contributor, and critic. He prepared the timelines for each chapter and was chief author of the Master Planning chapter. Kevin also involved members of his staff who have been important sources of information, specifically Jim Jensen, Scott Tillman, and Bryan Duncan (who completed the Master Planning chapter).

Kevin met frequently with me and our research assistants and, in the manner of a good architect, he asked strategic questions with an eye on keeping things ordered and moving forward. Thanks to Laurie Wojak, who while a student, provided research assistance that yielded volumes of materials that formed the basis for my writing.

Another research contributor, Mike McCormick, Vigo County Historian, has knowledge of Terre Haute and its history that is surpassed only by his passion for story-telling. Mike serves on the board of the Vigo County Historical Society and Museum whose director, Marylee Hagan, also provided assistance with the research and making available helpful information.

Thanks to the Archives staff at Cunningham Memorial Library, lead by Katie Sutrina-Haney, for making available photographs from the Martin collection. Thank you to Robin Crumrin, Dean of Library Services, and her staff and students who helped retrieve a significant quantity of material aiding my research.

My heartfelt appreciation to Greg Goode, who served admirably as liaison to government offices in Indianapolis and Washington during my presidency. He worked connections constantly and the buildings completed during my administration, some completed during President Bradley's presidency, and recent projects now underway during the Curtis presidency owe to his efforts.

President of the Board of Trustees when I was hired was Dr. Charlotte Zietlow. Charlotte was known for posing difficult (but necessary) questions and it is to her credit that she challenged plans to demolish University Hall (former Lab School) and Normal Library (now Normal Hall) during the Landini administration. These have both been recently renovated to a high standard and now serve to connect us with our past.

Santhana Naidu, Associate Vice President for Marketing and Communications, and Tony Campbell, Manager of Multimedia Services, provided invaluable support for this book. Santhana provided financial support and the assistance of his staff. Many of the images in this book owe to the work of Tony and his office. I appreciate his talent and generosity in making these images available.

Thanks to Teresa Exline, Chief of Staff to the President at ISU, for serving on the internal manuscript review committee (with Santhana) and for her advocacy and support for this project. Her only pressing request was that the book be completed before the university Sesquicentennial Celebration was passed – this year.

Many thanks to Shelly Greving and her team at Emerge Marketing Solutions for editing and designing this book. Shelly has been patient, responsive, insightful, and refreshingly creative.

Deepest thanks to my wife, Wieke van der Weijden Benjamin, who often provided encouragement and reminded me of the importance of this work. This is the third major writing endeavor in my professional career where she has read critically and made suggestions to improve the text. She has shared part of her professional life helping me and I am forever grateful. To my children, I trust this book will provide some recompense for the hours I spent writing and not engaging with them and their families.

Lloyd W. Benjamin III, Ph.D.
President Emeritus

INTRODUCTION

Not surprisingly, this book's historical journey begins with the word "university," which stems from the Latin "universitas magistrorum et scholarium" or "community of teachers and scholars."[1] This community of teachers and scholars, in turn, calls to mind matters such as shared attitudes, interests and goals and a certain fellowship among its members.

Another important element in the idea of community is a shared sense of place. For an academic community such as Indiana State University (ISU), its campus, and its provisions for learning and professional growth fulfill that function.

University buildings and grounds are the nexus of transformational experiences. They are also places of great beauty and inspiration. That beauty may stem from nature, or it may exist in the design of campus buildings, landscape, and public spaces. These elements help shape the community's spirit.

Today, ISU is comprised of 72 buildings and it covers 200 acres with an adjacent 300 acres.[2] It is a community of nearly 13,000 students who come from all over the world but with the largest percentage being Hoosiers. The campus is, today, thoughtfully designed, well manicured, and, especially in the spring and fall, engagingly beautiful. Growing from a single Spartan building in 1867 with cows grazing on its grounds to its current size is a remarkable story and is a testament to the vision and energy of generations of faculty, students, staff, administrators, and citizens of Terre Haute.

While we wish to enlighten readers about the campus' external beauty, this book is more than just a study of the formal evolution of the architecture of the campus. It stands as an interpretative record of the history in which each building, monument, spatial organization, or work of art that is part of it, has a unique story to tell.[3] Unknown to many is the fact that Indiana State Normal School was built through the generosity of the people of Terre Haute – an act that determined the course of university-community relations for years to come. While tied to the broader community, a university is also a place where traditions and rituals complete its identity.

Indiana State began as an underfunded teacher preparatory school near the crossroads of America.[4] The core mission was to meet the need for public school teachers in the state, and it continues to fulfill that responsibility. Today, its various colleges offer programs of study for students who wish to gain professional skills; for those who take pleasure in understanding their own and other people's cultures, past and present; and for those who seek to live a life grounded in positive values and beliefs.

Overall, this book seeks to illustrate the development of ISU through the various architectural styles that have defined the campus's buildings through the years. Each individual chapter is intended to play a part in renewing our knowledge of the University's history, as well as that of our forerunners who step by step built this campus. The chapters are arranged chronologically by President beginning with President William A. Jones (1869-79) and continuing to the present day. Each chapter includes a historical overview of a specific presidency, followed by information about the buildings constructed during that presidency. Also included is information about campus master planning, and artwork.

This book is also an addition to the 150th year celebration that provides an opportunity to delineate and comment on events that are a part of our history.

A vast amount of historically-relevant information, more than could be accommodated in a volume of this size, was collected and studied while conducting the research for this project. A website is under consideration. The information is copious, but I believe by creating this site new material can be added regularly so that future scholars or interested persons will be able to "dig" as deeply as they desire into the architectural history of Indiana State University and continue to build its legacy.

"It is our hope that this book may come into the hands of those who have gone forth … and that they may find again that sense of comradeship which was theirs back in their student days …"[5] ■

Introduction

THE BEGINNING

Terre Haute was a dynamic city during the second half of the 19th century. The population grew at a steady rate from about 4,000 residents in 1850 to over 36,000 by 1900. One of the most significant factors influencing its growth was its strategic position as a transportation hub located on the Wabash River, the National Road, and the Wabash-Erie Canal. Rail increasingly played an important role in its growth. Indicative of its increased prosperity, Terre Haute hosted the 15th annual state fair at Memorial Stadium in October 1867.

Dr. Edmund T. Spotswood    Baskin E. Rhoads

In 1865, Governor Oliver Morton addressed the General Assembly, and in his speech, spoke to the importance of establishing a state normal school in order to better prepare teachers for Indiana's schools. He attributed the sluggishness in state growth to the absence of qualified teachers.[6]

The Indiana General Assembly passed the original Enabling Act that created Indiana State Normal School (ISNS) in 1865. Baskin E. Rhoads, Representative from Vermillion County, had introduced the bill to establish a state normal school.[7] Governor Morton called a special session of the Legislature, and on December 20, 1865, the bill became law. The seed of Indiana State University's future had been planted.

Normal schools developed to address the need for prepared teachers. Although the view that teaching (like science) was a methodology that could be taught was gaining currency, it was not a unanimously supported belief.[8] Dr. William T. Daily, President of Indiana University, proclaimed normal schools were "humbugs." Others believed teaching was an inborn ability and attributes of a good teacher required knowledge of subject matter and upright character. In Indiana, and elsewhere in the Midwest, poor teachers frequently populated rural schools while larger cities generally were able to offer a higher-quality education.

ISNS was created at a time in history when it could ride the crest of growing interest in improving public education. The School Law of 1852 was an important first step in the creation of a statewide system of public education. Over the next two decades, the school year increased from 61 to 130 days and the number of students needing schooling grew from slightly over 200,000 to 500,000. This growth required more teachers, and the number of public teachers grew from about 4,000 to 13,000.[9]

During this time, the purpose of normal schools was to inculcate teaching standards or "norms," thus its name. Normal schools in the United States trained primary school teachers. The term "normal school" derives from the French term "école normale." The first école normale was located in the city of Reims, France. It was designed to be a model (laboratory) school with properly outfitted classrooms where student teachers could practice under supervision.

In the United States, normal schools were created to train high school graduates to become teachers. However, not all who attended the normal school were high school graduates. Some may have had some coursework at the high school level and were able to teach after having passed a test supervised by the county superintendent. Given the low pay, teaching was not a highly respected nor sought after profession, and it did not always attract the best and the brightest. Many who did teach often quit within a few years. "The relegation of persons unfit for other positions in life to teaching school seems to have been a distinct factor in the ... early history of Indiana."[10]

The responsibility for the creation and management of ISNS was assigned to a four-member Board of Trustees appointed by the Governor.[11] The State Superintendent of Public Instruction (George W. Hoss) served in an ex-officio capacity. The purpose of the school, as defined by the General Assembly, was the "preparation of teachers for teaching in the common schools of Indiana."[12]

The enacting legislation did not specify a location for the school. The gubernatorially-appointed Trustees and the Superintendent were given the responsibility for locating a suitable site. An opportunity was provided for any town or city in Indiana to make an offer in order to receive state support and the new school. One important caveat was that the citizens in the selected location be committed to cost-share with the state by providing $50,000, as well as the

Barnabas Hobbs

necessary land.[13]

In 1866, representation from Terre Haute, comprised of W. R. McKeen, J. H. Barr, and John M. Olcott, presented the offer of $50,000 and property valued at $25,000. Olcott was the Superintendent of Terre Haute City Schools and played a key role in determining the site for the campus and its first building. The selected site was a building previously occupied by the County Seminary of Vigo County, located east of Sixth Street between Eagle and Mulberry Streets.[14]

It was an auspicious time for the development of ISNS because the state had begun to recognize the need for a better-educated population in order to be competitive with other states, such as Ohio, Illinois, and Michigan. The period of 1870 to 1890 was characterized as the "Period of the Great Awakening." Educating the populace had gained legislative support, the economy began to grow stronger following the Civil War, and educated leaders who supported public education were identified to fill key positions, such as State Superintendent.

The growth in population required a requisite increase in available teachers.[15] Passage of legislation in 1867 enabled cities, towns, and townships to tax and collect funds to pay teacher salaries and provide needed

The Beginning

support for public education.[16] The public's willingness to support public education was not ubiquitous in Indiana. Urban centers were more supportive of these efforts than rural areas. Terre Haute's public demonstration of support for education ran counter to popular opinion elsewhere in Indiana.

The Trustees accepted the plans for the Normal School building developed by architect J. A. Vrydagh on August 10, 1886. The budget was set at $100,000 and the building was to be built in the Gothic Revival style.[17] In 1867, the General Assembly voted to provide $50,000 for the purpose of erecting a building for the school. In 1869, the General Assembly, following a visit by a delegation to inspect the new structure, provided an additional $79,000 for construction.[18] The final cost of the normal school building amounted to $189,000.

The cornerstone for the new normal school was laid on August 13, 1867, with, according to contemporaneous reports from that time, a "universal outpouring" of the people of Terre Haute. Placed in the cornerstone was a petition that had been signed by 1,500 residents of Terre Haute, requesting the city council agree to the terms of the 1865 Enabling Act.[19] In contrast to other parts of the state where divisiveness over funding public education hindered forward momentum, it was a credit to the people of Terre Haute that they generously supported the creation of ISNS in their town.[20]

Indiana State Normal School opened its doors on January 6, 1870, with an enrollment of 21 students – 13 women and eight men. The faculty consisted of William Albert Jones, President of the Faculty, and four teachers. The school was not complete, scantily furnished without equipment, and the library held two books – a dictionary and a Bible. State Superintendent Barnabas C. Hobbs led the chapel exercises. Following his reading of scripture, Hobbs knelt on the bare floor and prayed for divine guidance in the management of the school and its success.[21] ■

Introduction & The Beginning References

1 Encyclopedia Britannica "University" retrieved February 10, 2018.

2 Information provided by Kevin L. Runion, Vice President for Facilities Management (emeritus), June 5, 2014. Note: throughout this book, he will be referred to as Kevin Runion.

3 Dr. Robert LaFollette wisely observed that "the value of a building depends on what transpires within." Glenn White, The Ball State Story, Muncie: Ball State University Press, 1976, p. 5. Dr. LaFollette was a higher education specialist with the Agency for International Development.

4 Lyndon Johnson was the first President to graduate from a teachers college. Alan Carson Rankin, Inaugural Address, p. 7.

5 Normal Advance, 1922, np.

6 Journal of the House of Representatives, 44, Sess. Ge. Assembly, 1865, pp. 22-27. An earlier attempt to form a normal school failed in 1855 after Dr. E. T. Spotswood introduced a resolution into the General Assembly. Spotswood was a representative from Vermillion County. He favored prohibition and when the vote was taken on the bill, a canon was fired for every YES vote. The next day, hundreds of pounds of plastering fell on his seat in the House. Samuel E. Earp and Alembert W. Brayton, eds., Indianapolis Medical Journal, No. 17, 1914, p. 218. See also Biographical and Historical Record of Vermillion County, Chicago: Lewis Publishing Co., 1888.

7 Rhoads was a strong advocate for public education. During his term in the legislature, he was instrumental in drafting the bill to create Indiana State Normal School. He, in essence, was the "founding father" of the school. He served on the Board of Trustees, and in 1965, was honored by having Rhoads Hall named after him. See: http://politicalstrangenames.blogspot.com/2013/08/baskin-eply-rhoad.

8 Indicative of the resistance to the formation of a normal school is this remark by Superintendent of Public Instruction William C. Larrabee (1857-59) in his first official statement. "Our Indiana law makes no provision for them." "… I doubt if such schools, however important and valuable they may be in some states, would not comport with our circumstances, or suit our genius, or meet our wants." Richard G. Boone, A History of Education in Indiana, New York: R. Appleton and Co., 1892, p. 387. For Daily's remark, see Boone, p. 388.

9 William O. Lynch. A History of Indiana Teachers College. Bookwalter Company: Indianapolis, 1946, p. 1. (hereafter noted as "Lynch.")

10 Will D. Anderson, "A History of Indiana State Normal School," ISNS Yearbook, 1913, np.

11 The four Trustees were John Ingle, Jr. (Evansville), Isaac Kinley (Richmond), Barnabas C. Hobbs (Bloomingdale), and William C. Hannah (LaPorte). Lynch, p. 15.

12 Journal of the House of Representatives, pp. 22-27.

13 Approximately $682,000 today. See: http://www.measuringworth.com/uscompare.

14 Lynch, p. 18. Terre Haute was fortunate to have John M. Olcott as Superintendent of Schools. Terre Haute High School opened in 1863 and in 1867 its schools were considered the best in Indiana.

15 Lynch, p. 11.

16 Lynch, p. 7. Earlier court decisions in 1854 and 1857 effectively prohibited levying these taxes owing to popular opposition. Movement toward a state-wide education system began in 1873 with the passage of the County Superintendent Law. R, G. Boone, A History of Education in Indiana, New York: D. Appleton and Company 1892, pp. 240-251.

17 Lynch, pp. 18-19. The building actually contained both Gothic and French Renaissance elements.

18 It is ironic that the Legislature boasted having $7 million in the School Fund. More, they claimed, than any other state, yet the support for the new Normal School was so frugal.

19 Lynch, p. 20.

20 August 10, 1867, the City of Terre Haute increased its commitment to the school when it entered into an agreement with the Normal School Board to "pay forever one-half the cost of maintaining the Normal School and its grounds." Unfortunately, disagreement between the city and Normal School regarding paying half the insurance premium meant the school was uninsured when it burned in 1888. Lynch, p. 127.

21 Lynch, p. 32.

CHAPTER 1

1ST PRESIDENT
WILLIAM ALBERT JONES
(1869-1879)

December 20, 1865
The Indiana General Assembly passed a bill establishing the Normal School.

August 13, 1867
The Normal School cornerstone ceremony was held.

May 15, 1866
The City of Terre Haute offered $50,000 for building the school and a plot of land valued at $25,000.

November 2, 1869
William Albert Jones was appointed the first President.

Born: June 17, 1830

Died: November 13, 1905

Wife: Caroline E. Wilson (married 1852)

Positions held at Indiana State University: President (1869-79)

January 6, 1870
The Normal School opened its doors to 21 students.

June 25, 1872
The first graduating class was comprised of nine students.

1875
The legislature appropriated $10,000 to complete the basement and third floor of the school.

Summer 1879
The Board accepted Jones' letter of resignation.

Chapter 1 President Jones

William A. Jones, Indiana State Normal School's First President,

dedicated his life to education during an auspicious time for the state. The 10 years he spent at Indiana State Normal School (ISNS) coincided with a growing demand for better-trained teachers in the post-Civil War era. By the time of his retirement, Jones had made a significant imprint on the school and the teaching profession. His legacy has remained vitally important to the institution's heritage and continues today in the life of the University.

President Jones was born in East Haddam, Connecticut on June 17, 1830 and died of pneumonia November 13, 1905 in Hastings, Nebraska. He attended local schools and graduated from Williston Academy in 1849.[2] His formal education did not extend beyond high school. Later in his career, he was listed in the Normal School catalogs with a Master of Arts (A.M.) degree.

In 1856, at the age of 26, he moved his family to Illinois where he was Superintendent of the Altoona Schools, serving in this role until 1863, and then moved to the Aurora School District for six years.

As the first Headmaster of ISNS, Jones' two major accomplishments were to develop the school's academic program and to hire the first faculty. Enrollment, however, did not increase at a rate the Board had anticipated, and Jones was criticized for not increasing it aggressively. Most faculty members he hired were graduates of the ISNS. They were individuals in whom he had inculcated his philosophy about public education and the methodology for preparing teachers.

Conditions at ISNS during the early part of his tenure must have seemed as bleak as winter fields in Indiana. The building was incomplete and contained little equipment. The school had two books in its library – which was located in the President's office – a dictionary and the Bible. Donaldson noted the Trustees were so hard-pressed for funding to operate the school, they were unable to build a wooden fence around Normal Hall to keep the cows out of the school yard.[5] The budget for the new school was meager. In 1870, nearly one-third of the budget paid Jones' salary ($3,500).[6]

The ISNS faced several difficult challenges during the period of 1870-73. Enrollment was problematic. In

"The fact in the thing, the law in the mind, and the method in both."
– President William Jones[1]

"He laid broad and deep the foundations of this institution."
– President William Parsons

His relationship with the ISNS began in 1869 when Barnabas C. Hobbs, State Superintendent of Public Instruction for the State of Indiana, and ex-officio member of the state's Board of Trustees, traveled to Chicago to inquire about potential candidates for the ISNS presidency. During his trip he met Hiram Hadley, a former Hoosier educator living in Chicago, who highly recommended Jones. Hobbs paid Jones a visit, and based upon the excellent condition of the Aurora schools, eagerly recommended Jones for the job.[3]

Jones was elected President and Head Master on November 2, 1869 and welcomed the first class of 21 students to ISNS on January 6, 1870. Included in this inaugural class were William W. Parsons, who would become the third President of the Normal School, and Howard Sandison, who was elected to the position of Vice President in 1886 during Parsons' presidency.[4]

1871, the student population was 36, down about 10 percent from 39 in the preceding winter term. Jones' fastidiousness and insistence on high standards, along with his unique pedagogical model, may have adversely affected enrollment. The growth of private normal schools located closer to where students lived may also have had a negative impact on the school's enrollment. The absence of on-campus room and board meant students needed to pay prevailing prices in town. The period was marked by inflation following the Civil War that ended abruptly in the Wall Street panic of 1873 and ensuing depression that lasted five years. Finally, the depression caused the legislature to lower salaries paid by state schools.

After 1873, anxiety over enrollment lessened. By 1874, spring enrollment reached 279 (a ten-fold increase in 48 months) and presented a new problem – overcrowding.[7] By 1875, the legislature at last appropriated sufficient funds ($10,000) to equip the new ISNS building, landscape the grounds, and complete the third floor. By 1878, the interior of the school was nearly complete.

Jones' administrative mission was twofold: shape an appropriate curriculum for "common school" teachers (the equivalent of an 8th grade education), and provide leadership in developing the faculty. The no-nonsense curriculum Jones established was designed to fulfill the primary mission of ISNS – to train "common school" teachers. It consisted of eight disciplines: spelling, grammar, reading, writing, arithmetic, geography, physiology, and U.S. history. These were grouped into five subject areas: metaphysics, language, mathematics, natural science, and geography-history. It was designed to provide students with the equivalent of a high school education and, at the same time, instruction in teaching methods.

During his 10 years as president, Jones personally hired all faculty members. He met frequently with the small staff and impressed his ideas and practice upon them. The early graduates of ISNS were deeply influenced by Jones and his pedagogical methods. William Parsons, one of the first graduates, would become the third President of ISNS. He held President Jones in the highest regard as a teacher and mentor.

The conditions under which Jones served proved to be stressful. The absence of adequate and dependable funding and pressures to increase enrollment by lowering standards took their toll. The Board was critical of him and in 1877, it passed a motion requesting the secretary of the Board to, "inform President William A. Jones that a judicious association with his own teachers, and with the teachers of the city, of the state, and other states, will meet the approval of the Board of Trustees."[8] Jones' salary was dramatically reduced from $3,600 to $2,500 annually, an action that owed in part to the depression of the mid-1870s.[9]

In failing health, Jones submitted his resignation to the Board in the fall of 1878, only to have it rejected. He was given a leave of absence in order to recover his health. In May of 1879, he resubmitted his letter of resignation. Again, this was not immediately accepted and was held in abeyance with the hope that his health would improve. Jones did not withdraw his letter, and at the end of the academic year, the Board reluctantly acquiesced to his request. He was 49.

Jones lived in Terre Haute four more years and then moved to Hastings, Nebraska where he resided until his death on November 13, 1905 at the age of 75. After leaving the presidency, Jones abandoned a career in education, except when he served as Superintendent of the Institute for the Blind and ran unsuccessfully for Nebraska Superintendent of Public Instruction in 1894.[10]

Jones' strength was his teaching. While President, he directed the formation of the academic program and hired all nine faculty, met with them frequently, and instilled in them his philosophy of education. Beloved by the faculty, he was occasionally at odds with the Board of Trustees, who were critical of him for not aggressively increasing enrollment and for his solitary nature in not engaging others beyond the campus. The faculty veneration of him presaged more difficult times for the next President.

As the founding President, Jones led the development of teacher education in Indiana and proved to be a highly respected and effective educator beloved by faculty, staff, and many of his students. By the time of his retirement, he had made a significant imprint on the institution.

President Parsons' "Twenty-Five Years as President" address (1910) contained the following:

"To President Jones and his associates, education meant not so much knowledge of English, mathematics, science, history, literature, etc. It stood for the inculcation of correct life ideals and principles … they believed that public school teachers, above all, should be men and women having correct views of life and education, and themselves possessed of worthy character. To this end, they adopted a sound philosophy of life and education, which they made the basis and foundation of the school's first work."[11]

Indiana State Normal School

Architect: Josse A. Vyrdagh & Son
Contractor: Myles and Hedden
Date: August 13, 1867 Cornerstone was laid

Cost: $189,000
Area: 67,275 GSF

As an attractive and effective educational resource, ISNS drew enthusiastic praise from its beginning. A reporter for the Indiana Sentinel of Indianapolis visited Terre Haute on December 14, 1870 to report on the city's growth. In his story, he effusively described this building.

"As an edifice of magnificent and complete architecture, the Normal School excels any other building in the state. It is capacious, substantial, and convenient and comprehends in its general plans … all the conveniences of a first-class normal school … It may be styled the best planned and the best finished building in the state."[12]

The earlier history of the building depicted a far more Spartan structure owing to the budget shortage. The basement and 4th floor were unplastered and left in the rough. The 2nd and 3rd floors were plastered and floored with most of the windows in place, but without light fixtures. The heating system was inoperative.

The history of the Normal School building formally began when Dr. E.T. Spotswood and Judge Baskin E.

Rhoads convinced the legislature to appropriate funds for ISNS.[13] Legislation creating the school passed on December 20, 1865. It required the newly appointed Board of the Normal School to find a location for the campus and erect a building. Earlier, the state had promised $50,000 in matching funds to any city that provided a site and financial match for the school.

To the credit of Terre Haute's citizens, it was the only city in the state that responded to the solicitation. By a special act in March 1867, the Indiana General Assembly voted $50,000 from the Township Library Fund collections to the Trustees of the Normal School and added $79,000 to the construction fund in 1869.[14]

The Board of Trustees, on August 10, 1866, selected Josse A. Vrydagh to design the Normal School building. Vrydagh, born in Louvain, Belgium, moved to Terre Haute in 1866. He was an accomplished architect who, in addition to the Normal School, also designed the Terra Haute Opera House, the county court houses in Sullivan, Mt. Vernon, and Bedford, the East College Building at DePauw, and several local homes.[15]

The Vigo County Seminary that had operated from 1848 to 1853, and stood in the area of the present-day Gillum Hall, provided the land for the new building. The building housed the Vigo Collegiate Institute, a private school necessitated by the absence of public schools.[16] The Seminary was razed in 1867.

Vigo County Seminary

The cornerstone of ISNS was laid August 13, 1867, and numerous articles were placed in it for posterity. One of the items was the petition that 1,500 residents of Terre Haute had signed, requesting the City Council agree to the terms of the 1865 Act that required the city desiring the school to provide both land and money.

ISNS was a three-story structure measuring approximately 195 feet in width and 115 feet in depth. It was built in a hybridized revival Gothic style with some French Renaissance influence. It shares some characteristics with the Norman Romanesque-Gothic style of the Smithsonian Castle in Washington, D.C. In the U.S., Gothic Revival, sometimes referred to as "Collegiate Gothic," originated in the late 18th century but became more common in the 19th century. Buildings in this style have elaborate chimneys, steeply pitched roofs and gables, pointed arches, tall narrow windows, towers, and turrets.

The framing towers served a functional purpose as ventilation shafts.[17] A distinct Gothic element was the oculus or round window (in Gothic churches a rose window) over the main entrance that recalls Gothic churches of France, such as Notre Dame and Chartres.

The building exhibited a nice balance between horizontality (the linear stringcourses separated the floors, balustrades formed bases for the triple arcade windows, and a heavy dentilated cornice) and verticality emphasized by strong triangular pediments and ascending framing towers. The central entrance was defined by double flights of limestone steps rising on either side of the central landing, a slightly projecting portico, and central oculus window.

The building had a basement with a floor three feet below grade and 11-foot ceilings. The upper floors had 16-foot ceilings, with the exception of the lecture room, museum, and library, located on the third floor, that had 22-foot high ceilings.

The basement contained a gymnasium, chemistry lecture hall, laboratory, and play rooms for primary children attending ISNS. The west entrance was accessed by a double stairway which entered onto a reception room and secretary's office. The front hall was crossed by a major hall running north-south. The north and south entrances were also reached by double flights of steps. One entrance was used by men and the other by women, a decision reached by the Board on December 3, 1869.

A room for high school classes, two reference libraries, and four classrooms were located on the east of the long hall. The west side of the north end featured intermediate schoolrooms, and the south end included primary school rooms and four dressing rooms.

The second floor was used principally by ISNS. It contained two reference libraries, an assembly room, eight classrooms, and dressing rooms. A gentle light

Chapter 1 President Jones

entered the second floor through the round window on the west façade.

The third floor was most capacious and contained a large lecture hall and three rooms used as a museum and library. These rooms could be opened to create a large lecture hall. It also contained two "society halls" and music halls.[18] The building was designed for steam heat but was heated by stoves in the absence of a complete heating system.[19]

Inauguration ceremonies for the new building were held on January 5, 1870 in a large assembly room on the second floor. State Superintendent Barnabus C. Hobbs presided. Speakers included Governor Conrad Baker, who criticized the legislators for not supporting the development of a school system in Indiana until 1849. The principle speaker was Colonel Richard W. Thompson, an attorney in Terre Haute, member of the Board, and a person who, in the President Hayes administration, served as Secretary of the Navy. He used his well-developed oratorical skills to speak specifically to the value of the establishment of normal schools in the state.

ISNS officially opened on January 6, 1870 to a meager class of 21 students (13 women and eight men). President Jones and his staff of five faculty welcomed them in what must have been a very cold and sparsely furnished building. The building, from the exterior, was striking, but the grounds were littered with construction debris. There were no sidewalks, grass, or trees. Equipment was not found and there was no laboratory, not even a map.

The school's library holdings were miniscule. In 1873, Chauncey Rose made a gift of $4,000 for the purchase of materials that were kept in the President's office. President Jones was responsible for book acquisition. In his 1877 report to the Trustees, President Jones stated, "The library is used. It is not an ornamental appendage to the institution. It contains no rubbish."[20] ■

1888: Building Destroyed by Fire

President Parsons

On April 9, 1888, the building and most of its contents were completely destroyed by fire. The new heating apparatus that had been recently installed, new furnishings, laboratory equipment, and about 1,900 books in the library were all lost. The loss was estimated between $200,000 and $250,000. Unfortunately, the building and its contents were not insured because of a disagreement between the Normal School and City of Terre Haute about what portion of the insurance premium each should pay.[21]

After the fire, President Parsons and Vice President Howard Sandison announced classes would resume the very next day at 8:30 a.m. Local churches and private citizens made space available for classes. The Centenary Methodist Church served as the main center of activities until the second floor of the city high school was put in shape and served as headquarters until the end of the school year. After the fire and rebuilding of the main building, $15,000 was reserved for library purchases, and the President's secretary, Helen Gilbert, served as librarian, in addition to other duties.[22]

Chapter 1 References

1. For a fuller discussion of Jones' dictum, see Howard Sandison, The Problem of the Method, Terre Haute: The Inland Publishing Company, 1904. Sandison taught Psychology at ISNS. See: http://babel.hathitrust.org/cgi/pt?id=uc2.ark:/13960/t3kw5cf1m;view=1up;seq=13.

2. John Donaldson, "President William A. Jones," Indiana Magazine of History, 1934, Vol. 30, Issue 3, p. 2.

3. Lynch, p. 24. Hiram Hadley (1833-1922) created his own normal school in Richmond, Indiana, and in 1888, became president of Las Cruces College, New Mexico. Simon F. Kropp, "Hiram Hadley and the Founders of New Mexico State University," Arizona and the West, Vol. 9, No. 1, Spring, 1967, pp. 21-40. Hadley was known as the "pioneer educator."

4. Lynch, p. 120.

5. Donaldson, p. 5. The fence was completed in 1878.

6. In 2010 dollars Jones' salary would be equal to $58,333. See: http://oregonstate.edu/cla/polisci/sites/default/files/faculty-research/sahr/inflation-conversion/pdf/cv2010.pdf.

7. Lynch, p. 49.

8. Trustee Minutes, November 1, 1877, I, p. 278.

9. Lynch, p. 75.

10. Indiana State University Archives: President William Jones. See: http://library.indstate.edu/archives/exhibits/President/jones.htm.

11. John Donaldson, "President William A. Jones," Indiana Magazine of History, 1934, Vol. 30, Issue 3, pp. 242-254. See: http://scholarworks.iu.edu/journals/index.php/imh/article/view/6771/7263.

12. Indiana Sentinel, December 14, 1870. Cited in Mike McCormick, "Historical Perspectives," Tribune Star, Mar 22, 2014. See: http://www.tribstar.com/history/x1984797240/historical-perspective-indiana-sentinel-lauds-1870-terre-haute-landmarks. In a report of the Visiting Committee one reads, "Its external appearance is imposing and substantial. It is free from the useless ornamentation that characterizes the architectural design of so many public buildings …" Report for 1889-90 to the State Supervisor of Public Instructions and to the Board of Trustees of the Indiana State Normal School, p. 70.

13. Spotswood was also named the "chief poet of Vermillion County." Biographical and Historical Record of Vermillion County, Chicago: Lewis Publishing Co., 1888, p. 203.

14. Laws of the State of Indiana passed at the 45th Regular Session of the General Assembly, Indianapolis: 1867, Alexander H. Connor Printer, Chapter XCIII, p. 177. See: https://babel.hathitrust.org/cgi/pt?id=inu30000050074651;view=1up;seq=185.

15. Vrydagh designed the St. Nicholas Hotel in Dallas, Texas that also burned in 1860. The burning of the Patent Office in Washington provided the opportunity for Vrydagh to submit the winning design for the Treasury in Washington, D.C. for which he received $1,000. Unfortunately, politics came into play and the commission was given to Cluss and Schulze, who designed the reconstruction of the Smithsonian Castle after it burned in 1865. See: Smithsonian Preservation Quarterly, Spring, 1993, n.p. He served as supervising architect of the Treasury Department 1881-82. Charles C. Oakey, Greater Terre Haute and Vigo County: Closing the First Century's History of the City and County, Vol. 2, Terre Haute: Lewis Publishing Co. 1908, pp. 843-844.

16. The land (out-lot 43) was purchased from William C. Linton, agent for the heirs of William and Joseph Montgomery, for $100. Vigo County Seminary, 77. See: http://www.vigo.lib.in.us/archives/specialhist/PUBLSCHO/Volume1/pt17.pdf.

17. The new Power Plant on campus likewise encloses smoke stacks within an Italianate tower.

18. Frank Leslie's Illustrated Newspaper, February 5, 1870, pp. 357-358 cited in Indiana State Normal School Fire Centennial Observance 1888-1988, published by Indiana State University, np.

19. At the September 30, 1959 Trustee meeting, Allison Vrydagh, grandson of J.A. Vrydagh, presented the architect's drawing of the original building and a photograph when it was completed. These have been lost.

20. Lynch, pp. 67-68.

21. Lynch, pp. 127-128.

22. See: http://lib.indstate.edu/about/units/admin/facil.html.

CHAPTER 2

2ND PRESIDENT
GEORGE PLINY BROWN
(1879-1885)

July 1879
George Pliny Brown was appointed second President of the Indiana State Normal School.

May 26, 1881
58 trees were planted on the campus.

November 18, 1881
A course for graduate students was offered.

Born: November 10, 1836

Died: February 1, 1910

Wife: Mary Louise Seymour (married 1855-1910)

Education:
Grand River Institute

Positions held at Indiana State University: President (1879-85)

May 24, 1882
The Department of Music was approved.

June 15, 1882
The Trustees approved a $1.00 lab fee to be paid each term.

1885
The Indiana State Normal School Advance began publication.

Chapter 2 President Brown

Perhaps it was the middle name Pliny that suggested he was somewhat of an elitist.

In volcanology, a Plinian occurrence denotes a violent eruption. George Pliny Brown endured such an eruption at the Indiana State Normal School (ISNS), which has defined, arguably inappropriately, his place in the history of the institution. Memory of his brief tenure (six years) is lost and the campus has no physical reminder of his presidency, such as a monument or building. Yet George Pliny Brown was, in his lifetime, recognized as a "modern" educator, prolific author, and distinguished publisher.[2] In the early history of ISNS, Brown was the most professionally prepared of the Presidents who preceded and immediately followed him, and left a legacy of increased enrollments, financial stability, and enhanced prestige.

Brown was born on November 10, 1836, in Lenox, Ohio (Ashtabula County in northeastern Ohio). He graduated from Grand River Institute (formerly known as the Ashtabula County Institute of Science and Industry) in Austinburg, Ohio. He was teaching at the age of 16 in Waynesville, Ohio and became superintendent of Union School in 1858 at the age of 22. In 1860, Brown moved his family to Richmond, Indiana where he served as Superintendent of Schools for seven years, and then served in New Albany for one year.

He began his first publishing efforts in 1869, something to which he devoted more of his time after his presidency at ISNS, and a brief time in Topeka, Kansas. Subsequently, he purchased the Illinois School Journal, served as editor, and then became President of the Public School Publishing Company in Bloomington, Illinois. He was a productive writer and authored numerous books, in addition to the many articles he wrote for the Public-School Journal and School and Home Education Journal.[3]

Brown was appointed President of ISNS during the summer of 1879. He envisioned a new direction for ISNS that would directly impact the established curriculum and methodologies. He presciently recognized the need for ISNS to attract and graduate more students better pedagogically prepared to meet the needs of a growing public school system in Indiana. Brown saw his role was to be responsive to the needs of the state expressed by political leadership in Indiana. He emphasized pedagogy, teaching methods, and the importance of students understanding how to prepare themselves in content areas. This new direction was indicated in the 1879 annual report which stated, "The instruction given in a Normal School should regard, primarily, methods of teaching."[4]

The small faculty (10) he inherited had been hired and worked closely with President Jones. As is so often the case, change threatened the status quo.[5] This was an exceedingly loyal group who had deep respect for Jones and his ideals that had shaped ISNS. The Board, however, was steadfastly supportive of Brown and empowered him to bring about changes.

At its March 1881 meeting, the Board passed new rules regarding the authority of the president and

> "President Brown was a man of keen educational insight and of extended, varied, and successful experience in all kinds of public school work. This intimate knowledge of the schools enabled him to bring the work of the Normal School into closer harmony with the schools of the state and in this way he rendered a very great service during the six years of his presidency."[1]
>
> – President William Parsons

responsibilities of the faculty. The response was a "rebellion" prompted by five faculty members who submitted a formal protest to the Board.[6] The Board, in response, formed a committee to consider the substance of the protest and report back. The committee found "no reason why a working harmony should not prevail."[7] The Board supported Brown, resulting in the five faculty members resigning.[8]

With 50 percent of the faculty gone, Brown had to hire replacements. Those hired, ironically, had also formerly worked under President Jones, and this group, combined with those who remained and were sympathetic to Jones, set the stage for further conflict, although their complaints were managed out of the public eye. Indeed, Brown made few changes in the current curriculum and the conflicts may have owed to Brown's broader experience, high expectations, and attempt to steer the institution toward better meeting contemporary state needs, as well as concerns about the credentials and qualifications of some of the faculty.

President Landini (Eighth President, 1975-92) clearly championed Brown in a Founders' Day address delivered on January 16, 1980. In it, he suggests Brown wished the faculty to give more emphasis to the subject matter being taught than to the pedagogy of teaching. President Jones, Landini said, had built the curriculum on the craft of teaching while Brown sought a subtle shift in emphasis.

Interestingly, Brown was supported by Professor Lucy M. Salmon, a graduate of the University of Michigan and first member of the American Historical Association from Indiana. In her classes at the ISNS, she emphasized the subject matter to be taught by the future teachers. She resigned in 1885, two years after she had arrived, and finished her career at Vassar. Landini stated, "They probably missed each other's company, educational philosophy, and conversation."[9] Brown and Parsons, together with faculty and Trustees, are "more than responsible for the distinguished history of the university."[10]

President Brown was also criticized by the faculty for being too lenient toward students "and not sufficiently considerate of the interests of teachers."[10] Brown admitted, in an interview with a writer for the Gazette, that he had restored to classes a student who had been dismissed for wrong-doing. He stated he had been opposed to some actions of the faculty he considered "to reflect unjustly and with unnecessary severity against the students."[11] Brown's position was supported by a Board of Visitors who evaluated the school in 1882 and 1884, and in the latter review, questioned the severity of criticism of students in practice teaching and in courses for teaching "educational doctrine, or in the psychology of the teaching art."[12]

Brown was an experienced and widely respected administrator. While he served as Superintendent of the Indianapolis Schools, his strongest supporters were among the faculty, quite in contrast to his faculty relationship at ISNS. Lewis H. Jones, principal of the training school in Indianapolis, wrote that Brown was a "thoughtful man, a true teacher of teachers" whose "principles for which he contended were well-sustained."[13]

Brown submitted his letter of resignation on May 1, 1885. He remarked that his problems with the faculty played only a small role in his decision. He expressed eagerness to take on new challenges. No doubt, Brown had found the mode of instruction at ISNS too outdated, regimented, dogmatic, and inadequate in meeting the contemporary needs. Despite his difficulties, Brown could point to the growth in enrollment that made ISNS one of the largest normal schools in the nation.[14]

No major construction was undertaken during Brown's tenure. To his credit, he created the Department of Music and was the first President to have a telephone. The installation was problematic and the Board, at its April 1884 meeting, voted to have the telephone company detach "the wire from the elm tree in the yard."[15] The grounds remained unimproved since the wooden fence was installed in 1878. An 1880 graduate described the school yard in mock admiration. He wrote, "… the beauties of the ground surrounding the Normal building furnished a diagram of river and lake systems which was of assistance in botanical studies by specimens of dog fennel, catmint, and penny-royal with which it abounded."[16]

President Parsons, in the second of his semi-centennial addresses, captured the importance of President Brown's contributions to ISNS. He said,

> "Under President Brown's direction the school made …important advances. The courses of study were broadened…larger appropriations were secured for maintenance…and more was done to popularize the school and bring its work to the attention of the people of the state." "[17] ∎

Chapter 2 References

1. Trustee Minutes, April 18, 1884, I, p. 384.

2. Among his publications are: A Course of Composition and Grammar for the Primary and Grammar Grades of the Indianapolis Schools (1877); Religious Instruction in State Schools (1891); Elements of English Grammar (1889); The Story of Our English Grandfathers (1903); The King and His Wonderful Castle (1904); On the Teaching of English in Elementary and High Schools (1906); Physiology and Psychology of Education (1908), and In Memoriam: William Torrey Harris (1910).

   William Torrey Harris (1835-1909) was an outstanding Superintendent of St. Louis schools and served as U.S. Commissioner of Education. He established the first public kindergarten in St. Louis, made high school essential, expanded the common curriculum, and included art and music as a new curriculum area. Brown also added music to the normal curriculum and shared his interests in Hegel and Froebel.

3. Karen Campbell, George Pliny Brown-Educator, Administrator, Publisher, and Author. See: http://wanyesgenhis.blogspot.com/2005/11/george-pliny-brown-edu. Herbert Rissler, Strengthening the Beginning. Indiana State University Archives. Accessed 5/24/2014, http://library.indstate.edu/archives/exhibits/Presidents/brown.htm.

4. Lynch, pp. 86-88.

5. Brown's successor, President Parsons, pinpointed the crux of the controversy in his remarks made during the 50th anniversary of ISNS when he stated, "Moreover, to a considerable extent, somewhat abstract terminology adopted and employed in the early days of the school was abandoned to give place to language more current in educational and literary circles." Herbert Rissler, George Pliny Brown: 1879-1885, in the Indiana State University Archives. See: http://library.indstate.edy/archives/exhibits/Presidents/brown.htm Accessed 5/24/2014.

6. Lynch, p. 93.

7. Lynch, p. 95.

8. Briggs, Murray, Report of the Trustees. n.d., 1881, p. 1. Murray Briggs was President of the Board of Trustees.

9. Richard G. Landini, Founders' Day Address, January 16, 1980, pp. 3-4.

10. Lynch, p. 110.

11. Terre Haute Gazette, May 23, 1885.

12. Annual Register of the Indiana State Normal School, 1883-84, pp. 13-16. Lynch, p. 109.

13. Lewis H. Jones, "The Politician and the Public School," Atlantic Monthly, January 1896, LXXVIII, pp. 816-817.

14. Lynch pp. 110-113 and Annual Report of the Board of Trustees of the State Normal School of the State of Indiana, 1880, p. v22. Enrollment term average: Jones: 1870: 47; 1878: 272; Brown: 1879: 261; 1885: 419

15. Trustee Minutes, April 18, 1884, I, p. 384.

16. Lynch, p. 117 from the Terre Haute Gazette, June 17, 1881.

17. "The Semi-Centennial Celebration of the Indiana State Normal School," Indiana State Normal School Bulletin, Terre Haute: Indiana State Normal School, Vol. XIII, No. 4, 1920, pp. 25-26.

CHAPTER 3

3RD PRESIDENT
WILLIAM WOOD PARSONS
(1885-1921)

July 1, 1885
William Wood Parsons became the third President.

April 9, 1888
Indiana State Normal School was destroyed by a fire.

July 15, 1890
Arthur Cunningham was appointed the first librarian of Indiana State Normal School.

February 16, 1889
The General Assembly voted for $100,000 to complete the rebuilding of the school.

March 6, 1893
General Assembly approved $40,000 for building North Hall – the second campus building.

Born: May 18, 1850

Died: September 28, 1925

Wives
Harriet Emily Wilkes
(married 1883-1916)
Martina C. Erickson
(married 1917-25)

Education
High School: Tuscola, IL

Indiana State Normal School

Positions held at Indiana State University
ISNS Degree (1872)
English Grammar and Composition teacher (1876-83)
Department Head (1879-82)
Vice President (1883-85)
President (1885-1921)

1894
Baseball, football, and basketball were introduced on the campus.

December 2, 1915
The third campus building – Vocational Education – was formally accepted.

1919
The first homecoming parade took place.

1908
The first bachelor's degree was awarded.

June 25, 1917
The Science Building was opened.

November 11, 1918
Armistice Day

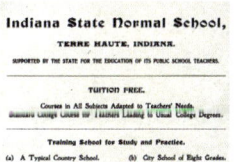

Chapter 3 President Parsons

William Wood Parsons was a dedicated educator who played a major role in the development of Indiana State Normal School (ISNS) and the promotion of teacher education in Indiana and surrounding states. His influence was magnified by ISNS graduates who taught and administered in schools around the Midwest.

Parsons was born May 18, 1850 in Terre Haute, the son of physician Dr. Thomas Parsons, who had moved from Maryland to Terre Haute in 1819. At the time of his birth, Terre Haute was an unincorporated village. He attended the Vigo County Seminary that was located on the site where the first ISNS building was erected. The family moved to Tuscola, Illinois where he attended high school and graduated in 1869. He was a member of the first class admitted to ISNS when it opened on January 6, 1870 and was in the first class to graduate in 1872. President Parsons died September 28, 1925, at the age of 75, after a 45-year association with the school.

After completing his study at ISNS, Parsons taught school in Arcola, Illinois, was superintendent of schools in Gosport, Indiana for a year, and taught high school for two years in Indianapolis. In 1876, four years after graduating, Parsons returned to his alma mater as a teacher of English grammar and composition. (To the students, he was known as "Uncle Billy.") By 1879, he was made department head. In 1883, he became Vice President, and in 1885, succeeding George Pliny Brown, he became the third President of ISNS.[1] The Trustees met on June 11, 1885, and heard three petitions (one from the faculty, a second from the alumni association, and the third from the student body) asking them to elect Mr. Parsons to the presidency.

Parsons' successful tenure as President (36 years), while the longest in the institution's history, was not without difficulties. Four major challenges stand out.

On April 9, 1888, fire destroyed the ISNS building. Owing to a misunderstanding between the school and the City of Terre Haute, the building and its contents, valued at approximately $225,000, were uninsured.[2] Parsons responded heroically to the challenges this disaster presented. He addressed students and faculty and made arrangements with other schools and churches in the area for classes to be held the very next day. This stemmed the feared diaspora of students and diminished the possibility that the state might move ISNS to another location. Once again, the citizens of Terre Haute provided substantial support for a new

Top: Original Vrydagh designed Normal School
Middle: 1900 Classroom   Bottom: President Parsons' office

building, which was opened for fall classes in 1889.[3]

The second major problem Parsons faced was a student revolt instigated by the dismissal of a faculty member popular among the students. It was alleged to the Board of Trustees that Professor Arnold Tompkins (Department of Reading, Rhetoric, and Literature) had, in his home, criticized the management of the school.[4]

An investigative hearing was held on November 11, 1892, and at the Board meeting of June 2, 1893, the Trustees voted not to continue Tompkins' employment beyond the current contract, arguing that it was not "in the best interest of the school."[5] The Board requested his immediate resignation. Tompkins refused to resign (probably because his contract would terminate at the end of the month.) The student body of about 800 was unaware of the problem until after the Trustees had acted. Their response was to hold a mass meeting. They selected 15 students to represent the student body. This committee demanded a report from the Trustees giving the reasons Tompkins was terminated. Their prepared statement was sharply critical of the school leadership for terminating a skilled teacher who they respected, while other teachers "narrow in scholarship and inefficient in teaching" were retained.[6] A second statement was submitted to the Board, who was convinced the Committee of Fifteen was launching a rebellion, that included an incendiary sentence stating: "We sincerely hope that the school management will receive that discipline which it evidently needs."[7]

turn of the century. Normal schools were required to elevate themselves to college rank, meaning all courses were required to be at the college level. Graduates of ISNS did not possess a more valued degree, and the ISNS faculty members were "given a lower rating in educational circles because they taught at a school not offering a course leading to a degree."[12]

For a limited time, 1874-76, an advanced course of study was established, but it was not continued. As Lynch notes, "It was a calamity that this advanced course was not continued …"[13] Modification of the common course of study could have been accomplished "without lessening their value through eliminating mental gymnastics when given for the sake of mental gymnastics."[14] ISNS was slow to get off the blocks and did not offer a program leading to a degree until after the 1907 legislation had passed. According to Lynch, "Parsons … never became much interested in degrees

"Parsons always gave the fullest measure of devotion to his native state, to the city in which he lived, and to the institution for which he served." – *Unknown, University Archives*

Parsons met with the student committee in an effort to resolve the issue. Because this problem had played out in the newspapers, the Board clearly felt publicly maligned. Parsons' proposal was for the committee members to sign a statement disapproving of public criticism of the Board. The Board met on June 29, and unexpectedly, the President of the Board rejected Parsons' action and insisted instead that each student sign a statement disavowing their previous actions and statements. Commencement was canceled, and the Board refused to provide certificates of graduation to the 50 or more students who had declined to sign the prepared statement.[8] Parsons showed considerable skill in his efforts to resolve the dispute and he would have succeeded had the Board's response been more tactful.

The preceding President, Brown, commented that this was "the old fight of dead formalism against the spirit of growth and freedom in institutional life."[9] Lynch, reflecting on the event 44 years later, wrote, "… the Normal School was never the same again. The 'revolution of 1893' led to a period of tolerance in marked contrast to what had preceded. The 'czarship' of the faculty came to an end, and the man at the head of the school became a wiser President …"[10]

A third problem was ISNS was disadvantaged by not pioneering the offering of advanced degrees of study provided by other institutions.[11] The transition from normal schools to teacher colleges began at the

… Perhaps he did not give enough thought to them and to what they could have done for the students of Normal School, the members of the faculty, and the institution itself."[15]

There was no major change in ISNS's enrollment during the last decade of the 19th century. Average three-term enrollment increased from 524 in 1890-91 to 676 in 1900-01. Restricting factors were the Great Depression of 1893, inadequate funding, competition from private normal schools that provided students the opportunity to study close to home, and tardiness in offering advanced degrees beyond the Common School certificate.[16] Parsons adhered strictly to the enabling law of 1865 that defined the mission of ISNS to "one thing-the preparation of teachers for teaching in the common schools of the state." ISNS was required to accept students who planned to become teachers, although a sizeable number did not have high school degrees.

In the interim, Indiana University and Purdue University, as well as other colleges in Indiana, could refuse admission unless the student was a high school graduate or could demonstrate comparable preparatory study. Further, graduates from other colleges were awarded bachelor's degrees, but it wasn't until 1908 that ISNS began to do so; prompted, no doubt, by enrollment and reputational concerns, as well as the fact that in 1907, the General Assembly defined public schools as consisting of both elementary and high school. This necessitated more advanced study for future high school teachers. Changes in the public schools drove changes at the institutions that prepared teachers – some more quickly than others. This important change in definition provided the impetus to later transform ISNS into the Indiana State Teachers College (ISTC).

The fourth major event to comment upon was the creation of the Eastern Division of ISNS. An earlier attempt to establish another normal school in Muncie failed, in part because of Parsons' opposition. By 1918, the effort succeeded, owing primarily to the sharp drop in enrollment in Terre Haute. Parsons feared a protracted war in Europe and saw a financial benefit in the creation of the Eastern Division. A gift of land and buildings was offered by the Ball brothers to the State Board of Trustees January 3, 1918. The General Assembly accepted the gift during the 1918 short session, and operating control was given to ISNS, which it retained until 1929.[17]

Major accomplishments during Parsons' amiable administration were: salving wounds and bringing normalcy back to the campus following the upheaval during Brown's presidency, developing baccalaureate degree programs, raising admission and graduation standards, increasing enrollment, advocating successfully with the Legislature and Governor for operating support and new buildings, making ISNS the model normal school in the state, and creating the Eastern Division of the ISNS in Muncie, Indiana, which later became Ball State University.[18]

The campus grew extensively during Parson's presidency. Five buildings were erected. The first was North Hall in 1895, and the second, the Training School, in 1905. These were built adjacent to Old Main and reflect the style of the earlier building. The third building, Normal Library, was dedicated on June 21, 1910 during a campus celebration of Parsons' 25 years of service as President. This accorded with the annual meeting of the alumni association, and its members presented Parsons with a handsome portrait of the President by the celebrated Indiana artist T.C. Steele. The painting now hangs in the Heritage Lounge in Tirey Hall. Normal Library accommodated approximately 114,000 volumes and was one of the largest teacher-education libraries in the country.[19]

The fourth building was the Industrial Arts (Vocational Building) completed in 1915. It faced north on Mulberry Street and housed industrial arts and home economics, as well as the school's press. The fifth, the Science Hall (later renamed the College of Business and the Classroom Building), was erected in 1917. Finally, Parsons Field was acquired prior to October 31, 1906, for $875.

Reeve Hall cornerstone

In June 1897, the Attorney General of Indiana stated ISNS had the right to establish courses in physical education. In 1894, football and basketball were introduced on campus. The first recorded basketball game was played against the Terre Haute YMCA. From 1908 through 1920, football was banned by the faculty.

North Hall faced north on Eagle Street and provided much needed space for library and science laboratories, as well as a gymnasium for men and women. The new sport of basketball (invented in 1891) was played in the basement of North Hall in a space with padded columns supporting the floor above. This proved especially challenging for visiting teams.

No doubt, one of President Parson's disappointments was not being able to secure funding to build a women's dormitory. The need was critical for women who were not residents of Terre Haute. They had to find housing off-campus that was expensive, unpleasant, and ill-suited for students.[20] A women's dormitory would provide many advantages for the campus. Most importantly, it would improve housing off-campus by creating competition, as well as attract more women to study at ISNS. It would take 20 more years until the cornerstone for Reeve Hall, ISNS's first women's residence hall, was laid on November 19, 1924.

The politics surrounding gaining approval and funding for new buildings are obscured behind building facades. For example, in 1904, ISNS requested $10,000 to complete the fourth floor of the Training School, and $100,000 to secure property and build a women's dormitory. The Governor nixed the Training School request. The House Ways and Means Committee and the Senate Finance Committee recommended an appropriation of $50,000 for a dormitory, but nothing for the Training School. When the bill was brought before the House, it did not contain the $50,000 recommended by the joint committees. The bill passed the House, but in the Senate the $50,000 was added back in. In the Conference Committee, the $50,000 was removed and $10,000 for the Training School was reinserted. Ultimately, when the bill was finally voted upon, no appropriation was made for either project.[21]

Parsons' personal life was filled with family misfortunes. One son died in infancy and his second son, Robert, died shortly after graduating from Wabash College at the age of 21. His wife, Harriet Emily Wilkes, died of pneumonia at the age of 55 in 1916.[22] In 1917, Parsons married his second wife, Martina C. Erickson, ISNS's first dean of women. She served in that role from 1905 to 1910. She died on August 23, 1959 at the age of 88, and in 1962, Erickson Hall was dedicated in her honor.

Parsons died four years after retiring in his home located on 1444 South Center Street on September 28, 1925. ∎

Old Main

Architect: W. L. B. Jenney & Otis[23]
Contractor: W. A. Atkins[24]
Collins and Ohm (1938-39 remodeling)
Date: 1888-89

Cost: Approx. $150,000[25]
Area: Approx. 67,000 GSF
Renovation: 1938-39 (President Tirey)
Razed: 1950

Normal School after April fire

The ISNS burned spectacularly on the morning of April 9, 1888. Strong winds in advance of a rainstorm fanned the flames. Morning classes had begun and about 600 people were in the building. The fire consumed almost all of the contents of the building, save some laboratory equipment, a few library books, and the record of Trustee meetings that was scurried out of the burning building by Parsons' secretary, Miss Helen L. Gilbert, after she dutifully locked the door behind her.[26]

The building was totally consumed and this loss was exacerbated because it was not insured. The city of Terre Haute had been reluctant to provide 50 percent of the insurance premium ($900) despite the prior agreement that the city would provide half the cost of operation of the school in perpetuity. The Trustees determined they would not pay ISNS's share of the premium unless the city met its obligation. The citizens, however, once again, rallied in order to keep the school, and on April 17, presented a petition signed by 1,000 citizens to the City Council, which voted to provide $25,000 for its rebuilding.[27]

On June 3, an additional $25,000 was pledged for rebuilding ISNS. In addition to the funds from the City of Terre Haute, the Legislature provided $100,000 to complete the building and heating plant, as well as provided books for the library, and purchased science apparatus and furniture.

Following the fire, plans were made to rebuild as quickly as possible. Portions of walls from the burned school remained, suggesting the old building could be restored, but this proved structurally impossible.

It was decided that a new structure could be built incorporating the old foundations, using only portions of the usable original structure. The Board awarded a contract for $2,750 to Shrover and Christian of Indianapolis to remove the debris caused by the fire and to "prepare the Normal building for reconstruction as specified in the architect's specifications …" It was also decided the building should be completed in a new style.[28]

A committee comprised of Trustees, President Parsons, the Mayor (Jacob C. Kolsem), and City Council members reviewed plans submitted for the new building. Submissions had been received from Jenney & Otis, J. A. Vrydagh & Son, and John A. Gaddis.[29] The vote was seven for Jenney & Otis, two for Vrydagh & Son and one for Gaddis.[30] A contract with Jenney & Otis was prepared by ISNS (President Parsons) and the city.[31]

A document remains, "Repairs to the Indiana State Normal School, Terre Haute," from the W. L. B. Jenney and W. A. Otis architectural firm in Chicago.[32] It is without date, but one assumes it was prepared in 1888. It provides detailed instructions for the contractor to follow. It states that the contractor was to take down the ruins to the top of the first story windows and the west front wall, between the corner turrets and to the top of the third story window sills over the balance of the building. It also states the contractor was to "take down the center of the west front and all other portions of the ruins that are not wanted in the new construction and all such parts with too much damaged to be safely repaired." The contractor was also required, "to make all necessary excavations for the foundation of the new tower in center of front elevation and for the foundation of the new circular ends of the pavilions on either side of said tower …"[33]

In contrast to the earlier ISNS, this building was heavier in appearance, reflecting the Chicago School influence. The new structure had two stories above the basement rather than three, as in the earlier building. The heating plant was placed outside of the building, which provided more interior space compared to the ISNS building it replaced. The original Normal School, on the third floor of the older structure, was located on the second floor.

The selection of the Jenney & Otis firm is most interesting because it shows the Board was interested in the new (modern) Richardsonian Romanesque style emanating from Chicago.[34] Typical of the Romanesque revival is the apparent massiveness of the building, emphasized by the heavy horizontal limestone banding

Old Main

for sills and cornices, and the diaper-patterned terra cotta belt cornice at the second story level of the two pavilions. Round-headed arches constructed of substantial masonry on the third-story level and in the dormers are also a characteristic feature of the Romanesque. The central arched entry is heavily framed in limestone.

The massive centralized tower rises from this heavy base and is punctuated with triple arched openings in the upper floor. The tower culminated in a dramatically rising triangular spire. Apparently, the Trustees and/or President Parsons believed Jenney's sketches of the proposed building did not display the "imposing" effect they wanted. Jenney responded that raising the height of the building by increasing the height of the stories could be done but would be expensive.

To contain costs and give a more impressive appearance, he proposed increasing the height of the tower in lieu of the stories. The tower was brick and Jenney stated the cost would be $250 per foot of height. In a letter on November 22, 1888, Jenney estimated the cost of rebuilding and adding a separate boiler house to be $126,068.[35]

Replacing the library was a formidable undertaking without adequate funding from the state. On March 17, 1891, the Board initiated the first student fee, charging each $1.00 per term. The fee was termed the "Janitor's Fee," but the money was used to buy books and supplies. In October of that year, President Parsons was authorized to purchase a new invention, the mimeograph, for faculty use. (The mimeograph was first licensed in 1887).

Classes were held for the first time in the building in September 1889, and the Board of Trustees held its first meeting in Old Main on September 13, 1889. ∎

Chapter 3 President Parsons

Power Plant Smokestack Topples

President Tirey

Date: April 7, 1953

The first reference to a determination to raze Old Main and North Hall appears in Trustee Minutes from September 21, 1949. "Whereas Indiana State Teachers College has no further use for the old Administration Building and Annex located on the College Campus; Now therefore be it resolved, that the President and Business Manager of the college are hereby authorized to take such steps as are legally necessary for the razing and/or sale of said buildings."[36] In 1950, the contract for demolition was awarded to Cleveland Wrecking Com., for $19,467.[37] The old Power Plant followed.

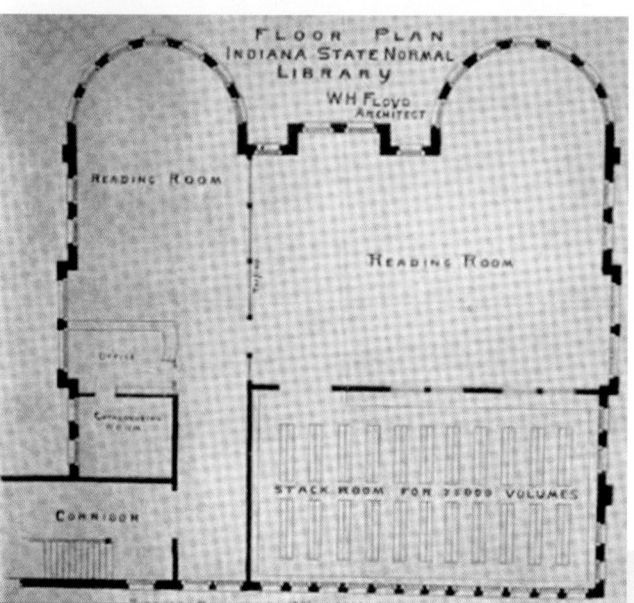

North Hall

Architects: W. H. Floyd and Guy Stone

Contractors: Jungclause and J. A. Schumacher

Date: 1894-97

Cost: $60,500

Razed: 1950

North Hall was the second building on the campus and was a contiguous addition to the Normal School facing north on Eagle Street.[38] North Hall was born out of several issues dictating the need for a new building on campus. First was the continued student population growth. Both the laboratory and library spaces were inadequate.[39] The Board of Trustees noted in their most recent annual report that odors from the chemistry labs in the basement permeated the entire building. Parsons noted the increased possibility of fire beginning in the laboratories and stressed that everything of value to the school was in one building.[40] Working under the pressure of a very limited budget, President Parsons was presented with two possibilities.

The first was to limit enrollment, request funds for new equipment, enlarge the library, and increase faculty salaries.[41] The second was to pursue a new building while trying to address some of the other needs. At their December 16, 1892 meeting, the Trustees reviewed and adopted the plans for North Hall submitted by W. H. Floyd and Guy Stone, Terre Haute architects.[42]

With the support of the Trustees, Parsons pressed for funds for the new building. In 1893, the Legislature voted and agreed to devoting $40,000 for the construction of North Hall. Construction began but funds were insufficient for its completion. The next General Assembly voted to allot an additional $20,000 to complete the building. Additional funds were found to provide for furnishings.

By 1895, Biology, Physics, and Chemistry, together with the library, moved into the new building and occupied the second and third floors.[43] The first and fourth floors remained unfinished.[44] A men's and women's gymnasium occupied the basement. The supporting columns in the basement had to be padded to prevent players from injuring themselves since the supports ran through the middle of the gymnasium. Later in its history, the building housed the graduate school, deans' offices, and classrooms for Art, Commerce, Education, and Mathematics.

Architect W. H. Floyd was born in Evansville in 1852 and learned his trade as a stair builder, and then studied mechanical engineering and architecture. He began his architectural career in 1880 and was active in Chattanooga, as was Guy Stone, until 1892 when he returned to Terre Haute. He earned a reputation as a builder of hotels and large-scale buildings. Among his more noteworthy buildings were the West Baden Springs Hotel in French Lick, the Filbeck Hotel in Terre Haute, Fairbanks Library, the Terre Haute House, the Grand Opera House, and his work on the ISNS campus.[45] He and his partner, Stone, also made a design proposal for the Masonic Temple. The contractors, Jungclause and Schumacher, worked in partnership running a plaining mill and selling lumber until 1895 when the partnership dissolved.[46]

The style of North Hall respects the Romanesque Revival style of the recently constructed Old Main building of 1889. It was a three-story structure with a central entrance bay flanked by two bays that advanced slightly in front of the central block. It had a heavily rusticated stone base as well as heavy cornices above the basement and first-story windows. Hipped roof dormers extended forward from the steeply gabled roof. The third-floor windows repeated the shape of the fourth story windows of Old Main. The central entry was comprised of double wooden doors set within a round-arched, thick, rusticated stone frame. The round Roman arch-shaped archivolt was supported by truncated columns set in the jambs. Floyd did not adopt the heavy terra cotta bands (belt cornices) seen above the third floor of Old Main but opted for a more simplified treatment of the wall surface. The building, like Old Main, reflects the heavy Richardsonian Romanesque style popular in Chicago during this time. The former Filbeck Hotel and Terre Haute High School shared many stylistic similarities.[47] ■

Country Training School

Lost Creek Township School No. 6.

Date: ca. 1870

Location: Chamberlain's Crossing, Lost Creek Township. Formerly five miles east of Terre Haute on the interurban line.

Chapter 3 President Parsons

In 1902, ISNS entered into an agreement with the trustee of Lost Creek Township, Mr. Joseph Ripley, in order to utilize this one-room school house, School No. 6, for training teachers. The majority of students who attended ISNS and became teachers would not teach in multi-room school buildings. On the contrary, the majority would practice in very simple, under-equipped, one-room schoolhouses. This rural school building provided an ideal training site.[48]

The builder of this schoolhouse has remained unknown, but it is proposed here that the builder was Mr. Isaac Myers. Myers came from Pennsylvania and settled in Vigo County in 1859. He farmed, but also practiced as a carpenter. It is recorded that he built five of the schoolhouses in Lost Creek Township, as well as three in Riley. He seems to have been an exceptionally civic-minded person who contributed significantly to his community.[49] A high school was eventually built on this site and the ISNS rural program was relocated.

The ISNS's programmatic involvement with the rural training school earned very favorable evaluations by the State's Board of Visitors and was a point of pride for President Parsons and Wm. H. Armstrong, President of the Normal School Board of Trustees. Armstrong wrote:

> "So far as is known, this is the only normal school in the United States maintaining a distinct rural school as an integral part of its training school. A large proportion of the students of the institution come from the country and go back to rural districts to teach. It has been deemed important, therefore, to add to the facilities for observation and practice in a typical country school."[50]

The Board of Visitors (1904-05) commented favorably:

> "… we desire to record our unqualified approval of the provision made for a model school in the country. Moreover, this feature is … peculiar to the Indiana State Normal School."[51]

Finally, the Board of Visitors (1905-06) stated:

> "The plan of having a model country school to enable seniors to learn by observation and practice … is an excellent one and should be continued. The establishment of a township consolidated school, under the control of the Normal School authorities, and accessible to students by trolley, would serve as a model … and greatly stimulate the establishment of consolidated schools."[52]

While a model, in the near future consolidation, the automobile and public transport would lead to the decline in one-room schools. By the turn of the century, progressive educators believed the one-room schoolhouse with "a local board of farmers was inefficient, unprofessional, and sectarian."[53]

In 1920, President Parsons informed the Trustees that the rural one-room schoolhouse would be abandoned at the end of the winter quarter.[54] ■

The Training School

Architects: J. F. Alexander and Son (J. Frank)[55]

Contractors: H. B. Walter (General Construction); The Andrews-Johnson Co. (Heating/Ventilation); D. W. Watson's Sons (Plumbing)[56]

Date: 1905

Cost: Approx. $79,500[57]

Area: Approx. 39,600 GSF

Razed: 1952[58]

Renamed: Stalker Hall, 1936[59]

The Training School

President Tirey

Date: 1952 The Training School was razed.

The Training School (later renamed Stalker Hall in honor of Francis Marion Stalker) allowed teacher training for all grade levels to be accommodated in one building.[60] It was constructed in 1905 adjacent to Old Main and faced Mulberry Street.[61] Together with the North Building, the two formed bookends for Old Main. The necessity and great advantage of this building was that it accommodated all 12 grades and brought all teachers and teaching preparatory courses under one roof.

Its construction was prompted by the state's new policy that made high school a part of the common school. This necessitated the extension of training for teachers to include four more years of high school study. The rooms in Old Main were not adequate and the combination of teacher training with scores of children and adolescents with older students was impracticable. The school recognized the need for a new building and an appeal was made to the legislature in 1903 for $50,000 appropriation.

The General Assembly appropriated $50,000 and, with that, the four-story brick and limestone Training School building was constructed. The cost of the land and construction totaled $33,812 over the appropriated amount. The fourth floor of the building, when it opened, was also incomplete. A request for an additional appropriation of $10,000 was made to the Governor to complete the fourth floor. His response was that the institution should find the additional funds from tax revenues. By "practicing rigid economy" the necessary funds were obtained, and the fourth floor was completed during the summer of 1907.[62]

The original purpose of the building was to house the "model school" that served as a site for observation and practice teaching. When the new Laboratory School opened (1937), the training school program was moved to the new facility. The basement of the Training School was used for manual training. Grades one through six occupied the first floor, and the upper floors accommodated the high school. When the training school function moved to the new Laboratory School, Stalker became the home of the Departments of Education and Social Studies.

The façade showed a tripartite division with the central entrance block advancing forward slightly. The double-door entry was enhanced by the limestone surround. Two columns rest on the entablature of the entrance and rise vertically three floors. The semi-circular arch of the doorway is repeated in the triple windows of the arcade at the top. Dormers emerge from the sharply pitched roof. Typical of Alexander's work are the horizontal limestone bands across the façade. A rusticated limestone cornice rests atop the basement windows and is repeated in ashlar masonry across the top of the third-floor windows. The bands are also prominent across the dormers and crowning triple arcade.

The building appears less ornate than some of Alexander's other buildings, perhaps reflecting a limited budget and aesthetic decision not to detract from Old Main and the North building. Many of the same elements, such as the limestone banding, rounded arches, and continued Romanesque stylistic influence that characterized Old Main and North Building, as well as the new Training School, can be seen in several high schools Alexander designed about the same time. Among them are Linden High School, West Lafayette High School, and Madison Township Public School.

In a report to the Trustees in 1946, the building was considered very unsafe.[63] It was not until six years later that the Trustees voted to raze this building together with the old Power House.[64] ■

President William Wood Parsons served as President of the institution for 36 years, the longest term served by any president in the school's history.

Normal Hall (Library)

Architects: James F. Alexander and Son (J. Frank)[65]
Contractor: August Ohm Sr.[66]
Glass Dome: Louis J. Millet[67]
Date: 1910
   Dedication: January 21, 1910[68]

Cost: $155,000
Area: Approx. 24,000 sq. ft.[69]
Location: 650 Eagle Street

Normal Hall is "the handsomest building in the state devoted to library purposes and is a durable and magnificent monument to (Indiana's) system of public education."[70]

Normal Library (aka Normal or Normal Hall) today is decidedly one the most handsome buildings on the campus and is the only remaining structure from the early period of campus development. A portion of the land the Library was located on was sold to ISNS by Arthur Cunningham, who had come to ISNS in 1890 from DePauw University. Cunningham played a major role in the growth of the Library in the late 19th and early 20th centuries.[71] The building was located facing south on Eagle Street and was planned from the outset to provide security for the holdings, sufficient storage for a growing campus, better accommodation for users, and beauty.

The choice of a neo-classical style, quality of materials, and proportions of the structure all contribute to the building's enduring presence.[72] The location of the library prior to Normal was North Hall. North was considered insufficient because it posed two important problems: it was not safe from fire and the growth in the student population rendered it congested and insufficient.[73] An appeal was made for a Legislative appropriation of $99,970 for the building. Additional funds were found for stacks, furniture, and fixtures. The contract for the new Library was let on August 6, 1907. The building was officially delivered to the Trustees on December 17, 1909, with a dedication ceremony on January 21, 1910. The total expense was about $155,000.[74]

The principle architect for Normal Library was J. F. Alexander and Son, whose architectural firm was located in Lafayette, Indiana and operated until 1917. It was a reputable firm and was responsible for some of the finest buildings in the region.[75] One of its most prominent was the Indiana Knights of Pythias Building in Indianapolis (1906-07), constructed just prior to the Normal Library. The firm also designed other libraries, for example, the Hoopeston Public Library in Hoopeston, Illinois (1904-05) and, ascribed to their firm, the Tipton Public Library (1902-03). Alexander also designed the Tippecanoe County Courthouse and the Administration Building on the Ball State Campus (the Eastern Division of ISNS). The firm was also responsible for building the Training School (1905 - renamed Stalker Hall in 1936, razed in 1953). The contractor for the new Normal Library was August Ohm Sr., a Terre Haute resident (died in 1920).

The new Library, in its initial configuration, could hold about 100,000 volumes. When three more tiers of shelving were added, it could accommodate about 250,000 volumes, making it one of the best collections for training teachers in the entire country.[76] The stacks had glass floors, which provided more light. The stacks were also "open," which provided immediate access for students and offered the wonderful element of serendipity, which comes from being able to look through the stacks and find new sources about a topic (something closed stacks and the card catalog system could not provide). The central reading room measured 60 x 80 feet and was crowned with a rotunda and dome, which was carried on marbleized Ionic columns on marble bases on the first-floor peristyle, and Corinthian columns carrying a peristyle and balustrade beneath the dome.[77] The light filtering through the decoration of the dome provided a gentle, if not inspiring, light for the readers beneath. In the history of art, light is a symbol for truth and inspiration. The space was floored with a "noiseless cork carpet."[78]

In the stained-glass dome there was a reproduction of a scene drawn from Raphael's tondo titled "Philosophy" in the Stanze della Segnature in the Vatican apartments. In the original painting the words "Causarum Cognitio" (Knowledge of Causes) can be read, which reflects Aristotle's emphasis on wisdom as knowing why something occurred, therefore knowing the causes.[79] Below was a series of 24 wreathed medallions, each with a flaming torch and open book (or scale of justice) in the center of the wreath. Below the wreaths were the names of 24 philosophers and educators.

Of the latter group, six were Indiana educators and President Parsons' name was included, no doubt, as a fitting tribute to his long and successful tenure with ISNS. On the lowest part of the dome were several inscriptions. One was quoted from the Ordinance of 1787, which gave educational freedom to the Northwest region. A second drew from the 1816 State Constitution, while a third was an extract from the Act of 1865, which established ISNS.[80] Interior stairways on the southeast and southwest corners were made of marble and bronze and communicated with rooms on the second floor and the basement beneath.

On the second floor at the front were two large rooms. One was used by children in the training school who were taught how to use the library. The second was used for storing more precious objects such as art books, rare books, and pictures. The sides were equipped with small seminar rooms for professors' and advanced students' use. The corridor on the second floor was used, occasionally, for art exhibitions. The basement housed a lecture room, book binding, and storage rooms, closets, and coat storage.

The exterior of the Library, done in limestone and brick, is in an Italian Renaissance-inspired, neo-classical style.[81] The building is two-story and rests on a basement finished in rusticated masonry. The deeper cutting of the stone gives the impression of a heavy and stabile base for the structure. A strong cornice resting on brackets under each window separates the basement from the first floor. The ashlar masonry terminates below the

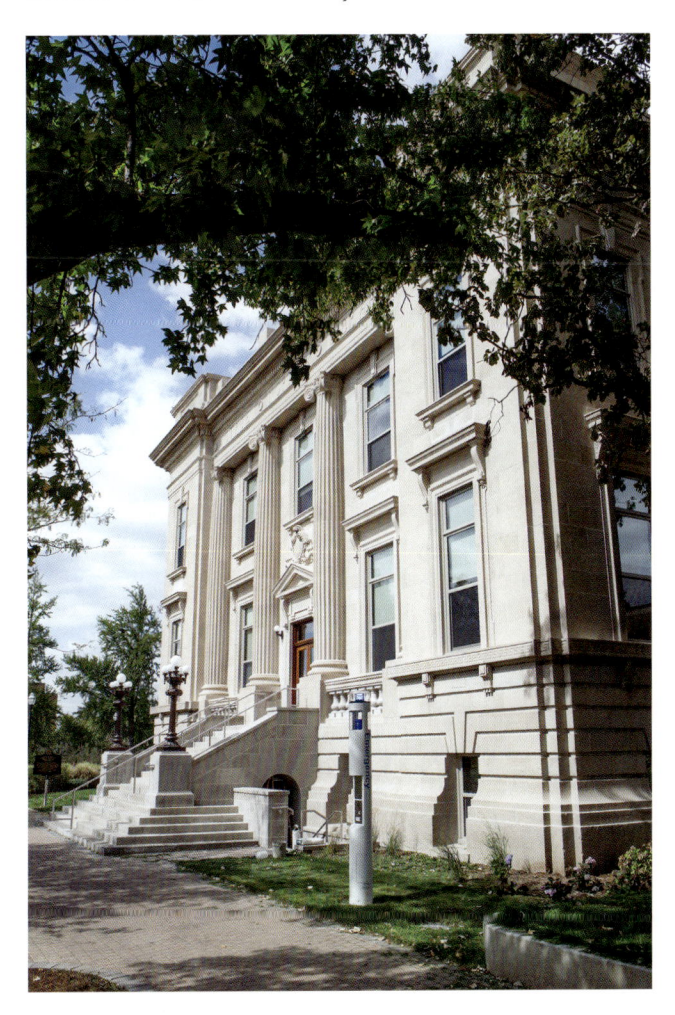

Chapter 3 President Parsons

cornice and the remainder of the building's surface is smooth-textured. The building shows a distinct axiality with emphasis placed on the South façade with the main entrance. The facade shows a tripartite division with the ornate entrance-way bracketed by two pavilions, or bays, at the southwest and southeast corners that step forward slightly, thus framing the central entry.

The entry appears monumental and dramatic owing to the four engaged fluted limestone Ionic columns, and more plastic treatment of the doorway flanked by two of the columns and a triangular pediment over the doorway. The original entrance was a double door with transom and stone cartouche over a console-supported triangular pediment.

The door is recessed into the front wall and the resulting shadow cast by the recession and canopy over the door, as well as the shadow created by the heavy entablature inscribed with "State Normal Library" resting on the Ionic capitals, add an element of drama. Above the entablature is a cornice with classically inspired dentils that runs around three sides of the building. Above that is a parapet wall.

A balustrade runs horizontally from the corner blocks to the bases upon which the columns rest. Horizontality is also picked up in the pediments above the windows that play off against the verticality of the central columns and window surrounds. The theme of the corbels supporting the lower stringcourse reappears beneath the sills of the upper story windows, as does the keystone seen in the basement windows that is repeated above in the shouldered architraves with keystones in the second story windows.

The windows of the first floor have stone surrounds and console-supported flat hoods. On the east and west sides of the building, the seven upper floor windows continue the design from the façade in a simple 'A' 'A' 'A' rhythm. The first-floor windows have triangular pediments that repeat the shape of the pediment over the door inserted in every other bay creating an 'A' 'B' 'A' rhythm down the length of the building.

One entered the building by means of 17 steps.[82] It seems fitting that students and faculty "ascended" into the Library which, like Raphael's School of Athens fresco suggests, was the center of teaching and learning – a kind of academic Acropolis. ■

"Stack Room"

President Tirey   **Date:** 1937

President Tirey was authorized by the Board to go to the State Budget Committee to request funds for adding five floors to the "stack room."[83]

The first item in the Capital Project requests for the years 1953-55 was submitted by ISTC for the addition to the Normal Library. The addition would have additional stacks and the existing building would receive new stairs and entrances. The current stairs delivered students directly into the reading room, so it was at this time the original steps were planned for removal.

Indiana State University Building a Legacy

New Stacks and Entrance

President Holmstedt

Architect: Yeager and Associates

Contractors: Snyder Construction; Neff Hardware and Electrical; Christman Co.

Date: 1955-57

Cost: $472,500 (estimate provided by Yeager Architects)[84]

Area: 68,115 GSF

An original estimate was for $472,500, based upon a plan developed by Yeager. The plan called for a box-like addition on the east side of the building that would allow for additional stacks. The plan also addressed the need for air conditioning, enlarging the reading room, and adding new entrances to divert traffic from entering directly into the reading room. The new entrance to the lower level on the south side required the removal of the original steps.[85]

Historical Importance

President Landini

Concern was raised during the Trustee meeting of December 2, 1988 that buildings of historical importance should be kept. They constitute what the alumni remember. Landini stated he thought of Normal Library "as a bridge between the present students and their predecessors, the alumni, as the symbol of ISU." Trustee Breeden spoke in support of preservation and suggested the library entrance be reconstructed with steps as an original part of the building. The Foundation Director stated that "in terms of fund raising the project is under way." The results of that initiative are unclear.[86]

National Register of Historic Places

President Benjamin

During President Benjamin's presidency, the building was listed on the National Register of Historic Places and the Indiana Register of Historic Sites and Structures. Early in his presidency, Benjamin made the statement that the restoration of Normal was an important priority and formed a committee to begin to explore opportunities. Initial plans would have moved the President's office and Alumni Affairs to the original building with the 1957 addition removed. Benjamin's plan for putting the alumni office and its functions in that building would allow visitors to be embraced by the history of the campus.[87]

Chapter 3 President Parsons

Normal Hall Renovation

President Bradley

Designer: arcDESIGN

Date: 2015-16

Cost: $15.1 million[88]

Area: 65,393 GSF; 42,435 ASF

Contractors: Weddle Bros. Construction Co.[89]; R. E. Dimond and Assoc. (Mechanical); Lynch, Harrison & Brumleve (Structural); Myers Engineering Inc. (Civil); The Garland Co. Inc. (Roof and Building Envelope); Conrad Schmitt Studios (Restored Dome and Scagliola Columns)

In September 2013, the Trustees authorized the administration to request approval to spend up to $16 million previously approved by the General Assembly to renovate Normal Hall.[90] Renovation on Normal Hall began in May 2014 and was completed in 2015. The project architect was arcDESIGN of Indianapolis, and R. E. Dimond and Associates served as Mechanical Engineers. Weddle Brothers Construction Company was responsible for all the remodeling. The project received an AIA Indiana Design Award for Preservation/Adaptive Reuse/Renovation.

The "storage box" addition of 1957 was removed, and a modern addition took its place. All of the building services, restrooms, mechanical rooms, elevators, etc., were moved to the new addition, enabling arcDESIGN to focus attention on historic materials, fabrics, finishes in contrast to the addition that is more contemporary in design with materials that contrast with the original building while not detracting. Every effort was made to salvage doors, original hardware, and restore or reproduce plaster moldings and to return the building to its former stateliness.

The restoration also brought the 1910 structure up to current ADA and OSHA standards. Two major restoration accomplishments were to restore the marble and bronze staircase and the stained-glass dome.[91] The dome surmounts the central rotunda and is supported by 20 original columns.

President Bradley dedicated the building that houses the Center for Student Success and University College to "student success." He said, "When completed, the project will provide a valuable new resource to students while preserving and re-energizing a significant historic structure in the heart of the campus."[92]

Normal Library unites the past, present, and future on the ISU campus. ∎

Indiana State University Building a Legacy

Science Hall

Architect: Clarence Martindale
Contractor: Almond Winfield (A. W.) Stoolman
Date: 1917
Cost: $132,000
Area: 37,200 GSF; 25,921 ASF
Location: 626 Eagle Street
Renamed: College of Business, 1962; Classroom Building, 1981

The original architect of Science Hall was Clarence Martindale (1866-1937).[93] He was an Indianapolis-based architect who became a member of the American Institute of Architects in 1901.[94] He was active in architectural circles in Indianapolis and served as the secretary of the newly formed Architects Association of Indianapolis in 1909.[95]

Martindale was an author and produced a book titled Modern Architecture. Among his other important buildings that bear some stylistic similarities to the Science Building are the Danville, Indiana Court House, designed in an Italian Renaissance-Second Empire style (dedicated September 8, 1915), and the Hendricks County Court House (1912-14), built in an Italian Renaissance style popular during the early part of the 20th century. Greek and Roman architectural elements, such as Doric and Ionic columns, classical ornamentation, and triangular pediments formed a part of his vocabulary, and similar elements were to be seen in the Science Building façade.

The footprint of the brick and limestone building was in the shape of a capital I. The façade was divided into three bays with brick quoins on the corners and a pronounced emphasis on the central bay - the corps de logis - which provided access through a central doorway. The second floor was treated like a piano nobile in French and Italian classicizing architecture. The balustrade, limestone panels above the windows, and Tuscan-style columns confirmed this style. The pilaster strips that extended from the second to the third floor carried a limestone cornice which united the facade horizontally. The central vertical axis culminated in a cartouche with swags.

The vocabulary of elements bear comparison with the Hendricks County Court House, where one finds a strongly emphasized central bay with framing piers and free-standing columns atop a rusticated base. The central pavilion (projecting element of the façade), with its reference to a Roman temple façade, reveals the influence of French architectural style such as one finds at the Louvre and Versailles. The more ornate central block compensates for the lack of visual interest in the bracketing bays, noteworthy for the simple treatment of the double-hung windows without pediments or decorative framing.[96]

A.W. Stoolman was a highly respected contractor. He was born in Paxton, Illinois, graduated from the University of Illinois (1897), and established his principle office in Champaign, with subsidiary offices in three other states and the cities of Indianapolis and Terre Haute.[97] Aside from the Science Building, he was also the contractor for the Terre Haute Masonic Temple, adjacent to the ISU campus at Eighth Street and Larry Bird (begun in 1915), and the Illinois Central Railroad Depot in Mattoon, Illinois (completed in 1918).

Significant additions to the curriculum in 1907-08, the gradual growth in enrollment and faculty, and the unhealthy location of science labs in North Hall contributed to the necessity of building a facility for the sciences.[98] Enrollment grew from 881 in 1913-14 to 1,207 in 1915-16.[99] The number of departments expanded from 21 in 1910 to 23 in 1920. The increasing interest in the sciences, combined with faculty with specializations in specific scientific fields, contributed to the creation of the departments of Physics and Chemistry.[100] ∎

Chapter 3 President Parsons

Remodeling Science Hall

President Holmstedt

Architect: Yeager Architects, Inc.[101]

Contractors: Hannig Construction (General Construction); Potter Electrical and Engineering (Electrical); Freitag-Weinhardt (Plumbing, HVAC)[102]

Date: 1961-62

Cost: $521,000[103]

Yeager prepared plans for general remodeling of the building. The building was considered in excellent condition, and with the addition of air conditioning, it was assumed it would "provide excellent instructional space for many years to come."

Fourth Floor Addition

President Rankin

Architect: Ewing Miller [104]

Contractors: Kuykendall Const. (General Construction); Freitag-Weinhardt, Inc. (Mechanical); Sanborn Electric Co. (Electrical)[105]

Date: 1969-71

Cost: $293,823[106]

Area: 41,304 GSF; 27,745 ASF

Ewing Miller presented a preliminary plan for an additional floor in April 1969 that was approved by the Trustees.[107] Cost was estimated at $247,000 without professional fees. This addition of a top floor to the original Science Hall provided 42 new offices of varying dimensions, study areas for students and 3 seminar rooms that could be opened to create an assembly room and deck. Miller stated a thorough study of the building had been completed and it was decided to build using a light steel frame and "considerable" reflective glass.[108]

Remodel First and Second Floors

President Landini

Architect: Walter Scholar and Associates, Inc.[109]

Contractors: Shelton Hannig, Inc. (General Construction); Harrah Plumbing and Heating Co., Inc. (Plumbing and Heating); Commonwealth Electric Co. (Electrical)[110]

Date: 1980-81

Cost: $881,523[111]

Renovations were made in this, one of the oldest structures on campus, for School of Technology and Music programs. The first two floors were remodeled to accommodate the Aerospace Technology Department and a new drafting facility. New lighting, electrical, and fire alarm systems were installed.

Razed

President Moore

Contractor: S&G

Cost: $144,767[112]

Razed: 1998

Indiana State University Building a Legacy

Chapter 3 References

1. The role of President was quite different from more recent presidencies. Parsons, as with other presidents, was referred to as President of the Faculty and it is clear the Board was directly involved in management. Some duties were repugnant. In 1914, The Board instructed "the President of the Faculty to consider the question of enlarging the men's toilet, or relieving in some way certain objectionable features that prevail there." Trustee Minutes, June 10, 1914, p. 457. Portrait by T.C. Steele

2. Terre Haute Evening Gazette, April 9, 1888. See also Lynch, pp. 126-130. The Gazette reported, "There was never a handsomer fire in Terre Haute or one that could be viewed so satisfactorily."

3. Lynch, p. 130. Terre Haute Gazette, April 11, 1888.

4. Lynch, p. 139.

5. Lynch, p. 139.

6. Lynch, p. 145.

7. Lynch, p. 146.

8. Lynch, pp. 149-151.

9. Lynch, p. 153.

10. Lynch, p. 153.

11. Lynch, p. 200.

12. Lynch, p. 200; pp.222-224. Most students who attended ISNS prior to 1907 had no high school experience; Parsons remained staunchly committed to admitting students without high school credentials. By 1921, ISNS had dropped its preparatory program for this population.

13. Lynch, p. 200.

14. Lynch, p. 201.

15. Lynch, p. 202

16. See Richard White, The Republic for Which it Stands: The United States During Reconstruction and the Gilded Age, 1865-96. Oxford History of the United States, 2017.

17. Lynch, pp. 257-261. The agreement to merge was reached on April 4, 1918. In addition to a drop in enrollment, Parsons had excess faculty who were anxious to remain employed.

18. Lynch, p. 262. A direction not taken that may have continued to benefit the school in the future was the offer made by the Trustees of Vincennes University to transfer its property, endowment, and equipment to ISNS on one condition; that ISNS would pay roundtrip rail for all students commuting from Vincennes to Terre Haute during the time it took for them to complete their degree. Trustee Minutes, February 5, 1919, p. 111.

19. Historical Sketch, p. 22.

20. How ill-suited is reflected in the great concern about the red-light district adjacent to the campus. President Parsons, Secretary Jump, and Judge Denny met with the Terre Haute Mayor in an effort to hire a detective to collect information about the district so action could be taken. Wisely, the Mayor suggested the detective not be someone local. Trustee Minutes, p. 114.

21. "Report of the Indiana State Normal School for the Fiscal Years Ending October 31, 1905 and October 31, 1906," pp. 29-30 in Annual Reports of the Officers of State of the State of Indiana, 1907, Indianapolis, Wm. B. Burford, Contractor for State Printing and Binding, pp. 1643-1644.

22. Trustee Minutes show that President Parsons was absent from the Trustee meeting February 3, 1916 "… on account of the critical illness of Mrs. Parsons." Trustee Minutes, February 3, 1916, p. 199.

23. The Board selected Jenney & Otis "to be the elected architects to provide plans for rebuilding." Trustee Minutes, April 21, p. 469.

24. The contract with W. A. Atkins for $47,200 was approved by the Trustees July 6, 1888. The contract stated a completion date of December 15. On October 12, 1888 a resolution was passed stating the building was not proceeding as rapidly as it should, and it put the contractor on notice for responsibility to meet deadlines or be fined.

25. The Legislature provided $100,000 and the City of Terre Haute provided $50,000. No doubt, there were other miscellaneous costs.

26. Trustee Minutes from April 9, 1888 (p. 461) stated about 100 books were saved, 100 more were in the hands of students, and 13 microscopes were recovered.

27. Ibid.

28. At one point during the process to decide how to proceed, Trustee President Briggs moved to substitute a two-story building for the old one. The motion was unanimously approved but was later supplanted by the Jenney & Otis plan. Trustee Minutes, April 20, p. 467.

29. Jenney had written to Mr. Jos. Strong, a highly respected businessperson in Terre Haute, on April 10, 1888 asking him to please "kindly say a word in my favor" and indicating his interest in serving as the architect for the rebuilding. Indiana State University Library Archives, Papers of William Wood Parsons, Records Group 1.2.

    Gaddis was John W. Gaddis (1858-1931) whose office was in Vincennes. He was responsible for a number of buildings currently on the National Register of Historic Places.

30. J. A. Vrydagh & Son received a payment of $100 for preliminary studies. No record of payment to Geddis has been found. The Jenney and Otis firm was paid $4,469 during the 1888-89 period. Annual Reports of the Officers of State of the State of Indiana, Indianapolis: 1889, p. 79. Between 1888 and 1890, W. A. Atkins was paid $29,418; Collins and Ohm $57,663 and Frank Prox $5,000 for the heating system.

31. Trustee Minutes, April 21, 1888, p. 470.

32. Indiana State University Archives.

33. The "Specifications" written by Jenney & Otis provide interesting information about contemporary building techniques. It states the contractor should cover the foundations in manure to protect them from freezing weather. Specifications for Repairs to the Indiana State Normal School …, p. 3.

34. William Le Baron Jenney (1832-1907) and Henry Hobson Richardson (1838-86) initiated the Romanesque Revival in Chicago. Characteristics of this style included heavy, rough stone exteriors, steeply pitched roofs, heavy half-round arches over windows and doorways, towers and projecting bays – all to be seen in Jenney's design. Buildings in this style were most frequently used for public buildings such as train depots and courthouses. The compact plan and use of heavy masonry produced a medieval fortress appearance.

    Jenney was a distinguished architect and is considered one of the founders of the Chicago School of architecture. He had studied in Paris and was a classmate of Gustave Eiffel, designer of the Eiffel Tower. He built his first skyscraper, the Home Insurance Building in Chicago in 1883-85. Among his apprentices was Louis Sullivan, famous for the innovative Wainwright Building in St. Louis. By 1890, Jenney was the most advanced architect in the world in building tall buildings using new materials and techniques.

    The influence of the "Chicago Style" in Terre Haute is interesting, but not unusual. Mr. Ewing Miller, principle architect during the Holmstedt and Rankins eras, stated in an interview (June 26, 2018 with the author) that in the early 20th century there were 13 Chicago satellite architectural firms working in Terre Haute.

35. Apparently, the heating system did not function properly. On January 23, 1890, the Trustees sent a letter to Mr. Frank Prox, who was under contract (September 1, 1889) to "thoroughly heat and ventilate … the entire Normal School Building." The letter continues, "Such apparatus has at no time met the requirements of your contract. It has proven very defective and totally inadequate to the purposes for which it was designed." Extreme cold threatened to shut down the school.

36. Trustee Minutes, September 21, 1949, p. 422.

37. Ibid, February 2, 1950, p. 477.

38 Payment was made in 1890 to B. V. Marshall for the lot east of Old Main for $3,000. It is assumed this is the lot on which North was built. Annual Reports of the Officers of State of the State of Indiana, Indianapolis: 1890, pp. 79-80.

39 Between 1888, when Old Main opened, and 1895, when North Hall was under construction, the average term enrollment had grown from 449 to 574 (28 percent). The total number of different students served in a year went from 936 in 1888 to 1,580 (a nearly 70 percent increase) in 1895. Report of the Indiana State Normal School for the Fiscal Year beginning October 31, 1899, p. 13.

40 Biennial Report of the Indiana State Normal School. Indianapolis: Wm B. Burford Publisher, 1892, p. 64.

41 The Board of Trustees (April 25, 1895) did implement a plan to limit enrollment at Normal by adding new admission requirements.

42 Trustee Minutes, December 16, 1892, p. 201.

43 The school had purchased 100 new chairs for the library but found they made too much noise. They then purchased rubber pads for the chairs that "… proved to make just as much noise as the old ones." (Annals, np.)

44 Lynch, pp. 160-161. Students attending the fall term helped move the library and science equipment to the new building.

45 Charles C. Oaky, Greater Terre Haute and Vigo County, Vol. 2, 1908: Chicago and New York: Lewis Publishing Company, pp. 613-614.

46 David J. Bodenhamer and Robert G. Barrows, eds., The Encyclopedia of Indianapolis, 1994: World Distributor, p. 1430.

47 Another fine example of Richardsonian Romanesque is the Old City Hall in Fort Wayne constructed by Wing and Mahurin in 1893.

48 Mr. Ripley fought in the Civil War and later went to Kansas where he served on the Santa Fe stage coach road. Later, he returned to Vigo County where he was born, and farmed.

H. W. Beckwith, History of Vigo and Parke Counties, Together with Historic Notes on the Wabash Valley. Chicago: H. H. Hill and N. Iddings Publishers, 1880, p. 399.

49 Ibid, p. 402.

50 Wm. H. Armstrong in Report of the Indiana State Normal School for the Fiscal Years Ending October 31, 1905 and October 31, 1906, Indianapolis: Wm. B. Burford Publisher, 1906., p. 9.

51 Alfred I. Bayliss, R. I. Hamilton, and George H. Tapy, "Report of the Board of Special Visitors,1904-05," Report, p. 22.

52 E. O. Lyte, Harold Barnes, and Edson B. Sarber, "Report of the Board of Special Visitors (1905-06)," Report, p. 27.

53 Andrew L. C. Cayton, Richard Sisson, and Chris Zacher, eds, The American Midwest: An Interpretive Encyclopedia. Bloomington: Indiana University Press, 2006. p. 796.

In 1900, the Superintendent of Public Instruction wrote, "The favorite expression of one of Indiana's foremost State Superintendents … was 'Establishment of a rural school at every crossroads.' This stimulus to rural schoolhouse construction multiplied those schools unduly, and many of them need to be abandoned at this time." Frank L. Jones, The Rural Schools: Pages from the Biennial Report of the Superintendent of Public Instruction of Indiana 1900, Indianapolis: 1900, p. 521.

54 Trustee Minutes, May 6, 1920.

55 Alexander must have had considerable respect among his peers, evidenced by the fact that he served on four committees simultaneously in the Western Association of Architects, one of which was to serve as representative to the national AIA. His fee was established at 5 percent of the total cost of the building. Trustee Minutes, December 15, 1903, p. 367. The Trustees approved the contract with Alexander in December 1903. Trustee Minutes, December 15, 1903, p. 365.

56 Trustee Minutes, March 21, 1904, pp. 385-386.

57 H. B. Walter (General construction-$44,820); The Andrews-Johnson Co. (Heating/Ventilation-$6,575); D.W. Watson's Sons (Plumbing-$3,674).

58 President Tirey told the Trustees that removing the Power Plant and Stalker was essential to the completion of the campus plan. Trustee Minutes, February 19, 1952, p. 196. Trustees voted to remove the old Power Plant and, if classroom space could be found, to remove Stalker at the same time. Trustee Minutes, April 23, 1952, p. 210.

59 The Trustees unanimously voted the name change to Stalker Hall. Trustee Minutes, December 7, 1936, p. 278.

60 Stalker became head of the Department of Education in 1923. Lynch, p. 293.

61 The lot was purchased from Caroline and Edward Huestis for $15,600. From budget report prepared by Joshua Jump, Secretary of the Board of Trustees. The agreement was reached via the telephone on October 8, 1903. Trustee Minutes, October 8, 1903, p. 338.

62 There are records of payment to the architect J. F. Alexander and Son ($7,700) and contractor H. B. Walter ($24,870), recorded by Joshua Jump, Secretary, Board of Trustees, in his budget report for fiscal years 1905-06.

63 "There are storage rooms under all the stairways in the basement. These facts make this building a constant fire hazard." Trustee Minutes, January 15, 1946, p. 666.

64 Tirey discussed with the Board the need to remove this building and the Boiler Plant. Trustee Minutes, February 19, 1952, pp. 196-197. The Board voted for the removal of both buildings and hiring an architect to prepare plans for a new classroom building. The topic was again raised in the September meeting of the Board, but with additional properties included for demolition and Tirey's recommendation that an architect be hired to develop plans for razing Stalker and the Heating Plant. Trustee Minutes, September 27, 1952, pp. 286-287. Demolition cost was $25,000. Tirey also informed the Board an additional $120,000 would be required to complete the new power plant and service building. That was a significant sum and currently would be equal to over one million dollars. See: www://data.bls.gov/cgi-bin/cpicalc.pl.

65 The Alexander firm was established in Lafayette, Indiana in 1872 and was liquidated in 1918. The Inland Architect and News Record, Vol. 10, September 1887, p. 23.

66 It appears from correspondence of the time that President Parsons was exceedingly concerned that Mr. Ohm (1853-1920) had accomplished nothing since the contract was signed on August 27, 1907. Parsons reminded Ohm that the building was to be completed by December 1908 – ten months hence. He wrote, "Nearly half of the time has elapsed, and nothing has been done except to do some excavating and fill the street with materials." Parsons Letter to Mr. August Ohm, February 13, 1908. Ohm was a highly respected contractor. Among his buildings in Terre Haute were the Northern Hotel built for Albert R. Monninger and Charles J. Dressler (razed by ISC in 1969), the Big Four Passenger Station, and he also built the Indiana State Building at the World's Columbian Exposition in Chicago (1893).

67 For Millet, see: David Hanks, "Louis J. Millet and the Art Institute of Chicago," Bulletin of the Art Institute of Chicago, vol. 67 (1973), pp. 13-19. Louis J. Millet taught at the Art Institute's school from 1886 until 1918 and directed its department of decorative design until his retirement. He was a collaborator with the famed Chicago architect Louis Sullivan and participated in establishing the Chicago School of Architecture in 1893. See: https://network.architexturez.net/pst/az-cf-162163-1081913562.

68 The dedication of the Library coincided with a week-long celebration of President Parson's 25 years as president.

69 Total area after the addition of the east wing in 1956 was 65,393 GSF; 42,435 ASF.

70 From the Dedication Program, June 21, 1910.

71 The cost for the land was $7,924.50. "Report of the Secretary of the Board of Trustees," Annual Reports of the Officers of State of the State of Indiana, Volume 2 (Indianapolis: Wm. B. Burford Contractor for State Printing and Binding, 1906, 34. See also: Herbert Rissler, "The Heart of the University," Alumni Magazine, Winter, 1979, pp. 1-5. Cunningham was able to have the administration agree to a $1.00 per term fee paid by students. Eventually the fee was increased to $2.00, which provided $5,000 each year for acquisitions and salaries.

72 After the Chicago World Columbian Exposition (1893), the revival of the classical architectural style gained in popularity. At the Normal School, the new classicizing Library marks a distinct break with the Romanesque style building prevalent in earlier buildings on campus.

73 Wm. H. Armstrong, President of the Board of Trustees, noted in his report to the Governor that Normal had a collection worth approximately $100,000 in a building without fire-proofing. He wrote that property for a new library had been purchased, plans and estimates had been obtained, and he requested an appropriation of $99,970. Report of the Indiana State Normal School for the Fiscal Years Ending October 31, 1905 and October 31, 1906, Indianapolis: Wm. B. Burford, 1906, p. 1624 in Annual Reports of the Officers of State of the State of Indiana, Indianapolis: 1907, Wm. B. Burford, Contractor for State Printing and Binding.

74 It is difficult to estimate comparable value in current dollars. The relative value ranges from $2.7 million to $7.4 million. See http://www.meauringworth.com/uscompare/relativevalue.php. In light of the campus experience with fire, the heating plant was carefully removed to a site 200 feet away from the building.

75 J. F. Alexander also served as secretary of the Western Association of Architects at the November 16, 1887 meeting in Cincinnati. W. L. B. Jenney (Chicago) served as secretary of foreign correspondence. One year later, Jenney would be engaged in rebuilding the Normal School. The Inland Architect and News Record, Vol. 10, September 1887, p. 23.

76 At the time of the dedication, the number of volumes was estimated as 50,000 to 80,000. A major source of funding for additions to the collection came from students who paid a $1/term fee (originally titled a "janitors" fee). From the Dedication Program, 2. At the time the Library was built, approximately 2,700 volumes were being added each year. In 1935, the fourth, fifth, and sixth floor stacks were completed as a WPA project.

77 The transition from the Ionic to Corinthian order can be found in Roman architecture, such as the second and third floors of the Colosseum in Rome. The faux marble columns were created using a method of painting termed "scagliola" from Italian meaning "chips." It required experienced and skilled craftsmen.

78 From the dedication program of 1910.

79 This recalls President Jones' favorite dictum, "The fact in the thing, the law in the mind …" See also: Teresa Exline, The Search for the Names of the Normal Hall Dome," State Magazine, September 24, 2015.

80 From the dedication program of 1910. (isua-library-dedication-1910-20).

81 The World's Columbian Exposition (Chicago, 1893), introduced Beaux-Arts classicism. This new style replaced interest in the heavier Romanesque Revival style seen, for example, in Old Main, North Hall, and the Training School.

82 The steps were removed in 1954.

83 Trustee Minutes, June 14, 1937, p. 332. "Library Enlarged at Indiana State," The Indianapolis Sunday Star, January 9, 1938, pt. 1, p. 11, C6.

84 Trustee Minutes, July 28, 1952, p. 262.

85 Trustee Minutes, July 28, 1952, p. 262. This information was part of the budget appropriation request for 1953-55.

86 Ibid, December 2, 1988, Section III, p. 21.

87 Plans to demolish the Elks Building, owned by ISU since 1970, prompted Professor Robert Clouse to state, "We need to keep some of the buildings. Alumni like to come back to ISU and see buildings they recognize. They can identify with buildings." Quoted in the Indiana Statesman, Friday, April 27, 1990, p. 16.

88 Indiana State University Facilities Management Completed Projects, June 30, 2016, III-1. The Gayle and Bill Cook Foundation donated $1 million to the renovation.

89 Weddle Bros. received the Indiana Subcontractors Association "Project of the Year" award.

90 Trustee Minutes, September 6, 2013, pp. 14-15. Johnson's Urbana-Champaign.

91 The stained-glass dome was recreated by Conrad Schmitt Studios in Wisconsin. For more about the restoration, see: Teresa Exline, "Normal Hall Restored to its Former Glory," State Magazine, September 25, 2015.

92 From "Indiana State University Newsroom", September 6, 2013. See: http://www2.indstate.edu/news/news.php?newsid=3677.

93 The Board formally raised the issue of a new science building and authorized the President to present the matter to the State Board of Finance for approval as required by law. Trustee Minutes February 29, 1916, p. 217.

94 The American Institute of Architects Quarterly Bulletin, Vol. 1, No. 4, (January 1901), p. 161.

95 American Architect and Architecture, Vol. 95 (March 24, 1909) p. 11.

96 Apparently, structural problems developed in the building. President Hines reported to the Board that he had received a report from the architectural firm Johnson, Miller, Miller, and Yeager, that piers were overly stressed by the load they were carrying and would require immediate repair. The situation was sufficiently dangerous that the architects advised the President to cease using the building until the repairs had been completed. The repair was assigned to Mr. Muehler under the supervision of the architects. The price was estimated to cost between $8,000 and $10,000. Fortunately, as work progressed, the cost was reduced to $3,000. Trustee Minutes, December 8, 1925, pp. 455-456.

97 Johnson's Urbana-Champaign office, Illinois City Directory: (Champaign-Urbana, Illinois: Clark-Ewell Co., 1919-20), 3. See: https://ia600306.us.archive.org/21/items/johnsonsurbanach191920love/johnsonsurbanach191920love.pdf.

98 Lynch, p. 242. For a discussion of curricular changes and addition of A, B, and C Courses, see Lynch, pp. 224-225.

99 Lynch, p. 255.

100 Lynch, p. 240. The Department of Domestic Economy was created in 1914 as well. It was located in the Vocational Building in 1915. Of the new faculty, Lynch states this new group "steadily lifted the work of the Normal School to a higher level of scholarship." Lynch, p. 242.

101 Plans were approved and authorization to solicit bids was given. Trustee Minutes, July 20, 1961, X.

102 Trustee Minutes, September 21, 1961, III.

103 Hannig Construction (General Construction- $201,831), Potter Electrical and Engineering (Electrical-$61,994), Freitag-Weinhardt (Plumbing, HVAC-$213,286).

104 The Trustees authorized advertising for bids for the new addition. Trustee Minutes, July 16, 1969, p. 9.

105 Trustee Minutes September 19, 1969, Exhibit A, Sec. II.

106 Trustee Minutes, September 19, 1969, Sec. II., A. Kuykendall Const. (General Construction-$174,350); Freitag-Weinhardt, Inc., (Mechanical-$93,500); Sanborn Electric Co. (Electrical-$25,973).

107 Trustee Minutes, April 17, 1969, II: N.

108 Trustee Minutes, April 17, 1969, Sec. II: N.

109 Trustee Minutes, June 15, 1979, F.

110 Trustee Minutes August 29, 1980, pp. 48-49. Includes fees and contingencies.

111 Shelton Hannig, Inc. (General Construction-$505,323); Harrah Plumbing and Heating Co., Inc. (Plumbing and Heating-$138,300); Commonwealth Electric Co., (Electrical-$237,900).

112 Indiana State University Physical Plant Projects: 1999-2000, p. 23.

Chapter 3 President Parsons

CHAPTER 4

4TH PRESIDENT
LINNAEUS NEAL HINES

(1921-1933)

1921
Allendale property was purchased.

1927
The Graduate Division was established.

1929
The Normal School was renamed Indiana State Teachers College (ISTC).

November 19, 1924
The cornerstone ceremony for Reeve Hall, the first women's campus residence, was held.

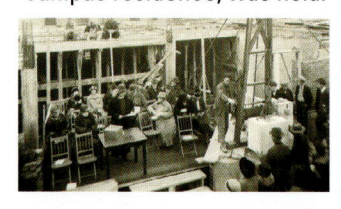

February 21-22, 1928
The (Women's) Physical Education Building was dedicated.

Indiana State University Building a Legacy

Born: February 12, 1871

Died: July 14, 1936

Wife: Berthe Georgia Wiggs (married 1907-36)

Bachelor's Degree
Indiana University
Mathematics

Master's Degree
Indiana University

Honorary L.L.D. Degree
Indiana University

Positions held at Indiana State University:
President (1921-33)
Director of the Extension Division and Placement (1933-36)

1930
The North Central Association accrediting body admitted ISTC to the highest level of teachers colleges.

1932
Franklin Roosevelt defeated Herbert Hoover.

1929-39
Unemployment during the Recession.

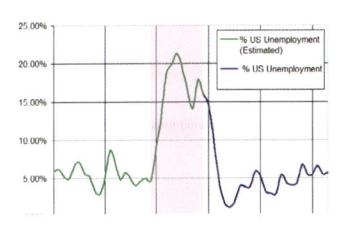

1932
Plans for the Training School (Laboratory School) were completed.

Chapter 4 President Hines

Linnaeus Neal Hines was born on February 12, 1871 in Carthage, Missouri.[1]

Leaving Carthage, his family moved to Noblesville, Indiana, where he attended elementary and high schools. He graduated from Indiana University (IU) in 1894 with a degree in mathematics.[2] While at IU, he lettered twice in football, and in 1893, became the manager of the team. Over a seven-year period, he taught mathematics and served as Assistant Principal at Evansville and Shortridge High Schools in Indianapolis (1899-1901).[3]

The next 18 years he served as superintendent of city schools in Union City (1901-06), Hartford City (1906-08), and Crawfordsville (1908-19).[4] During this time, he completed a master's degree at IU (1908). Hines was elected State Superintendent of Public Instruction in 1918 and served from March 15, 1919 until September 30, 1921.[5]

On October 1, 1921, at the age of 50, he resigned this position to accept the presidency at Indiana State Normal School (ISNS), succeeding President Parsons. He served as President until June 30, 1933, when he resigned the office but continued to work at the college as Director of Extension and Placement until 1936.[6] Similar to Parsons, Hines also served as President of the Eastern Division (Muncie) until 1924, when Benjamin F. Burris succeeded him.[7]

An inauguration ceremony was conducted at ISNS January 6, 1922 and at Muncie on January 13. In his inaugural speeches, Hines introduced his agenda – an agenda he worked on persistently during his presidency. In Terre Haute, he proposed changing the name of the school to Indiana State Teachers College, advocated the establishment of a rural school department (at both campuses), development of extension and correspondence courses, strengthening the college course (degree program), further development of the teacher training school (and adding one in Muncie), and reviving the recently closed rural training school.[8]

Concerning the name change, Hines stated, "There is a strong movement to change all normal schools to teachers' colleges. With us, since we already have four-year courses, and grant degrees, we need only change the name to Indiana State Teachers College, add some courses ... and the deed is done."[9]

He also noted the need for additional resources in order to realize the full potential of ISNS. These included more faculty, better salaries, a large auditorium, gymnasia for men and women, more housing facilities, a larger cafeteria, and creation of a graduate department. The growth, as well as aging of the campus, required the creation of a "building program," no doubt to earmark resources for repairs, and a fund source for planning new structures.[10]

During his presidency, an event of singular importance was the separation of what was to become Ball Teachers College from ISNS. A major figure driving the separation movement was Lemuel A. Pittinger, who was named President of Ball Teachers College on July 15, 1927.[11] Between 1923-27, a movement developed in the General Assembly to separate the budgets of the two institutions. Pittinger led this movement. Pittinger reached an agreement with Hines to support legislation

"The advancing educational standards of this institution have been given formal and official recognition." – President Linnaeus Hines

creating two distinct schools. House Bill 187 passed both Houses in February 1929, and Governor Leslie signed it into law March 7, 1929.[12] Indiana State Normal School became Indiana State Teachers College (ISTC).

In March 1930, both Ball State and Indiana State were approved by the North Central Association of Colleges and Secondary Schools to be moved from the list of teacher training schools to the list of universities and liberal arts colleges. Graduates from both institutions had complained in the 1920s that it was increasingly difficult to obtain teaching positions in secondary schools with their normal school credential-preference going to college and university graduates.[13]

In the period after the First World War, enrollment steadily increased. One of the consequences of this increase in Terre Haute and Muncie was that many more students were completing the four-year college curriculum rather than the two-year programs for becoming public school teachers.[14] Both the growth in the college curriculum and the addition of a graduate department contributed to the need to change the name of the school from ISNS to ISTC.[15] With the change of name, Hines had attained one of the major goals of his inauguration speech.

Enrollment growth also necessitated additional faculty. Hines directed the consolidation of academic departments, and despite objection, reduced the number from 27 to 13.[16] He recognized the need for new programs and led expansion efforts until his resignation from the presidency in 1933.

Enrollment growth, and the expectations of a new generation of students, contributed to several significant building projects, including the first women's residence hall (Reeves Hall) and a Physical Education Building erected on North Seventh Street. Athletics and student organizations increased. During his tenure, a Faculty Women's Club and the Indiana State Teachers College Foundation were formed.

The growth in college instruction required better-credentialed teachers with significant graduate level education. The change in name and development of more advanced curriculum necessitated a review by the accrediting organization, North Central Association of Colleges, in 1932. In their report, two findings stood out. The review noted the level of faculty achievement did not meet the Association's standard.[17] In response, President Hines encouraged faculty to take leaves of absence to pursue advanced degrees. Second, the current location of the college was a significant issue. The Association believed it would be better situated for further growth in a less dense and trafficked location.

President Hines, at a meeting of the Association, stated the college would forego accreditation if it meant having to move to a new site. The college was granted a two-year extension with an additional review set for 1934.[18] The concern about location raised by North Central delayed the decision to build the Laboratory School on its present site.

Expansion slowed during the Depression era as Hines had to lead the institution during a period of declining resources. The Depression, deflation, business stagnation, and loss of tax revenues put considerable stress upon all public institutions.[19] The budget for 1930-31 totaled $618,126, while in 1932-33 it was approximately $501,800, necessitating cuts in faculty and staff salaries.[20] The Hines presidency saw a significant loss of faculty who had been with ISNS for years. Many retired or passed away and were replaced with new faculty with advanced degrees who indelibly changed the institution.

While Hines was no longer President when the Laboratory School opened, he had played an important preparatory role. First, he had determined the best site for the new Lab School would be Heminway Park, owned by the city of Terre Haute. Previously, Chauncey Rose's home stood on that property. It was known for its beautiful grounds. On September 8, 1925, his home was razed and converted into Heminway Park.

Protests were vociferous and Hines fielded numerous letters and even an editorial in the local paper giving advice on where the school should be located.[21] Hines remained steadfast regarding the location and insisted that the building would be designed by local architects.[22] In 1932, he appointed a committee to begin developing tentative plans for the new school, and in 1934 a successful grant was submitted to obtain partial funding through the Public Works Administration (PWA) program.

President Hines' legacy included, in addition to numerous buildings and the institutional name change, faculty growth in both number and degrees held, curricular growth, and the establishment of a graduate department. Hines left the presidency at a time when future circumstances would worsen for the college.[23] In 1932, Hines suffered a stroke and was confined to a wheelchair, and on June 8, 1933, he submitted his resignation and departed the office on August 10, 1933. He left his position reluctantly.[24]

President Hines died on July 14, 1936, at his residence at 1504 S. Sixth Street and was interred in Roselawn Memorial Park, Terre Haute. In 1966, Hines Hall was dedicated in his honor.

Following President Hines' resignation, Dr. Lemuel M. Pittenger, President of Ball State Teachers College, served as interim president at ISTC until Dr. Ralph Tirey assumed the office on January 1, 1934. Governor Paul V. McNutt charged President Pittenger with undertaking an evaluative survey of ISTC. Pittenger made his final report to the Board on December 4, 1933.[25] In it, he outlined a series of recommendations to improve the quality of ISTC and further cooperation between the two institutions to develop "a quality program of teacher education."[26]

An insightful recommendation was to develop a campus master plan for ISTC to assure deferred maintenance was done and the physical plant improved.[27] In the midst of his study, a rumor surfaced that there was a plan proposed by a "high state official" to abolish ISTC while continuing Ball State Teachers College.[28] The rumor proved false. ■

Allendale Lodge

Date: Land purchased 1921;
Additional property purchased 1941

Sold: 1999 to Sisters of Our Lady of Mount Carmel

Area: 8.3 acres

In 1921, ISNS purchased an 8.3-acre tract of land six miles south of campus.[29] The land was bounded on the west by Highway 41 (earlier Seventh Street Road) and the Sullivan interurban line. Acquisition of the property was ardently advocated by Professor Fred Donaghy, who envisioned creating an "experimental farm" on the property.

Donaghy graduated from ISNS in 1914 and completed a master's degree at Indiana University in 1915. He succeeded Dr. Roscoe R. Hyde in 1918, and in 1920, was made the head of the Department of Biology and Agriculture. By 1929, he had earned his doctorate degree from Johns Hopkins University. He was passionate about his work and enthusiastically engaged students in his fields of interest. Unfortunately, he died on July 8, 1938. Donaghy Day was initiated in 1976 as a day set aside for the faculty, students, and community to help beautify the campus and downtown.

The property became a learning environment for many students in the 1920s and 30s. Donaghy, with students, planted gardens, orchards, trees, and shrubs native to Indiana. It served as a site for teaching botany and zoology, and the lodge provided a place for student educational and social activities.

Allendale Lodge was a rustic stone and wooden structure with a large fireplace and screened porch. Students provided the labor to build the Lodge with support from the National Youth Administration, and the college paid for the cost of building materials.[30]

The Lodge served as the site for President Tirey's luncheon on June 15, 1945. This event included special guests attending the Jubilee Celebration, marking 75 years since the Legislature gave approval to establish the ISNS. The Lodge was used occasionally by outside groups for wedding receptions and other occasions, which provided welcomed income.

Lodge Constructed

President Tirey

Date: 1939

Cost: Approx. $12,000 (Land and Lodge)

Area: Approx. 2,000 sq. ft.

President's Residence Added[31]

President Holmstedt

Architect: Yeager Architects

Contractor: W. H. Sanford

Date: 1954

Cost: $35,056.78[32]

Location: Allendale

Bids were received for the President's residence on February 23, 1954. It was noted that none of the bids, save one, met the requirements for public bidding because they contained no non-collusion affidavits.[33]

New bids were received and opened at the March 10, 1954 Trustee meeting. The contract was awarded to W. H. Sanford Co., for a total of $30,000.[34] The Holmstedt home was a single-story, wood frame 1,800 sq. ft. building with partial basement and an attached garage.

President Moore

President Moore reported to the Trustees that the administration determined the Allendale property was no longer essential to the University because most functions were now held in the Hulman Memorial Student Union.[35]

Indiana State University sold the Allendale Lodge and surrounding property to the neighbors to the north, the Sister of Our Lady Carmelites, in 1999. ■

Chapter 4 President Hines

Women's Residence Hall
(Reeve Hall)

Architect: Johnson, Miller, Miller, and Yeager[36]

Contractors: North Raffin, Co. (General Construction); Prox and Burget (Plumbing); Freita-Weinhardt Co. (Heating and Ventilation)

Date:
Cornerstone Ceremony: November 19, 1924[37]

Dedication: October 19, 1925

Cost: $105,000

Location: 660 Mulberry Street

President Parsons had recognized as early as 1904 the need for affordable and safe housing on campus. Parsons saw the lack of proper student housing to be an impediment to enrollment growth, especially for women whose homes were far from Terre Haute. Students had to contend with cramped, uncomfortable rooms off-campus at excessive prices, given there was little competition among renters for student trade.

Not only would new housing attract students, but it was believed it would improve off-campus housing conditions as well. One former student summarized conditions in this way, "Among the disadvantages of the rooming houses may be mentioned poor furnishings, lack of adequate housekeeping, poor lighting, poor heating ..." and so forth.[38] An attempt to provide nourishing and well-priced meals was made in 1920 when the school acquired property at 663 Eagle Street and installed a cafeteria. Seating was limited to about 150 students.[39]

Mary J. Anderson, a member of the Department of Grammar and Composition, was an early advocate for women's housing. She was a graduate of the University of Michigan, and at ISNS, served as a quasi-dean of women without compensation. She supervised a home for women near campus established by the YWCA, which provided room and board and was a model for development of the residence hall.[40] By her work and insight, she helped define the need for a Dean of Women position.

Another advocate for a women's residence was Charlotte S. Burford, who joined the faculty in 1903 and was named Dean of Women in 1910.[41] Helen

Helen Reeve, Dean of Women, 1954

Stage 2: Remodel First Wing and Add Second Wing "Annex"[42]

Architects: Miller and Yeager

Contractors: Adams and Sanford (General Construction); Prox and Burget (Heating); O. A. Toelle (Plumbing)[43]

Date: 1929

Cost: $180,668[44]

Typical student room

Reeve was the first Residence Hall Director (1926-47) and succeeded Charlotte Burford as Dean of Women in 1947, serving until 1956. In 1947, Florence M. Thompson became the Director of the Women's Residence Hall, and in 1956, she became the Dean of Women. Miss Margaret Wilson replaced Thompson's position as Director in 1956.

For President Parsons, gaining approval and funding for the new residence hall proved an arduous task and took many years to complete. A tax that was levied in 1921 provided some funds for construction. As early as September 1922, President Hines attempted to have "local capitalists" build a dormitory and have ISNS purchase it with rentals. In April 1923, Hines proposed to the Trustees that a campaign for funds be mounted for the Women's Residence Hall and the gymnasium.[45]

In April 1924, a Mr. North of North Raffin Construction Co. proposed to the Trustees that his company would build a dormitory with the understanding ISNS would ultimately own the structure. The proposal was not acted upon after it was learned the process involved steps that would violate state law.[46]

On November 16, 1924, preceded by a marching band, President Hines and the Trustees marched into the Normal Hall and then to the site where the residence hall was to be built. The location was 660 Mulberry Street. The cornerstone was ceremonially laid in place following several speeches. The building opened October 5, 1925 and accommodated 100 women. The dedication was held on October 19, 1925 and included a reception and evening banquet.[47]

The initial residence hall was a four-story brick structure built in a Neo-Jacobean style. The Jacobean Revival style, based loosely upon a commingling of Gothic and Renaissance styles in 17th century England, became popular in late 19th century and a part of the commercial builder's portfolio through the first 20 years of the 20th century. Eventually, all three wings of the enlarged Reeve Hall would share the same interior plan. Floors above the first floor had bedrooms designed for double occupancy on either side of a central corridor.

The building rested on a stone plinth. The various floors were articulated by beveled double belt courses between the first and second floors. Sills and hood molding on the third floor, as well as a stringcourse, separated the third and fourth floors. Above the fourth floor was a frieze with brick and stone panels.

The first building was more decorative with four gambrel gables, one on each side and one on each end. Below each gable there was a two-story oriel that projected from the second floor. Stone gargoyles projected from the parapets of the oriels. Tracery pinnacles were located on the ends of the building.[48] Exterior ornamentation was more abundant in the first building but was reduced in the next two building phases.

A main entrance was created to join the added east and west wings. An ornate gate was placed in front of the entrance. Gnome-like figures representing music, physical education, chemistry, and home economics were positioned over the entrance door. The gate was salvaged when the building was razed and was repositioned in the area formerly occupied by the building. Likewise, the gargoyles were repurposed and formed the legs of a semicircular bench commemorating the site where this once grand building, rich with history, stood.

V-12 sailors move into Reeve Hall, 1943

Chapter 4 President Hines

President Tirey

Early in Tirey's presidency, Reeve Hall presented a budgetary problem. Revenues were insufficient to make bond payments.[49] With the continued growth of the school, President Tirey suggested the urgent need for an addition to accommodate more women students. He indicated a budget of $600,000 was available with $100,000 from reserves and $500,000 from bond sales. A motion was made by Board member Ahlgreen to appoint Yeager architects to develop plans and bid documents, but the motion died for lack of a second.[50]

While an addition was proposed, President Tirey reported to the Trustees that only 119 women resided in Reeve Hall, and in order to make payment on the outstanding bonds, a minimum of 145 or 150 needed to be in residence. He proposed offering scholarships to 30 women with outstanding high school records and "splendid teaching personalities" with the stipulation they live in Reeve Hall.[51]

Third wing was completed.

President Holmstedt

Architect: Yeager and Associates[52]

Contractors: Wilhelm Construction (General Construction); Christman Co. (Plumbing); Freitage-Weinhardt, Inc. (Heating; Ventilation); Sanborn Electric Co. (Electrical); Wall-Away Co. (Cabinets); Westinghouse Electric Corp. (Elevator)[53]

Date: 1955-56
Cost: $627,133[54]
Area: 26,300 GSF addition

President Holmstedt, at the September 28, 1954 Trustee meeting, reported the addition may cost up to $650,000, and that the facility would accommodate an additional 150 to 160 women in 76 rooms.

Bids for the addition were opened November 12, 1953, and the addition was completed in 1956, transforming the "U" shaped footprint into a "W." This addition added modern conveniences such as three lounges, a recreation room, laundry facilities, and other amenities, making it a suitable and secure home away from home for 340 women students.

Reeve Hall gate

Originally titled "Women's Residence Hall," it provided accommodations for all freshmen and sophomore women who were required to live on campus. It also served as Naval barracks for the V-5 and V-12 programs in 1994-96.

The Faculty Women's Club requested the Women's Residence Halls be named after Mrs. Charlotte Burford and Miss Helen E. Reeve and was eventually renamed Reeve Hall in 1959.[55]

On the evening of September 18, 1962, a fire occurred in room 422 of Reeve Hall. Damage in that room was severe, and smoke damage was found on the fourth floor east and central areas and stairwells. Damage was estimated to be in the $25,000-$30,000 range.[56]

President Rankin

Owing to increased costs, age of the building, and increased vacancies, Reeve Hall was closed as a residence in 1971 and transformed into offices and classrooms. ∎

Asbestos Abatement

President Moore

Contractor: Abatement Group
Date: 1997-98
Cost: $134,000[57]

Demolition

Contractor: Verkler
Date: 1997-98
Cost: $235,000[58]

The gargoyles from the exterior were repurposed and the entry gate was installed on the north side of Oakley Plaza.[59]

Reuse

Project Manager: Scott Tillman

Physical Education Building

Architect: Johnson, Miller, Miller, and Yeager
Contractor: Glen W. North Construction Co.
Date: Dedication: February 21-22, 1928
Cost: $307,623
Area: 53,260 GSF; 41,435 ASF

Initially, athletics was not considered central to the mission of the Normal School and there were no facilities for training, practice, and competition. In 1895 a gymnasium was included when North Hall was constructed which, with supporting piers in the space, added the element of obstacle course to the game of basketball. The first basketball team competed in 1894. (See: North Hall regarding this space).

The Department of Physical Education was established in 1897 after the State Attorney General ruled ISNS had legal right to provide courses in this discipline. The Students' Athletic Association then petitioned for grounds for practice and competition. Baseball was the first outdoor sport, followed by football in the fall of 1894. To accommodate the need for a field was impossible on the limited site of the campus, so the school purchased Parsons Field on South 17th Street in 1903. It was replaced in 1909 by the second Parsons Field, located on North Second Street.[60]

When Birch E. Bayh Sr. arrived on campus, athletic competition was erratic due to the difficulty in scheduling and creating teams, since students were not consistently enrolled from quarter-to-quarter and year-to-year. Bayh coached and taught physical education courses from 1918 to 1923, followed by Arthur L. Strum. Bayh's .640 winning percentage at ISU ranks him as the sixth-winningest coach in the school's history. During the decade of 1920-30, inter-collegiate

Chapter 4 President Hines

competition was regularized, contributed to student life, and became a point of pride defining the school.

As physical education became an important curriculum discipline and aspect of the student experience on campus, the need for adequate facilities supporting these activities grew. The new Physical Education Building was created as a spectator sports facility that could also accommodate large audiences attending university functions – something the school had been without since its inception.[61]

The Physical Education Building opened its doors in 1928 with dedication ceremonies on February 21 and February 22.[62] The new facility contained a floor for men's athletics and one for women, offices, classrooms, storage, and locker rooms. The men's gymnasium could accommodate approximately three thousand people and had a stage at the north end used for campus functions.

Hines had a challenge to obtain funding. The Depression was underway and the school had not fared well in previous biennial budgets.[63] In a letter from L. A. Pittenger to President Hines, dated February 26, 1925, he wrote, "I did all I could to assist Terre Haute in securing needed appropriations, but the $125,000 for your gym got mixed up with the Riley Hospital matter in a jam."[64] In 1927-28, he was finally successful in obtaining the $75,000 necessary for completion of the Gymnasium.

Gymnasia are typically unadorned functional boxes of space. The ISNS Gymnasium was a functional facility that did receive design detailing that made it distinctive. The entire exterior was brick with two stories of windows surmounted by an attic level on the east and west sides. The south façade was the principle entry. It was divided into three units – two pavilions on the east and west ends and a central section with three round-headed arches rising two stories. The attention to detail merits comment. Brick corbels were positioned above the pavilion windows. A diaper brick pattern was situated above the first-floor windows, creating an interesting textured surface. Over the central bay,

Women's basketball practice

Exterior of the Physical Education Building

rowlock arches framed the large central windows. A stone ornament was placed atop each pavilion and stone panels above the first-floor windows of the center bay read 'Physical Education Building.'[65]

Remodel Auditorium

President Holmstedt

Date: 1956
Cost: $170,053

Destroyed by Fire

President Landini

Contractor: A & C Excavating Demolition
Date: July 24, 1984
Cost: $98,322

The Women's Physical Education Building caught fire in the early evening on July 24, 1984. The cause was not conclusively determined, but inspection suggested an electrical short. Only one person inside the burning building, as well as three firemen, suffered minor injuries, but the building was destroyed beyond repair.[66] Ironically, President Landini, in the 1983-85 Capital Improvement Budget Request, asked for funding to demolish this building, Walden Apartments, and five portable classroom buildings.[67] The fire advanced the schedule.

The remains of the building were razed, creating a landscaped open space later to be occupied by the Music Rehearsal Building (Landini Center for Performing and Fine Arts). ■

Indiana State University Building a Legacy

College Bookstore (formerly Central Christian Church)

Architect: Alfred Grindle[68]

Original Contractor: Charles A. Pike

Contractors: Glenn W. North Construction Co. (General Construction); Holthaus and Carney (Heating); Wissell and Christman (Plumbing)

Date: Acquired February 11, 1932[69]

Cost: $12,000[70]

Area: 11,280 ASF

The Central Christian Church was located at 639 Mulberry Street between Sixth and Seventh Streets. This placed it between Reeve Hall to the east and Condit House to the west. The building was built in a hybrid medieval style with large clerestory windows along the nave that provided ample lighting for the interior. The building is characteristic of Grindle's style. One might compare this church with Trinity Episcopal (1909) and University Lutheran Church (1930) in Bloomington, Indiana. He was also the architect for the Glossbrenner Mansion in Indianapolis. The Bookstore is a good example of an eclectic building combining Romanesque-Gothic revival elements together with early Christian details such as the Lombard bands across the façade that can be traced back to early Christian buildings in Ravenna, Italy (for example, Galla Placidia.)[71]

Prior to being converted into the College Bookstore, Ernestine Myers purchased it. It had also served as the Shrine Temple. In the 1920s, Myers transformed it into the "Ernestine Myers School of the Stage," which opened on June 27, 1927.

In 1932, the College Foundation acquired the building that had not been used as a church for years.

The façade was modestly remodeled. The central entry, with its simple but impressive stone work framing the entry on the north side, was retained. A wrought iron light and incised stone work reading "Bookstore," as well as a College insignia set in roundels, were added above the impressive double doored entry. The nave provided the large space needed for sales displays and the side aisles were equipped with counters. At the south end of the nave, a small lunchroom, complete with a soda fountain, was installed. Renovation work completed the conversion of the space from church to bookstore.

The desire to extend Reeve Hall with an additional wing to the west where it would encroach upon the area occupied by the College Bookstore, combined with the expense to be incurred with a necessary renovation of the old structure, led to the decision to raze the building.[72] This structure was replaced with a new bookstore located further north on the campus, across from the Home Economics Building. ■

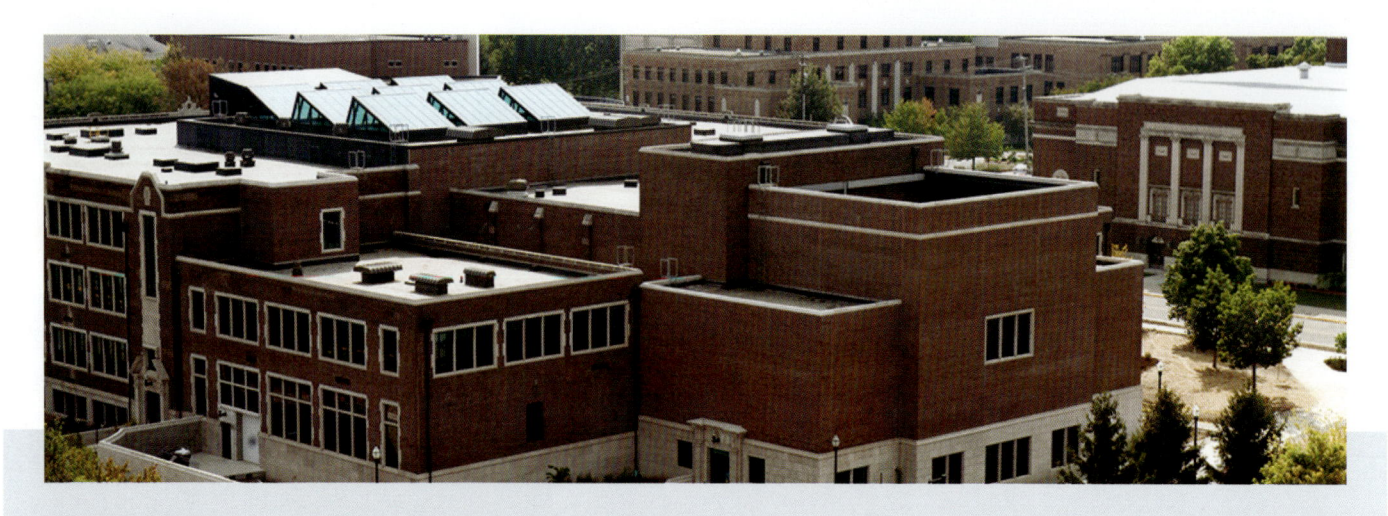

Laboratory School[73] (University Hall)

President Tirey

Architects: (Warren) Miller and (Ralph) Yeager

Contractors: Glenn W. North Construction Co. (General Construction); Freyn Bros. (Heating; Plumbing)

Cost: $407,958 (Public Works Administration grant of $120,000 for Phase 1 and $119,000 for Phase 2)[74]

Date: Cornerstone Laid: September 8, 1934

Phase One Completed: July 1935

Phase Two Completed: 1937

Dedication: November 12, 1937[75]

Area: 157,119 GSF; 94,591 ASF

Location: 401 N. Seventh Street

Hines initiated planning for the Laboratory School, but he left office for health reasons by the time construction was completed. The building was dedicated by his successor, President Tirey. The need for a new laboratory school had long been recognized, but securing the required funding was difficult. The country was still recovering from the devastation caused by WWI, the outbreak of the Spanish Flu (1918-19), and the Great Depression (the years 1932-33 were considered the worst).[76] The election of Franklin Roosevelt and the introduction of the PWA (Public Works Administration) helped provide the necessary seed money for the building.

During President Hines' administration, initial planning had begun for the Laboratory School. In a letter dated January 19, 1929, Hines wrote to Robert Frost Daggett in Indianapolis stating "… the local firm of architects–Johnson, Miller, and Yeager–is doing the work on our new building."[77] Permission was granted by the Trustees to pay Miller and Yeager $1,500 for special expenses involved with plans for the school.[78] At the April 11, 1932 meeting of the Board, the Controller, Mr. Connelly, was instructed to request from the Budget Committee permission to spend $450,000 from the Education Improvement Fund for the erection and furnishing of the Training School.[79]

On May 12, 1933, Hines wrote John Heller of Decatur, Indiana asking for his help in securing early approval from Governor McNutt to proceed.[80] He references the building program (PWA) President Franklin Roosevelt was to initiate as a potential source of funding. Eventually, funding was secured from revenue obtained from a two-cent state tax improvement fund and a federal PWA grant for $122,385. The initial building, completed in 1935, cost $407,958.[81]

In the same letter to Heller, Hines states, "We have the site for the building, the plans, and specifications and everything ready to go here."[82] Securing the site had presented its own challenges. University Hall is located on property that once belonged to Chauncey Rose. The grounds had been renamed Heminway Park, and anticipated removal of trees from the site prompted public disagreement that played out in the Terre Haute Star and in personal letters sent to Hines. Some suggested the expansion should be west of Sixth Street, or maintained within the vicinity of the current buildings of Old Main and adjacent structures. The frequency of traffic through the campus, combined with pressure brought by the accrediting agency that recommended moving the campus to another location, certainly supported considering another site. Hines, however,

Laboratory School view from southwest

prevailed and secured the support of the Lions Club and Terre Haute Chamber of Commerce, both supporting the donation of Heminway Park to the State Teachers College.[83] This decision represented the commitment to keep an urban campus. One of the least pleasant letters admonished Hines to keep "… your buildings between Sixth and Seventh Streets and Chestnut and Mulberry Streets where they belong." He further advised Hines to "… stop fighting for this park. Be a gentleman once in your life."[84]

Additional pressure had been applied by the North Central Association that stated it found the campus too restricted by the town and indicated it would withhold accreditation if the campus was not moved to a more favorable location, allowing expansion and reducing annoying and dangerous traffic. Trustee Keltner expressed the opinion, "If change of site is necessary to North Central approval, the college would forgo North Central accreditment (accreditation)."[85] By January 1932, the purchase of Heminway Park was approved and Johnson, Miller, Miller and Yeager were appointed architects for the project.[86]

The Laboratory School was built in a neo-Jacobean style at 402 North Seventh Street at the corner of Chestnut and Seventh. It was a cast-in-place concrete structure except for the auditorium, made of structural steel. The exterior was constructed of face brick masonry with limestone trim. The Board approved giving oversight to the laying of the cornerstone to the "Terre Haute Social Lodge No. 86 F.A.M."[87] The initial building and addition comprised a quadrangle with an inner courtyard originally.[88] It is a three-story brick veneer structure with limestone accents at the windows, entrances, and quoins.[89] The original main entry faced Chestnut Street.

This south facing façade has two flanking pavilions on the east and west sides that serve to bracket the building. These pavilions rest on a one-story stone polygonal base and are ornamented with stone relief panels, pinnacled parapets, and gargoyles (continuing the playful ornamental theme of Reeve Hall). Seven bays occupy the space between the pavilions, with a decorated central bay that serves as the entrance. Pilasters frame the double-door entrance that is surmounted by an open pediment resting on consoles. Inscribed in the parapet above is "Indiana State Teachers College." The windows are consistently framed with Gibbs surrounds which, in addition to the large panels of polychrome brickwork on the south side, are pleasing decorative additions consistent with the Neo-Jacobean style.[90]

The Laboratory School provided a setting for future teachers to practice and it served the educational needs of children of the district as well as faculty and staff children.[91]

Renovated Laboratory School second floor

View toward the atrium

Chapter 4 President Hines

Addition on north side of Laboratory School

President Tirey

Architect: Miller and Yeager

Contractor: Glenn W. North (General Construction)[92]

Date: Work Commenced: September 29, 1936
Dedication: November 12, 1937

Cost: Estimated $257,820[93]

By 1936, during the Tirey administration, an addition was made on the north side of the building that contained two gymnasiums, the Sycamore Theatre, music rooms, and Special Education facilities. The decision to proceed with designing and financing the building was made at a special meeting of the Trustees September 8, 1936.[94] Building was to commence October 1, 1936 and be completed by October 1, 1937. Tirey reported the acceptance of the completed addition by the PWA office in Indianapolis.[95]

The Gilbert Wilson murals in the south entrance were completed in 1936. (Great care was taken to preserve these murals during the renovation and restoration.)[96]

President Landini

Date: 1978

The high school was discontinued in 1978 and the entire school closed in May 1992 during the Landini administration.

Renovation of Laboratory School

President Benjamin[97]

Architect: Schmidt and Associates

Contractors: R. E. Dimond and Associates (Consulting Engineers); Weddle Brothers (General Construction); B&S (Plumbing); NRK (Electrical)

Date: 2006-08

Cost: Approx. $32 million[98]
State contribution was $26.88 million

Indiana State University Building a Legacy

Laboratory School, atrium ceiling

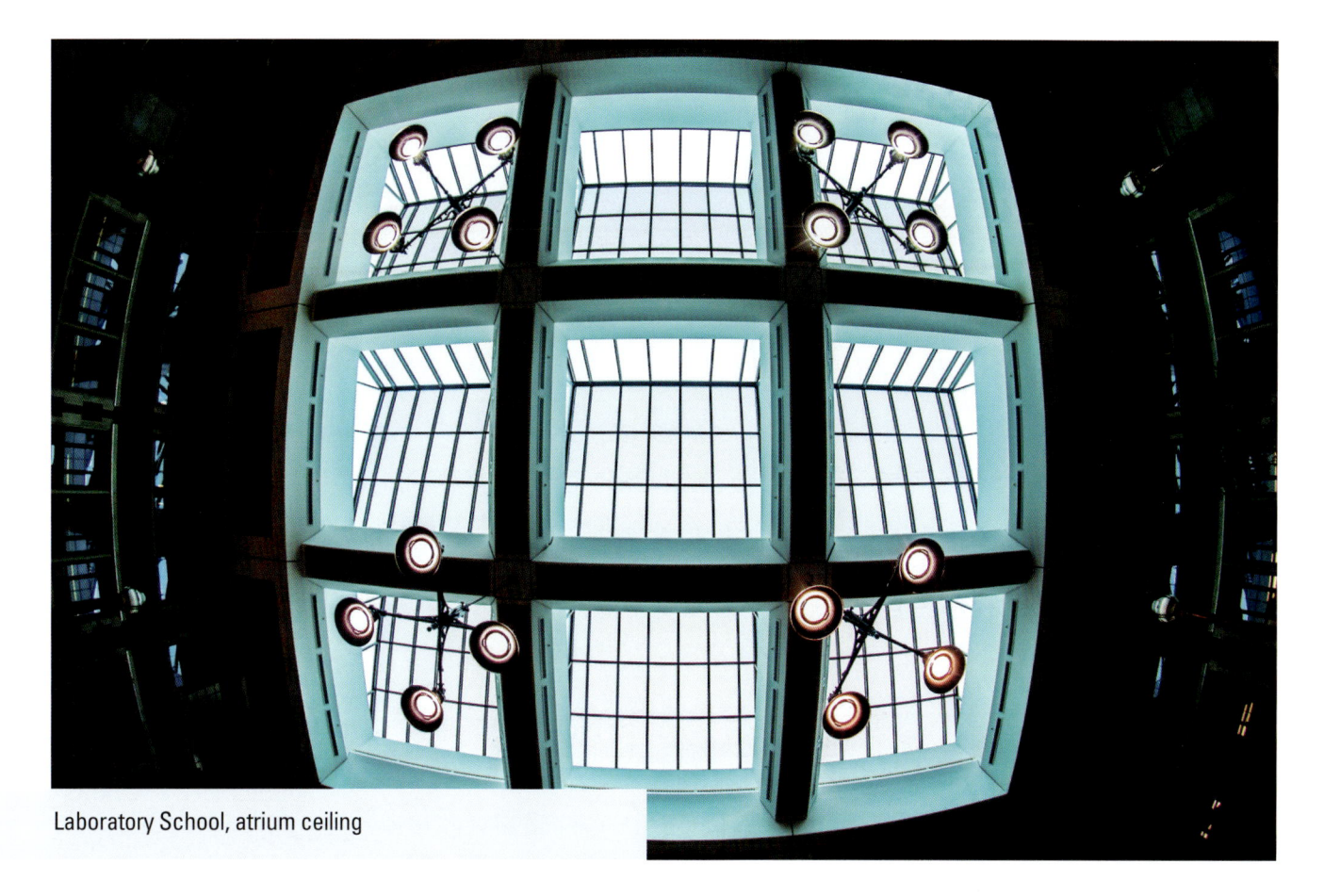

> "We have the opportunity to create a space that honors the past but brings life, energy, excitement, and light where it never existed previously."
> Wayne Schmidt

Benjamin outlined 6 goals for the renovation of the building:

1. Reflect the heritage of teacher training in this building.
2. Be technologically advanced and adaptable.
3. Through the design, provide opportunities for "accidental interaction" between faculty and students, as well as different departments.
4. Contribute greater visibility to the college.
5. Respect the character of the original building.
6. Create a covered atrium that can serve as a pre-event gathering place and site for student-faculty interaction.

During the Benjamin Presidency, plans were developed, and funding secured, for the renovation of the University Hall and the Federal Building. In the initial proposal to the state, funding was requested to renovate the K-12 school and add additional space to accommodate both the School of Education and School of Business.[99] In May 2005, the Schmidt architectural firm, knowing the Federal Building would be acquired by ISU, asked that the current contract for the renovation of the Lab School be extended to include the Federal Building, in order for it to serve as the new home for the School of Business. The contract specified that Schmidt would be responsible for interior and exterior renovation, site development, HVAC, technology, electrical upgrades, and creation of a new entrance on the south side of the Federal Building.

Grosjean Counseling Clinic in University Hall

Chapter 4 President Hines

Auditorium before/after renovations

The contract also specified Schmidt would develop a plan to "put back" the footprint affected by the demolition of Statesman Towers.[100]

Receipt of base bids occurred in June 2007. The entire base bid and change orders totaled over $29 million.

It had become clear the Statesman Towers that had been converted into the College of Education and College of Business were obsolete. Originally built as residence halls, the buildings had structural piers standing in the classrooms obstructing everyone's view. A further obstacle was the absence of central air-conditioning that necessitated maintaining over 550 individual window units. The units consumed an enormous amount of electricity and their noise level competed with the trains nearby.[101]

Initial stages of planning to vacate both Towers focused on moving both Business and Education to the former Lab School/University Hall complex. It was determined this would not provide sufficient space for both colleges. In the meantime, President Benjamin, together with Mr. Greg Goode, Executive Director of External Affairs, entered into discussion with the U.S. Postal Service and Senators Bayh and Lugar to see if the Federal Building (the city post office located on the corner of Seventh and Cherry), might be donated to Indiana State University. That building, combined with a renovated Lab School/University Hall, could provide grand spaces for both disciplines.

A major challenge was to convince the Indiana Commission of Higher Education to agree to support this plan and, with the Board's approval, to secure funds from the State. With the Federal Building (future home of the College of Business) agreement being favorable to ISU, ISU pledged to raise funds for the renovation of the building if the state would fund the renovation of University Hall (future home of the College of Education). The General Services Administration agreed to the transfer of the Federal Building and $6 million in funds were secured for the initial phase of the Federal Building renovation.

Representative Kersey and Greg Goode helped move this project through the legislature. The University received final approval to begin construction September 29, 2006. The state appropriated $22.88 million and the University agreed to provide the difference of approximately $2.92 million. (At the time, this was the largest state-funded project in ISU's history). The project was a textbook example of carefully planned adaptive reuse of a building of historical importance.[102] Exterior details were preserved including the conservatory cantilevered off the third floor east façade. Special attention was also given to restoring the auditorium, particularly in the selection of colors and finishes.[103] President Benjamin and his wife, Dr. Wieke Benjamin, were involved in the renovation and especially the restoration of the theater. The architect, Wayne Schmidt, brought in a restoration specialist who identified the original colors of the auditorium and stage that were subsequently used for the renovation. The auditorium now functions as a mid-level performance venue.

Benjamin suggested the open atrium area between the south and north buildings be enclosed to create a reception space before the beautifully renovated auditorium, as well as serve as a food court and informal gathering place for faculty and students. The interior atrium is open, airy, and filled with sunlight that, together with the plant material, connects with the exterior environment and creates an exciting light-filled space. Schmidt & Associates subcontracted with Architectural Energy Corporation (Boulder, Colorado), for a thorough lighting analysis of the atrium. A key problem was how to lower summer heat gains while raising winter illuminance. Another issue was being able to get the steel necessary for the steel skeletal structure into this enclosed area. Concrete had to be pumped through the building to the site. Nevertheless, difficulties were overcome and the openness of the space belies the construction obstacles.

Schmidt commented on his approach to renovation "… the beginning point is to come to know the character of the current structure. "Buildings speak to you," he said. He wanted to retain the feeling of a school since it was formerly bustling with children scampering down hallways and banging locker doors. He retained that feeling in the renovation. Especially noteworthy are the arched ceilings of the hallways with rooms on all sides. Schmidt is also keen on including artwork in his projects. Here, special care was taken to stabilize and protect the Gilbert Wilson WPA mural at the south entrance.

Continuing its efforts to reduce energy consumption, the building was LEED certified. Construction was too far along to receive the highest level of LEED certification, but scoring 26 out of 27 points meant the building could be eligible for "Achieved" certification.[104]

Auditorium stage

The renovation of University Hall was recognized by American School & University as among the best in the nation in its 2011 Architectural Portfolio. One element that was praised was the enclosure of the exterior courtyard into an atrium, "establishing it as the building's 'town square.'" [105] ■

Renamed University Hall the Bayh College of Education

President Bradley

Date: April 16, 2010

The Trustees approved renaming University Hall the Bayh College of Education.[106]

Sen. Bayh and his father, former Sen. Birch Bayh Jr., had advocated for educational issues. Birch Bayh Sr. served as ISU's first athletic director.

Chapter 4 President Hines

"Arthur's Odyssey" by Michael Dunbar

Michael Dunbar "Arthur's Odyssey" was dedicated September 2, 2009. The white steel, 9-ton sculpture was produced by K&M Steel Manufacturing in Cassopolis, Michigan.

The piece was installed at the northeast corner of the building. Dunbar directed the Art in Architecture Program for the State of Illinois since its inception in 1977 and, like the ISU program, earmarked a percent of the building cost for the acquisition of artwork.

Restoration of Gilbert Wilson murals

The WPA, in 1936, funded the Gilbert Wilson murals in the south entry of University Hall.

Restoration of the Gilbert Wilson murals in the south entry (dating from 1936) was performed by Terre Haute artist Bill Wolfe, utilizing the same medium-Rembrandt pastels. The mural had sustained water and mold damage and had to be stabilized before work could begin.

Gilbert Wilson summarized the mural by writing "It is an attempt to state thru (sic) the medium of form and color the greatest problem facing civilization today. That problem is WASTE. Waste of the earth upon which we live and waste of human life."

Indiana State University Building a Legacy

Interim President Lemuel M. Pittenger

Lemuel M. Pittenger was the Interim President of Ball Teachers College (which became Ball State Teachers College during his tenure) from 1927-42. After President Hines submitted his resignation in June 1933, Pittenger was appointed to manage the Indiana State Teachers College. As a representative of the Trustees, he was made acting President and served until President Tirey began his presidency in January 1934.

Chapter 4 References

1. Lynch, p. 283. Lynch mistakenly gives his birthdate as February 13, 1871, purportedly in a log cabin.
2. Indiana University Alumni Quarterly, Vol. 9, p. 204.
3. In June 1899, he took some postgraduate work at Cornell University.
4. Lynch, p. 238.
5. Educator Journal (February 1922) XXII, p. 108.
6. See: http://indstate.edu/archives/collections/findingaids/Hines-Linnaues-Neal-institutional.pdf. He was also the editor and co-owner of the Educator Journal.
7. Burris had served as Assistant State Superintendent during Hines' tenure as State Superintendent.
8. Indianapolis News (January 6 and 13, 1922). The General Assembly approved the name change in 1929. Lynch, pp. 287-288. Hines' speech was preceded by an address of Superintendent B. J. Burris who spoke emphatically about the need for the Normal School to address the needs of rural education. He noted that 60 other normal schools had organized departments of rural education. See: M. P. Helm, "L.N. Hines Inaugurated President of Indiana State Normal School," The Educator Journal (Bloomington, IN., February 22, 1922), p. 333. He also addressed the need for a new gymnasium, Inaugural Address, p.12.
9. Ibid, p. 336.
10. Ibid, pp. 336-337.
11. Pittenger was an adept politician. He spent six years in the lower house of the Indiana General Assembly, served as Republican floor leader and "… took charge of the expansion requirements of the two normal schools …" Glenn White, The Ball State Story, p. 67. President Hines, during a visit to Muncie, asked Pittenger to replace Professor Erle Clippinger to teach English at the Indiana State Normal School in Terre Haute; a position he accepted.
12. Edmonds, Anthony O. and E. Bruce Geelhoed, Ball State University: An Interpretative History, Bloomington, IN: Indiana University Press, 2001, pp. 82-85. "… passage of this legislation signified the triumph of the 'Muncie men'."
13. Ibid, p. 95.
14. According to the Historical Sketch, "In 1924, all regular college curriculums were raised to a college basis …" p. 21.
15. The Graduate School was established in 1927 and offered courses required for administrative licenses for supervisors, principals, and superintendents and the Masters in Education. In 1923, the General Assembly prescribed a year of graduate study for the licensing of first-grade school administrators and supervisors.
16. Lynch, p. 292.
17. This was not a new finding. In 1928, seven years after Hines assumed the presidency, the North Central Association stated ISNS "must increase the number of advanced degrees … or they would be put on the list of secondary schools." The Association gave three years to meet this requirement. Ibid, p. 290. Hines had inherited a large number of faculty from the Parsons era. As Lynch noted, "Until President Parsons retired in 1921, the school retained a familiar atmosphere because he was still surrounded by faculty members who had served the institution for many years."
18. Minutes, March 2, 1932 XI, p. 60.
19. The budget situation was so dire that serious consideration was being given in the General Assembly to close Ball Teacher's College. President Pittenger called on his friends in the legislature to curtail the effort. Glenn White, The Ball State Story, p. 75.
20. Lynch, pp. 319-320.
21. An anonymous letter of July 28, 1930 stated, "I believe if you were a life-long resident of Terre Haute … you should not be so selfish as to take this small park away from us. Show the people you like the City of Terre Haute and are not so narrow as you seem to be by wanting the Normal to have our Heminway Park."
22. In a letter to Robert Frost Daggett on January 19, 1929, Hines stated, "In reply (I) will say that a local firm of architects, Johnson, Miller, and Yeager, is doing the work on our new building."
23. The college's budget was heavily dependent on enrollment. The entering class of the fall quarter, 1933, showed a nearly 20 percent drop from the fall quarter of 1931.
24. His departure was prompted by a report given by L. A. Pittenger, who was serving as Interim President until a replacement (Tirey), was appointed. Pittenger wrote: "President Hines seemingly did not realize the full import of the Board's action on relieving him of the executive duties of the college and insisted on remaining in the President's room where he could be a member of all conferences and act as President in my absence. In the belief that this arrangement would not be in the best interests of the college, Mr. Hines was told he could no longer exercise the powers of President and that he should immediately begin his work as head of the Division of Extension and Placement." Trustee Minutes, August 10, 1933, p. 374. Hines' difficulty in leaving the position can also be seen in a letter from Pittenger to Hines in which he writes, "… never in my life have I had quite so hard a task as I experienced the day I came over to Terre Haute to take over your duties. Money could not have hired me to take that job … I steeled myself to do it the best possible way I knew. I knew your heart was breaking, but I should like for you to know that mine was aching." Letter from L. A. Pittenger to Dr. L. N. Hines, May 4, 1934. By September 28, Hines had not received a contract for the next year. He wrote President Pittenger, "My present contract expires this week. If you will, I wish you would see that I get a notice of employment as other members of our faculty have received." Letter from L. N. Hines to President L. A. Pittenger, September 28, 1933.
25. Governor McNutt attended an executive Board of Trustees meeting June 28, 1933 and stated that Mr. Hines "give up his duties as President at once …" Trustee Minutes, June 28, 1933. In a preliminary report to the Board, Pittenger noted a lack of definition and coordination on the campus and stated, "Individual efforts ever so good cannot, when added together, make an institution." Trustee Minutes, October 2, 1933, p. 420. He noted an administrative organization that was deficient. Trustee Minutes, October 2, 1933, p. 420. Pittenger delivered his report, but the Board deferred its acceptance. Trustee Minutes, December 4, 1933, p. 458.

26 Lynch, p. 327.

27 Ibid, p. 328.

28 Ibid, p. 327, n. 14.

29 The 8.3-acre lot was purchased for $2,490 from Julia Donham. In 1941, a 1.545-acre tract on the southwest corner was purchased from Paul and Frances Bronson and Carson and Marion Sims for $1,500.

30 Trustee Minutes, June 19, 1939, p. 581, and September 18, 1939, p. 629. In June, drawings for the improvement of the lodge and arboretum were approved.

31 Yeager Architects presented plans that were approved by the Trustees, with authorization to advertise for bids. Trustee Minutes, January 26, 1954, p. 456. Bids were opened February 23, 1954. Trustee Minutes, February 23, 1954, p. 458.

32 Trustee Minutes, March 9, 1955, VI and IX.

33 Trustee Minutes, February 23, 1954, p. 459.

34 Trustee Minutes, March 10, 1954, p. 464.

35 Trustee Minutes, May 9, 1997, Sec. II: A.

36 Three lots on Mulberry to serve as the building site had been purchased and the architects selected by the July Board meeting. Trustee Minutes, July 8, 1924, p. 247. At this meeting, the Board selected the brick face made by the Hydraulic Pressed Brick Co. of Brazil, shade 356, Saraband Chincillas.

37 The cornerstone celebration consisted of a parade, the school song, a prayer by President Emeritus Parsons, various presentations, naming the facility, laying the cornerstone, and singing "America." Trustee Minutes, November 19, 1924, p. 304. The committee assigned to select a name for the new building recommended "Women's Residence Hall." Trustee Minutes, November 19, 1924, p. 303.

38 Lynch, p. 269.

39 Ibid, p. 290.

40 Lynch, pp. 209-210.

41 Lynch, p. 206; 241.

42 Trustee Minutes, August 25, 1928, pp. 434-435.

43 Adams and Sanford (General Construction, $116,874); Prox and Burget (Heating, $11,667); O. A. Toelle (Plumbing, $12,404).

44 Trustee Minutes, August 25, 1928, p. 434. The bids were divided into two contracts, one for new construction and the second for remodeling the earlier building. New construction without fees and contingencies totaled $140,945.

45 Trustee Minutes, April 9, 1923, p. 79.

46 Trustee Minutes, April 1, 1924, p. 207.

47 Reeve Hall 1925, Indiana State University Archives. See: http://library.indstate.edu/archives/exhibits/architecture/ReeveHall.htm

48 The National Register of Historic Places Inventory Subdistrict Number Five Indiana State University-North Seventh Street, 1980, pp. 67-68 provides a very detailed description of the architectural features of the building.

49 The school's dormitory fund was insufficient to make the August 31, 1934 debt service payment. The residence hall was at capacity the first year it opened but the number fell each year until, in 1932-33, fees were reduced by approximately 30 percent. Despite this effort, the number of residents continued to fall. Income for 1933-34 was 35 percent less than receipts for 1929-30. Trustee Minutes, June 25, 1934, p. 22.

50 Trustee Minutes, June 25, 1953, p. 352.

51 Trustee Minutes, December 3, 1934, p. 58. It was reported in 1946 that 192 women were in residence. Trustee Minutes, January 15, 1946, p. 664. Achieving full occupancy, necessary to make payments on outstanding debt, was an ongoing issue.

52 Trustee Minutes, January 26, 1954, p. 447. Yeager Architects was paid $33,716. Funding was chiefly through bonds ($501,181).

53 Trustee Minutes, November 12, 1953, p. 397.

54 Wilhelm Construction (General Construction, $377,584); Christman Co. (Plumbing, $56,500); Freitage-Weinhardt, Inc. (Heating and Ventilation, $50,500); Sanborn Electric Co. (Electrical, $30,124); Wall-Away Co. (Cabinets, $61,500); Westinghouse Electric Corp. (Elevator, $11,744).

55 Trustee Minutes, May 27, 1959, p. 71. The letter was exhibit 'L' in the Minutes.

56 Trustees Minutes, September 28, 1962, VI, p. 599.

57 Ibid, June 30, 1998, p. 30.

58 Ibid.

59 Scott Tillman, campus architect, was responsible for the gateway project. Cost was $41,200. Indiana State University Facilities Management Completed Projects, June 30, 2000, p. 24.

60 Lynch, p. 187.

61 The stage was generous and measured 66' x 17', or about 1450 sq. ft.

62 Two speeches emphasizing the importance of physical education were delivered by Arthur L Tresler (Permanent Secretary, Indiana High School Athletic Association) and Major John. L. Griffith (Commissioner of the Big Ten). Tresler's speech was "The Status of Physical Education in Indiana" and Griffith's was "The Meaning of Physical Education in Modern Life." Program of the Dedication Ceremonies of the New Physical Education Building.

Progress building the gymnasium must have been delayed initially. President Hines reported to the Trustees that no progress was made erecting the gymnasium because the "citizens of the Chamber of Commerce of the city had not collected the money necessary to purchase a site." Trustee Minutes, February 17, 1926, p. 197.

63 In a review of specific appropriations for education institutions, State Normal received nothing for the years 1911-23, and $75,000 for the 1925-27 biennium. By contrast, State Normal in Muncie received $125,000 for 1921-23, $230,000 for 1923-25, and $250,000 for 1925-27. During this same period, Purdue received over $2 million, while State Normal's total was $259,470. Distribution of an 8-cent levy and mill tax totaled $938,960.

64 Pittenger was serving in the House of Representatives and was chair of the Ways and Means Committee. He was President of Ball Teachers College from 1927-42.

65 The construction drawings for the gymnasium are located in the Architecture Library at Ball State University and are dated April 4, 1927. A second set of drawings dated May 29, 1929, included changes/modifications to the building. A significant one was to change the name from Indiana State Normal School to Indiana State Teachers College.

66 Numerous articles appeared immediately after the conflagration describing the event. See the Indiana Statesman, Vol. 90, No. 117, July 25, 1984, and Vol. 90, No. 118, August 1, 1984. The facility was demolished by A&C Excavating ($98,322).

67 Indiana State University Capital Improvement Budget Request 1983-85 (August 1, 1982), Attachment A.

68 Alfred Grindle was born in Manchester, England. Later in life he resided in Bloomington, Indiana. He designed the Glossbrenner Mansion in Indianapolis and University Lutheran Church in Bloomington, Indiana. Thanks to Mike McCormick, Vigo County Historian, for locating the name of the architect. The building was finished in 1911.

69 Trustee Minutes, February 11, 1932, p. 1.

70 Glenn W. North Construction Co. (General Construction, $10,947); Holthaus and Carney (Heat, $2,230); Wissell and Christman (Plumbing, $1,147).

71 Lombard bands refer to decorative blind arcades seen forming a decorative band across the upper reaches of the building below the roofline.

72 In an earlier report to the Trustees, it was stated, "The first floor has a great deal of sag in the center. Its general appearance and condition seem to justify its condemnation …" Trustee Minutes, January 15, 1946, p. 666.

73 During the development phase of this building, the Trustees determined the name of the school would be "The Indiana State Teachers College Demonstration School." Trustee Minutes, June 4, 1934, p. 7. At the June 25 meeting, however, Tirey reported several faculty had recommended changing it to the "Indiana State Teachers College Laboratory School." Trustee Minutes, June 25, 1945, p. 19. This name was adopted. In President Landini's era, the name was again changed to University School. Trustee Minutes, December 13, 1979, p. 74.

74 Glenn W. North Construction Co. (General Construction, $306,933); Freyn Bros. (Heating and Plumbing, $93,875).

75 Parsons Hall was dedicated the same day.

76 Gasoline cost .09 cents per gallon, bread .08 cents per loaf, and the stock market was around 144.

77 L. N. Hines letter to Robert Frost Deggett, January 19, 1929. University Archives Cunningham Memorial Library. Earlier, in a letter of February 5, 1928, Hines wrote to Murray A. Dalman of the architectural firm Perkins, Chatten, & Hammond. "… The plans for this piece of construction are yet so remote and indefinite that it is hard for us to give much information other than that in all probability local architects will be employed … It may be 2 or 3 years before we can begin anything." The Trustee Minutes for September 30, 1932 (p. 188) note the approval to pay $8,500 to Miller & Yeager to complete the payment of $13,500 for the plans for the Training School, based on an estimated cost of the building of $450,000.

78 The Board approved hiring Miller and Yeager Architects to "revise the plans and specifications …" Trustee Minutes, December 4, 1933, p. 459.

79 Trustee Minutes, December 15, 1932, p. 223. Trustee Minutes, September 30, 1932, p. 188. These show "Mr. Connelly was instructed to pay Miller and Yeager $8,500 to complete the payment of $13,500 for the plans for the Training School." The architects submitted plans for the building June 15, 1932, according to Trustee Minutes, p.119.

80 At the December 4, 1933 Trustee meeting, Governor McNutt "… instructed the Board and officials … to prepare immediately applications for this federal aid." Trustee Minutes, p. 458.

81 This was the first building on campus to be supported, in part, by federal funds.

82 Hines letter to John Heller, May 12, 1933. University Archives, Cunningham Memorial Library. Heller was publisher of the Decatur Daily Democrat and Secretary of the State Democratic Convention from 1912-14.

83 Hines wrote to Mr. Harry Fitch, Secretary of the Lions Club, thanking the Club for its resolution of support. (Hines letter to Fitch, July 15, 1930. The Chamber sent a resolution recommending "… Rose Park, otherwise known as Heminway Park … be made available by gift … to the Indiana State Teachers College for use in the extension of its building program." Letter from Morton F. Hayman, Executive Secretary, Terre Haute Chamber of Commerce, July 23, 1930.

84 Anonymous letter to Hines, July 28, 1930. University Archives, Cunningham Memorial Library.

85 Trustee Minutes, March 25, 1932, p. 69.

86 Trustee Minutes, January 12, 1932, p. 39.

87 Trustee Minutes, June 4, 1934, p. 7.

88 This courtyard was replaced with a covered atrium in the 2007-09 renovation.

89 Considerable attention was given to the selection of brick. A committee of four was appointed in April 1934 to recommend the type of brick and source the materials. The committee selected face brick and cull brick made by the Terre Haute Vitrified Brick Company (West Terre Haute). Trustee Minutes, June 4, 1934, p. 9. For a photograph of the plant see: http://visions.indstate.edu:8888/cdm/ref/collection/vchs/id/2650.

90 James Gibbs, December 23, 1682 – August 5, 1754. English architect strongly influenced by the classicizing Italian architect Andrea Palladio. The building was formally accepted October 7, 1935, Trustee Minutes, p. 143.

91 The school published the first annual named the "Analyst."

92 Trustee Minutes, September 8, 1936, p. 228. Glenn W. North (General Construction, $245,698)

93 Trustee Minutes, September 8, 1936, p. 228..

94 Trustee Minutes, September 8, 1936, p. 225.

95 Trustee Minutes, September 29, 1937, p. 358.

96 Gilbert Wilson, "An Interpretation of the Gilbert Wilson Murals in the Laboratory School," Terre Haute, n.d.

Wilson wrote about his murals, "As an artist, I have put myself as the youth who lies poring upon the clean, clear fall of water." It is an attempt to state, through the medium of form and color, the greatest problem facing civilization today. That problem is 'Waste.'"

97 An agreement with Schmidt and Associates for initial design work was concluded May 30, 2005. The design fee was $2,253,976. The project manager was Michael W. Engledow.

98 The Indiana Commission for Higher Education had approved the expenditure of $29.8 million for University Hall in 2005. Final approval came in September 29, 2006. This was the largest state-funded building project in the history of ISU. Greg Goode, Executive Assistant to the President for External Affairs, remarked that this "was truly a great day for the university" and noted it created over 100 construction jobs involving 32 trades.

99 Indiana State University Capital Budget Request 2003-05, June 15, 2002, p. 4. To provide the same amount of space both schools occupied in the Towers would require an addition of approximately 38,000 square feet.

100 Letters dated May 27 and May 30, from Schmidt and Associates to Mr. Bryan Duncan (Director Capital Planning and Improvements, ISU).

101 Schmidt & Associates did a feasibility study in 2004 and recommended Business move to the Federal Building.

102 The Lab School is listed on the Indiana Division of Historic Preservation and Archaeology's Historic Sites and Structures lists.

103 Restoring the auditorium and equipping it to be useful as a medium-sized auditorium coast approximately $3.2 million.

104 Letter from Schmidt & Associates to Bryn Duncan February 15, 2008. The cost to pursue LEED certification was estimated at $590,000-$727,000 for University Hall and $225,000-$282,000 for Federal Hall.

105 See: http://www2.indstsate.edu/news/news.php?newsid=3005.

106 See: http://www2.indstate.edu/news/news.php?newsid=1991.

CHAPTER 5

5TH PRESIDENT
RALPH NOBLE TIREY
(1934-1953)

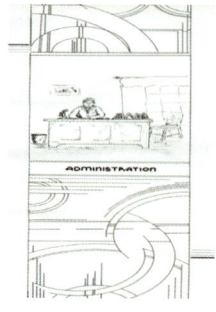

January 1, 1934
Ralph Noble Tirey became the fifth President.

February 4, 1935
Tirey presented his 10-year campus improvement plan.

December 7, 1941
Pearl Harbor was bombed.

September 8, 1934
Cornerstone ceremony was held for the Laboratory School.

March 15-17, 1940
The Student Union and Fine Arts Buildings were dedicated and Eleanor Roosevelt attended.

Indiana State University Building a Legacy

Born: November 10, 1882

Died: August 16, 1964

Wives: Io Short (married 1906-20)
Inez Bonham (married 1922-41)
Ruth B. Hill (married 1946-64)

Education:
Southern Indiana Normal and Practical Business Institute

Bachelor's Degree
Indiana University, *Education*

Master's Degree
Indiana University, *Education*

Honorary L.L.D. Degree
Indiana University

Positions held:
President, Indiana State Teachers College (1934-53)

June 13, 1948
Groundbreaking for Dreiser Hall and the Administration Building.

April 7, 1953
The smokestack for the old power plant was toppled.

May 7, 1945
Germany surrendered to Allies.

February 19, 1950
Demolition of Old Main, North and Stalker Halls begins.

Chapter 5 President Tirey

President Tirey was born on November 10, 1882 in Mitchell, Indiana. He was the fourth son born to William Henry and Nancy Jane (Ganges) Tirey. After graduating from Southern Indiana Normal and Practical Business Institute, he became a schoolteacher and began his teaching career in a one-room schoolhouse in Lawrence County.[1] The next year, 1901, he moved to Springville and took the position of Principal of the school. Three years later, he moved to Oolithic and served as Principal until 1906.

Tirey became Superintendent of the Lawrence County schools in 1906 and married his first wife, Io Short.[2] Five years later, he moved to the town of Vevay and served as their Superintendent of Schools. He briefly attended Harvard University, studying school administration. Following World War I, he became Superintendent of Washington, Indiana schools. He moved to Bloomington in 1922, serving as Superintendent from 1922 to 1934. He also accepted a position as lecturer in the Indiana University (IU) School of Education, where he taught the 1933-36 period that he co-authored a number of educational books. They included "My Playfellows Workbook" and "New Paths" (1934), "My Friends to Make Workbook" (1935), and "Life Use Speller" (1936). He was a frequent contributor to educational journals and an active member of several academic and social clubs.

Tirey, like earlier presidents, recognized the need to unify and beautify a campus that had developed in a constricted space, crisscrossed by streets laden with traffic. They posed a threat to student safety, interfered with teaching, and contributed heat and dust during the summer.[6] The degree to which the traffic was a disruptive hazard is underscored by Tirey's recommendation that a pedestrian tunnel be built under Seventh Street at the new Laboratory School. Tirey needed to find a solution to this worsening situation, especially since the college had not taken advantage of the opportunity to change locations when the Main Building, North Hall, and Stalker Hall were the only structures needing to be replaced. With the construction of the Normal Library, Industrial Arts Building, and Science Hall, the die was cast.[7]

> **"My friends, the plea that I make this morning is that we may be able to produce great teachers ... teachers who can put their feelings and their knowledge into action for the betterment of humanity."** – President Ralph Tirey

courses in school administration.[3] While at IU, he completed B.A. and M.A. degrees in education and received an honorary L. L. D. degree in 1945.[4] In 1929, he was elected President of Indiana State Teachers' Association. Tirey was a pitcher on the baseball team while at IU, and later was a recipient of a Z.G. Clevenger Award, presented to alumni who had made significant contributions to IU athletics.[5]

In 1933, Governor McNutt appointed Tirey, who was 51, to become the fifth President of Indiana State Teachers College (ISTC), a position he held for 19 years. He officially took office January 1, 1934, and was inaugurated April 27, 1934. Major architectural achievements of his administration included completing the new Laboratory School (planning and funding began under President Hines), and Parsons Hall in 1938 (the first men's dormitory on campus). In 1940, the Fine Arts and Commerce Building and Student Union Building (later Tirey Hall) were dedicated. Later, Dreiser Hall (housing Mathematics and Communication) and Gillum Hall (known then as the Administration-Health Building) were completed.

1934 was a busy year for President Tirey. It was during

President Tirey introduced a ten-year improvement plan to the Trustees on February 4, 1935. Street closing was a high priority. In 1937, Tirey reported to the Trustees that property on the west side of Seventh Street between the Elks Club and Fairbanks Library had been purchased by the Foundation at a cost of $30,000. By 1938, Tirey was successful in having Mulberry and Eagle Streets closed, and as a result, had a landscape design developed that served to unify and create a proper collegiate setting.

This improvement project included landscaping, grading, and construction of access drives and sidewalks. Property would need to be purchased that included buildings in poor repair. The total cost was estimated at $25,000 for property acquisition, and $50,000 for implementing the design. Tirey introduced the concept to the Board of Trustees, who then referred it to a committee. A year later, the Board approved closing the streets and acquiring the property. Tirey's proposal was contingent upon securing a Works Progress Administration (WPA) labor grant that was forthcoming and accepted by the Board at its April 1938 meeting.[8] Tirey had taken up in earnest the task of modernizing and enlarging the campus, and with the growth in student population following World War II, the issue was even more pressing.[9]

Clearly, an important part of President Tirey's legacy was the acquisition of property, closing streets, and developing a plan for a more cohesive and traditional college campus. The result of his efforts, which included the razing of Old Main, was the creation of the campus quad. To carry out plans for expanding and improving the campus, he established the Physical Plant Department. Tirey graciously recognized the city, its citizens, the Foundation, Mayor Sam Beecher, and many others for supporting the street closings and property acquisition.[10]

As he was leaving the presidency, Tirey was engaged in trying to add additional real estate that included four city blocks west of the campus (west of Sixth Street) between Mulberry and Chestnut Streets. Projecting forward, Tirey spoke to the need to add a wing to Reeve Hall and the Student Union Building (Tirey Hall), build a field house, develop better athletic facilities, and add to the library.[11]

Tirey was equally attentive to the academic enterprise, and expanded teacher education and school administration programs. He also added new programs in order to address workforce needs of the state.

Another significant achievement of his administration was to enhance the quality of student life on campus.

Tirey had an affable character and developed a reputation for being accessible to students.

Toward the end of his presidency, Tirey discussed his administrative philosophy in which he encouraged the faculty to be "kind" to each other and the students. He acknowledged the Faculty Advisory Council but suggested there was growing tension between the administration and faculty.[12]

For much of the early history, one relies on Lynch's History of Indiana State Teachers College (Indiana State Normal School, 1870-1929), published by the school in 1946. It was President Tirey who had asked Lynch to undertake writing the history for the 75th anniversary (June 1945). In February 1947, Tirey wrote Lynch saying, "I suppose there is no prefatory statement you wished me to make in the book." Two days later, Lynch wrote back, "It will be correct and fine if you wish to prepare a short message to alumni to be printed just before or after my 'preface.' You may have a page and a half or two pages as readily as one page."

President Tirey died on August 16, 1969 at the age of 81 and was buried in Highland Lawn Cemetery in Terre Haute. ■

Parsons Hall

Architect: Miller and Yeager[13]

Contractor: Robert E. Meyer[14]

Date: Dedication: November 12, 1937[15]

Cost: $164,200[16]

Area: 45,111 GSF; 23,766 ASF

Location: Sixth and Eagle Streets

The original Parsons Hall was named for William Wood Parsons (President 1885-1921) and was the first men's residence hall located on the campus.[17] Partial funding was provided by the Public Works Administration (PWA), which had also provided funding for Reeve Hall and several other buildings constructed during the 1930s. The PWA grant totaled $70,200 and required work on the facility to begin no later than January 11, 1937, and be completed by January 11th of the following year.[18]

An addition was made to Parsons Hall in 1950, bringing total occupancy to about 540 men. The student rooms were designed for double occupancy and were situated along double-loaded corridors. It also provided a new dining room, kitchen, activity rooms, and new quarters for the dormitory director. Funds came from several sources, including a $150,000 bond issue, dormitory reserves, and additional non-state funds.[19] ■

Chapter 5 President Tirey

Addition to the Building

Architect: Ralph O. Yeager

Contractor: Glenn W. North (General Construction)

Date: 1951

Cost: $458,611[20] *(Total costs including fees, furnishings, etc., $502,028.[21])*

Area: Addition 6,300 GSF

President Tirey introduced a proposal to make an addition to Parsons Hall in 1950. He pointed out the urgent need for more housing, noting there were now three boys in rooms intended for two, and 96 boys were living in temporary metal buildings.[22]

Remodeled

President Rankin

Date: 1969

During President Rankin's administration, the building was converted into faculty office space.

Building was razed

President Landini

Contractor: Jeffrey A. Bell Construction (Excavating)

Date: 1991

Cost: $296,306

Asbestos removal added to the cost of building demolition. Articles raising concern about asbestos affecting students ran in the Statesman in November and December 1991.

Student Union Building (Tirey Hall)

Renamed: Ralph N. Tirey Memorial Union[23]

Architect: Miller and Yeager

Contractors: Robert E. Meyer (General Construction); Neff Hardware and Electric Co. (Electrical); Prox and Burget (Heating and Plumbing)[24]

Date: Dedication: March 15-17, 1940

Cost: $427,488[25]

Area: 95,257 GSF; 52,078 ASF

Location: 220 North Seventh Street

ISTC benefited greatly from the PWA program. The Student Union Building is a case in point. The project received $191,728 in federal funds.[26] Plans for the building were approved, and bids from contractors were due November 21, 1938.[27]

The building, a highly modified Romanesque/Art Deco style, was designed with arms extending east and west from a massified central block, which was defined by three recessed doorways leading to the main floor. One approached the building from stairs on either side of an arched opening, which provided an entry into the basement level of the structure. The exterior brick facing included several shades of brick ranging from red to tobacco brown, which contrasted nicely with the limestone plinth course base of the structure. Rising from the ground level are wall buttresses with limestone caps that, at that time, would have echoed some of the architectural features of the Central Christian Church (Book Store) to the south.

The college, in cooperation with the city, closed portions of Eagle and Mulberry Streets, replacing brick streets with landscaping, which provided much needed relief from the traffic crisscrossing the campus. This was an important step in the development of a sense of "campus." Dr. Fred Donaghy, for whom Donaghy Day is now celebrated, provided advice for the grading and landscaping. Street closure was an important step influencing the siting of the new building. The Board discussed the site in September 1938. It was noted the new structure would require razing an old frame building known as the Student Union Building, and an old brick storage building.[28]

The Student Union was a remarkable building for some aspects of the engineering required to create Tilson Auditorium, named after Professor Lowell Mason Tilson, faculty member and head of the Department of Music (1915-40), and as a stimulus to the local economy. Newspaper accounts cited the 60,000 feet of wiring provided by Neff Hardware and Electric Company (32 North Sixth Street), over 2 million bricks prepared by Terre Haute Vitrified Brick Works, C. G. Mayrose Plaining Mill for the beautiful woodwork (including English hardwood in the ballroom and Appalachian white oak on the lowest level), glass provided by Edward S. Lammers

Beam raised to support balcony in Tilson Auditorium

Paint and Glass, and thousands of square feet of slate roofing from Hartman Company.[29] The contractor, Meyer, discussed the particular challenge posed by placing a single steel beam to provide primary support for the balcony in Tilson Auditorium. The beam was produced by Bethlehem Steel Corporation and was claimed to be the largest single piece of steel ever manufactured by the firm. In all, over 600 tons of steel were used in the building. Meyer remarked that installing the heavy roof supports over Tilson Auditorium was the most difficult aspect of the construction. Great care was taken in the selection of paint for the interior spaces.

Grill expansion underground

Renovation and Expansion

President Rankin

Architect: Ewing Miller and Associates

Contractors: Repp & Mindt, Inc. (General Construction); Sanborn Electric (Electrical); United Piping Corp., (Mechanical); Hillman's Equipment, Inc. (Food Service)

Date: 1971-73

Cost: $3 million

The Trustees, in view of enrollment growth, recognized the need to renovate and expand facilities and in 1971 authorized the expansion of the Tirey Memorial Union Building.

The $3 million expansion was begun in the spring of 1971 and was completed 18 months later. It consisted of, in addition to renovations, adding an underground grill and lounge area and the Link Building (See Rankin) between the Union and south annex (Old Elks Club now functioning as a student activities area). The new grill rose up to ground level in the terrace and could accommodate nearly 600 patrons.

Chapter 5 President Tirey

Interior spaces on the lower level included a cafeteria, kitchen, dining room, recreation room, and a 30' wide x 75' long swimming pool located beneath Tilson Auditorium. The second floor had a vestibule, foyer, ballroom, offices, alumni office, women's faculty clubroom, student lounge, and auditorium entrance. The auditorium was equipped with 1,318 seats on the main floor and 414 in the balcony. The third floor had meeting rooms, the men's faculty clubroom, balcony entrance, and seven hotel rooms.

The Student Union Building, together with the Fine Arts and Commerce Building, were dedicated simultaneously in an elaborate program that lasted three days and included an address by Mrs. Franklin D. Roosevelt on March 16, as well as a concert presentation by Rose Bampton (1907-2007), who was a distinguished soprano from the Metropolitan Opera Company.[30] ■

Remodel

President Landini

Architect: Walter Scholer and Associates, Inc.[31]

Date: March 4, 1988 The Board authorized selecting an architect to develop schematic designs.[32]

Cost: $11.8 million (for 3 combined projects)

President Landini oversaw the remodeling of Tirey Memorial Union and the Link Building, as well as new construction to house Central Computing.[33]

This was the third major project identified in the Master Plan completed during Landini's presidency.

Renovation of Tirey Lobby, State Room, Corridor, Heritage Lounge, and Ballroom

President Moore

Architect: Schmidt & Associates

Date: April 3, 1997-2000

Cost: $520,036

In September 1998, University Arts Curator, Ms. Christie Wells, and Mr. Kevin Runion, Associate Vice President for Facilities Management, submitted a plan to Mr. Robert Schafer, Vice President for Administrative Affairs, suggesting a revitalized Heritage Lounge devoted to displaying the history of the university. Central to their proposal was to display all the painted portraits of past university presidents.[34] To enhance the ambience, new carpeting, restoration of the wooden panels, improved lighting, and new furniture were proposed.

On January 24, 2000, the university dedicated the Hall of Presidents, with all the portraits now together in one building.

Tilson Auditorium Upgrades

President Benjamin

Date: 2001-02

Tilson Auditorium received several upgrades, including a new curtain for the 87-inch stage, repairs to the ceiling and lighting, and the replacement of seats on the ground floor, with reconditioned seats purchased from the old Century Theater in New York. The restrooms on the balcony level were also updated.

State Room Renovation

Date: 2004

Cost: $71,000

President Benjamin suggested changes be made in the State Room (the meeting place of the Trustees). These included removing the small stage on the west side of the room, rearranging seating for the audience, installing new technology, creating a small room on the southwest corner for refreshments, and installing a plaque to recognize past Trustees.

Repair Steps on South Side

President Benjamin and President Bradley

Contractor: Garmong

Date: 2008-09

Cost: $149,447

In addition to the interior renovation of the Trustee Meeting room, Benjamin recognized the need to restore the entry steps that had badly deteriorated. The work was completed during the Bradley presidency.

Fine Arts and Commerce Building

Architect: Miller and Yeager[35]

Contractors: James McHugh Construction Company[36] (General Construction); Porter, Glore, and Glass (Electrical); Fred Christman Company (Plumbing)[37]

Project Manager: Alvin Avey (for McHugh Construction Co.)

Date: Completed: 1940
Dedication: March 15-17, 1940[38]

Cost: $367,272[39] (Public Works Administration $165,272; State $202,000)

Area: 63,379 GSF; 36,989 ASF

Location: 649 Chestnut Street

The Fine Arts and Commerce Building was constructed on property called the Hussey block, purchased for the sum of $34,000 by the College Foundation, with funds donated by Terre Haute citizens and companies.[40] Funding came from a PWA grant and the State Improvement Fund.[41] Bids for the building were opened on December 19, 1938, and the McHugh firm was selected as general contractor.[42]

Fine Arts and Commerce Building south facade prior to renovation

A minor controversy developed over the orientation of the building ... should the facade face north or south? The decision was made to have the building face Chestnut Street. June Reynerson, chair of the Art Department, returned from a trip to Mexico to find the facade faced north while the classrooms faced east, west, and south. She, like most artists, preferred the art classrooms face north in order to take advantage of the natural light.

Art occupied the first floor and included two studios, a crafts shop, lecture rooms, offices, and pottery kilns. The second floor was occupied by the Commerce Department with separate classrooms for teaching penmanship, typewriting, and dictation, as well as lecture rooms. Revealing the imprint of new technology, an "office machine room" was included, and classrooms were equipped with greenboards rather than blackboards. Music occupied the third and fourth floors. The art gallery was renamed after William T. Turman, who served as the art chair from 1894-1934.[43]

Stylistically, the building is done in a restrained classicizing Art Deco style and echoes the Federal Post Office, also designed by Miller and Yeager and completed December 1, 1934. Art Deco derives from the 1925 Exposition Internationale des Arts Decoratifs et Industriels Moderne. It was especially popular during the movie palace era but waned in importance with the approach of World War II, with austerity replacing ostentation. The horizontal massing of form, evident in the Federal Building with an emphasis on symmetry, may also be labeled "streamline moderne."

Constructed with fire clay face brick masonry and limestone trim, the Fine Arts and Commerce Building was built of light brown brick with stone details. It stands three stories tall with a fourth story penthouse that occupies most of the roof area. The central block is flanked by wings that project on the east and west ends, forming an inverted "U" footprint.

The facade consists of five bays articulated with fluted stone convex pilasters. Each wing has one matching pilaster. The brick spandrels contain sculpted stone panels, and similar panels sit above the pilasters.[44] A stone frieze atop the third floor has decorative fruit festoons and a molded cornice. The penthouse is surmounted by a stone entablature with cornice and dentils. Two art deco-style lamps are located at the front of the building. The architectural features of the facade are continued in the entry hallway, which was handsomely finished in marble with terrazzo floors.[45]

By 1952, the current lighting in the building was considered inadequate and $159,000 was spent to add a freight elevator and upgrade the lighting.[46] ∎

Office Remodel

President Holmstedt

Architect: Yeager

Date: Completed 1957-61

Cost: $112,580

In 1957, additional offices were added to the second floor to accommodate growth in the business faculty. Further remodeling was done under the direction of Miller, Vrydagh, and Miller during the 1959-61 budget period.

Business Department Moves, Building Remodeled

Architect: Yeager Architects[47]

Date: 1962-63

Cost: $521,084 (estimated)

The Commerce (Business) Department moved out of the building in 1962. At the April 27, 1962 meeting of the Board of Trustees, Yeager Architects was contracted to undertake the remodeling of Fine Arts, to be done after the Business Department moved into the remodeled Old Science Building. The remodeling was completed in 1963.

Renovation to Add Space for Music

President Landini

Architects: Boyd/Sobieray & Associates, Inc.[48]

Contractors: C.H. Garmong & Son, Inc. (General Construction); Harrah Plumbing & Heating Co., Inc. (Mechanical); Commonwealth Electric Co., (Electrical)

Date: Bids reviewed January 9, 1981[49]

Cost: $479,690[50]

Landini oversaw renovation of the Fine Arts Building and Classroom Building to provide more serviceable space for music. These were two separated, yet connected, projects. Music was taught in the Fine Arts Building, the old Classroom Building, and several scattered derelict houses.

President Landini was authorized by the Trustees to request the university be allowed to take steps to realize the project. This included engaging architects and developing a financing plan that included fees and bond sales.[51]

Music Facilities Phase 2

Architect: Boyd/Sobieray Associates, Inc.

Contractors: CDI Corp. (General Construction); Harrah Plumbing and Heating; Midwest Electric Co., (Electrical)

Date: 1981-82

Remodel School of Music with the practice and studio rooms, instrument repair shop, and soundproofing.

Remodel First Floor of Fine Arts

Architect: Schmidt and Associates, Inc.[52]

Contractor: Hannig Construction

Date: 1989-90

Cost: $120,000

Chapter 5 President Tirey

Renovation

President Moore

Contractors: Hannig (General Construction); Harrah Plumbing and Heating/AAA (Electrical)

Date: 1998-99[53]

Cost: $1.8 million

This work consisted of electrical and HVAC upgrades. It represents a small portion of the $6.5 million requested previously.

(Left) Normal Hall; (Right) Renovated Fine Arts

Renovation of 1940 Building

President Bradley and President Curtis

Architect: arcDESIGN[54]

Contractors: Weddle Bros. Building Group, LLC, (General Construction); R. E. Dimond & Associates, Inc. (Mechanical, Electrical, Plumbing); Lynch, Harrison & Brumleve, Inc. (Structural Engineers)

Project Manager: Bryan Duncan

Date: Renovation began: 2018

Cost: Estimated at $15 million[55]

This is a comprehensive renovation that vastly exceeds the earlier plans for $6.5 million updating. Renovation includes replacing outdated mechanical and electrical systems, reconfiguring interior spaces to make better use of available space and to improve accessibility, and renovating classrooms, studios, and laboratories. The quality of the built environment is an important aspect of teaching effectiveness and student learning and success.

Plans include creating a new south entrance, restoring interior and exterior structures, replacing windows (to improve energy efficiency), as well as new mechanical, HVAC, plumbing infrastructure, and fire protection system.[56]

Walden Apartments

Date: Acquired 1941
Cost: $75,000[57]

Area: 24,312 ASF
Location: North Seventh Street and Chestnut

The Walden Apartments, prior to ISTC ownership, opened in 1904 as a modern apartment building. It offered multi-room apartments with bath, hot and cold water, and steam heat.[58]

The growth in enrollment and the addition of the Navy V-12 program necessitated the acquisition of suitable properties in the vicinity of the campus to relieve the housing shortage. The apartment building served multiple purposes before it was razed in 1988. It provided housing for women in the honors program. By 1951, it was described as a faculty apartment building with 12 apartments. It served as a practice site for students in the Home Economics program. Female students, usually around 33 seniors, lived there for eight weeks when they were not student teaching. They received credit for managing the household budget and preparing meals for apartment residents. It was also known as the Walden Design Center because some women students in the Interior Design program lived and worked there. Later, it provided office space for the Department of Economics staff, and then a daycare center. The building was razed during President Landini's tenure to make room for new construction. ∎

President Landini
Contractor: S&G Excavating
Cost: $69,500[59]
Razed: June 30, 1988

Chapter 5 President Tirey

Administration and Health Building (Gillum Hall)[60]

Architect: Ralph O. Yeager Jr.

Contractors: Glenn North Construction Company (General Construction); Christman Company (Plumbing, Heating, Ventilation); Moorehead Electric Company (Electrical)[61]

Date: Groundbreaking: June 13, 1948
Dedication: April 14, 1950

Cost: $804,251[62]

Area: 48,830 GSF; 31,814 ASF

Location: 217 North Sixth Street[63]

Gillum Hall was originally named the Administration and Health Building. The original Gillum Hall was a residence hall built in the 1960s. The name Gillum was transferred to the current building, allowing the former residence hall to be renovated and renamed the Hulman Memorial Student Union, constructed during the Landini presidency.

On the exterior, this building might be considered the twin of Dreiser directly to the north. It is a three-story structure. The second and third floors are faced with light-brown multi-toned bricks and cut stone trim. The ground floor is clad in ashlar stone. Like Dreiser, Yeager included "vision panels" of glass block at the stairwells that eventually leaked badly and were replaced with curtain glass to provide illumination for the stairways.

Dr. Harry V. Wann, "Dedication to Service," Bronze, 1940

The new building allowed the administration to move out of Old Main and was designed to accommodate many of the administrative offices (admissions, business, registrar, student financial aid, the president, and three vice presidents), as well as the health and computer centers.

Ewing Miller commented on the two buildings. He noted that they were separated by a large flight of steps providing entry from Fifth Street, and he contrasted Yeager's modernism to the more traditional work done by Miller and Vrydagh. "Ralph, Jr. was back from the University of Illinois where he had been trained in this modern style, and so they launched into what was Terre Haute's sort of first beginnings with a contemporary or modern statement through the use of glass block."[64]

Together with its companion building Dreiser, these two buildings mark a decided turn toward a more modern style of building on campus. They reflect the influence of Eliel and Eero Saarinen Buildings at Cranbrook, and the Wermuth House in Fort Wayne. Ralph Yeager was especially an admirer of the Saarinens.

The facility proved not to have sufficient space as the student population grew. By Rankin's time, the clinic

Renovation

President Holmstedt

On April 27, 1962, the Board approved hiring Weber and Curry to develop plans for adding additional office space in the basement with a budget of $50,000.[65]

served between 250 and 300 students each day in a small section of the building. Relief came in 1972 when the new Student Health Building opened at 530 North Fifth Street.

A seven-foot bronze sculpture, created by the head of the Department of Foreign Languages, Dr. Harry V. Wann, entitled "Dedication to Service," was unveiled at the east entry on the day of dedication, April 14, 1940.[66]

Remodeling

President Landini

Architect: Schmidt Associates Architects, Inc.[67]

Contractors: Mussett Nicholas and Associates (Mechanical); Lynch, Harrison, and Brumleve (Structural)

Date: 1989 (architect appointed)

Cost: $4.5 million[68]

A major renovation was proposed for Gillum Hall toward the end of the Landini presidency. It included completely gutting the interior to accommodate offices and support facilities and code changes. All mechanical and electrical systems dating to 1948-49 needed to be replaced. Space was created to house Information Technology and Communications, an Audio-Visual Center, and Television Services. This renovation was part of the 1986 Master Plan for the campus.

Renovations

President Moore

Contractor: Springhill Plumbing and Heating

Date: 1994-95

Cost: $279,469

First Floor Air Conditioning Upgrades

Date: 1999

Cost: $100,000 est.

Significant renovations amounting to about $100,000 were made to the building in 1999, prompted by the growth of the Foundation and Computer Center activities.

Second Floor Renovation to the Graduate School

President Bradley

Contractor: Evan Ryan

Project Manager: Bryan Duncan

Date: 2016-17

Cost: $643,505[69]

Chapter 5 President Tirey

Dreiser Hall (Former Language and Mathematics Building)

Architect: Ralph O. Yeager Jr.

Contractors: J. L. Simmons Company Inc. (General Construction); Christman Company (Plumbing, Heating, Ventilation); Moorehead Electric Company (Electrical)[70]

Date: Groundbreaking: June 13, 1948

Dedication: April 14, 1950

Cost: $983,890[71]

Area: 51,809 GSF; 28,943 ASF

Location: 221 North Sixth Street

Dreiser Hall is a three-story structure built with face brick masonry and limestone trim. It was originally designed to serve as a classroom building to house the Language and Mathematics Departments in the College of Arts and Sciences. The building also housed a 300-seat theater, as well as the radio and TV studios. It was renamed Dreiser Hall in honor of Theodore Dreiser, an American novelist and journalist of the naturalist school. Dreiser was born in Terre Haute in 1871 and died in Hollywood, California on December 28, 1945.[72]

Ralph Oscar Yeager, Jr. was a graduate of the University of Illinois. His buildings, such as Dreiser and Gillum, contrast with all the earlier buildings on campus that harkened back to period styles such as the Romanesque, Renaissance, and Neo-Renaissance styles. The ornamental Art Deco style was considered "contemporary" and can be seen in the Post Office Federal Building (Scott College of Business) and the Sheldon Swope Art Museum.

In contrast with these older styles, Yeager Jr. ushered in a new direction, reflecting his exposure to the new International Style that emerged at the Bauhaus in Germany, Italy, and elsewhere in Europe and South America. It was especially influential on Chicago architects owing to the presence of Mies van der Rohe.[73] Dreiser Hall represented the beginning of a contemporary or modern statement in campus buildings. The International Style describes buildings that are rectilinear, having plain surfaces devoid of excessive ornamentation. The use of glass, steel, and reinforced concrete comprised the basic language of this style. Specifically, in Dreiser, Yeager used glass blocks by the entry (which was quite modern), concrete block, and porte-cocheres.[74] It is devoid of ornamental excrescences found in period style buildings – elements such as Greek-style columns with ornate capitals and bands of Greco-Roman influenced moldings, or Romanesque-inspired gargoyles. Ewing H. Miller, responsible for most of the buildings during the Holmstedt and Rankin periods, commenting on

Dreiser Hall from the southeast

Rudy Valee signs theater wall in Dreiser 1943

the new style, referred to it as "Mussolini modern."[75]

Dreiser and the Administration Building mirror each other and were built at the same time. Dreiser, however, according to a 1961 report, "was not as well constructed." There were roof leaks, the exterior brick work required early tuck pointing, and the materials used in construction were of lesser quality.[76]

For many years, the building hosted a variety of activities ranging from English coffee hours and poetry readings to theater performances and radio broadcasting.[77] ∎

Renovation

President Landini

Architect: Schmidt and Associates

Contractors: Hannig Construction (General Construction); Williams Plumbing (Plumbing); AAA Electric (Electrical)

Date: July 21, 1989[78]

Cost: $2.34 million[79]

Renovations were completed to accommodate several new departments.

Theater Upgrades Phases I and II

President Bradley

Contractor: Crown

Date: 2011-13

Project Managers: P. Teeters, B. Duncan, S. Culp, S. Porter

Cost: $344,803

Power Plant

Presidents Tirey and Holmstedt

Architect: Yeager

Contractor: Glenn W. North (General Construction)[80]

Date: 1952

Cost: $763,305[81]

Area: Boiler House 8,400 sq. ft.[82]

Location: 528 North Eighth Street

Power Plant and maintenance shop was remodeled with addition of $500,000 boiler.

At the Board of Trustees meeting on February 19, 1952, President Tirey advised that Stalker Hall (originally the Training School) and the extant power plant should be removed at the same time. He stated this was necessary in order to complete the campus plan, which had entailed street closings and the beginning of the formation of a traditional quadrangle.[83] The razing of Stalker necessitated the creation of a new classroom building, and he recommended architects be employed to develop

Chapter 5 President Tirey

preliminary plans to be presented at the March 19, 1952 meeting of the Board.

Tirey had to deliver some bad news as well. He informed the Board that completion of the new power plant would cost an additional $120,000. The Board directed him to go to the State Budget Committee and the Governor for permission to spend $120,000 of funds then held by the college.[84]

A study of capacity was conducted by A. & E. Engineering, Inc., and showed the need to add an additional boiler and other equipment in order to meet the needs of the campus as it expanded into the 1960s. Additional boilers 3, 4, and 5 were added during the Holmstedt and Rankin eras.

The Power Plant could generate two 4,500 lbs. of steam per hour, had machinery for unloading coal cars and depositing it in a bunker, and equipment for removing clinkers and ashes. Tirey stated the new plant could provide adequate heat for a campus twice the size of ISTC.[85]

Boiler 3 Added
President Holmstedt

Boilers 4 & 5 Added
President Rankin

Boiler Converted to Burn Oil
President Landini

Engineers: M & E Engineering Service, Inc.

Date: 1978

Cost: $173,994[86]

The General Assembly, during the summer Special Session, appropriated $173,994 for the modification of boiler 5 to enable it to burn oil rather than coal. The university had not reached its goal for carbon dioxide emissions.[87]

Education and Social Studies Building (Stalker Hall)

Architect: Ralph O. Yeager[88]

Contractors: J. L. Simmons Company, Inc. (General Construction); Sunbeam Electric Company (Electrical); Prox and Burget (Plumbing); Freitag-Weinhardt, Inc. (Heating and Ventilation)[89]

Date: Dedication: September 20, 1953[90]

Cost: $850,000[91]

Location: 621 Chestnut Street

Area: 46,972 GSF; 28,616 ASF

The Education and Social Studies Building is a three-story (above grade) building situated on Chestnut Street. Today it stands on the north side of the central campus quadrangle. It was constructed of brick masonry and limestone with limestone trim. Stylistically, the building is similar to the appearance of Gillum and Dreiser, which flank the western side of the quadrangle and share similar modern stylistic characteristics. The building was designed to house the two largest programs, the Education and Social Studies departments, as well as laboratories, offices for Nursing Education, and audio-visual support for the campus. The building was divided into east and west wings to house the two departments. The Yeager architectural firm sought design recommendations from education faculty members Dr. Fred Swalls and Dr. Lloyd N. Smith.

Indiana State University Building a Legacy

Renamed Stalker Hall in Honor of Francis Marion Stalker[92]

President Holmstedt

Francis M. Stalker had a long and distinguished career at ISTC from 1892-1929.[93] In addition to serving as Dean of the Department of Education, he, with two colleagues, created summer courses that led eventually to creating a regular summer session. He was known for his education creed, and in 1940, a plaque was placed in Stalker Hall. It reads:

> "To have and to keep a sane healthy soul in a sound healthy body; To think straight; To appreciate beauty in nature, in fine arts, and in the deeds of men; To act nobly; To work skillfully with the hands as well as with the head; To realize that there is work to be done in the world; Above all to be consumed with a burning desire to do a full share of the world's work – These are the marks of a completely educated man or woman."

Major Renovation

President Benjamin

Architect: Steve Arnold, MMS

Contractor: CDI, Inc.

Date: 2003-05
Rededication ceremony: September 23, 2005

Cost: $5.06 million[94]

Van Alstine, "Via Solaris," 2005

President Bradley

Bradley oversaw renovation of the lower level of Stalker Hall to accommodate Information Technology offices, serving students' computing issues.

Contractor: Evan & Ryan

Date: 2012-13

Cost: $263,709[95]

Renovated South Façade Stalker Hall

Chapter 5 President Tirey

Stalker Hall lobby

Today, Stalker Hall currently houses the Offices of the Dean of Arts and Sciences and several other departments. This college is home to approximately 4,000 undergraduate and graduate majors. During the Tirey era, the building had been constructed without an elevator – a problem that was finally remedied with the major remodeling done throughout the structure in 2003. Electrical, heating, and air conditioning systems were upgraded, an elevator was added, and the ground floor lobby was added, equipped with a coffee bar and place for students and faculty to meet informally. The reconfiguration of interior space enabled the consolidation of departments and programs. For example, the History department had offices scattered about the building.

Because the building faced northward and the south facade was hidden by the Library and the earlier Science/Classroom buildings, its importance was diminished, and the north face served as the principle entrance to the building.[96] Demolition of the Classroom building in 1998 provided an opportunity to address the aesthetics of the south face.

President Benjamin developed an idea for the facade, based upon Italian Renaissance and French Baroque architecture, that would provide a fitting conclusion to the north end of the quadrangle and connect the building to other buildings facing the quad. Benjamin's rendering for the facade was further developed by Mr. Runion, Associate Vice President for Facilities Management, and Mr. Arnold, project architect.[97]

Today, pavilions on the east and west ends step forward about 14 feet (an idea based upon 16th century Italian Renaissance building and French 17th century design), and the main entry on the south was given more prominence so that today it "participates" in the quadrangle. New limestone and brick were used to create the pavilions, serving to tie the building to neighboring structures. Face brick and limestone trim formed the standard vocabulary for many of the campus buildings.[98]

The original building had two separate entrances at the east and west ends of the north side. A more distinguished entrance was developed that helps students and visitors locate the principle entrance. On the south side, the building appeared to be asymmetrical. That was rectified in part by adding emphasis to the south entrance.

Upon entering, a commons area with a coffee bar was designed, making it a pleasant place for students and faculty to gather between classes. The design reflects elements one finds in some of Frank Lloyd Wright's buildings.

All of the restrooms were made ADA compliant, and additional accommodations were made for disabled faculty, staff, and students. Air conditioning was added creating a barrier-free interior and upgrading finishes and lighting were advanced to create a better-designed learning environment.

A light sculpture, designed by the Dutch artists Frans and Marja de Boer Lichtveld, was purchased utilizing funds provided in the Percent for Art program. The sculpture, located at the second-floor level, is visible at night from the quadrangle. Art work from the university permanent collection was placed throughout the building, and another monumental sculpture, "Via Solaris" by John Van Alstine, was installed in the courtyard area north of the building that directs visitors to the north entrance. A central axis is thus created running north-south through the building.

The university was presented the "Outstanding Contributions in Area of Design-Public Sector Award" on May 16, 2007, by Downtown Terre Haute, Inc. for the renovation of Stalker Hall. ∎

De Boer Lichtveld, "Three Elements," 2008

Chapter 5 References

1. Another graduate of this school was State Representative John W. Summers (1889).

2. While serving as Lawrence County superintendent, he published a journal that was sent to the teachers and patrons of the schools in the county. In it he provided reading plans and information on various subjects. In one journal he wrote, "The most effective supervision requires a close personal touch and contact of the supervisor and teachers."

   The Educator Journal, Vol.10, No. 6, p. 304. This gives good insight into his administrative talents and philosophy that informed his presidency at ISTC.

3. Lynch, p. 330.

4. Tirey received his honorary doctorate one year after the famed war correspondent Ernie Pyle. The degree was presented by Herman B. Wells, the eleventh President of IU.

5. Clevenger was both coach and athletic director at IU. In 1904, he was captain of the baseball team and coached the sport from 1904-05. Tirey was in the first group to receive this award in 1963.

6. "The expansion of the business section northward, the deterioration of residences to the north and west … the increased street car and motor traffic on Sixth Street, motor traffic on Mulberry and Eagle Streets, and the large areas of pavement surface about and near the buildings that reflected heat – all of these features made up ever-present annoyances and discomforts affecting faculty and students at work." Lynch, p. 336.

7. The North Central Association of Colleges did comment in its 1932 accreditation review that movement of the campus would be required – a position challenged successfully by President Hines.

8. Trustee Minutes, April 19, 1937, XII, 322, Ibid, June 14, 1937, XII, p. 332, Ibid, April 11, 1938, CXII, p. 409. Lynch, pp. 337-338. The Federal Government furnished $83,694 and the Board approved spending $36,463. The final cost surpassed $120,000. Other items in Tirey's plan included adding an auditorium, gymnasium, library, and art room in the new Laboratory School, improving the athletic facilities, building a new stack for the power plant, creating a fine arts and museum building west of the Vocational Building, adding an extension to the Normal Library, creating a student commons and adding tennis courts and parking for a total of $1.26 million.

   In the period 1944-45, Mr. Hulman proposed a gift of property comprising roughly 47 acres lying between South 25th Street, Brown Avenue, Wabash Avenue, and Poplar Street, valued at $70,500. Apparently, there was an additional eight acres of land in that tract because Arthur Strum, Director of Physical Education, and Glenn Curtis, Director of Athletics, wrote Tirey encouraging him to ask for the full 55 acres and to purchase any additional properties in the area for athletic use. Letter dated 12/21/44.

9. In 1946, the landscape architect Lawrence Sheridan was hired to study and make recommendations for the continued improvement of the campus. Sheridan was born in 1887 in Frankfort, graduated from Purdue, and attended the Harvard School of Landscape Architecture. See: https://tclf.org/pioneer/Lawrence-Sheridan. Sheridan completed a landscaping plan for the inner quadrangle in 1953. Modernizing included the razing of the first Stalker Hall (Training School) and the old Power House.

10. Trustee Minutes, December 19, 1938, pp. 524-525.

11. Ralph Noble Tirey, Exciting, Exacting and Expansion Years at Indiana State Teachers College 1934-53. President's Report to the Teachers College Board of Indiana. 1953, pp. 23-24.

12. Minutes of Faculty Meeting, March 18, 1953, np. University Archives, Cunningham Memorial Library. Earlier, President Tirey had remarked that a "… college cannot be run as a pure democracy with the faculty voting on every issue." Trustee Minutes, April 28, 1934.

13. They were approved by the Trustees in December 1936. Trustee Minutes, December 7, 1936, p. 282. Parsons Hall was built on property purchased from Minnie Cottom and Mary C. Cooper for $21,000. Tirey approached the Board with plans to close Eagle and Mulberry Streets between Sixth and Seventh Streets. The Trustees approved it at their next meeting. Trustee Minutes, May 10, 1937, p. 325.

14. The recommendation by the architects for general contractor was Robert E. Meyer for $122,338. Trustee Minutes, January 8, 1937, p. 302.

15. Parsons Hall was dedicated the same day as the Laboratory School.

16. Includes fees, land, furnishings, and construction. Trustee Minutes, December 7, 1936, p. 282.

17. The second Parsons Hall was built on the site of the former Elks Lodge Building and contains administrative offices, bursar, and registrar. Today, it is connected via the Link Building (Rankin Hall) to the east wing of Tirey.

18. Trustee Minutes, November 9, 1936, p. 271.

19. Tirey, *Exciting*, p. 21.

20. Glenn W. North (General Construction $365,522) Trustee Minutes, January 17, 1951, p. 111.

22. Trustee Minutes, April 21, 1950, p. 503.

23. The Student Union Building was officially named in honor of President Tirey by the Trustees in June 1963. Trustee Minutes, June 21, 1963, IV, B, p. 733.

24. Trustee Minutes, November 21, 1938, pp. 509-511.

25. Trustee Minutes, November 21, 1938, p. 512. Robert E. Meyer (General Construction, $286,425); Neff Hardware and Electric Co. (Electrical, $22,567); Prox and Burget (Heating and Plumbing, $74,200).

26. Tirey had received a telegram from Regional Director of the PWA in Chicago showing a federal allotment of $191,782 for a "Student Building." He was advised to forward plans and specifications to the PWA. Trustee Minutes, August 19, 1938, p. 452. Tirey received another telegram dated September 31 (which must be in error since the Board was meeting on September 29) stating the Federal PWA had made an allotment of $165,272 for the project. Trustee Minutes, September 29, 1938, p. 478.

27. Trustee Minutes, October 13, 1938, p. 497 and 499.

28. Trustee Minutes, September 7, 1938, p. 469.

29. The Student Union Building was officially renamed the Ralph N. Tirey Union and the auditorium was named the Lowell M. Tilson Music Hall at the Board of Trustee meeting, June 21, 1963, p. 733 of the Trustee Minutes.

30. Tickets were required to attend her performance with prices ranging from $.75 to $1.50.

31. Trustee Minutes, May 6, 1988, Section I, p. 7. The Scholer group had recently completed the School of Technology addition and the addition to the arena.

32. Trustee Minutes, March 4, 1988, H, p. 8.

33. The Board authorization to accept proposals and select an architect to prepare a design for remodeling and new construction. Trustee Minutes, March 4, 1988, Section I, p. 8.

34. Three presidents did not have portraits. These would have to be created from old images.

35. Warren Miller and Ralph Yeager were appointed in September 1938. Trustee Minutes, September 7, 1938, p. 469.

36. McHugh Construction of Chicago was founded in 1897 by James D. McHugh, an Irish bricklayer. The company specialized in elaborate masonry work.

37. Trustee Minutes, December 19, 1938, p. 526.

38 The Commerce and Fine Arts Building was dedicated at the same time as the Student Union Building (Tirey Memorial Hall).

39 James McHugh Construction Company (General Construction, $239,965); Porter, Glore, and Glass (Electrical, $17,323); Fred Christman Company (Plumbing, $19,997).

40 $15,000 was paid from a state appropriation to the college in 1939. Tirey thanked the College Foundation for purchasing the Hussey block and advancing $156,000 to make possible the PWA grant. He also credited Mayor Sam Beecher, Helen Condit, the Elks Club, the Public Works Board, and citizens who contributed generously to make the building possible. This is another instance in which the community contributed to the growth of the Teachers College. Trustee Minutes, December 19, 1938, pp. 524-525.

41 Tirey was authorized to file an application with the PWA for a grant-in-aid for the Fine Arts and Commerce Building estimated to cost $340,000. At the same meeting, he was authorized to hire Miller and Yeager to provide preliminary plans. Trustee Minutes, June 20, 1938, p. 435. Tirey announced at a later Board of Trustee meeting that he had received a telegram from D. R. Kennicott, Regional Director of PWA of the Chicago office of a federal grant of $191,782 made by the Public Works Administration. Trustee Minutes, August 19, 1938, p. 452. Tirey officially accepted the building April 25, 1940. Trustee Minutes, April 25, 1938, p. 708.

42 Trustee Minutes, December 19, 1938, p. 526.

43 A Percent for Art program was established by President Benjamin. It called for a set aside of 1 percent of the cost for a new building or major renovation to be used to purchase artwork specific to that structure.

44 The term "spandrel" is also used to indicate the space between the top of the window in one story and the sill of the window in the story above and is often used when there is a sculpted panel or other decorative element in this space.

45 A certificate of completion was accepted by the Board. Trustee Minutes, January 8, 1940, pp. 684-685.

46 Yeager Architects was contracted to make several changes in Fine Arts including new lighting, adding corridors to the elevator and rear entrance, enclosing the rear porch for gallery storage, and reorganizing space on the third floor. Trustee Minutes, June 11, 1954, p. 533. At the same meeting, Yeager Architects was contracted to add an elevator to the Science Building, improve campus lighting, and remodel the Industrial Education Building.

47 Yeager presented final plans and specifications. Trustee Minutes, May 24, 1963, XII.

48 Trustee Minutes, July 31, 1981, p. 7. Appointed to the Fine Arts renovation project, Boyd and Sobieray Associates formed in 1975 and were known principally as Health Care Consultants.

49 Trustees approve bids. Trustee Minutes, January 9, 1981, p. 238.

50 Boyd/Sobieray Associates ($39,500); C.H. Garmong & Son, Inc. (General Construction, $296,185); Harrah Plumbing & Heating Co., Inc. (Mechanical, $86,785); Commonwealth Electric Co., (Electrical, $57,220).

51 Ibid, June 5, 1981, p. 398.

52 Appointment. Ibid, September 15, 1989, H. p. 9.

53 The University requested $5.9 million in the Capital Budget Request for 1991-93. Funds were not appropriated. Indiana State University Capital Improvement Budget Request 1993-95, Schedule E. The project was resubmitted August 1992 as priority 2.

54 arcDesign was responsible for the renovation of Normal Hall.

55 The project was approved by the Trustees October 19, 2017.

56 See: http://www2.indstate.edu/news/news.php?newsid=5104.

57 Trustee Minutes, May 4, 1948, p. 172.

58 Trustee Minutes, June 15, 1943, p. 332. Tirey commented "… through the help of the college foundation and the generosity of Mr. Ben Blumberg, Crawford Failey and his, sister Alice Failey Sherman, the Walden Apartments … have been purchased …". Trustee Minutes, May 4, 1948.

59 Physical Plant Projects Fiscal Year 1987-88.

60 This Administration Building was renamed Gillum Hall in July 1989. Trustee Minutes, July 21, 1989, Sec. 1, M, p. 10.

61 Trustee Minutes, January 17, 1951, Exhibit D.

62 Ibid. Glenn North Construction Company (General Construction, $582,647); Christman Company (Plumbing, Heating, Ventilation, $116,186); Moorehead Electric Company (Electrical, $24,906).

63 The location of this building represents an important step in the development of the campus quad.

64 Ewing H. Miller, interview by Jane Hazledine, Terre Haute, Indiana, April 13, 1981, 3, transcript, Vigo County Oral History Project, in Local History Books Online: Oral Histories, Vigo County Public Library. p. 19.

65 Trustee Minutes, April 27, 1962, XXII, C, p. 502.

66 In a 1975 edition of the Advance, the sculpture was referred to as "Gertrude," and by 1989 the title had changed to "Venus." The statue is now located to the west of Tilson Auditorium and is enveloped in new lore.

67 Appointment made in September 1989. Trustee Minutes, September 15, 1989, H, p. 9.

68 This was the estimated amount. Indiana State University Capital Improvement Budget Request 1991-93, "Special Repair and Rehabilitation," Attachment A. Funds were not appropriated.

69 Indiana State University Facilities Management Completed Projects, June 30, 2017, n.p.

70 Trustee Minutes, January 17, 1951, p. 113.

71 J. L. Simmons Company Inc. (General Construction, $697,699); Christman Company (Plumbing, Heating, Ventilation, $137,434); Moorehead Electric Company (Electrical, $71,853).

72 Dr. James Bush, professor of English, recommended Dreiser's name. Trustee Minutes, January 20, 1966, XIX.

73 Probably the leading proponent of the International Style was Mies van der Rohe, who had been the last director of the Bauhaus before it was closed in 1933. Mies had relocated the Bauhaus to Berlin after the Nazis forced the school to close in Dessau. The Berlin school was located in an abandoned telephone factory which was raided by the Gestapo in April 1933. Mies was appointed head of the School of Architecture at the Illinois Institute of Technology in 1938 where he exerted tremendous influence on the transformation of building into the "modern" style.

74 The glass block stairwell window wall deteriorated and leaked and was replaced with a curtain wall window. Physical Plant Projects Fiscal Year 1984-85, p. 63. This afforded a view onto the Quad. Annual Report of the Physical Plant 1985-86, p. 63.

75 Hazledine Interview.

76 "A Quality Analysis of the Academic Buildings at the Indiana Four State Schools, Trustee Minutes, November 17, 1961, Exhibit B.

77 Sycamore, 1960, p. 8. Miller, Ewing H. Interview by Jane Hazledine. See: http://www.vigo.lib.in.us/archives/OralHistory/miller/miller.php.

78 Trustee Minutes, July 21, 1989, Sec. 1, I, p. 6.

79 Physical Plant Projects 1988-89. House Bill 1530 passed in the Special Session on May 9, 1989, giving bonding authority of $3.5 million for the renovation of Holmstedt and Dreiser Halls and the Bookstore. Indiana State University Facilities Management Projects, 1991-92, p.1.

80 Trustee Minutes, November 15, 1950, p. 91. The Power Plant was one of the few buildings on campus named by its function.

81 President Tirey provided information regarding the expense. He also stated, "the building is modern in every respect with two large 4,500 lbs. of steam per hour boilers" and equipment to automate unloading coal and disposing of ashes and clinkers. Ralph N. Tirey, Exciting, Exacting and Expansion Years at Indiana State Teachers College: 1934-53, p. 21. Glenn W. North (General Construction, $289,572).

82 A facilities report submitted to the Federal Security Agency, Office of Education dated 1951, states a new heating plant and service building were under construction and were to be completed in about a year. It provided 1300 H. P. 125 P. S. I. A Report of Facilities at the Indiana State Teachers College Terre Haute, Indiana, March 15, 1951, Part IV, 5.

83 Trustee Minutes, February 19, 1952, pp. 196-197.

84 Trustee Minutes, February 19, 1952, p. 196. $120,000 would be equivalent to approximately $1.07 million. Total inflation from 1952 to 2015 was about 814 percent. See: www.data.bls.gov/cgi-bin/cpicalc.pl and www.calculator.net/inflation-calculator.html.

85 Ralph Noble Tirey. 1953. p. 21.

86 Ibid, November 9, 1978, pre-136.

87 Trustee Minutes, August 24, 1978, p. 44.

88 The Trustees approved Ralph O. Yeager to design the new building in April 1952. Trustee Minutes, April 23, 1952, p. 209. The Trustees asked the architect to develop plans for a three-story building. The building appeared in the "List of Needs as Reported to the State Budget Committee New Construction 'A' List" as the second item immediately after land acquisition. The cost was set at $920,000. Trustee Minutes, July 19, 1950, p. 8.

89 Trustee Minutes, July 28, 1952, pp. 258-259.

90 Final inspection and acceptance of the building by the Trustees occurred November 12, 1953. The Trustees moved to name the building in honor of Dr. Stalker at their June 1965 meeting. Trustee Minutes, June 18, 1965, XXI: C, p. 65.

91 Trustee Minutes, July 28, 1952, p. 258. Board authorized administration to request the State Budget Committee allocate $804,493 to build the new Classroom building. In December 1953, after bids had been received and alternates deducted, the total cost was given as $595,648. This does not include furnishings. Trustee Minutes, December 10, 1953, p. 444. J. L. Simmons Company, Inc. (General Construction, $588,172); Sunbeam Electric Company (Electrical, $48,244); Prox and Burget (Plumbing, $33,040); Freitag-Weinhardt, Inc. (Heating and Ventilation, $89,500).

92 Trustee Minutes, June 18, 1965, XXI: C.

93 Francis Marion Stalker (1892-1929) had a 37-year career at the Indiana State Normal School. He was named Dean of the Department of Education in 1923, a position he held until 1927. He contributed generously to the Cunningham Memorial Library's Indiana Collection. In 1898, he was named President of the Indiana State Teachers Association. It was this organization earlier in the state's history that advocated the creation of a Normal School.

94 Indiana State University Facilities Management Completed Projects, June 30, 2006, p. 13. The cost was approximately $84.85/sq. ft. February 6, 2003, the State Budget Committee approved $4.5 million for the renovation. The university had received bonding authority in 2001, but the budget shortfall delayed approval to move forward.

95 Indiana State University Facilities Management Completed Projects, June 30, 2013, n.p.

96 Remodeling the north side of the building required moving a mature black maple tree at a cost of $30,000. Fortunately, with special attention, the tree survived.

97 Also involved in the design process were Bryan Duncan (Director of Construction and Planning) and Scott Tillman (University Architect). A more detailed account of the renovation and its impact can be found in Martin Blank, "Welcome to the new Stalker Hall," Indiana State University Magazine, 2005, pp. 17-21.

98 A planning meeting was held November 24, 2003 to consider scheme 'F' that included improved aesthetics for the north and south facades and north entry.

CHAPTER 6

6TH PRESIDENT
RALEIGH W. HOLMSTEDT
(1953-1965)

July 1, 1953
Raleigh Warren Holmstedt became the sixth President.

October 18, 1959
Burford Hall was dedicated.

April 25, 1961
Science Building was dedicated.

November 9, 1956
The Home Economics Building opened.

1960
Sparkettes began to perform.

July 1, 1961
Indiana State Teachers College became Indiana State College.

Indiana State University Building a Legacy

Born: March 24, 1899

Died: January 6, 1988

Wife: Mary Sarah Power (married 1930-78)

Education:
Bachelor's Degree
Hastings College

Master's Degree
Columbia University Teachers College

Ph.D. Degree
Columbia University Teachers College

Positions held at Indiana State University:
President (1953-65)

1961
The School of Graduate Studies was established.

1962
The College of Art and Sciences and School of Nursing were named.

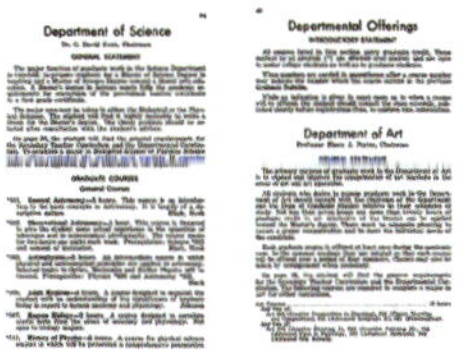

1963
The MBA program began.

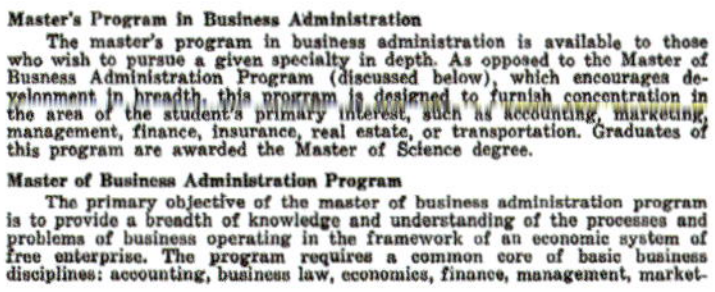

December 1, 1962
The Physical Education Building (Arena) was dedicated.

January 18, 1963
Condit House (the oldest building on campus) vested with the College.

1964-65
Sycamore Towers were dedicated.

February 8, 1965
The Governor signed a bill changing Indiana State College to Indiana State University.

Chapter 6 President Holmstedt

Raleigh Holmstedt was born in St. Edward, Nebraska on March 24, 1899. He was the eldest of 15 children. He earned his bachelor's degree with honors from Hastings College in Nebraska (where he was awarded with the Bronco Award in 1924) and later earned his master's degree (1924) and Ph.D. (1932) from Columbia University Teachers College. One can discern from his numerous publications and academic appointments his areas of expertise were school administration and finance.[1]

ISTC Campus 1963

In 1930 President Holmstedt married Mary Sarah Power. While he came from a family of 15 siblings, she was orphaned early in her life. Both graduate assistants, they met while he was teaching statistics at Columbia. She graduated from Massachusetts General Hospital. On the same day Holmstedt took his final doctoral examination, they went to city hall to obtain a marriage license. She was the first woman to serve on the Bloomington City Council.[2]

The Holmstedt era was one of major change, property acquisition, and construction.[4] During his tenure, nine residence halls and nine academic/service buildings were constructed, and five were remodeled.[5] Among the new buildings were the Science Building (replacing a structure from the early 20th century), Physical Education Building (known as the Arena), and student residence halls Erickson, Sandison, Blumberg, Cromwell, Gillum, and Pickerl Halls. Miss Helen Condit

The history of our institution suggests we do not change the name of our college in advance of quality programs which merit name change.
– President Raleigh Holmstedt

Holmstedt began his academic career as an instructor in mathematics and coach at the Nebraska School of Agriculture in Curtis, Nebraska. He joined the Indiana University (IU) faculty as an assistant professor in 1929. He advanced rapidly, becoming an associate professor in 1934 and professor in 1935. He authored the "State Aid Bill" that provided a formulaic approach for state financial support for public schools in Indiana. In 1942, he was consultant for the Survey of Administration and Finance for the New York City school system and performed a similar role in Washington, D. C. in 1948. He served in World War II and was Chief of Education and Religious Affairs in Kassel, Germany. He was later discharged at the rank of major. By 1951, he was serving as Assistant Dean of Graduate Studies at IU. He assumed the presidency at Indiana State Teachers College (ISTC) in 1953.[3]

Holmstedt's appointment was owed considerably to student action on campus. Prior to a meeting of the Trustees on October 4, 1953, students had learned that Dr. Ralph Watson, Business Manager, was under consideration to be named President. Approximately 1,000 students, led by heads of various student organizations, attended the meeting to voice their concern. The Trustees relented and indicated the Board would study the question further. Later, Raleigh W. Holmstedt was named the sixth President of ISTC.

left her home to the school following her death in 1962.

The size of the campus also increased through the acquisition of available properties. The Terre Haute campus grew by 30 acres, and 60 acres were added to the Brazil campus. The school changed from the quarter to the semester system. One should not underestimate the work entailed in this change. The curriculum had to be adapted, the entire advising and record keeping processes needed to be changed, and some programs had to be revised. During his tenure, the WISU radio station began broadcasting. It was during the Holmstedt presidency that the Board expressed interest in exploring the establishment of a medical school and school of architecture on the Terre Haute campus.[6]

The piecemeal acquisition of many parcels of real estate over time had created a disorganized patchwork of properties. Acquisition accelerated dramatically during Holmstedt's time. This necessitated development of a design for the campus to help strategically organize what had been acquired, and to guide the future of the university. The Board approved hiring Metropolitan Planners to prepare a campus master plan and appropriated $3,750.[7]

In August 1962, Educational Research Services, Inc., an academic planning firm, presented a long-range building plan for the college. It contained several strategic points that influenced decisions made during Holmstedt's presidency, but its influence continued into the future. Of major concern was enrollment. Indiana State Normal School (ISNS) had been the slowest among the major public institutions in the state to award the bachelor's degree (beginning in 1909). This was one deterrent affecting growth because degrees conferred by other institutions were held in higher esteem. Another was the absence of a broad array of programs at the undergraduate and graduate levels.[8] Third, because demographics is destiny, the report showed that the traditional catchment area for students was Vigo and contiguous counties. Unfortunately, this part of Indiana lagged in economic growth and had the lowest birth rate.[9]

The campus also had a high number of commuting students who were not full-time. This had important implications because it meant that if the school was to prosper, it needed to broaden its appeal to students from outside the five-county area and enlarge and diversify its degree programs and facilities. The future, the report stated, depended heavily on creating needed housing.[10]

By 1962, Reeve Hall and Burford Hall were the only residences for women on campus. Before Parsons Hall was built (1937), men lived off-campus.[11] Following World War II, births peaked in 1947, and in 1965, that group of 18-year-olds was ready for college. It was projected that between 1961 and 1972, the percentage of college-age students would increase by about 45 percent. This would have a serious impact on colleges.[12] For ISTC to absorb a larger number of students, it would need to increase significantly its academic facilities, including the library and residence halls.

Projected enrollment by 1972 was estimated at 12,567 – a number that no doubt fueled the construction of a large number of residence halls by the end of President Rankin's term in 1975.[13] The Planning Report concluded the total amount needed for campus development between 1962 and 1972 at $44.1 million.[14]

In 1961, ISTC became Indiana State College, a move not strongly favored by Holmstedt, and in 1965 it attained university status. The Trustee Minutes record the Act, authorizing the name change and establishment of a Board of Trustees.

"In accordance with the proclamation of Lieutenant Governor Richard O. Ristine, acting for Governor Matthew E. Welsh, issued July 7, 1961, the Acts of the Indiana General Assembly of 1961 were promulgated and became in full force and effect July 6, 1961 at 4:40 p.m., C.D.T."

Chapter 141, Acts of 1961, "An Act to change the name of Indiana State Teachers College; and establishing a Board of Trustees, transferring powers and duties of the State Teachers College Board to the Board of Trustees created by this act and preserving certain rights and remedies, became effective as of the date and time designated …"[15]

A change in the Board of Trustees in 1961, something also not favored by Holmstedt, brought pressure to begin the process of organizing the various professional schools (Education; Nursing; Business; and Health, Physical Education, and Recreation), and the local members of the Board pressed for a broader array of programs and an upgrade from college to university status.[16] Holmstedt, whose disciplinary background was education, strongly supported the traditional role of the school in preparing teachers for the normal schools.[17]

Another important milestone was the awarding of the first doctoral degree jointly awarded with IU. By 1948, Ball State University offered jointly, with IU, the Ed.D., and in 1957 established a joint Ph.D. degree program with Purdue University in guidance and counseling.

In 1965, the college was renamed Indiana State University (ISU).[18] This event was not without controversy. President Stahr of IU, together with President Hovde of Purdue, protested the change of name, arguing the similarity to IU would evoke confusion.[19] President Stahr suggested ISC follow examples in Michigan and Illinois and consider adopting the name "Indiana Western University" or "Terre Haute State."[20] A formal resolution adopted by the Indiana University Board of Trustees opposing the adoption of the name "Indiana State University" was presented at the February 2, 1965 Trustee meeting, but to no avail.[21] The change in name became effective February 8, 1965. Because this change has been so much a part of the university's identity, it warrants presenting the notice of official action. The change of name of Indiana State College to Indiana State University became effective on passage of a bill and signature of the Governor to amend Section 2, Acts 1961, and Chapter 141, adding a new section designated as Section 11:

> *Section 11. Following the effective date of this section, the name of Indiana State College, wherever the same appears in the foregoing act, is changed to read and shall be Indiana State University, and the name Indiana State College Board, wherever the same appears in the Act, is changed to read and shall be Indiana State University Board of Trustees.*

The Act became official February 8, 1965.[22]

Rapid change can be stressful and Holmstedt resigned from the presidency in 1965 before the age-related

Chapter 6 President Holmstedt

mandatory retirement deadline. No doubt, President Holmstedt endured considerable stress owing to external developments that impacted the college. The budget during the 1963-65 biennium was well below expectations.[23] The appropriations for current operations for 1965-66 and 1966-67 were insufficient.

In 1965, President Holmstedt stated, "... unless we get back the latest $4 million cut, we will have no choice but to raise fees again. We cannot keep our current faculty at the present salary schedule."[24] Expectations of developing new undergraduate and graduate programs at a time of dwindling resources must have put considerable pressure on President Holmstedt. Across the country, a pervasive trend that emerged during this time was to raise student costs regularly in order to finance higher education necessitated by the decrease in state support.

His interest in developing a medical school and school of architecture failed to gain adequate support to proceed. In 1964, Purdue and IU presented a plan to develop regional campuses offering four-year undergraduate degree programs. It was clear that Ball State and ISU were not central to the planning, and President Holmstedt voiced concerns about the potential negative impact on ISU's enrollment.[25] This was especially worrisome when one considers ISU emphasized undergraduate education and had failed to add advanced-level professional programs, except in the education field. Holmstedt responded to the state-wide plan for regional campuses, and in it, he noted the Ball State Faculty Senate had voted to become a university, and that a sizeable part of the expansion of graduate programs in the state takes place at ISU and Ball State. He also stated ISU would move toward university status "as rapidly as possible."[26]

During the 1960s, important steps were taken to implement the evolving mission of the university. The North Central Association (1965) approved the offering of the Ph.D. in several fields. Professional schools were developed to address student interest and provide a workforce able to advance the economic interests of the state. The Schools of Education; Business; Health, Physical Education, and Recreation; Nursing; Technology; and Graduate Studies were all developed.

Another development that came late during Holmstedt's presidency was an interest in developing a presence in the Evansville area.[27] Members from ISU met with the Mayor of Evansville and representatives from business, education, and government. They expressed enthusiastic support for ISU to develop a regional campus in Evansville. Plans were made to lease the Centennial School there to offer classes in that facility beginning September 1965.[28]

Holmstedt's retirement was announced by the Board President on October 26, 1963 – a date well before his retirement officially began.[29] The year before his retirement, he suffered a coronary attack and suffered from angina often.[30] Raleigh Holmstedt died January 6, 1988 in Bloomington, Indiana. He was buried in Paxton Cemetery, Keith County, Nebraska. Holmstedt Hall, built in 1966 during the Rankin Presidency, was named in his honor, and today, houses several College of Arts and Sciences departments and classrooms.

Afterword

Resolution – University Status for Indiana State College

WHEREAS Indiana State College has made significant progress in changing from a single-purpose teacher education institution to a multi-purpose college with a variety of undergraduate programs and an expanded graduate program embracing all of the basic fields of study, and

WHEREAS during the next decade there will be a very large increase in the enrollments in all levels of college and university education and a corresponding need to meet the growing demands of business, industry, government, and the professions for trained and educated people, and

WHEREAS Indiana State College, as a public institution of higher learning, has the obligation and the responsibility to serve the people of Indiana. With high quality educational programs which will promote the social, cultural, and economic development of our state and will provide for the youth of Indiana educational opportunities that will best prepare them for citizenship and a highly productive life, and

WHEREAS plans have been projected to further develop programs in several professional and vocational fields and to extend graduate and professional study to advanced levels, by the necessary legislative action.

BE IT RESOLVED, that the Indiana State College Board hereby endorses and supports the development of Indiana State College to university status as rapidly as is administratively possible and the necessary resources can be obtained, and

BE IT FURTHER RESOLVED, that this development be recognized by a change in the name of Indiana State College to Indiana State University by the necessary legislative action.[31]

Home Economics Building (Family and Consumer Science Building)

Architect: Miller, Vrydagh, Miller

Contractors: G. W. North Construction Company (General Construction); Prox & Burget (Plumbing, Heating, Ventilation); B-A Incorporated (Electrical)[32]

Date: Dedication: November 9, 1956

Cost: $482,950[33]

Area: 22,847 GSF; 13,226 ASF

Location: 318 North Sixth Street[34]

Renamed: Family and Consumer Sciences, 2000

The Home Economics Building was constructed on the southwest corner of Sixth and Chestnut Streets. It was the first academic classroom building not located on the quadrangle completed during the Tirey administration. It was considered one of the best-designed structures for home economics education at the time. It was built with brick masonry, aluminum trim, glass, and blue metal porcelain panels.

The principle architects for the building were Miller, Vrydagh, and Miller.[35] Ewing Miller credits President Holmstedt for selecting his firm following several buildings designed by Ralph O. Yeager Jr., whom President Tirey favored.[36] It was designed as a one- and two-story building with functionally articulated parts that contained laboratories for food, nutrition, family living, textiles and weaving, and classrooms.[37] Ewing Miller credited Dr. Anne Lee, Chairperson of the Home Economics department, with influencing the design. Miller stated, "She wanted a functional building that … reflected a contemporary approach to things because home economics at that time was going from the standard food and housekeeping kind of thing … into interior design and house planning …"[38] Miller also credited the Board with being supportive of the new style. "When we presented it (the plans) to the Board, they said, absolutely this is what we want … a statement where people know where we are, but we want to be Modernist, contemporary … we had a great Board. And two very good presidents that went along with it."[39]

Modernist refers to one of the important principles of contemporary architecture that "form follows function." The close working relationship between Miller and Dr. Lee reflects Miller's sensitivity to how a building was to be used. His later residence halls show a similar interest in optimal designing to meet the needs of the occupants. The geometric organization of the exterior, stripped of old-fashioned ornamentation found on earlier buildings on the campus, reflects the new "less is more" aesthetic popularized by post-Bauhaus architects.

Chapter 6 President Holmstedt

The building was oriented to allow maximum usage of northern light in the laboratories in the two-story wing of the building. The single-story portion of the building included an exhibition hall, meeting rooms, faculty offices, faculty and student lounges, and a living-dining area.[40]

Ewing Miller described this as an "international style" building influenced by contemporary architecture he had seen recently in Scandinavia and England.[41] He noted the use of new building materials, specifically the panel wall on the north side, comprised of blue metal porcelain and glass he described as a "skin."[42] He discussed how this was an "open-ended" building, and that the porcelain and glass panels that were inserted in an aluminum frame could be readily removed, allowing the building to expand to the west or south. Miller wrote, "I used the curtain wall as a means of showing that the elevation was temporary and if the adjacent street were closed, the building could be extended … and class size doubled … when needed."[43]

One might compare, for example, the General Motors Technical Center in Warren, Michigan, where one finds glass and panels set in a metal armature. The rectilinear articulation of the building's surface can also be found in Eliel Saarinen's First Christian Church in Columbus, Indiana. Miller also noted that the proportional relationship of the one- and two-story elements was an international feature and could be found in the work of Saarinen at Cranbrook.[44] It also reminds one of Walter Gropius' Bauhaus building in Dessau, Germany (1925-26). ∎

Studio Space Renovation for the Interior Design program

President Landini

Contractor: CDI

Date: 1988-89

Cost: $303,742

Remodeled

President Bradley

Architect: Ratio

Contractors: CDI (General Construction); Pixel Density Design LL.C. Technology Package[45]

Project Managers: Steve Culp and Bryan Duncan

Date: 2011-12[46]

Cost: $2.69 million[47]

Renamed: John W. Moore Welcome Center

The 2011-12 renovation was extensive. Departments in Family and Consumer Science moved to new quarters in the College of Technology and College of Nursing, Health, and Human Services, and this building was transformed into the President John W. Moore Welcome Center.[48]

The new center reflects the qualities of its namesake – the educator and advocate. The Center is the "front door" to the campus and provides a warm, personalized, and informative welcome to higher education, and is indicative of President Moore's expressed belief that ISU is the place for each student to succeed. The main area is designed as a living room and has 11 interactive touch screens students can use to learn more about the campus or ISU's academic programs and services.

The Center's occupants include the Office of Admissions, the New Student Transition Program, the Scholarship Office, a Veterans' Services Office, and university testing.

At the rededication ceremony, past President Moore, in his characteristic self-effacing way, stated, "We honor single individuals; I think symbolically it's a good thing to do. But we have to remember that contributions are made by people who will never get their names put on a building and that's why I feel somewhat embarrassed and so grateful and appreciative of the efforts and contributions of so many people here at Indiana State …"[49]

Burford Hall

Architect: Miller, Vrydagh, and Miller

Contractors: J. L. Simmons Company Inc.; Sanborn Electric Company (Electrical); Burton Plumbing-Heating (Plumbing and Heating)

Date: Dedication: October 18, 1959[50]

Cost: $1.45 million[51]

Area: 59,912 GSF; 43,728 ASF

Location: 200 North Sixth Street

Burford Hall was the second women's residence hall on campus and was named after Charlotte Schweitzer Burford, who served as Dean of Women from 1910-46. Dean Burford came to ISTC at a time when finding safe, adequate housing for women required a strong commitment and determination. She championed ISTC becoming an affiliate member of the American Association of University Women. To qualify, the college was required to have a residence hall for women. The qualification was met with the construction of Reeve Hall. The continued growth in the student population necessitated enlarging the residence hall program. Prior to President Holmstedt, 23 years had elapsed since a residence hall had been built.[52] During his administration, seven more were in use and more were planned.

Burford Hall is a six-story structure which, in its original configuration, had 30 rooms, service areas, and a lounge on each of the five upper floors. The exterior was made of face brick masonry with glazed block and stone trim. Construction began in March 1958, and 300 female students moved in September 13, 1959. It was financed through a Federal Housing and Home Finance Agency loan to be repaid from student fees.

Burford Hall was the first of three L-shaped residence halls arranged around a central dining facility.[53] The second structure was Erickson Hall (dedicated November 4, 1962) and Pickerl (dedicated November 3, 1963). The buildings shared many of the same features. Miller described the complex as "orthodox" and further stated the building was not architecturally significant.[54] One of Miller's familiar motifs was the insertion of glazed ceramic tile that divided the rows of windows, a feature he had seen in some low-income apartments in London.[55] Miller wrote, "Although dormitories were meant to define the academic campus and be background architecture, I used brick to define the building ends and glazed tile on the spandrels under the windows ... to define the living area from the group usage of the building. (An) all-brick building with holes punched for individual windows could be taken for public housing."[56]

One aspect of Miller's approach to architecture in the mid-twentieth century that distinguished him from other designers was his collaborative approach to design. He was especially interested in the behavioral and social sciences. As early as 1958, Miller collaborated with experimental psychologist Lawrence Wheeler. Wheeler was born in Indianapolis and attended the University of Pennsylvania from 1941 to 1942. He entered the service during World War II and afterward attended the Indiana University, where he earned a BFA (1948), MA in experimental psychology (1950), and Ph.D. in the same discipline (1962). Miller and Wheeler were friends, but the war separated them. In 1955, Miller met Wheeler at a concert at IU and from that point on, they became collaborators. This collaboration may be one of the first instances of an architect and social scientist working together designing a residence hall.

Wheeler began his research in 1962 in Burford Hall, surveying and interviewing residents to determine their response to the building's strengths and shortcomings. Residents were quick to complain about the long halls with rooms on either side and the noise disturbance, which owed to the double-loaded corridor plan. Common wisdom of the time suggested dormitories should have public areas where students could gather to study and recreate. In practice, students preferred to study in their rooms with their doors open.[57]

Miller did a series of buildings during the Holmstedt administration. Many of them were residence halls, necessitated by the rapid growth in enrollment. Lessons learned from Burford influenced the design of Sycamore Towers, and research done in Sycamore Towers influenced the design of Hines, Jones, and Statesman Towers, and eventually, Lincoln Quad.

While the height of Burford would soon be surpassed by 12-story Blumberg Hall, Ewing Miller commented on the scale of his buildings. He said, "… the Board (Trustees) wanted an expression … that was different from all other colleges. Muncie was low-rise, Indiana University was collegiate gothic … and low-rise buildings. Purdue was more classic and condensed but it didn't have much in the way of high rise. So, Indiana State wanted its expression for itself."[58] Miller also stated his style was appropriate for an expanding school that was an urban school rather than a country school.[59] ■

Renovation and Upgrading Suites

President Benjamin

Architect: David R. Snapp & Associates

Contractor: CDI

Date: 2006-07

Cost: $7.35 million[60]

This was one of the first major residence hall renovations undertaken because it was apparent that outdated housing was a deterrent to enrollment growth.[61] Every double room was equipped with a private bathroom, replacing the gang showers disliked by students. The exterior was given an insulating skin and new windows were installed. Several nicely-furnished public areas were included, as well as a small stage for performance by the residents. The goal, according to Benjamin, was to create housing with amenities desired by students in order to increase enrollment. Floors were reserved for students in the same major fields, such as music. Programming in the residence hall was intended to contribute to student retention.[62]

Tutoring Center (Success Center)

President Bradley

Cost: $467,800[63]

Date: 2010-11

Science Building

Architect: Miller, Vrydagh, and Miller[64]

Consulting Architect: Walter Scholer Sr.[65]

Contractors: F. A. Wilhelm Construction Company (General Construction); F. G. Christman Company (Plumbing and Ventilation); Hatfield Company (Electrical); E. H. Sheldon Equipment Company (Laboratory Equipment)

Date: Dedication: April 25, 1961
1960-68 Different phases of construction

Cost: $2.54 million[66]

Area: 266,768 GSF; 129,579 ASF

Location: 600 Chestnut Street

Ewing Miller described the Science Building as "very functional, very straightforward."[67] President Holmstedt appears to have been supportive of the Miller, Vrydagh, and Miller firm, and was receptive to a more contemporary style in architecture that broke with the style of preceding buildings on campus. The Science Building, as Ewing Miller described it, was shaped by its function and the infrastructure that makes it perform.[68] In stating this, Miller was echoing the key principle of modernist architecture.

The phrase "form follows function" became a design mantra in the 20th century. The adage was originally coined by Louis Sullivan (known for the revolutionary Wainwright Building in St. Louis) in an article published in 1896.[69] New building materials, the desire for a modern style, and the constraints of state funding meant that traditional styles of the past no longer provided the aesthetic language for a new building, rather, it was the purpose or function of the building that factored heavily in design. That principle, combined with Miller's interest in the new "International Style" of building, meant that superfluous ornamentation no longer appeared, and buildings tended to be defined by simplified geometric shapes created in steel, concrete, and glass.

Flexibility is essential in a science building as research and technology evolve. Miller designed the durable and useful building with "knockout walls," meaning room sizes could be more readily changed to accommodate increased enrollments and changes in the instructional and research programs of the various disciplines. Miller continued to introduce a practical modernism in which function influenced design.

Chapter 6 President Holmstedt

The Trustees appointed Miller, Miller, and Associates to prepare plans for an addition to the Science Building in May 1964.[70] He described one of the major external influences on his design concept was the changing nature of teaching. As he said, "We were concerned about making classrooms very habitable for a very different form of education … this was audiovisual which was heavy in the life sciences."

Miller, Miller, and Associates presented completed plans with specifications to receive bids on December 18, 1965. On the exterior, the building was made of face brick with precast concrete panels and precast concrete trim. The interior was designed with a solar controlled shading system to cut down on heat gain and glare. The building had several windowless laboratories requiring advanced systems for air conditioning, air filtration, and air exhaust. This required a major installment of accessible climate control equipment. That element of mechanical functionality influenced the rectangular shape of the building to house the equipment and create a functional distribution system.

As Miller stated, "I designed the building around a spine for mechanical supply and exhaust systems that served each laboratory individually and the classrooms collectively."[71] This is a good example of form following function, but in a creative way. ∎

Science Building Addition

President Rankin

Architect: Miller, Miller, and Associates

Contractors: Shelton Hannig, Inc. (General Construction); F. G. Christman (Plumbing, HVAC); B-A, Inc. (Electrical); Hamilton Manufacturing Company (Laboratory Equipment)[72]

Date: Groundbreaking February 24, 1966
Dedication: April 16, 1969

Cost: Approx. $4.29 million[73]

Area: 270,660 GSF (with additions)

Location: 455 North Sixth Street or 600 Chestnut Street

(Above-Below) Science Building renovated lounges

John L. Laska, "Prometheus," bronze, 1962

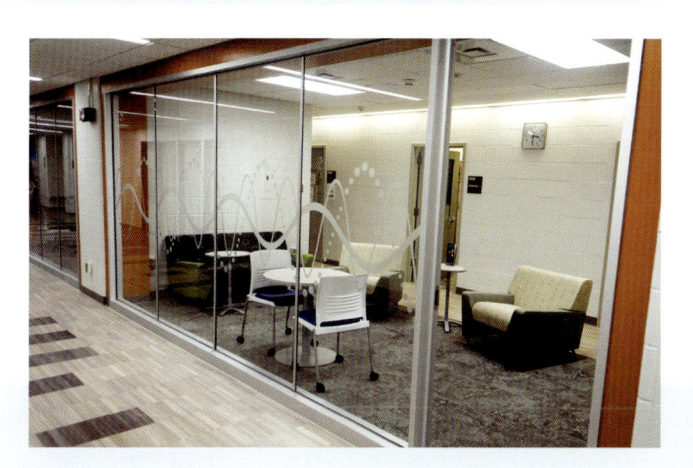

Science Building renovated hallway

President Moore

The science facilities were in dire need of upgrading in order to enable students to work in a contemporary science environment conducive to their classes and research. In the early to mid-1990s, a significant ($10.75 million) infusion of grant funding, plus additional bond funding, provided approximately $13 million, used to create new labs in Physiology and Microbiology, upgrading fume hoods, a new distilled water system, lab upgrades, improving air flow and ventilation, and making the facilities handicapped accessible. The original labs were designed for old forms of instruction, and the new labs included computer and data ports, and were designed with flexibility in mind, so students could work in clusters on specific projects.[74]

In the Faculty-Staff Convocation on September 18, 1995, President Moore announced that a total of nearly $14 million had been secured from government sources for Science Building renovations.

President Benjamin and President Bradley

In subsequent years, during the Benjamin and Bradley administrations, laboratories continued to be upgraded, a new exhaust and heat recovery system was installed, OSHA and ADA standards were addressed, new lighting was added, and aesthetic improvements were made. The images above show the recently renovated interior spaces.

A total of approximately $7.7 million was spent during the period 2008 through 2017. In addition, a $14.8 million Satellite Chiller Plant was added to meet the new load demands necessitated by this addition and new construction.

Chapter 6 President Holmstedt

Bookstore

Architect: Miller, Vrydagh, and Miller

Contractors: W. H. Sanford (General Construction); Prox and Burget Company Inc. (Plumbing and HVAC); Hatfield Electric (Electrical)

Consultant: Ken White Associates[75]

Date: 1962

Cost: $250,000[76]

Area: 12,930 GSF; 8,284 ASF

Location: 231 North Sixth Street

The new bookstore introduced a modern and imaginative design aesthetic to the campus.[77] It was a split-level building with a glass-curtain facade, comprised of bold geometric shapes formed by the box-shape of the building, elongated rectangular windows, doorways, and landscape planters. It was an example of the new International Style of interest to Ewing Miller, and it reflects the work done in the Yale School of Architecture and by noted architect Louis Kahn. The glazed facade and geometric clarity might also recall buildings by Mies van der Rohe, such as Cromwell Hall at the Illinois Institute of Technology.[78]

The cost of the building was estimated at about $250,000 and was built as a pendant to the new Home Economics Building by Miller, and in a similar style.[79] The building was approximately 12,900 sq. ft., air conditioned throughout, and contained an inventory not only of textbooks, but sportswear, school-related items, children's books, and convenience-store items. Miller described a conflict with the bookstore consultant who wanted every interior wall to be windowless. The compromise, he wrote, was "I got the front elevation to open up the building and he had the other three walls free of windows. This produced a long brick wall along Sixth Street. This gave me the opportunity to hire John Laska to relieve the monotony."[80]

Ewing Miller, the designer, owing to his time abroad and familiarity with a tradition of art in architecture going back to ancient times, wanted to incorporate art into the initial design of the building, or as he said, "trying to bring art into the building form."[81] He hired a sculptor, John Laska, to design an interesting brick panel that served as a model.[82] The bricks were laid in a specific manner. Some were turned on the short end and protruded about 4-6 inches in order to cast a shadow on the other wall of bricks. It was, in essence, a type of bas-relief sculpture. The actual engagement of an artist in the architectural design process was a very modern step, quite in contrast to the more typical practice of placing an object as an afterthought in front of the finished building – an object that might not be related to the building, its users, or the environment around it.

When completed, the Bookstore, although small, was well laid out and imaginative in design. The design adapted the structure to existing differences in grade. Miller concluded, "It was a bright little jewel."[83] ∎

Remodeled- Student Computing Center

President Landini and President Moore

Architect: Wayne Schmidt and Associates

Contractors: CDI; Sycamore Engineering; Williams Plumbing Company; White's Creative Landscape

Date: 1989-Opened Fall 1993[84]

Cost: $1.44 million[85]

In 1991, the Bookstore was moved into the Hulman Memorial Student Union and the building was renovated to accommodate computer laboratories and services. This renovation represented the third phase of implementing the 1986 Campus Master Plan.

It would have been unthinkable to build a separate building for student computing at the time the Bookstore was constructed, but in the early 1990s, student computing was more ubiquitous. Computer labs with desktop computers began to multiply across campus, but not all departments had their own computer labs. It was essential to construct a centralized facility for student use. By this time, the Center was in the new heart of the campus adjacent to the new Student Union and Commons.

The university was authorized to renovate the former Bookstore, but the decision was made to build an entirely new structure, preserving one small portion of the earlier foundation in order to satisfy the terms of the authorization that this was a renovation. ∎

Remodeled

President Bradley

Contractor: Hannig Construction[86]

Project Manager: Scott Tillman

Date: 2012-13

Cost: $643,333

President Benjamin

When originally constructed, the Bookstore occupied a central location on campus. Today, the Bookstore is located to the south on Cherry Street at Fifth Street, on property purchased during the Benjamin administration. Benjamin envisioned locating some campus departments there, such as the Center for Community Engagement and a business incubator in order to enhance campus and community relations.

This building, located at Sixth Street and Chestnut, formerly the Student Computing Center, was remodeled to be the University Career Center.

The current Bookstore on the corner of Cherry Street and Fifth Street was built during Bradley's presidency. It was funded by Barnes & Noble® and the ISU Foundation.

Chapter 6 President Holmstedt

Erickson Hall

Architect: Miller, Miller, and Associates

Contractors: J. L. Simmons Company, Inc. (General Construction); The Sanborn Electric Company (Electrical); Fred G. Christman (HVAC)[87]

Date: Dedication: November 4, 1962

Cost: $1.51 million[88]

Area: 78,690 GSF; 41,035 ASF

Location: 218 North Sixth Street

Erickson Hall, a six-story residence hall, was the second of three units built in close proximity within a short period of time. Each was designed to house 300 female students. Similar to Burford, the exterior was built of face brick, glazed tile, and metal trim. The urgency with which the new residences were built reflects both the growth of enrollment in the 1960s and the pressing need to develop adequate and safe housing for women. The building included dining facilities, lounges, and recreational areas. It's a fitting tribute to Martina C. Erickson, who served as the first Dean of Women from 1905 to 1910. She had spent her professional career advocating for the welfare of female students and set high expectations for their learning and character.

It was President Parsons who, on April 29, 1905, first advocated for creating a Dean of Women position. He again spoke to the need at the May 27, 1905 Board meeting.[89] He recognized that women constituted a significant proportion of the student population at ISNS, and it seemed imperative that an administrative position be created with the chief responsibilities of looking after female students' health and interests. Miss Marina C. Erickson was appointed on August 5, 1905.[90] Part of the Dean's role was to "give special attention to the matter of health, manners, morals, and general deportment of women," as well as serve as counselor and advisor. She retired August 31, 1910 and was succeeded by Charlotte Schweitzer (Mrs. Burford).

Burford, Erickson, and soon Pickerl were built in a similar "orthodox" dormitory style, in which functionality and budget were prime considerations, but the attention to textural surfaces and rhythmic punctuation of the glass blocks are characteristic Miller attributes. Also typical for a Miller design, a spacious lounge was located strategically on the ground floor.

Following a decline in enrollment, Erickson was converted into academic offices during the Moore presidency. ∎

Renovation

President Moore

Contractors: Jungclaus-Campbell Company (General Construction); Sycamore Engineering Inc. (Mechanical); NRK (Electrical)[91]

Date: 1997

Cost: $4.69 million[92]

Erickson reopened in 1997 following extensive renovations. Formerly a residence hall, the building housed the School of Graduate Studies, the Departments of Communication and Social Work, the Office of Continuing Education, the Office of International Student Services, Army ROTC, and the Employee Assistance Program.

Renovation included a new exterior envelop achieved by installing thermally insulated glass windows. Upgrades were made to the mechanical, heating, and air conditioning systems, as well as the restroom facilities to make them ADA compliant.

Chapter 6 President Holmstedt

Erickson Hall entrance northeast corner

Renovated Erickson Hall

President Bradley

Architect: Browning, Day, Mullins, Dierdorf, Inc.[93]

Contractor: Garmong & Son, Inc.

Project Managers: Steve Culp and Seth Porter

Date: 2011-13[94]

Cost: $8.82 million[95]

The six-story building was remodeled in 2011-13, converting it back into a residence hall for 260 students. It received a new entrance at the northeast corner and exterior skin. Each floor has 25 double occupancy clusters around a pod, shared toilet, and shower room with pod-style living rooms. The first floor has a spacious lounge, laundry, mail, and vending facilities. Other amenities include a student porch, laundry and snack facilities, the Office of Residential Life Services and additional multi-purpose meeting rooms and classrooms.

Following a trend begun in Burford Hall, housing is devoted to specific disciplines. In the case of Erickson, the themed communities are Criminology/Criminal Justice and Psychology.[96]

Indiana State University Building a Legacy

Sandison and Gillum Residence Halls

Unit 1 Sandison

Architect: Yeager Associates[97]

Contractors: George Bahre Company (General Construction); Freitag-Weinhardt, Inc. (HVAC and Plumbing); Hatfield Electrical Company (Electrical)[98]

Date: Dedication: November 4, 1962

Cost: $1.65 million[99]

Area: 64,707 GSF; 44,422 ASF

Location: 440 North Fifth Street

Sandison Hall is a nine-story structure originally designed to accommodate 300 students. The exterior is made of face brick masonry with precast concrete trim. It was named after Howard Sandison, an 1872 alumnus, member of the faculty, and a Vice President at ISNS (1881-1917).[100]

Sandison Renovation

President Landini

Contractor: Neighy Construction

Date: 1988-89

Cost: Estimated at $1.11 million[101]

The renovation included upgrading electrical and plumbing systems, painting, carpeting, ceilings, casework, coverings, and drapes.[102]

Sandison Renovation

President Bradley

Architect: David R. Snapp & Associates, Inc.

Contractor: Garmong

Date: 2009-10

Cost: $9.19 million[103]

The initial estimate of $10 million was raised to $11 million by the Trustees in February 2009. The State Budget Committee approved the project in May 2009. Sandison had been closed since 2006. Final expenditures were less than estimated. The renovation updated double occupancy rooms with private baths for 240 men and women and made changes to the facade to blend in with adjacent buildings, particularly the Hulman Memorial Student Union. Updating also included air conditioning, WiFi, and a fire suppression system.

The residence featured themed housing that has been shown to improve student performance and persistence. Five of the floors are populated by students interested in nursing and health care. The addition of the McKee Nursing Center (dedicated September 10, 2010) on the first floor, equipped with the latest technology, creates an innovative living-learning facility where residents have hands-on learning opportunities in health care.[104] Sandison is also home to the Leadership Learning Community, with two resident peer advocates prepared to assist students with leadership skills and community service endeavors.

Unit 2 Gillum[105]

President Holmstedt

Architect: Yeager Architects

Contractors: Shelton Hannig, Inc. (General Construction); Freitag-Weinhardt, Inc., (Plumbing, Heating, etc.); Ernest Miller (Electrical)[106]

Date: Dedication: November 3, 1963[107]

Cost: $1.48 million[108]

Area: 47,812 ASF

This second dormitory of the same design soon followed. The Trustees accepted the preliminary plans submitted by Yeager Architects, and bids were received in February 1962.

Indiana State University Building a Legacy

Photo depicts later renovation

Student Union and Food Court Renovation

President Landini

Architects: Schmidt Associates; Architects, Inc.; Mussett, Nicholas, and Associates, Inc.

Date: Completed October 1991

Cost: $7.69 million

Renamed: 1990, Hulman Memorial Student Union

The renovation of Gillum was a repurposing of the building. A food court was created on the ground floor level and the balance of the building formed a new Student Union complex, meeting rooms, and President's dining area on the top floor. Construction and renovation associated with the Student Union is one of the first steps toward implementation of the Master Plan (1986) approved by the Trustees. The creation of the food court, which was a new idea for the campus, enabled private sector vendors in Terre Haute to now conduct business on the campus.

HMSU Sycamore Banquet Center

President Bradley

Architect: RATIO Architects

Contractor: CDI

Date: 2011-12

Cost: $3.69 million

Chapter 6 President Holmstedt

Physical Education Building (Arena)[109]

Architect: Miller, Vrydagh, Miller
Contractor: J. L. Simmons Co., Inc.[110]
Date: Dedication: December 1, 1962[111]
Cost: $2.9 million[112]
Area: 293,846 GSF; 179,081 ASF
Location: 401 North Fourth Street

Sports arenas present their own unique design problems. One of them is noise – shouting voices and pounding balls in a cavernous space. The second is that arenas may also be utilized as instructional space. A third is how to bridge a great distance while not compromising the views of spectators. Typically, arenas were built on a post and lintel (or beam) system with steel trusses spanning the playing area. Unfortunately, the supporting beams were posts placed in front of spectators. Ewing Miller, the design architect, pointed out that there was structural experimentation going on in Italy at the time, notably in the work of Pier Nervi.[113] Miller's discussions with his structural engineer led to the design for this innovative and daring folded-plate roof.

The Arena and Physical Education Building was put into use in February 1962, and the formal dedication was held in December 1962.[114] Constructed of brick and glazed tile masonry, architecturally, the building was a tour-de-force for its folded plate roof, which was the largest roof of its type in the world.[115] It spanned about 265 feet without the use of interior supports, enabling the creation of a large gymnasium (210' x 155') for basketball games. It could be subdivided into three separate gyms for teaching and practice.[116]

Miller decided the folded concrete plate roof could be sprayed with sound-absorbing material to lessen the noise, particularly when the arena was used for instruction. The electrical consultant Ralph Stuart recommended a new lighting system that provided a very even light over the floor. However, the noise-dampening ceiling muffled the sound of the cheering crowd much to the consternation of the coaches, and the mercury vapor lights turned peroxided blond hair pastel green.

The building could seat 5,500 people, and in addition to the gymnasium, it accommodated gymnastics, wrestling, dressing rooms, an Olympic-type pool, trainer's room, and offices. The Arena was recognized by The University of California Conference on Creative Use of New Materials at the International Conference of Engineers held in Rome, Italy. The building was listed as one of the 10 most outstanding buildings completed in 1961.[117] Miller concluded, "It remains a marvelous piece of engineering."[118]

Another point of pride – Indiana State University was one of the first three universities in the United States to offer an accredited Athletic Training Program. ∎

Indiana State University Building a Legacy

Northern Addition

President Landini

Architect: Walter Scholer and Associates[119]

Contractors: CDI, Inc. (General Construction); Sycamore Engineering, Inc. (Mechanical and Electrical); F. E. Gates (Synthetic Floor Surface)

Date: Groundbreaking: May 2, 1986

Dedication: April 19, 1988

Cost: $11.61 million[120]

Area: 170,086 GSF; 89,620 ASF (For the addition only) Total 293,846 GSF; 175,360 ASF

Renamed: Health and Human Services Building

On May 2, 1986, a groundbreaking ceremony was held for a northern addition to the original building. The addition of 121,000 sq. ft. was designed by Walter Scholer and Associates. It included basketball, badminton, volleyball, racquetball and tennis courts, a jogging track, classrooms, and faculty offices. In 2003, a climbing wall was dedicated in the north gym arena.[121]

This building was included as a high priority among the proposed projects in the Capital Improvement Budget Request for 1983-85. It had been proposed previously but was not funded. The Commission for Higher Education listed it as the only construction project cited as "high priority" that was not funded by the 1981 General Assembly.

The justification for the request was compelling. Indiana State University was the only institution in the country that had accredited undergraduate and graduate programs in athletic training. The university, out of necessity, had to use old residences and commercial property. The addition, it was argued, would make it possible for the university to demolish several dilapidated structures and the Women's Physical Education Building (1924).[122] The Women's P.E. Building burned and insurance money helped fund the northern addition. ■

Weight Training Facility Expansion

President Benjamin

Date: 2005

Cost: $1.66 million[123]

The courtyard was enclosed to make a weight training facility.

Chapter 6 President Holmstedt

Aerial view of the College of Health and Human Sciences

Renamed College of Health and Human Services

HVAC, Remodeling

President Bradley

Contractor: Harrah Plumbing and Heating

Date: 2010-11

Cost: $1.17 million

Locker Room Renovation

Contractor: Garmong

Project Managers: Steve Culp and Bryan Duncan

Date: 2012-13

Cost: $681,187[124]

This project added HVAC to the south gym and lower level and upgraded electrical systems.

In 2009, Ratio Architects, Inc. presented a master plan for remodeling and new construction for the newly titled College of Nursing, Health, and Human Performance. In July 2010, the Trustees approved including Phase 1 in the 2011-13 Capital Budget Request. No significant upgrades had been made in the facility since its construction 55 years earlier. The facility did not meet current ADA or OSHA standards. ■

Deedee Morrison, "Our River-Our Future," stainless steel with laser cut and enameled steel elements, 2019

Expansion and New Construction

President Bradley
Architect: Ratio Architects
Contractor: Hannig Construction
Date: 2016-19

Ribbon Cutting: December 15, 2017
Cost: $64 million[125]
Area: 380,846 GSF; 229,081 ASF[126]

The strategic 2007 merger of the former College of Nursing and the College of Health and Human Performance led to the formation of the College of Nursing, Health and Human Services in an effort to support enhanced collaboration among the several disciplines.[127] Healthcare is drawing many students who anticipate higher-paying careers in high-demand professions. The college currently counts approximately 3,500 students in its various programs and is certain to grow.

The entire project, phases I and II, were guided by five goals:

1. Meet safety and ADA guidelines
2. Enhance instructional capabilities
3. Develop a socially responsive research agenda
4. Create a health and social wellness information center
5. Meet the state's workforce and economic development needs

College of Nursing, Health and Human Services

Chapter 6 President Holmstedt

The project consisted of two phases: Phase I was the construction of a new 87,000-square-foot expansion to house new academic programs of the recently formed college. Phase II included improving temperature control and ventilation in the old facility, some space reconfiguration to improve efficiency, and new technology. All work was done according to Leadership in Energy and Environmental Design (LEED) standards. The new addition contains smart classrooms and the newest technology to support the new programs and enable increased collaboration among the disciplines.

Phase I includes an outpatient clinic and various labs that are discipline-specific, such as neuro, physiology, motor skill, and applied science labs. It also includes two 150-person lecture halls, graduate research suites, offices, and a wellness garden.[128]

Phase II features a new four-story glazed atrium illuminating lounge spaces and a two-story open walkway with natural light. Aquatic and therapeutic pools were renovated, as well as classrooms and labs. The track renovation reflects the prestige John McNichols brought to ISU and this sport.[129]

Additional interior projects were completed during the Bradley administration. These included adding new air conditioning, replacing gym floors, creating a Dietetics area, and renovating locker rooms at a cost of over $3 million. ■

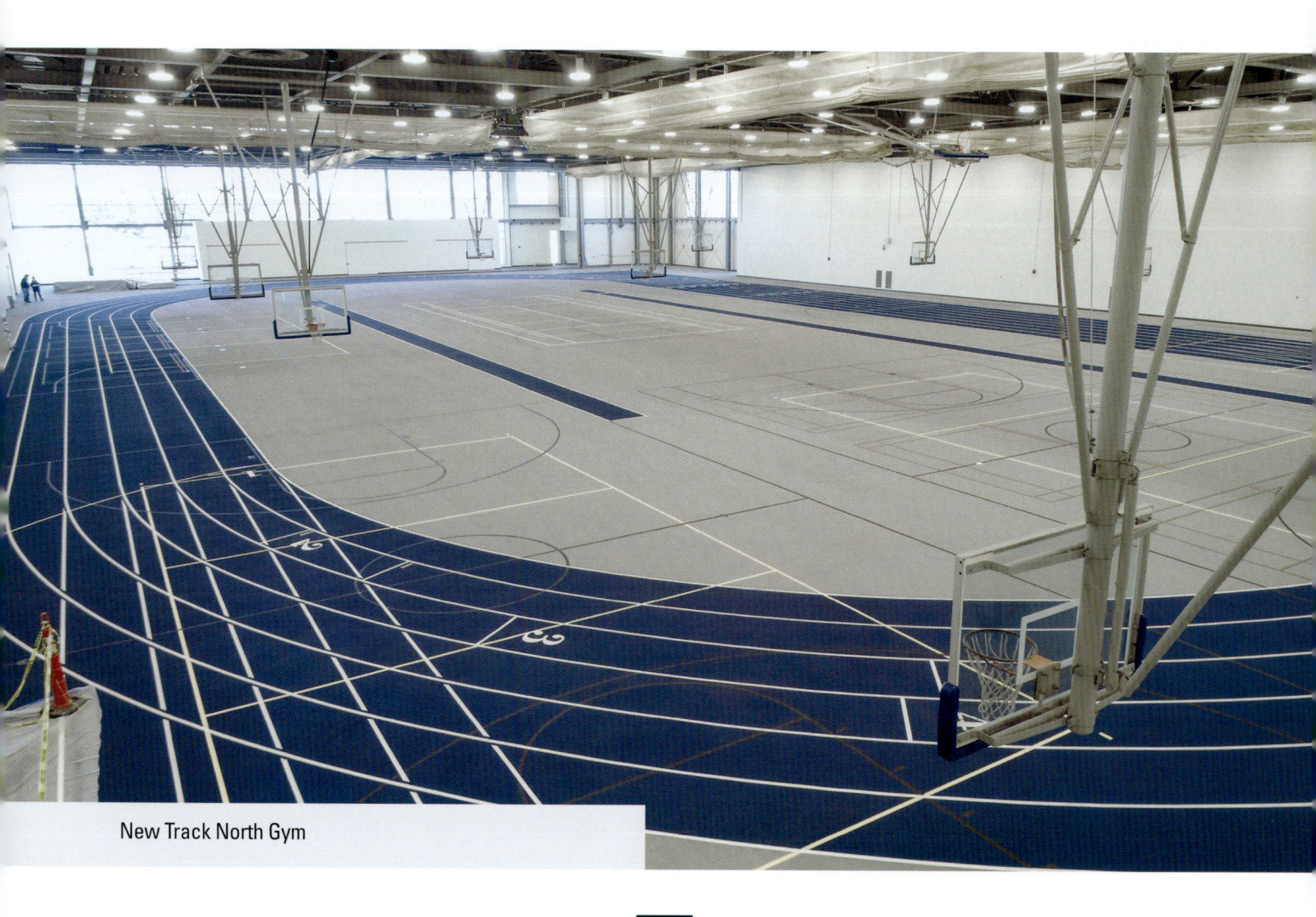

Interior, College of Nursing, Health and Human Services

New Track North Gym

Indiana State University Building a Legacy

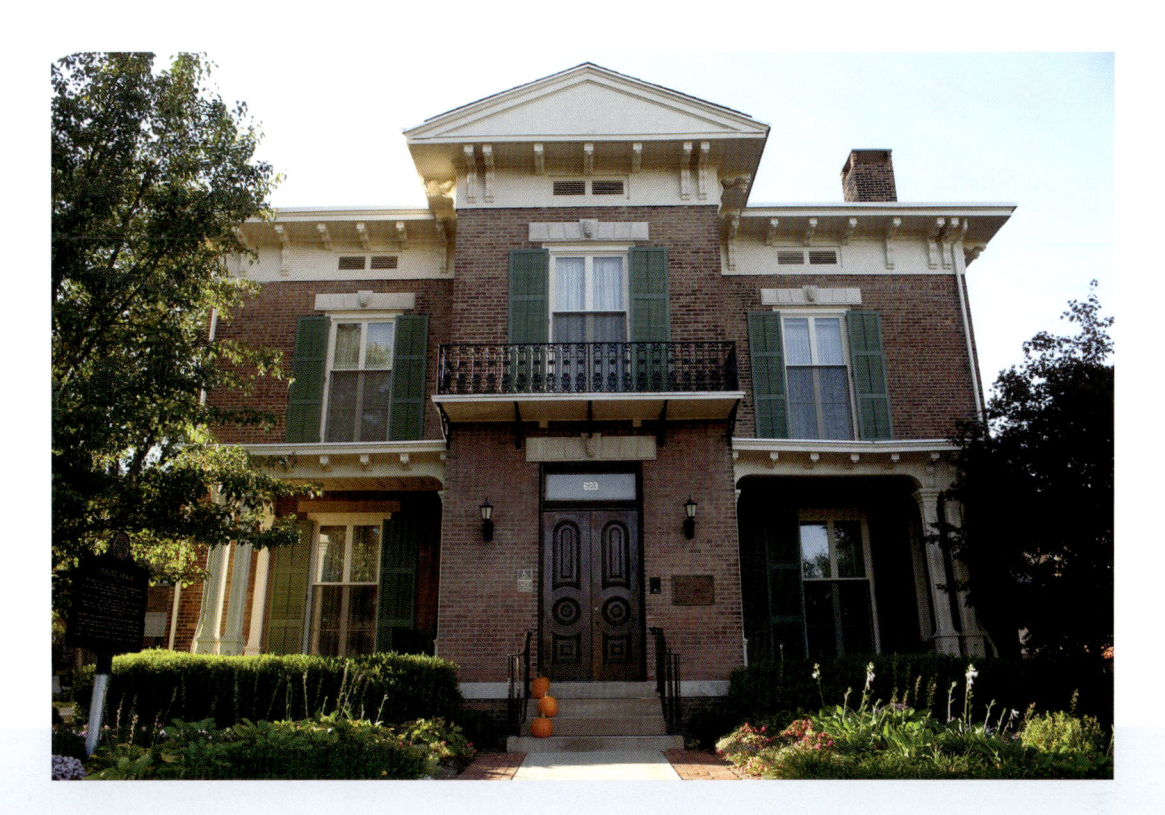

Condit House

Architect: Jabez Hedden
Date: 1860

Location: 629 Mulberry Street

Condit House was built in 1860 by Jabez Hedden, for Terre Haute resident Lucien Houriet, who was a watchmaker and jeweler. The house was located across the street from the Vigo County Seminary. He sold the home to Reverend Blackford Condit and his wife, Sara Louise Condit, in 1863.[130] Reverend Condit was the pastor of Central Presbyterian Church, and Mrs. Condit was the daughter of Caleb Mills. Mills was the second Superintendent of Public Instruction and founder of Wabash College in Crawfordsville, Indiana.[131] He often visited the family in Terre Haute and would have been one of its most illustrious visitors. Mills was an ardent leader of efforts to create a state school system, and he sponsored the Indiana Free Public School Law. He is rightly called the "Father of the Indiana Public School System."

The home passed to their daughter, Helen Condit, who lived there until her death on December 10, 1961. Helen Condit was actively involved in the Terre Haute community. She was the co-founder of and served on the Board of Union Hospital, and she contributed to the Swope Art Gallery. She was, like her maternal grandfather Caleb Mills, associated with Wabash College and contributed to the development of ISTC.

One of her lasting legacies was the establishment of the Caleb Mills Scholarship, awarded to a graduating senior who was training to be a teacher. She signed an agreement with ISTC in 1928, stipulating her intent to transfer ownership of Condit House to the campus upon her death.[132] It is ironic that the first thought of acquiring the Condit House arose in 1915 when Mr. Allen Condit (Helen's brother) intimated he would seek to enjoin ISNS "from operating such departments as may be annoying to the occupants of the property."[133] The plan was to locate the Vocational Building within a few feet of their home. The Trustees wrote Mr. Condit and offered him $15,000 for the property. He declined the offer.

Condit House has served a variety of purposes since it came to the university.[134] At the August 10, 1962 meeting of the Trustees, "authorization was given to prepare the Condit House for use by the Alumni Relations Office," even though the College did not yet have title to the property, with portions to be reserved as guest rooms. From 1963 until 1966, it housed the Office of Alumni Affairs and the Indiana State College Foundation.

Stylistically, Condit House was built in a provincial Italianate style. In appearance, it is symmetrical and somewhat formal. The central axis of the facade features a pavilion surmounted by a classical pediment. The exterior shows a hip roof, projecting eaves supported on brackets, and two chimneys. There are three long windows across the facade at the second floor, and two tall windows flanking the central doorway on the ground level. Stone beehives added a modest decorative element to the exterior. The steps required restoration, and in 1985, they were replaced with three large pieces of Bedford limestone.

A pair of rich wooden double doors with handsomely etched glazing opens onto a small entrance way. A second set is located at the back of the small entry. This set of doors opens onto a foyer. The second pair of doors matches the cherry wood balustrade that leads to the second floor. The two floor-to-ceiling windows on the front of the house and 12-foot high ceilings give the house a spacious and nicely illuminated ambience, and a pleasant view of the quadrangle.

Original mantel pieces and a sculptured ceiling medallion evoke the character of the time it was built. The rear wing of the house was restored and contained the kitchen and dining rooms. Several rooms had frescoed ceiling decoration.

A very interesting gift from the University Foundation to the home is a Steinway piano that came from the Alice Longworth family in Cincinnati. Alice was the eldest child of Theodore Roosevelt and married Nicholas Longworth, who was House Speaker and an Ohio Congressman. Known for her insouciant vitality, she frequented Cincinnati symphony events.

Alumni Center and Foundation Renovation
President Rankin

Contractor: H. Readinger & Sons, Inc.[135]

Cost: $132,000[136]

Area: 12,082 GSF; 7,011 ASF

President Alan Carson Rankin, together with the approval of the Trustees, supported the renovation of Condit House to be used as the President's residence.[137] Gaining approval to proceed with renovations was difficult. Miller and Associates was asked to develop revised plans after the initial proposal was rejected because of the excessive cost.[138] Revised plans were used to solicit new bids on January 18, 1966. The Board tabled consideration of the plans and bids and authorized "architectural consultations" to consider ways to enlarge Condit House at a lesser cost. The bids ranged in price from $62,186 to $80,000.[139] The Board, however, decided at the February meeting to ask the low bidder (Leon G. Heine & Son, Inc.) to allow the Board to consider the project further.[140]

At the February 19, 1966 meeting of the Board, Mr. Roll McLaughlin presented preliminary plans "illustrating possible alterations … which might result in Condit House being a desirable residence for the President of the University."[141] The Board moved to request approval of the Governor to appoint Mr. McLaughlin to prepare definitive plans and bid specifications, and that the bids that had been received previously by the Trustees be rejected.[142] By September 1966, McLaughlin presented a progress report stating a contract had been let to demolish the rear wing of the building, but materials such as bricks, doors, windows, shutters, etc., were being salvaged to be repurposed in the new construction.[143]

New bids were presented in October of that year. The contractor selected was H. Readinger & Sons, Inc., of Terre Haute, who had submitted a bid of $132,000.[144] The project was held in abeyance, and in December 1966, McLaughlin met with the building committee to review further changes to reduce cost.[145]

Renovation was completed in 1967, and the Rankin family moved into Condit House in February 1968. The socially-minded Rankins enjoyed Condit House and frequently entertained the Terre Haute citizenry there.

Presidents Richard G. Landini and John W. Moore resided here, although President Moore for only a few months before he moved off-campus. Condit House was converted into the Office of the President and served this role until July 2008, when it was once again converted into the President's residence. ■

Renovation and Remodel

President Bradley

Architect: Scott Tillman, University Architect

Contractors: Neff Construction (Garage, House, Kitchen, Windows); Earl C. Rodgers & Associates/Neff Construction (House)[146]

Date: 2008-11

Cost: $487,411

Condit House was once again renovated to become the presidential residence on campus. The Office of the President was moved to Parsons Hall.

Chapter 6 President Holmstedt

Pickerl Hall

Architect: Miller, Miller, and Associates[147]

Contractors: J. L. Simmons Company (General Construction); F. G. Christman (Plumbing, Heating); The Sanborn Electric Company (Electrical)[148]

Date: Dedication: November 3, 1963

Cost: $1.37 million[149]

Area: 59,823 GSF; 40,676 ASF

Location: 301 North Fifth Street (Originally North Fifth and Eagle Streets)

Renovation

President Moore

Contractors: Hannig (General Construction); NRK (Electrical); Springhill Plumbing and Heating

Date: 1998-99

Cost: $513,920

President Moore oversaw the renovation to accommodate Public Safety and ADA restrooms on the first floor.

The Trustees were informed that the dormitories currently under construction and scheduled to open in 1962 would not be adequate to house the influx of students wanting to attend the college. Trustee Kendall moved, and Miss Maehling seconded, a motion authorizing the administration to submit applications to the Housing and Home Finance Agency for $3 million to finance construction of the third women's dormitory, Pickerl, and the second men's dorm, Sandison.[150]

The firm of Miller, Miller, and Associates was approved to design Pickerl Hall. As was the case with Erickson and Burford Halls, it was designed to accommodate 300 women students. The Trustees accepted the preliminary plans for the women's dormitory at their October 19, 1961 meeting.[151] It was named in honor of Dorothea Maude Pickerl, a 1914 alumnus of ISNS. It was dedicated November 3, 1963, one year and a day after Erickson Hall.[152] Stylistically, it follows the designs of Burford and Erickson and might be characterized as residence "modernism." It retained the six-story elevation and L-shaped footprint of the Burford dormitory. The exterior was constructed of face brick, glazed block, and metal trim.

Pickerl Hall renovated interior

Indiana State University Building a Legacy

Renovation

President Bradley

Architects: David R. Snapp & Associates; R. E. Dimond & Associates, Inc. (Consulting Engineers)

Contractors: CDI, Inc.

Project Managers: Rex Kendall and Steve Culp

Cost: $8.22 million[153]

Date: 2010-11

Like Sandison Hall that reopened for the fall semester in 2010, the updating of Pickerl continued the process of renovating student residences and introducing themed housing, which has been shown to improve student academic performance and persistence to degree.[154] Pickerl is home to the University Honors Program learning community.

The building, a six-story structure, was remodeled on the interior and exterior and work was completed in 2011. The old dormitory plan was revised to include double rooms with private baths and individual climate control. A patio was added for outdoor activities. The entry lobby was given glass and marble wall surfaces, which, with the lighting, creates a dramatic entry. The exterior, like Burford, was given an insulated skin replacing the glazed tile, and new thermal windows for energy conservation. The interior also received new finishes using quartz, granite, and sisal.[155] Air conditioning was added, in addition to a new fire suppression system. Lounges and meeting rooms on the first and lower levels were reconfigured and updated.

American School and University named the renovation of Pickerl Hall as among the best in the nation in its 2011 Architectural Portfolio. Rex Kendall, Director of Residential Life, stated, "Careful and significant planning has to take place to make sure the renovations, once completed, reflect the current trends of residence halls …"[156]

Chapter 6 President Holmstedt

Hulman Center

(Deming Hotel)

Architect: Holabird & Roche

Contractor: Sheldon-Breck Construction Company (St. Louis)

Date: 1914
Acquired: 1963

Cost: $400,000 (Original)

Area: 135,000 GSF

Location: 615 Cherry Street

Renamed: Hulman Center, 1964

The Deming Hotel was built on the site of an earlier Congregational Church. Holabird and Roche was a Chicago firm that designed the structure in the Second Empire Style. Holabird and Roche both worked in the architectural firm of William Le Baron Jenney, the "father" of the American skyscraper. Jenney had been the chief architect for the building of Old Main after the disastrous fire of 1888. The Holabird and Roche firm was responsible for the Palmer House (1923-25) and Crane Company building (1913) in Chicago, which bear comparison with the Deming Hotel.

The Board of Trustees unanimously passed a resolution that "the necessity exists to acquire, operate, control, and manage the Deming Hotel and associated properties, to be known and operated as Student Union Facilities # 2 …"[157] Two months later, the Deming Hotel was officially named Hulman Center in honor of Anton Hulman Jr.[158]

Terre Haute Mayor Tucker appeared before the Board at its May 24, 1963 meeting to protest the college's acquisition of the Deming Hotel. He stated, "It was a step in the wrong direction." He asked the college to "refrain from expanding into the downtown of the city."[159] He cited the loss of tax revenue and parking as two major concerns. The Deming property included a garage, and the city was disturbed by the prospect of a loss of parking near downtown businesses. This prompted a discussion by the Board at the September 1963 meeting in which several proposals were presented, all of which recognized the campus also had a parking problem and that additional parking was needed. The Board decided to keep the Deming Garage to provide parking for students and the community, and to consider asking the Foundation to purchase the Bowman Milk Company Plant at Seventh Street and Pennsylvania Railroad, as well as other properties in the area to extend the campus northward to create additional parking.[160]

President Rankin

Renamed: Continuing Education Center (1973)

Renamed Conference Center (1974)

In 1968, $100,000 was transferred from reserves to cover costs associated with the rehabilitation of student housing rooms.[161] In October 1973, the Trustees approved the name "Continuing Education Center" to distinguish it from the new Hulman Civic University Center. Finding that name awkward, the Board then decided to rename the building the "Conference Center."[162]

President Landini

A special meeting of the Board was held on February 25, 1976 to discuss the expression of interest by Bethesda Corporation to purchase the building and convert it into apartments for the elderly.[163] President Landini reported to the Board in May 1976 that plans for the sale of the Conference Center building were progressing.[164]

Indiana State University Building a Legacy

Operation of the facility was not without difficulties. A first sign of financial problems is noted when the Board was informed that the fiscal operation of Hulman Center had been unsatisfactory, owing to remodeling costs, delayed preventative maintenance, and revenue shortfalls in the Gourmet Room. Vice President Moulton advised that immediate and substantial reduction in employees and "elimination of certain major expenditures" would rectify the situation.[165] In May 1964, it was learned that the Terre Haute Realty Company, which operated the hotel, had incurred a loss of $19,155. In accordance with the purchase agreement, the debt was added to the purchase price paid by the college for the property. Fortunately, the Hulman Foundation made a contribution of $20,000 to cover the loss.[166]

In December, the Vice President of Slater Food Service, in a letter to the Board, projected losses continuing into mid-1965 and sought relief from the Board. Barring agreement, Slater Food Service asked that this letter serve to start the notice period. Remodeling of the Hulman Center was entrusted to Miller, Miller, and Associates. In an interesting move, Board President Dr. Crockett appointed two Board members (Archer and Kendall) as a Board committee to engage in the planning procedures together with the architects and college officials.[167]

In October 1964, Ewing Miller of Miller, Miller, and Associates presented a report on the rehabilitation plans of Hulman Center. The plan proposed an increase of 25,000 sq. ft. at a cost between $1.03 million and $1.82 million. A loan would be required to finance the project but obtaining a loan would require a demonstrable income flow. The Trustees, to little effect, suggested the administration pursue grants from external foundations.[168]

By 1978, due to continuing revenue constraints, the Trustees were prepared to sell the property. ∎

Classroom Building (Holmstedt Hall)

Architect: Weber and Curry[169]

Contractors: Repp and Mundt, Inc. (General Construction); Christman (Plumbing and HVAC); Potter Electrical Engineering & Construction (Electrical)[170]

Date: 1964

Cost: $1.48 million[171]

Area: 99,324 GSF; 50,898 ASF

The urgent need for a general classroom building to house faculty and accommodate departments including Social Sciences, English, and Foreign Languages was taken up by the Trustees at their March 16, 1962 meeting. The Board, however, tabled voting on appointing architects until the April meeting.[172]

Chapter 6 President Holmstedt

In April, the Board tabled the decision until the May meeting. Finally, at the May 25 meeting, the Board appointed Weber and Curry to design the Classroom Building.[173] Preliminary plans had been developed by the August 10, 1962 Board meeting and shared with the Education Research Services, Inc. consultants, and the campus administration.[174] The Classroom Building was the campus' highest priority for capital appropriations submitted to the State Budget Agency between 1963-65.[175]

The architects, Weber and Curry, presented nearly completed plans for the Classroom Building in February 1964.[176] It was to include 30 classrooms of various sizes, space for the School of Nursing, two large lecture halls accommodating between 250 and 300 students, a study area for commuter students, and faculty offices. The selected site was east of the Science Building. The Trustees approved the plans and authorized the architects to proceed with preparing detailed plans suitable for bidding.[177] Final plans were submitted in May 1964, and the administration was authorized to advertise for bids to be received by June 24, 1964.

Holmstedt Hall has an exterior of face brick with stone limestone trim. Stylistically, the building exhibits mid-century modernism characteristics and bears a distant relation to Louis Kahn's Richards Medical Research Laboratories (1957-65). The architect, Ewing Miller, who had an extensive career designing buildings on the campus during the Holmstedt and Rankin eras, voiced his opinion of Holmstedt Hall. "…Weber and Curry did the little, low Holmstedt Hall in a more generic form. It's more organic … it's not a pure style. It has more little idiosyncrasies into it of the designer thing. I don't think either Wayne Weber or John Curry were the purists or historians that we were, and I don't think they had quite the grace that the Yeager dormitory had …"[178] ■

Renamed Holmstedt Hall in honor of President Emertius Raleigh W. Holmstedt[179]

President Rankin

Date: July 1, 1965

Center for Medical Education Remodel

President Landini

Architect: M&E Engineering

Contractor: Williams Plumbing and Heating[180]

Date: 1980

Cost: $170,019 (Included new laboratory furnishings)

New laboratories were developed in several rooms to accommodate the medical sciences program.

Architect: Schmidt and Associates

Date: 1989

Cost: $940,000[181]

With the completion of Root Hall, some departments housed in Holmstedt were moved to the new building. Some departments in Root Hall were moved to Holmstedt. The renovation represents the third phase of the Campus Master Plan.

President Benjamin

During the Benjamin presidency, upgrades were made to the HVAC system and renovations were completed in the large lecture halls.

Cost: See note[182]

ADA Updates

President Bradley

Architect: Ratio Architects, Inc.
Contractor: C. H. Garmong & Son, Inc.
Project Managers: Steve Culp, Bryan Duncan

Date: 2010-11
Cost: $517,890[183]

The plaza on the south side of Holmstedt Hall was made more environmentally friendly with improved ADA access.

Brandon Zebold, "ISU Sphere," Corten steel, 2012

Permanent Collection

Directly south of Holmstedt Hall, in what is now called Holmstedt Hall Plaza, a sculpture was installed entitled "ISU Sphere" (2012) by Brandon Zebold. It is made of corten steel and measures five feet in height and width. The engaged observer will begin to see both positive and negative shapes that reference the local iconography, such as the Sycamore tree and Wabash River.[184]

University Family Housing

Four buildings located in a four-block area bounded on the west by First Street, on the east by Third Street, on the north by Crawford Street, and on the south by Park Street.

Maehling Terrace
University Apartments

Architect: Weber and Curry

Unit 1
Contractors: F. A. Wilhelm Construction Company (General Construction); Freitag-Weinhardt, Inc. (Plumbing and Heating); B-A, Inc. (Electrical)[185]

Date: 1964

Cost: $1.36 million[186]

Area: 59,464 GSF; 43,976 ASF

Location: 100 Farrington Street

Unit 2
Contractors: Shelton Hannig, Inc. (General Construction); Fred G. Christman (Plumbing and Heating); AAA Electric (Electrical)[187]

Date: 1967[188]

Cost: $1.56 million

Area: 75,099 GSF; 51,531 ASF

Location: 200 Farrington Street

Renamed: Name changed from Family Housing to Maehling Terrace on January 4, 1968

Unit 3
Contractors: F. A. Wilhelm Construction Co (General); Construction), AAA Electric (Electrical); F. G. Christman (Plumbing-Heating)

Date: 1969

Cost: $2.7 million

Area: 97,784 GSF; 72,063 ASF

Location: 201 Crawford Street

Unit 4
Contractors: Glenroy Construction Company (General Construction); AAA Electric of Terre Haute (Electrical); Healy Mechanical Contractors, Inc. (Mechanical)

Date: 1971[189]

Cost: $2.75 million[190]

Area: 107,612 GSF; 81,618 ASF

The earliest mention of family housing can be found in the minutes of the November 16, 1962 Trustee meeting. ISU was working collaboratively with the Urban Development Commission and the Director, Mr. Morris Landsbaum, suggested a 10-acre area adjacent to Fairbanks Park should be considered for married student housing.[191]

President Holmstedt and the Trustees recognized the urgent need for family housing for students. Weber and Curry were charged with preparing plans for Unit 1 at the October 3, 1963 meeting of the Board. Unit 2 was to replicate Unit 1, but with an enlargement of community spaces in the basement, and reduction of laundry facilities and lobby space.[192]

The site chosen was between South Third and First Streets and about 1.3 miles from the campus. To assist in preparing designs for these facilities, married student and family housing at Indiana University, Michigan State University, Western Michigan University, the University of Michigan, and Ball State Teachers College were visited to study cost, room size, design, furnishings, and utilities.[193] Preliminary plans and specifications for construction were approved by the Board in February. A scale model of an apartment was constructed and displayed in the basement of Gillum Hall dormitory.[194] ∎

Family Housing and Daycare Center Expansion

President Rankin

When completed, the complex had two 80-unit buildings constructed between 1965 and 1967, and two 112-unit buildings finished between 1969 and 1971. All units were four-story brick buildings with basements. The exterior featured face brick masonry with precast concrete trim. When completed, there were 384 apartments in the four-building complex.

The two completed 80-unit buildings were named in honor of Hilda Maehling, J. J. Maehling, and Walter H. Maehling. Hilda Maehling was an alumna, teacher, and had served as a Trustee of the university.[195] J. J. Maehling also graduated from Indiana State and was a significant donor. Walter H. Maehling was a supporter of the university and was a realtor who served 20 years in the Legislature.[196]

A nursery school was established in Unit 2 of the complex.[197]

A call for bids went out in April and May of 1971 for Unit 3, but none were received, owing apparently to bond market conditions. The decision was made to combine Units 3 and 4 in a call for bids for sale at a later date.[198]

President Bradley

Contractor: Evan & Ryan Electric
Project Manager: Scott Tillman
Date: 2013-14
Cost: $493,048[199]

ISU's Child Care Center is located in the Family Housing complex. The Infant Care space was renovated in 2013, going from two rooms with 1,500 sq. ft. to four rooms with 4,000 sq. ft., a kitchen, administrative areas, and a new secure entrance. This was an important renovation that allowed the Center to enroll more children and provide additional space for ISU students to observe and practice teaching.

Before renovation

After renovation

Sycamore Towers
Blumberg Hall, Cromwell Hall, Mills Hall, and Rhoads Hall[200]

These four residence halls are treated as a group because they were conceived as an integrated complex. They shared similar floor plans and exterior treatment. They were all developed and put into service between 1964 and 1965. The Towers residents dined in Sycamore Towers Dining. This facility was renovated during the last three presidencies.

Chapter 6 President Holmstedt

Blumberg Hall

Architect: Miller, Miller, and Associates[201]

Contractors: F. A. Wilhelm Construction Company (General Construction); F. G. Christman (Plumbing and HVAC); The Sanborn Electric Co. (Electrical)

Date: Dedication: November 1, 1964

Cost: $4,61 million[202]

Area: 87,732 GSF; 61,968 ASF

Location: 410/400 Mulberry and 401/411 Chestnut Street

The extraordinary enrollment growth during Holmstedt's presidency necessitated the continued building of residence halls.[203] Miller, Miller, and Associates was commissioned to design four new halls.[204] Initially designed for women, the Sycamore Towers complex soon housed both women and men. Blumberg Hall was the first tower to be constructed. It was named for Benjamin and Fannie B. Blumberg.[205] Benjamin Blumberg was a businessman and served on the Indiana State College Foundation, helping to financially support the Foundation in its efforts to advance the College. Fannie Blumberg was an artist and author of children's books. Her special interest was the betterment of youth, and she gave a significant amount of money to support the special education program for children with disabilities.

Blumberg Hall was the first to be completed and it marked a new stage in the development of campus architecture for several reasons. It was designed as a high-rise structure far surpassing all previous campus buildings in height. The earlier residence halls by Miller were six stories high. Blumberg was 12. Several factors contributed to the decision to go upward. One was the availability and cost of land. Another overarching reason was the Trustee's interest in having this tall cluster of buildings visible from Routes 40 and 41, serving as a symbol of ISU's growth and prestige. Scale represented status. Finally, there was Miller's interest in experimenting with new building materials that further distinguished these buildings from his preceding designs.

Blumberg and the remaining three structures are all 12-story buildings connected to a one-story dining

Indiana State University Building a Legacy

facility. The buildings share the same floor plan with the exception of Cromwell and Mills, where the floor plans were inverted from the arrangement of Blumberg and Rhoads. The buildings were made using pre-cast concrete panels. This had not been done previously on campus. Miller's designs make use of the plasticity of concrete, meaning various parts could be shaped and cast repeatedly – a far less expensive method of construction than using brick and carved decorative elements, such as friezes, pediments, entablatures, moldings, etc.

The long walls of the exterior are lighter in hue than the walls of surrounding buildings. Miller was able to achieve this effect by using white quartz aggregate in the concrete mix.[206] The exposed aggregate concrete panels and modular construction with prefabricated elements were developed by the Ford Foundation and Toronto school system.[207] The height of the building and lighter color drew the attention of those coming to or passing by the campus.

Miller commented on his choice of materials.

> *After trying both curtainwall (Home Economic Building) and spandrels of glazed tile (first set of dormitories-Pickerl, etc.) I realized that a use of materials in context with the surrounding community was needed for this campus to coexist adjacent to the 19th century town center. It required masonry. We had very good brickworks and the advent of new technology, precast concrete, gave me materials I could sculpt, giving a surface of light and shadow in a variety of finishes. The choice of the white slip was both purposeful and fortunate, as it has worn well … and it sends a bright visual message.*[208]

Miller commented the dorms were originally designed to house women and, "I felt the design should reflect a restraint of strong structural articulation and have a lacey appearance reducing visually the bulk of the rectangular building."[209]

Miller composed the long walls of pre-cast concrete panels dividing the windows. This was the first time he had used this material on campus. The panels were more vertical than horizontal, which suggests they had some load-bearing character. The precast walls were attached to the pre-cast and pre-stressed concrete floors that were connected to a central supporting structural core. Miller was attentive to the play of light across the surface of the paneled facade and commented upon the play of light and shade to break up the "… monotony of flat surfaces and punched holes of conventional construction …"[210]

The gridded pattern of panels was applied on all floors, with the exception of the first and seventh floors. The seventh floor is identifiable by the raised windows and taller vertical elements. The seventh floor was reserved for common lounge areas, study rooms, snack machines, and the administrator apartment. The windows are set back from the concrete grid, creating an observation deck. It is worth pointing out that Miller emphasized the seventh floor, which visually corresponded with the roofline of the six-story residence halls built earlier.[211]

The first floor was the primary entry to the building and contained lounges, offices, and recreational areas. It provided a horizontal base for the tower that appeared to rest upon it. In an interview, Miller stressed that the base had a slight flair, which contributed visually to the impression of stability.[212] Evenly spaced piers (pilotis) support the base and within them are thin vertical windows. The space between the pier supports are filled with four-by-four paned windows, immediately suggesting the measured grid that governed the design. The highly geometricized grid had its origins in earlier 20th century curtain-wall buildings by architects such as Walter Gropius (Bauhaus, Dessau, Germany), and Mies van der Rohe (Lake Shore Drive Apartments, Chicago and Seagram Building, New York). The shape of these supporting piers was continued into the interior supporting members visible in the lobby.

The behavioral research undertaken by Lawrence Wheeler (a Miller collaborator), beginning with the residents of Burford Hall, influenced Miller's work on the Towers. Students in Burford did not use the large lounges for study but preferred to study in their rooms. The noise emanating from rooms on both sides of long corridors was disturbing, and students tended to remain in their rooms and congregate only with adjacent neighbors. Students complained that the lounge was too large and did not have sufficient private areas, and they disliked the small windows. Miller stated that despite research showing students preferred smaller, more intimate lounge areas, he was not at liberty to modify this aspect of the design.[213] One very interesting finding concerned the absence of built-in furniture. While the exclusion of built-ins (beds, desks) was initially a budgetary consideration, students enjoyed being able to move furniture about and personalize their rooms.[214]

These findings influenced Miller's designs for Blumberg and the other Towers. The 'L' shaped plan with long double-loaded corridors (rooms on both sides of the hallway) was abandoned for a rectangular plan with shorter arms. A single row of rooms was located on

Chapter 6 President Holmstedt

a hallway, while on the opposite side the mechanical systems were contained. This remedied the noise problem found in Burford. Rooms were built larger because students preferred to study there rather than in large public study rooms. The large lounges on the ground floor of the earlier buildings were sub-divided to create more private areas. Women, however, found large formal lounges more desirable than men.[215]

Surveys conducted among students in the Towers showed that students much preferred the second through fourth floors as opposed to the 11th and 12th floors. This finding was taken into consideration in future resident hall construction. It was also found that the location of the mechanical corridors on each floor created barriers to interactivity with students on the opposite corridor.[216]

The Master Plan adopted in 2009 noted the need for renovation of housing facilities. A renovation program for all four Towers began in 2013 and concluded in 2018. The Towers were over 50 years old and did not meet contemporary fire or ADA requirements. Further, the buildings needed air conditioning, replacement of the heating system, window replacement, power and data systems, and improved fire protection. These improvements made the residences more attractive, safer, and more efficient. ■

Renovation

President Bradley

Architect: Ratio

Contractors: Hannig Construction Inc.; R. E. Dimond and Associates; B&S; HEF

Date: 2015-16

Cost: $17.48 million[217]

Blumberg was the second of the Towers to be renovated. Student rooms were reconfigured. The bathroom down the hall was replaced with double occupancy rooms, each with a bath. HVAC was updated, as were the electrical systems and fire suppression.

Cromwell Hall

Architect: Miller, Miller, and Associates
Contractor: F. A. Wilhelm Construction Company
Date: Dedication: November 1, 1964
Cost: $8.26 million
Area: 87,378 GSF; 61,608 ASF
Location: 400 Mulberry Street

On June 16, 1964, Beecher Cromwell made a gift of property valued at $60,000 to the College Foundation, with another $40,000 anticipated in the very near future. Trustee Busby moved, and Miss Jesse seconded, that "one of the 12-story towers for men was named Beecher Cromwell Hall in recognition of Mr. Cromwell's generous gift."[218]

Renovation

President Moore

Date: April 19, 1995[219]
Cost: $2.21 million[220]

Floors one through 12, including a meeting area on the seventh floor, were renovated. The building was designated as a co-ed living learning center for first-year students. Upgrades were made to the heating and air conditioning systems, and the plumbing systems and restrooms were made ADA compliant.

Renovation

President Bradley

Architect: Ratio
Contractors: Hannig Construction Inc. and R. E. Dimond and Associates
Date: 2016-17
Cost: $20 million[221]

Student academic support services, tutoring and academic peer advocates populated the renovated areas, providing academic assistance in an effort to improve student persistence.

Chapter 6 President Holmstedt

Rhoads Hall

Architect: Ewing Miller Associates, Inc.

Contractors: Repp and Mundt, Inc. (General Construction); Freitag-Weinhardt, Inc. (HVAC); B-A, Inc. (Electrical)

Date: Dedication: November 19, 1965

Cost: $4.46 million[222] (For Mills and Rhoads)

Area: 86,760 GSF; 60,886 ASF

Location: 411 Chestnut Street

Units #3 and #4 are combined because both were designed and built at about the same time with similar plans. Miller, Miller, and Associates presented preliminary plans for the proposed Men's Dormitory Units #3 and #4.[223] The State Budget Agency approved the use of residence hall income, estimated at $4.28 million, for construction. The Housing and Home Finance Agency gave preliminary approval and reserved funds totaling $4 million.[224] Final plans for Units #3 and #4 were approved by the Trustees in February 1965.[225] The opening bid date was set for April 2, 1965. An early date was set because the Board was anxious for construction to begin as soon as possible.[226]

Rhoads Hall was named after a historical person who was fundamental to the establishment of ISNS. Judge Baskin Eply Rhoads (1834-95), a state legislator from Vermillion County who, during the 1865 legislative session, introduced the bill to create ISNS. He is recognized as the "founding father" of ISNS. He served as a Trustee until 1874.[227]

7th Floor Renovation

President Moore

Date: 1995[228]

Cost: $3 million

Remodeling for Honors College

President Bradley

Contractor: E. Rogers

Date: 2008-09

Cost: $223,300

Renovation

President Bradley

Architect: RATIO Architects

Date: 2017-18

Cost: $20.5 million[229]

The State Budget Committee approved the request for $23 million to update Rhoads Hall. This is the last of the four buildings to be remodeled, receiving air conditioning, fire suppression, mechanical systems, and lighting. Representative Clyde Kersey, a long-time champion of ISU, stated, "This entire four-year plan was a cost-effective means of better serving the university's student population while preserving the traditions of this great university." [230] Funding came from residence hall reserves and bonding.

Mills Hall

Architect: Ewing Miller Associates, Inc.

Contractors: Repp and Mundt, Inc. (General Construction); Fred G. Christman (Plumbing and HVAC); The Sanborn Electric Company (Electrical)[231]

Date: Dedication: November 19, 1965

Cost: $4.46 million[232] (For Mills and Rhoads)

Area: 87,610 GSF; 61,590 ASF

Location: 401 Chestnut Street

Mills Hall was named for Caleb Mills (1806-79). He was the first instructor at Wabash College in Crawfordsville, Indiana, where he taught Greek for 40 years and served as the first principal. Beginning in 1854, he served as the second Superintendent of Public Instruction and is remembered as "The Father of Public School Education" in Indiana. Mills was the author of the six unattributed "Messages" he penned between 1846 and 1852. They were intended to inform legislators about the lack of educational facilities in the state. His granddaughter, Helen Condit, bequeathed Condit House to Indiana State College following her death.

He is remembered today at ISU not only for Mills Hall, but for the highest academic award presented to faculty – which is the "Caleb Mills" teaching award. ∎

Renovation

President Bradley

Architect: RATIO Architects[233]

Contractors: Hannig Construction Inc. and R. E. Dimond and Associates

Date: 2015-16

Cost: $17.18 million[234]

R. E. Dimond and Associates was responsible for the mechanical, electrical, and plumbing design services. The company used advanced energy-saving technology to provide efficient heating, ventilation, and air conditioning. A silver LEED designation was one of the goals for the renovation project.

Sycamore Towers Dining Room Remodel

President Landini

Contractors: C & T and Nei Fhelendigh

Date: 1990-91

Cost: $845,668

Sycamore Towers Renovation to Dining Facilities

President Benjamin

Contractors: Jungclaus-Campbell Construction Co., Inc. and NRK, Inc.

Date: 2003-04   **Cost:** $1.53 million

Renovation

President Bradley

Architect: RATIO Architects

Contractor: Hannig Construction Inc.

Project Manager: Steve Culp

Date: 2019-20

Cost: Limited to $16.8 million[235]

The Sycamore Dining facility will be renovated to upgrade dining and food service operations. The thermal envelop will be improved, roof redone, new restrooms added, improved natural light and increased seating options. The facility will also be expanded by 2,000 sq. ft. and a new kitchen installed.

Chapter 6 References

1. Holmstedt produced 15 works in 48 publications. Among them were, "A study of the effects of the teacher tenure law in New Jersey," New York: Teachers College, Columbia University, 1932 (No. 526 in the Contributions to Education Series) and "The tenure of Indiana school administrators," Bloomington: Indiana University, 1953; The Indiana Conference on Higher Education, 1945-65, Bulletin of the School of Education vol. 43, no. 1, 1967, University of Indiana, Bloomington, Indiana.

2. Indiana University Bloomington Faculty Council Circular, B29-1988.

3. May 13, 1953, the Trustees met in Executive Session at the Columbia Club in Indianapolis to discuss the candidates for the Presidency. The motion was made to offer the position to Dr. Raleigh H. Holmstedt, Assistant Dean of Education at Indiana University and was approved by a vote of four to one. Trustee Minutes, May 13, 1953, p. 325. At Holmstedt's inauguration (January 6, 1954), President emeritus Tirey spoke with a keen sense of pride about the college, but he also interjected a note of self-deprecation. He recounted a story told by Chancellor Lindley (University of Kansas) who, during the last year of his administration, received a letter from an admiring student. She wrote, "I hear they have bestowed on you … the greatest honor that can be done a college president … namely they made you president emeritus." Then she added, "I don't see why they didn't make you that a long time ago."

4. To give one example, on April 30, 1959, the Trustees directed the administration to request the State Budget Committee to allocate $250,000 for the purchase of land. In 2016 dollars, that amount would be $2.05 million. See: http://www.saving.org/inflation/inflation.php?amount=250,000&year=1959.

    At the October Board meeting it was stated that "Since December 1, 1955, the College completed 136 real estate transactions at a total cost of $1.4 million." Trustee Minutes, October 28, 1959, VIII, c. That is the equivalent of over $11 million today. See: http://www.usinflationcalculator.com. A new reality confronting the campus was approval of Fallout Shelter Licenses. Trustee Minutes, November 16, 1962, XI, p. 618.

5. In a report to the Trustees it was estimated $44 million additional funds would be required for residences, buildings land, utilities, remodeling, and a student health center.

6. Trustee Minutes, January 18, 1963, XV, p. 640.

7. Metropolitan Planners was a firm directed by Lawrence V. Sheridan and Kenneth Schellie. Sheridan had been a consultant to the city planning commission in Terre Haute so he was, no doubt, quite familiar with the school's expansion and the need for the city and university to coordinate future growth. See: Lawrence V. Sheridan. Early Hoosier Landscape Architect/City Planner, n.p. n. l, 1981.

8. "Although the teacher training function is one which will continue … if the institution were to limit itself primarily to teacher education, enrollments would be less than if it were to continue expanding its degree offerings …" Educational Research Services, Inc., Long Range Building Program for Indiana State College, New York: 1962, p. 12. (Hereafter referred to as LRBP.) The report stressed the need for programmatic and curricular expansion, especially at the graduate level if Indiana State College will become a transformed institution of greater service to the State. LRBP, p. 17.

9. The population of Vigo county grew by nine percent in the years 1940-60, while Vandenburgh (Evansville) grew 27 percent and Monroe (Bloomington) 64 percent. Educational Research Services, Inc., LRBP, p. 6. In the fall term, 1961, about half of the freshmen came from five counties (Vigo and surrounding). LRBP, p. 7.

10. LRBP, p. 45. The Report stated, "… the rate of increase of enrollment at Indiana State College from the five counties has been slower than the rate from other counties. This is consistent with the assumption that Indiana State College is in a period of transition from a primarily regional state institution to a comprehensive college which will draw … from the entire state." LRBP, p. 56.

11. Parsons Hall was built in 1937 during the Tirey era and was enlarged in 1951 during Holmstedt's presidency.

12. LRBP, p. 12.

13. This number does not include the wooden frame constructed houses used as residences, all of which were demolished whenever feasible. The Report estimated 5,840 students would need to be housed by 1972. LRBP, p. 58.

14. LRBP, p. 75. This is equivalent to $116 million in today's dollars. See: http://inflationdata.com/Inflation/Inflation_Calculators/Inflation_Rate_Calculator.asp. The estimated academic space needed by 1972 was 701,000 sq. ft. LRBP, p. 37. Housing needs by 1972 were projected at 5,580 students. Trustee Minutes, June 20, 1962, XV: A, p. 561.

15. Trustee Minutes, July 20, 1961, II: B. A new seal was also adopted.

16. It is noteworthy that at the December 15, 1961 Board meeting, President Holmstedt "recommended that further organization of the academic departments into schools and/or divisions be deferred to a later date …" Trustee Minutes, December 15, 1961, XVIII.

17. A former employee observed that Holmstedt was an "old plainsman" from Nebraska, trained as an educator who adhered faithfully to the idea that the proper role of a normal school was the preparation of teachers. Interview with John Newton, March 27, 2018.

18. The Trustees passed a resolution that would direct the administration to take "the necessary steps to enable Indiana State College to reach university status during the 1965-67 biennium." Trustee Minutes, February 28, 1964, XIV. The Board passed a resolution on motion by Miss Jessee and seconded by Mr. Kendall, setting forth the intention of Indiana State College to seek university status. Trustee Minutes, April 17, 1964, Exhibit D. President Holmstedt presented to the Board a plan to introduce a bill to change the name to Indiana State University. Trustee Minutes, December 18, 1964, XX.

19. Trustee Minutes, April 19, 1963, XVII.

20. Trustee Minutes, January 15, 1965, Exhibit D.

21. Trustee Minutes, February 19, 1965, Exhibit H.

22. Trustee Minutes, February 19, 1965, IV.

23. Legal problems with the Indiana sales tax law in 1963 delayed classroom construction for two years.

24. Trustee Minutes, February 19, 1965, XVI.

25. Trustee Minutes, February 28, 1964, XI. See a copy of a letter sent from Holmstedt to the presidents of Purdue, Indiana University, and Ball State Teachers College, Trustee Minutes, March 20, 1964, Exhibit A.

26. Trustee Minutes, March 20, 1964, pp. 850-852. Letter from President Holmstedt to President Stahr (IU), President Hovde (Purdue), and President Emens (Ball State), March 9, 1964.

27. Norbert A. Stirzaker, Director of Extended Services, presented a report to the Trustees that contained information about estimated costs of staffing, facilities, and a library. No action was taken at the meeting, but the Board did authorize Dr. Stirzaker to explore further the availability of suitable facilities. Trustee Minutes, February 19, 1965, XIX.

28. Trustee Minutes, April 16, 1965, XV.

29. Trustee Minutes, October 26, 1963, XXI.

30. Information from Vice President Robert Schafer, June 2000 according to research by Dean Wood, Maryland. See: http://hem.fyristorg.com/hok/lee/RaleighUS.htm.

31. This is the draft of the resolution considered by the Trustees at the April 17, 1964 Board meeting. Trustee Minutes, April 17, 1964, Exhibit D.

32. Trustee Minutes, July 27, 1955, X.

33. Ibid, G. W. North Construction Company (General Construction, $335,813); Prox & Burget (Plumbing and Heating, Ventilation, $82,000); B-A Incorporated (Electrical, $37,800).

34. The site was approved by the Trustees in August 1954. Trustee Minutes, April 19, 1954, XIII. The site was owned by Mr. Taylor who asked $34,500 for property assessed at $11,500. The Board approved condemnation proceedings.

35. This architectural firm was selected by the Trustees at their May 13, 1954 meeting. Plans were approved by the Trustees June 23, 1955. Trustee Minutes, June 23, 1955, Sec. X: A.

36. Ewing H. Miller, interview by Jane Hazledine, Terre Haute, Indiana, April 13, 1981, 20, transcript, Vigo County Oral History Project in Local History Books Online: Oral Histories, Vigo County Public Library.

37. Dr. Anne Lee was department chair and provided oversight of the building design. She was responsible for introducing new professional programs that prepared students for careers outside of teaching. These new fields required appropriate facilities in the new building.

38. Flowers, p. 137.

39. Ibid.

40. Dedication of the Home Economics Building, Terre Haute: Indiana State Teachers College: 1956, n.p.

41. Following World War II, Miller returned to school at the University of Pennsylvania in 1945. He came under the influence of architects/teachers who had studied at the Bauhaus in Germany and were now teaching at places like the Illinois Institute of Technology (Mies van der Rohe) or Harvard (Walter Gropius) and introduced what Miller called the Modernist style. He also names Saarinen as an important influence.

42. This porcelain-enamel wall began to cause problems. The caulking, available at the time of construction, developed leaks. The panels allowed for heat loss and gain and the resulting moisture attracted dirt on their surface. A new plastic material used to cover wall surfaces did not stay in place because it was affected by condensation owing to interior/exterior temperature differential. LRBP p. 28.

43. Email to the author from Ewing Miller, July 30, 2018.

44. Ewing Miller, interview, p. 22. The Saarinens (Eliel and Eero) both designed churches in Columbus, Indiana. Eliel planned the First Christian Church (1942) and Eero designed the North Christian Church (1955), about the same time the Home Economics Building was underway.

45. The complete interactive technology package was $300,710.

46. Contract date is July 19, 2011.

47. Department of Facilities Management Annual Report 2011-12, III-1. Funds were to come from residence halls reserves and university reserves. The Trustees voted to rename the building in February 2017. Trustee Minutes, February 17, 2012, p. 14.

48. See: http://www2.indstate.edu/news/news.php?newsid=2462.

49. See: http://www2.indstate.edu/news/news.php?newsid=3240.

50. Preliminary plans and models were presented to the Board. Trustee Minutes, January 9, 1957, p. 327.

51. Allowable costs approved by the Housing and Home Finance Agency. Trustee Minutes, September 14, 1960, X. Cost for construction plus other expenses totaled $1.51 million. Trustee Minutes, April 26, 1961, VI and Exhibit D.

    Burford, Erickson, and Pickerl Halls were all constructed under the HH, a College Housing Loan Program.

52. President Tirey addressed the urgency of an addition to the Women's Residence Hall at the Trustee meeting on June 25, 1953. A budget of $600,000 was discussed, with $100,000 coming from reserves and $500,000 from bond sales. A motion was made to appoint Yeager Architects to make plans and detail biddable specifications. The motion failed for lack of a second and the issue was deferred to a future meeting. Miller, Vrydagh, and Miller eventually obtained the contract and one might speculate from this that the Board was interested in a more modern building of the type this firm could produce.

53. Miller stated that all three buildings were conceived at the same time but built sequentially. He also stated the residences were built in a "dicey" area and that he had planned a garden-courtyard area in front of the buildings to create a safety zone for the female residents. Interview with Ewing Miller, June 27, 2018.

54. Michael Flowers, Behavior and Design: The Architecture of Ewing H. Miller II. Unpublished Masters of Science thesis, Ball State University, May, 2015, p. 37.

55. Flowers, p. 37. "… the use of glazed tile in the spandrels of those buildings was right from the Pimenckel apartments done in London that was housing for lower income families."

56. Email to the author from Ewing Miller, July 30, 2018.

57. See Martin Heilweil, "The Influence of Dormitory Architecture on Resident Behavior," Environment and Behavior 5, no. 3, December 1973, pp. 377-412. In 2013, Miller received the Indiana Service Award from the American Institute of Architects Indiana. See: hhtp://aiaindiana.org/member-services/awards/2013-aia-indiana-service-awards. Mention was made of Miller's interest in behavioral research and its design implications.

58. Flowers, pp.136-137. Miller stated the glazed tile in the spandrels was taken from the Pimenckel apartments in London housing lower income families.

59. Flowers, p. 136.

60. Indiana State University Facilities Management Completed Projects, June 30, 2007, n.p.

61. The renovation was designed by David R. Snapp and Associates. The same firm designed the renovation of Pickerl in 2010 and Erickson.

62. The Burford renovation was featured in American School and University Magazine 2007 Architectural Portfolio.

63. Department of Facilities Management Annual Report 2010-11, pp. III-1.

64. The Trustees approved the plans and specifications in 1958. Trustee Minutes, December 18, 1958, p. 29. Ewing Miller had high praise for Ralph Stewart, who was responsible for the mechanical engineering, and Homer Howe for the structural. Howe advised on all the pre-cast concrete.

65. Walter Scholer was a prolific Indiana architect. He designed several buildings on the Purdue campus, including the Chemistry and Pharmacy Buildings and two hospitals in Richmond and Henry Counties. Plans were approved, and an authorization was given to advertise for bids. Trustee Minutes, December 18, 1958, XII.

66. Bids for the Science Building were opened February 1959. Trustee Minutes, February 11, 1959, V. Acquiring the property for the building was not without controversy. The Trustee Minutes give some indication of this. (March 28, 1959, p. 54). The possibility of an injunction suit being filed involving the Cutshall property was discussed at the August 12, 1959 board meeting, and continuing the Cutshall litigation, the Trustees also learned that ISTC was barred from using alleys as the building site for the new science building. F. A. Wilhelm Construction Company (General Construction, $894,230); F. G. Christman Company (Plumbing, Ventilation, $862,215); Hatfield Company (Electrical, $245,973); E. H. Sheldon Equipment Company (Laboratory Equipment, $395,000).

67. Hazledine, Interview, p. 29.

68. Miller stated the Science Building was the only building in the U.S. with a mechanical core down the center of the building. Miller Interview, June 27, 2018.

69. "The Tall Office Building Artistically Considered," in Lippincott's Magazine, March 1896, pp. 403-409.

70. Trustee Minutes, May 22, 1964, XIX. Preliminary plans were approved November 20, 1964. Trustee Minutes, November 20, 1964, XVIII.

71. Email to the author from Ewing Miller, July 30, 2018.

72. Bids opened. Trustee Minutes, February 4, 1966, Exhibit A.

73 Shelton Hannig, Inc. (General Construction, $1.44 million); F. G. Christman (Plumbing, HVAC, $1.56 million); B-A, Inc. (Electrical, $351,500); Hamilton Manufacturing Company (Laboratory Equipment, $450,248).

74 Trustee Minutes, February 3, 1995, Sec. I.

75 Advised on bookstore layout.

76 (General Construction, $133,600); Prox and Burget Company Inc. (Plumbing and HVAC, $61,675); Hatfield Electric (Electrical, $32,310). Does not include architect and other fees.

77 The firm of Miller, Vrydagh, and Miller Architects was appointed to prepare plans and specifications for the Bookstore, and Kevin White Associates, Inc., from Westwood, New Jersey, was appointed to prepare marketing, merchandising, and store planning. Trustee Minutes, May 27, 1959, XX, p. 71. Miller, et.al, presented final plans for the Bookstore. Trustee Minutes, September 14, 1960, XV. Initial bids exceeded budget and were rejected. Miller, Vrydagh, and Miller presented a revised plan with estimates of cost reduction. Trustee Minutes, November 18, 1960, V. New bids were received January 6, 1961.

78 Miller's design does not stress the industrial simplicity or steel frame construction typical of van der Rohe.

79 Funding came from bond sales to be repaid with bookstore earnings.

80 Ewing Miller email to the author, August 12, 2017.

81 Interview with Ewing Miller, June 27, 2018.

82 John Laska was also responsible for the Prometheus statue placed in front of the Science Building in 1963. Laska taught in the ISU Art Department (1954-81) and designed both the Debs Award and the Special Olympics Award.

83 Ewing Miller to the author, August 12, 2018.

84 The Trustees made this appointment. Trustee Minutes, July 21, 1989, Sec. 1, I, p. 6. House Bill 1530 passed during the Special Session on May 9, 1989, providing bonding authorization for $3.5 million for the renovation of Holmstedt and Dreiser Halls and the Bookstore.

85 Indiana State University Department of Facilities Management Annual Report, 2012-13, III-1. Facilities Management Department Project Update Year 1992-93, p. 124, and 1993-94, p. 102.

86 Hannig is first mentioned in association with the renovation of the Student Computing Complex (former Bookstore) in May 2013. Trustee Minutes, May 3, 2013, p. 66.

87 The Miller, Vrydagh, Miller firm was contracted to prepare plans and bidding specifications. Trustee Minutes, January 21, 1960, VII. Completed plans were presented by the architects and gained Board approval. Trustee Minutes, February 27, 1961, VII. Bids were opened April 26, 1961 and J. L. Simmons Company, Inc. was selected as the General Contractor. Trustee Minutes, April 26, 1961, VI. With other fees and contingencies, the total was $1.51 million.

Beginning September 1962, sorority suites were available in Erickson. Trustee Minutes, February 23, 1962, IX. Trustee acceptance of the finished building was made at the September 26, 1962 Board meeting. Trustee Minutes, September 26, 1962, IV.

88 J.L. Simmons Company, Inc. (General Construction, $909,481); The Sanborn Electric Company (Electrical, $123,800); Fred G. Christman (HVAC, $329,000).

89 Trustee Minutes, April 29, 1905, p. 474 and May 27, 1905, pp. 483-484.

90 Ms. Erickson was the wife of the third president of the University, William Wood Parsons.

91 Jungclaus-Campbell was founded in 1875 by a German ship carpenter. Purchases listed in Trustee Minutes, October 18, 1996, Sec. I.

92 Jungclaus-Campbell Company (General Construction, $1.67 million), Sycamore Engineering Inc. (Mechanical, $1.64 million), NRK (Electrical, $487,582).

93 This firm was formed in 1927 and is headquartered in Indianapolis. They have extensive experience in higher education, especially at IU Bloomington, Butler, and IUPUI.

94 The Trustees approved the concept and authorized the administration to seek authority to expend up to $10 million for the renovation. Trustee Minutes, October 14, 2011, pp. 7-8

95 Indiana State University Facilities Management Department Completed Projects Fiscal Year 2013-14, June 30, 2014, No. 15.

96 See: http://www.indstate.edu/news/news.Php?newsid=3654.

97 Yeager Architects, Inc. was selected to prepare plans for a new men's residence hall. Trustee Minutes, April 20, 1960, XX. p. 190. Completed plans and specifications were presented and approved at the January 9, 1961 meeting. Trustee Minutes, January 9, 1961, IV-V.

98 Other fees not included in total. Trustee Minutes, April 26, 1962, p. 325.

99 The Housing and Home Finance Agency approved $1.65 million for the men's dormitory for 300 occupants. Trustee Minutes, October 26, 1960, XVIII. George Bahre Company (General Construction, $1.28 million); Freitag-Weinhardt, Inc. (HVAC and Plumbing, $447,000); Hatfield Electrical Company (Electrical, $123,223).

100 On a motion by Trustee Dr. Crocket and second by Mr. Archer, Unit 1 was named Sandison Hall. Trustee Minutes, August 10, 1962, XVII. Howard Sandison's father was the owner of a saloon on Wabash Avenue, and in 1904, opened the Sandison Hotel at 516-518 North Ninth Street. See: http://vigo.lib.in.us/archives/genhistories/esareyvol3/part_8/pt203.pdf.

101 Physical Plant Projects, 1988-89.

102 Trustee Minutes, December 2, 1988, Section 1: J.

103 Funding from sale of housing and dining system bonds for $9.5 million and Residence Hall Reserves.

104 Nancy McKee was a nursing professor emerita and her husband, Dr. Dale McKee, served as ISU Foundation Director. The McKees created an endowment to fund programs and maintenance.

105 President Holmstedt informed the Trustees he had received a letter of appreciation from the Gillum family after they had been notified a residence hall would be named in their honor. Trustee Minutes, April 19, 1963, XV.

106 Bids were opened February 23, 1962. Trustee Minutes, February 23, 1962, V. The Board formally accepted the completed Gillum Hall at their June 1963 meeting. Trustee Minutes, June 21, 1963, XX.

107 The Trustees voted to name this residence after Robert Gillum in March 1963. Trustee Minutes, March 29, 1963, XXI.

108 Shelton Hannig, Inc. (General Construction, $993,780); Freitag-Weinhardt, Inc., (Plumbing and Heating, etc., $267,000); Ernest Miller (Electrical, $57,930).

109 The Trustees officially named the Men's Physical Education Building the "Indiana State College Arena." Trustee Minutes, January 9, 1962, XVII.

110 The Trustees approved the General Construction bid from J. L. Simmons, Inc. for $2.59 million. With other contingencies, the estimated total cost of the project was $2.9 million.

Trustee Minutes, July 21, 1960, V. A. Plans had been approved at the June 13, 1960 Board meeting.

Trustee Minutes, June 13, 1960, Exhibit C.

111 State approval for using student fees for constructing the building was given in November 1959. Trustee Minutes, April 20, 1960, XV.

112 State appropriated funds totaling $1.2 million, and the balance from sale of bonds to be paid from student fees. Includes architect and engineer fees, legal and administrative costs, interest during construction, and contingencies.

113 Pier Nervi (1891-1979). He was known as an architect-engineer who explored the formal and structural possibilities of reinforced concrete. One of his most memorable buildings was the Flamino Stadium, site of the XVII Olympics in Rome.

114 Holmstedt informed the State Budget Committee that the current Physical Education Building was above capacity and requested $54,000 for preliminary planning expenses. Trustee Minutes, August 12, 1959, VII, p. 186. The preliminary plans were approved at the September 1959 Board meeting. Trustee Minutes, September 30, 1959, VI. Miller, et.al. presented final plans and recommended distribution of bid documents. Bids were due July 21, 1960.

Trustee Minutes, May 18, 1960, VII and June 13, 1960. Bids were opened July 21, 1960.

115 The folded concrete roof design was developed by Homer Howe, a Miller associate. Flowers, Behavior and Design, p. 42.

116 Miller described the roof system in his interview with Jane Hazledine. The folded-plate span was created by using concrete that was folded with reinforcing rods or cables running through it. After the concrete set, the cables were drawn tight to create a slight arc in the roof. The process was known as camber. This method also meant that the concrete needed to be only six inches thick, which enabled spanning the large space without interior supports such as columns that would have presented problems in basketball games. Hazledine, Interview, pp. 32-33. The building was included in the proceedings of the 4th Federation Internationale de la Precontrainte, Rome-Naples, June 1962, and was presented at the World Conference on Shell Structures at the University of California, October 1962, for "Creative Application of Engineering Theory to Architecture."

See Trustee Minutes, October 26, 1962, VIII.

117 Trustee Minutes, October 26, 1962, VIII.

118 Comments provided by Ewing Miller in an email to the author, August 13, 2018.

119 The Trustees approved hiring Scholer in December 1984. Trustee Minutes, December 7, 1984, p. 14. Scholer and Associates presented schematic plans for Trustee approval in April. Trustee Minutes, April 19, 1985, p. 5.

120 This was the estimated cost submitted to the Commission for Higher Education in 1982. The total let in contracts was $10.11 million, which does not include other charges and fees. The university then requested the budget ceiling be raised to $12.4 million to reinstate alternates that were excluded when contracts were originally let. CDI, Inc. (General Construction, $6.61 million); Sycamore Engineering, Inc. (Mechanical and Electrical, $3.33 million); F. E. Gates (Synthetic Floor Surface)

121 Outdoor tennis courts were installed in 1988-89 for $310,835 by White Construction.

122 Ibid, July 23, 1982, p. 20.

123 Indiana State University Facilities Management Completed Projects, June 30, 2005, n.p.; Ibid, p. 13.

124 Indiana State University Facilities Management Department Completed Projects 2012-13, June 30, 2013, No. 1.

125 The Indiana State Budget Committee approved the $64 million request on March 15, 2016. This is the largest state-funded project in the history of the university. According to Greg Goode, Executive Director of Government Relations, "At $64 million, no other project ... has ever come as close to the magnitude of this type of investment." See: http:/www2.indstate.edu/news/news.php?newsid=5042.

126 Equivalent to $168 GSF and $270 ASF.

127 In the fall of 2006, President Benjamin assigned a Health Professions Task Force to develop a strategic plan for the development of a college for health-related professions. This would involve the merger of the College of Nursing with the College of Health and Human Performance. The change of name from the former to the College of Health and Human Services was formally adopted during the Bradley presidency. Trustee Minutes, February 20, 2015, p. 18.

128 Information from "ISU Unveils Phase I Plans for Health and Human Services." See: http://schoolconstructionnews.com/2018/01/03.isu-unveils-first-phase-plans-health-human-services/.

129 McNichols was the longest tenured coach at ISU and served as head coach of the track and field and cross-country programs. He died unexpectedly on December 21, 2016, having suffered a stroke on December 17.

130 Rev. Condit was a prolific author. Noteworthy here was his "The early History of Terre Haute from 1816-1840," published in 1900. Lucien Houriet left Terre Haute for California but returned in 1879 to visit his brother. The Saturday Evening Mail, November 8, 1879, p. 8, noted, "he had amassed wealth and waxed fat."

131 Caleb Mills (1806-79) graduated from Dartmouth College and Andover Seminary and then went to Wabash College as its first faculty member and principal of its preparatory school. He won awards as elected Indiana Superintendent of Public Instruction in 1854. At ISU, he is recognized through a residence hall named after him and the university's highest honor, the "Caleb Mills Teaching Award." See Osborne, James Insley, and Theodore Gregory Gronert (1932). Wabash College: The First Hundred Years, 1832-1932. R. E. Banta, Crawfordsville, Indiana. He is especially recognized for championing the creation of a state normal school and wrote anonymous messages signed "One of the People" between 1846 and 1852 urging the legislature to pass an act establishing a system of common schools supported by tax revenue.

132 Trustee Minutes, January 18, 1963, IX. By 1963, Condit House was vested in the Indiana State College Board.

133 Trustee letter to Mr. Condit dated September 30, 1915.

134 In 1962, the Trustees authorized preparing Condit House for use by the Alumni Relations Office with portions also to be used as guest rooms even though the college did not yet have title to the property. Trustee Minutes, August 10, 1962, XXV. Preliminary plans were presented to the Trustees in 1963. Trustee Minutes, April 19, 1963, XI.

135 This was a Terre Haute firm. Herman Readinger was born in 1921 and died in 2011. He was a brick mason by trade.

136 Trustee Minutes, October 22, 1966, IV. Governor Branigin rejected the contract and asked the Board to scale down plans and reduce cost. Trustee Minutes, November 18, 1966, XVI: C.

137 Restoration architects for the renovation were James Associates, Indianapolis and H. Roll McLaughlin (AIA). McLaughlin was born November 29, 1922. He had a long and distinguished career. He was president of James Associates, Inc. (Indianapolis), oversaw many restorations, served as a Board member of the National Trust for Historic Preservation, and was elected to the College of Fellows, American Institute of Architects. National Register of Historic Places Inventory-Nomination Form, prepared by Dr. Alan C. Rankin, August 7, 1972, pp. 2-4.

138 Trustee Minutes, November 19, 1965, XVII.

139 Trustee Minutes, January 20, 1966, Exhibit C.

140 Trustee Minutes, February 4, 1966, IX.

141 Trustee Minutes, February 19, 1966, XIV.

142 Trustee Minutes, February 19, 1966, XIV.

143 Trustee Minutes, September 9, 1966, XIII.

144 Trustee Minutes, October 22, 1966, IV.

145 Trustee Minutes, December 16, 1966, XV.

146 Garage cost: $103,171; House cost: $115,000; Kitchen and windows cost: $269,240. Indiana State University Facilities Management Completed Projects, June 30, 2010, n.p.; June 30, 2011, n.p.

147 Trustees appointed the architectural firm. Trustee Minutes, August 17, 1961, VI.

148 Ibid, February 23, 1962, IV.

149 The Housing and Home Finance Agency reserved $1.5 million for the building. Trustee Minutes, January 9, 1962, Exhibit A. J. L. Simmons Company (General Construction, $852,450); F.G. Christman (Plumbing and Heating, $248,647); The Sanborn Electric Company (Electrical, $110,764).

150 Trustee Minutes, July 20, 1961, IX.

151 Trustee Minutes, October 19, 1961, IV. The Board approved the final plans and specifications and gave authorization to go out to bid. Trustee Minutes, January 9, 1962, IV.

152 President Holmstedt informed the Trustees that he had received a letter of appreciation from Dorothea Pickerl after she was notified a residence hall had been named in her honor. Trustee Minutes, April 19, 1963, XV. The name was approved by Trustees in March 1963. Trustee Minutes, March 29, 1963, XXI.

153 Facilities Management Annual Report 2011-12, p. III-1. July 9, 2010, the Trustees approved the sale of bonds to finance the renovation. $1 million came from Residence Hall reserves and $9 million from bond sales.

154 Sandison offered themed housing for students in nursing and other health care fields, and space for informal faculty-student interaction and group study.

155 See: http://schooldesigns.com/Project-Details.aspx?Project_ID=4259 and Indiana State University Department of Facilities Management Annual Report, 2011-12, III-I.

156 See: http:/www2/indstate.edu/news/news.php?newsid=3005.

157 Trustee Minutes, April 19, 1963, XVII. The Trustee authorized the administration to obtain funds to purchase the Hotel. Trustee Minutes, March 29, 1963, VI: B.

158 Trustee Minutes, June 21, 1963, XIV: A.

159 Trustee Minutes, May 24, 1963, Exhibit K.

160 Trustee Minutes, September 20, 1963, XIV, p. 784. The college agreed to purchase Bowman Dairy for $110,000. Trustee Minutes, April 17, 1964, XVII: A. Pennsylvania Railroad property was acquired.

Trustee Minutes, September 20, 1963, XIII: C.

161 That was a significant investment. Adjusting for inflation, that is equivalent to almost $700,000 today. See: http://www.dollartimes.com/inflation/inflation.php?amount=100000&year=1968.

162 Trustee Minutes, February 16, 1974, H.

163 Trustee Minutes, February 28, 1976, p. 226.

164 Trustee Minutes, May 7, 1976, p. 268.

165 Trustee Minutes, February 28, 1964, XIV.

166 Trustee Minutes, May 22, 1964, XIV.

167 Trustee Minutes, June 26, 1964, XVII.

168 Trustee Minutes, October 23, 1964, XIX.

169 Weber and Curry were Terre Haute architects. Wayne M. Weber (1905-84) was an architect and Fellow of the American Institute of Architects. He made an extensive collection of covered bridge photographs that are now at Ball State University. See: http://libx.bsu.edu/cdm/landing-page/collection/WMWbrArch. Board appointment May 25. Trustee Minutes, May 25, 1962, XVII: A.

170 Trustee Minutes, June 26, 1964, VI.

171 Trustee Minutes, June 26, 1964, VI. Includes architect fees and contingencies. Repp and Mundt, Inc. (General Construction, $855,200); Christman (Plumbing HVAC, $343,768); Potter Electrical Engineering & Construction (Electrical, $166,098).

172 Trustee Minutes, March 16, 1962, IX.

173 Trustee Minutes, May 25, 1962, XVII: A. At the June meeting of the Trustees, the consulting firm Educational Research Services, Inc., that had been contracted to develop a 10-year plan (particularly major capital projects that would need to be built to accommodate increased enrollment). They estimated that needed classroom space by 1967 was 90,000 sq. ft., and by 1972 estimated need was 120,000 sq. ft. Trustee Minutes, June 20, 1962, XV: 2.

174 Trustee Minutes, August 10, 1962, XX.

175 The following projects were submitted in the 1963-65 capital appropriations request: General Classroom Building ($2.25 million); Land Acquisition ($800,000); Campus Improvement ($447,778); Industrial Education Addition II ($500,000); Library Addition II ($400,000); Storage Facilities ($200,000). Trustee Minutes, August 10, 1962, XVIII.

176 The administration was authorized by the Board to request the State Budget Agency allocate $42,000 to pay for preliminary planning expenses. Trustee Minutes, February 28, 1964, XII.

177 Trustee Minutes, November 16, 1962, IV. Trustee Crockett requested Educational Research Services, Inc. reconsider the site.

178 Hazledine Interview, p. 27.

179 Trustee Minutes, July 1, 1965, XI.

180 Ibid, August 29, 1980, Sec. 1, Exhibit G. Bid amount was $169,200.

181 Physical Plant Projects Fiscal Year 1984-85, p. 84. House Bill 1530 included bonding authorization of $3.5 million for the renovation of Holmstedt and Dreiser Halls and the Bookstore. Trustee Minutes, June 23, 1989, Sec. I, K.

182 The cost was originally estimated at $490,000. Payment SMC for $649,290. Trustee Minutes, February 27, 2004 Sec. 2. M. Jungclaus Campbell was also engaged, but the amount shown in the Minutes ($1.08 million) includes payment for both Holmstedt Hall and the renovation ongoing in Mills Hall.

183 Indiana State University Facilities Management Department Completed Projects Fiscal Year 2011-12. June 30, 2012, No. 21.

184 During Benjamin's presidency, the Percent for Art program was initiated. This required that one percent of the cost or a new or renovated building be dedicated to the purchase of artwork for the structure.

185 Trustee Minutes, August 28, 1964, IV.

186 F. A. Wilhelm Construction Company (General Construction, $886,692); Freitag-Weinhardt, Inc. (Plumbing and HVAC, $249,000); B-A, Inc. (Electrical, $107,400).

187 Shelton Hannig, Inc. (General Construction, $1.15 million); Fred G. Christman (Plumbing and Heating, etc., $292,918); AAA Electric (Electrical, $118,158).

188 The administration was directed by the Trustees to file an application with the Housing and Home Finance Agency for $1.4 million. Trustee Minutes, October 2, 1965, IX, 2. The Trustees approved the plans for Unit 2 at their April 22, 1966 meeting. Trustee Minutes, April 4, 1966, X, A. Contracts were awarded. Trustee Minutes, May 27, 1966, VI: C.

189 Trustee Minutes, May 22, 1970, Sec. II: A.

190 Glenroy Construction Company (General Construction, $1.77 million); AAA Electric of Terre Haute (Electrical, $437,615); Healy Mechanical Contractors, Inc. (Mechanical, $539,200).

191 Trustee Minutes, November 16, 1962, XV, p. 629.

192 Trustee Minutes, February 19, 1966, XV, p.185. The Trustees voted to offer $86,700 to acquire property from the Department of Redevelopment of the City of Terre Haute, approximately a four-block square, for additional family housing. Trustee Minutes, March 17, 1967, XII, p. 457.

193 Trustee Minutes, November 22, 1963, VII, p. 811.

194 Trustee Minutes, February 28, 1964, VIII: A, p.835.

195 Hilda Maehling was an activist in the Women Teachers' Association and played an important role in the National Education Association. She was also President of the Indiana State Teachers Association in 1936.

196 See: http://omeka.indstate.edu/document/164.

197 Trustee Minutes, July 19, 1968, XVI.

Chapter 6 President Holmstedt

198 Trustee Minutes, July 16, 1971, Sec. II: E.

199 Indiana State University Facilities Management Completed Projects Fiscal Year 2013-14, June 30, 2014, No. 16.

200 These four buildings are treated together because they were designed as a complex by the same architectural firm, share a common floor plan, and have similar interiors and exteriors. Each structure housed 430 occupants. The Trustees authorized submission of an application to the House and Home Finance Agency for a loan of $4.27 million to build the first west residence hall. Trustee Minutes, September 28, 1962, X, p. 599.

201 Miller, Miller, and Associates presented preliminary plans for the west residence project in October 1962. The design depicted a 12-story building. They were authorized to develop bid documents and detailed plans. The Trustees formally accepted the building at their July 1, 1965 meeting. Trustee Minutes, July 1, 1965, XXV.

202 Trustee Minutes, April 19, 1963, V. F. A. Wilhelm Construction Company (General Construction, $2.9 million); F. G. Christman (Plumbing, HVAC, $834,914); The Sanborn Electric Co., (Electrical, $356,487).

203 The consulting firm, Educational Research Services, Inc., was contracted to develop a 10-year plan for the campus. A specific element of a report addressed to the Trustees pointed out two critical needs: a general-purpose classroom and student housing. They endorsed the idea of a four-unit complex that would house about 350 students each. Housing needs through 1972, they projected, would require facilities for 5,800 students. Trustee Minutes, June 20, 1962, XV: 1.

204 The firm of Miller, Miller, and Associates was appointed to develop the Women's Dormitory Complex. Trustee Minutes, May 25, 1962, XVII. The administration was authorized to submit an application to the Housing and Home Finance Agency for a loan of $4.27 million to finance the construction of the first West Residence Hall, as it was then called. Trustee Minutes, September 28, 1962, X. Preliminary plans were approved on October 10, 1962 and the architects were authorized to proceed with detailed plans and specifications for bidding. Trustee Minutes, October 10, 1962, VII.

205 Trustee Dr. Crockett recommended that one of the new high-rise dormitories be named Blumberg Hall as a "tribute for his generous gifts." Trustee Minutes, August 10, 1962, XXVIII: Sec. A. The Trustees approved honoring the Blumbergs at the March 29, 1963 meeting. Trustee Minutes, March 29, 1963, XXI. President Holmstedt informed the Trustees he had received a letter of appreciation from the Blumbergs after they had been notified a residence hall would be named in their honor. Trustee Minutes, April 19, 1963, XV.

206 Flowers, p. 44.

207 Scott Meacham, Dartmouth College. New York: Princeton Architectural Press, 2008. p. 139.

208 Correspondence to the author June 27, 2018.

209 Email from Miller to the author August 5, 2018.

210 Flowers, p. 44. This was Miller's first use of pre-cast concrete. The skin of the building was made lighter by using white quartz aggregate in the concrete.

211 Burford, Erickson, and Pickerl.

212 Interview with Ewing Miller, June 27, 2018.

213 Email from Miller to the author, August 5, 2018.

214 Flowers, p. 45; Lawrence Wheeler, "Behavioral Research Survey Sycamore Towers 1967," May 1967, 7, box 13, folder 7, Miller Family Architectural Records, Drawings + Documents Archive.

215 Flowers, p. 46.

216 Flowers, p. 47. Ewing Miller Associates received a design award from the American Institute of Architects in 1968.

217 The Trustees had approved a budget request of $22.5 million. Trustee Minutes, May 2, 2014, pp. 105-106 and the appointment of RATIO Architects. Funding was taken from the residence hall reserve funds and long-term debt. Trustee Minutes, May 2, 2014, p. 105. Indiana State University Facilities Completed Projects, June 30, 2017, n.p.

218 Trustee Minutes, June 26, 1964, XVI.

219 The Trustees authorized the President to secure authority to expend $2.5 million for the renovation of the specified areas. Trustee Minutes, April 19, 1995, Sec. I.

220 Williams Plumbing, $592,381; Hannig Construction Inc., $1.16 million; Sycamore Engineering, $307,400. Trustee Minutes, October 18, 1996, Sec. I.

221 $4 million came from residence hall capital reserves and $16.1 million bonded. Trustee Minutes, May 6, 2016, p. 33.

222 This was the budget ($4.08 million) approved at a special meeting of the Board. Trustee Minutes, April 2, 1965, I. On April 16, the Trustees approved a total project budget of $4.46 million. Trustee Minutes, April 16, 1965, XXII. Repp and Mundt, Inc. (General Construction, $2.94 million); Freitag-Weinhardt, Inc. (HVAC, $806,000); B-A, Inc. (Electrical, $339,200).

223 Trustee Minutes, November 20, 1964, XVII.

224 Trustee Minutes, December 18, 1964, V, p. 100. The Board authorized the sale of bonds totaling $4.46 million for Units #3 and #4 in September. Trustee Minutes, September 9, 1966, p. 356.

225 Trustee Minutes, February 19, 1965, VI.

226 Total project cost was estimated at $4.46 million.

227 Units #3 and #4 were named by the Trustees in June 1965. Trustee Minutes, June 16, 1965, XXI.

228 The Trustees and the President requested authority to expend $3 million for the renovation. Trustee Minutes, March 31, 1995, Sec. I, p. 11.

229 Funds to come from Residence Hall Reserves and tax-exempt revenue bonds.

230 See: http://www.housedemocrats.org/final-phase-of-isu-residence-hall-renovations-approved.

231 Trustee Minutes, February 28, 1964, V.

232 Repp and Mundt, Inc. (General Construction, $3.03 million); Fred G. Christman (Plumbing, HVAC-$712,000); The Sanborn Electric Company (Electrical, $339,997).

233 RATIO Architects was engaged by October 2012 to begin design and engineering plans for the towers. Trustee Minutes, October 5, 2012, records payment of $1.35 million to RATIO.

234 Represents final cost. $3.5 million came from housing and dining reserves and the sale of up to $17.2 million in bonds. The Trustees, at their October 2012 meeting, authorized the university administration to gain state approval to spend up to $22 million for the first phase of a multi-year project. Funding came from residence hall reserves and bond sales. The Trustees authorized financing at their May 2014 meeting. Trustee Minutes, May 2, 2014, p. 101.

235 Five million of the cost was paid by Sodexo with the balance to come from cash reserves and bonding.

CHAPTER 7

7TH PRESIDENT
ALAN CARSON RANKIN
(1965-1975)

January 5, 1967
Jones and Hines Halls were dedicated.

September 16, 1967
ISU was the first university to have Astroturf surface.

September 20, 1968
The Aerospace Technology program was approved.

July 10, 1968
Groundbreaking for the College of Nursing took place.

November 21, 1969
The first unit of Lincoln Quads was dedicated.

Indiana State University Building a Legacy

Born: December 19, 1914

Died: February 24, 1999

Wife: Francis Margaret Goodnough Atkins (Rankin) (married 1958-99)

Education:
Bachelor's Degree
Kansas State College – Fort Hays
Political Science and Education

Master's Degree
Syracuse University

Ph.D. Degree
Syracuse University

Positions held at Indiana State University:
President (1965-75)

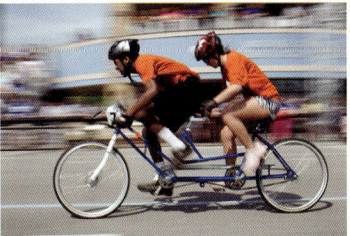

June 1970
The Tandem Bike Race began.

December 17, 1971
Groundbreaking for Hulman Civic Center took place.

January 15, 1971
Groundbreaking for Cunningham Library took place.

April 30, 1975
The Vietnam War ended.

Chapter 7 President Rankin

President Rankin was born December 19, 1914 in Hoisington, Kansas. It was a small town (population in 1910 was 1,975) and owed its existence to the Missouri-Pacific Railroad.[1] He was raised in an academic family. His father was a professor, his grandfather was a college president, and his mother taught school.

He received his undergraduate degree in political science and education from Kansas State College-Fort Hays and completed the Masters in Political Science and Doctor of Social Science both from Syracuse University.

While at Fort Hays, he was editor of the yearbook, president of the student body, and member of the student council, as well as being a cellist in the college orchestra and singer in the Glee Club. His ongoing interest in music was expressed by having the Pittsburgh Symphony Orchestra perform on campus at his inauguration, and through his support of bringing the Contemporary Music Festival to campus. He was honored by receiving the Alumni Achievement Award

> **"Indeed Alan Rankin is the person who has brought the university tradition to Indiana State."**
> – ISU Trustees

from KSC-Fort Hays – the highest honor given to alumni. During WWII, he was Chief of the Salary and Wage Administration section of the Panama Canal Department and the Caribbean Defense Command.

His first academic position was at Miami (Ohio) University from 1946-54. For the next two years (1954-56), he served as director of student personnel and assistant professor of Political Science at Cornell University. Rankin was brought to the University of Pittsburgh by Chancellor Edward Litchfield, who had worked with him at Cornell. Rankin served as Litchfield's executive assistant, responsible for managing the chancellor's office, as well as numerous special projects. Rankin provided the leadership for a group that, in 1957, proposed the creation of the Graduate School of Public and International Affairs.[2]

Rankin was nominated for the presidency at Indiana State University (ISU) by Dr. William P. Tolley, Chancellor of Syracuse University, in 1964. He was appointed President by Board of Trustee President James D. Archer and took office July 1, 1965. His inauguration was held on April 14, 1966.[3]

President Rankin served during one of the most contentious periods in the history of ISU. Indeed, from the 1960s into the 1970s, it was a turbulent time on campuses across the country. The baby boomers created the largest college population in U.S. history and a generation of educated and socially-aware activists.[4]

The activism was fueled by student movements to fight racism, poverty, the war in Vietnam, and to establish participatory democracy in the '60s. Sit-ins that had proven effective in the civil rights movement were used by students to protest restrictions on campus, and to gain a voice in university administration. The '70s had been described by Tom Wolfe as the "me decade." Personal freedom and rebellion against authority defined the decade.

Students occupy Administration Building

The murder of students at Kent State on May 4, 1970 revealed the intensity of protest movements and the committed reactions they stirred. This killing by National Guard troops heightened tensions on campuses nationally. Fortunately, ISU did not have to endure the death of protesting students on its campus. This owes considerably to the equanimity and willingness of President Rankin to engage all segments of the campus caught up in the tumultuous times when leadership and authority were continuously questioned and challenged. Rankin's administration faced sit-ins, streakers, anti-war demonstrations, and the burning of the American flag in a classroom.[5]

During the rededication of the Link Building honoring President Rankin, he commented on campus streakers. He related how several young men showed up naked outside Cunningham Library while he was making

Alumni Center/Hall

Historic Name: Marathon Oil
Architect: Unknown
Date Acquired: July 1966
Cost: $325,000

Location: Cherry Street[6]
Area: 36,740 ASF

President Landini
Renamed: Alumni Hall, 1989

President Moore
Razed: 1995

The three-storied building was acquired in 1966 to house the Alumni Center and several offices, notably, the Vice President for Development and Public Affairs, Placement, and Graduate School Dean.

The building faced Cherry Street. It was a conservative International Style Building, meaning it had little external ornamentation. It had a fine ashlar marble surface.

With the acquisition of the Marathon Building, Alumni offices were moved out of Condit House, which was later remodeled to become the residence, and during the Moore presidency, the office of the President.

---

a presentation. He noted they weren't angry and wouldn't throw rocks because they had no pockets.

One target of the student movement was to attack the *in loco parentis* rules that set curfews and dorm rules. Students pressed for several years for same-sex dormitories and bedroom visitation – something the Board and President Rankin initially opposed.

Affirmative action was something new for universities to understand and make a priority. Another issue Rankin faced was the call for the creation of an Office of Women's Advocate. Rankin opposed creating this position, indicating that the Office of Affirmative Action was responsible to represent all minorities on campus. His decision was rejected by the Faculty Senate.

During his tenure, the campus entered a period of unsurpassed growth in enrollment, programs, and faculty and, of necessity, buildings to house students, classrooms, and library holdings. Growth owed to the influx of baby-boomers, but, toward the end of his presidency, the university experienced several years of damaging enrollment decline. The boom in building led to an over-building of dormitories, and financial indebtedness that forced the university to consider declaring a state of financial exigency.[7] On April 21, 1973, "the Board of Trustees, recognizing the critical financial situation, adopted a resolution supporting the position set forth by the administration at that time in order to meet the financial exigency."[8]

Despite inflationary pressures, the budget increase recommended by the Indiana Senate Budget

Chapter 7 President Rankin

Subcommittee in 1973 for all public universities for the next biennium (1973-75) was $461 million.[9] President Rankin pointed out to the committee that the House recommendations would not cover unavoidable and inflationary costs. He projected a deficit of $125,000 with no certainty about where the money could be found. The Trustees recognized this was a serious matter and the administration should consider emergency measures and retrenching where possible.[10] Retrenchment is a term used in higher education that describes a reduction in faculty and staff (even tenured faculty) in the event of financial exigency. During periods of financial difficulty, all things bear scrutiny. The Trustees questioned the efficiency in the deployment of faculty across academic programs. How does one maximize the use of available faculty when faculty are tenured in specific departments? Apparently, the Commission for Higher Education also saw this as an issue unique to Indiana State and reduced the university's instructional support budget by $700,000, stating "Indiana State is substantially over-funded in relationship to other institutions in the instruction program area."[11]

The budget situation continued to worsen in 1973-74, owing to declining enrollment, debt service, and reduction in the state's instructional support budget. In March 1974, two documents relating to retrenchment were distributed to the Trustees, Faculty Senate, and Executive Council.[12] The worsening situation led to the postponement of the dedication of the new Hulman Civic-University Center. The Board of Trustees took the most drastic of measures, declaring financial exigency in April 1974. The Faculty Senate rejected the plan presented by the administration. Trustee Archer moved the Faculty Senate motion not be approved and reaffirmed that a financial exigency exits for the foreseeable future.[13]

Without doubt, the stress level for the President had risen unabated. Campus disruptions, which were a part of campus life in the late 1960s and early 1970s, paled in comparison to the budget shortfalls the campus had to manage, which required extreme and unpopular decisions.[14] In May 1973, President Rankin reported all budgets would be cut by 5 percent. For Academic Affairs, this meant not filling 55 vacant positions and giving notice to 27 faculty members that they would not be reappointed for the 1974-75 academic year. The President anticipated ongoing drops in enrollment, which would adversely affect budgets across the campus. Student fees were regularly increased, owing to the decline in state appropriations, loss of enrollment, and the need to provide $545,000 debt service on the Hulman Civic-University Center.[15]

The University of Southern Indiana was founded in 1965 as a regional campus of ISU. In 1974, the first bill was introduced to separate the Evansville campus from ISU but failed to be reported out of the Senate committee. Certain to pass in the near future, the impact on the ISU main campus would be adverse.[16] In February 1974, as the administration prepared budget projections for the fall term, it became clear that room rates would again have to be raised in order to cover debt service and that the newly constructed Statesman Towers residence halls would be closed, as would central food service in Sandison Complex. Students complained they had not been properly consulted before these proposals were put before the Trustees.[17] Trustee Hitch said the "University is gambling, hoping things will swing around." The trend to develop several associate degrees that focused on occupational training were discussed by the Trustees, a trend, no doubt, to combat enrollment loss.

This was a period of inflation and state support for higher education was diminished, forcing universities and colleges across the state to increase tuition and fees. This phenomenon was not limited to Indiana, and increasingly, the public became critical of higher education. It questioned the purpose of tenure, the importance of the liberal arts, and pressured to increase vocationally-oriented programs grew.[18]

While the movement to create an autonomous Evansville campus threatened ISU enrollment, the formation of a new Higher Education Commission presented additional exacerbating issues. In 1972, the Commission prepared two volumes, the first, "The Current Status," commented on the state of higher education in Indiana and a second titled "A Pattern for the Future" was a preliminary draft for public discussion. Rankin informed the Board he had yet to receive a copy.[19]

The Vice Chairman of the Commission, Mr. Beurt Servaas, was quoted in an Evansville newspaper saying that Ball State and Indiana State were "second class" institutions. One hopes Mr. Servaas either misspoke or was misquoted. It is likely he was referencing the Carnegie classification of institutions, which does distinguish between Type I research universities with selective admission standards and Type II universities, such as Ball State and ISU, with limited doctoral offerings and a more generous admissions policy.[20] Nevertheless, there was concern among Trustees that the Commission intended to control admissions at state schools.[21]

Much of the campus we enjoy today took shape during Rankin's presidency. Initially, the need for new classroom space was severe. Rankin wrote that ISU

> "... leased temporary buildings including Sunday School rooms, four old garages, four old apartment houses, five old houses, a dozen pre-fabs, a parsonage, and a former dairy" to accommodate growth.

Four units of Married Student Housing were built adjacent to First Street. Hines, Mills, Rhoads, Holmstedt, Lincoln Quad, and Statesman residence halls opened.[22] Cunningham Memorial Library was completed and dedicated on March 8, 1974.[23] Condit House was remodeled to become the President's home and the university acquired Memorial Stadium from the city. A major project was the completion of the 10 million-dollar Hulman Center – a project supported by the university, city, and private donors.[24] Academically, doctoral programs began and the first Ph.D. was awarded. A satellite unit of the Indiana University School of Medicine (known as the Terre Haute Center for Medical Education) was created. In the arts, Rankin was supportive of the Swope Museum and can be credited with supporting bringing the Contemporary Music Festival to ISU.[25] Mrs. Rankin shared her husband's interest in music. She had an opera-quality mezzo-soprano voice and performed often in Terre Haute Community Theater productions.

President Rankin's other successes included bringing the Hoosier Boys and Girls State Summer Conventions to the campus, developing the Indiana Special Olympics, and serving as one of the founders and the first executive director of Leadership Terre Haute.

An interesting, but unrealized, project was the development of a plan to move the Swope Museum closer to the campus. The Swope director, Howard E. Wooden, wrote President Rankin in February 1973, stating the Swope Board of Managers and Board of Overseers favored the project and asked that the Trustees of ISU be petitioned to consider leasing a site on the periphery of the campus and that the university be requested to supply heat and consider other forms of support.[26]

Rankin and Ewing Miller introduced yet another visionary idea for extending the campus. In 1969, Miller presented a master plan proposal to the Trustees that addressed the Riverfront development, something resurrected and acted upon during the Bradley period.[27] Miller envisioned this property might be used for organized sports, as well as Greek and married student housing.

President Rankin submitted a letter requesting he be relieved of his position as President on April 12, 1974.[28] He was succeeded by Dr. Richard Landini, who assumed the presidency on May 15, 1975.

President Rankin died on February 24, 1999 and was buried in the Mount Allen Cemetery in Hays, Ellis County, Kansas. The tombstone inscription reads simply, "Seventh President of Indiana State University." At the conclusion of his inaugural address in 1965, President Rankin quoted from the ancient drama Antigone where King Creon cries out, "It is easy to say 'no.' To say 'yes' you have to sweat and roll up your sleeves and plunge both hands into life up to your elbows." A profoundly fitting epitaph. In their April 20, 1974 statement following President Rankin's announcement of resignation, the Trustees stated most cogently, "Indeed Alan Rankin is the person who has brought the university tradition to Indiana State."[29]

Clinical Psychology Building

Contractors: Frank L. Johnson and Sons Development Company, Inc.

Date: 1968-69

Cost: $49,950

Area: 1,783 Sq. Ft.

Location: 424 North Seventh Street

Bids for the Psychology Building were received and the contract was awarded in October 1968. The building housed 12 experimental rooms and laboratory/workshop spaces.

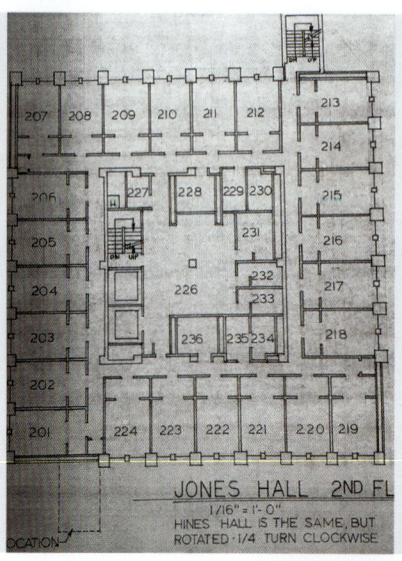

Hines Hall and Jones Hall

Architect: Ewing Miller Associates, Inc.

Contractors: Repp and Mundt, Inc.;[30] Freitag-Weinhardt, Inc.; B-A, Inc.[31]

Date: Dedication: January 5, 1967

Cost: $4.08 million

Area: 70,431 GSF, 46,885 ASF each

Location: Jones Hall: 455 North Fifth Street

Hines Hall: 460 North Fifth Street

Hines and Jones Halls were the third set of residences added to the campus. Jones Hall honors the first president of the ISNS, William Albert Jones (1869-79), and Hines Hall is named after the fourth president, Linnaeus Neal Hines (1921-33).[32]

The design for both buildings was guided by the behavioral research conducted in Burford and Sycamore Towers (the cluster of four high-rise buildings), and the preexisting buildings that were part of the Sandison complex designed by Yeager (Sandison and Gillum).[33] Research indicated there was a gender preference that influenced design. Women preferred larger and more formal lounges, and 57 percent of all students preferred being on the bottom three or top two floors.[34]

The floor plan was also changed. Yeager used a rectangular floor plan, while Miller chose a square floor plan, no doubt having seen how students better interacted in the Sycamore Towers. This design placed mechanical equipment in the center, and the shorter hallways encouraged greater interaction and less hall noise. Aesthetically, Hines and Jones appear denser and more sculptural than the Sycamore Towers, perhaps reflecting Miller's consideration that these were intended to be men's dorms.[35] The surface of Hines and Jones was done in concrete that contained pea-gravel, giving the concrete a darker color, contrasting with the Towers that had white quartz aggregate making the surfaces appear lighter.

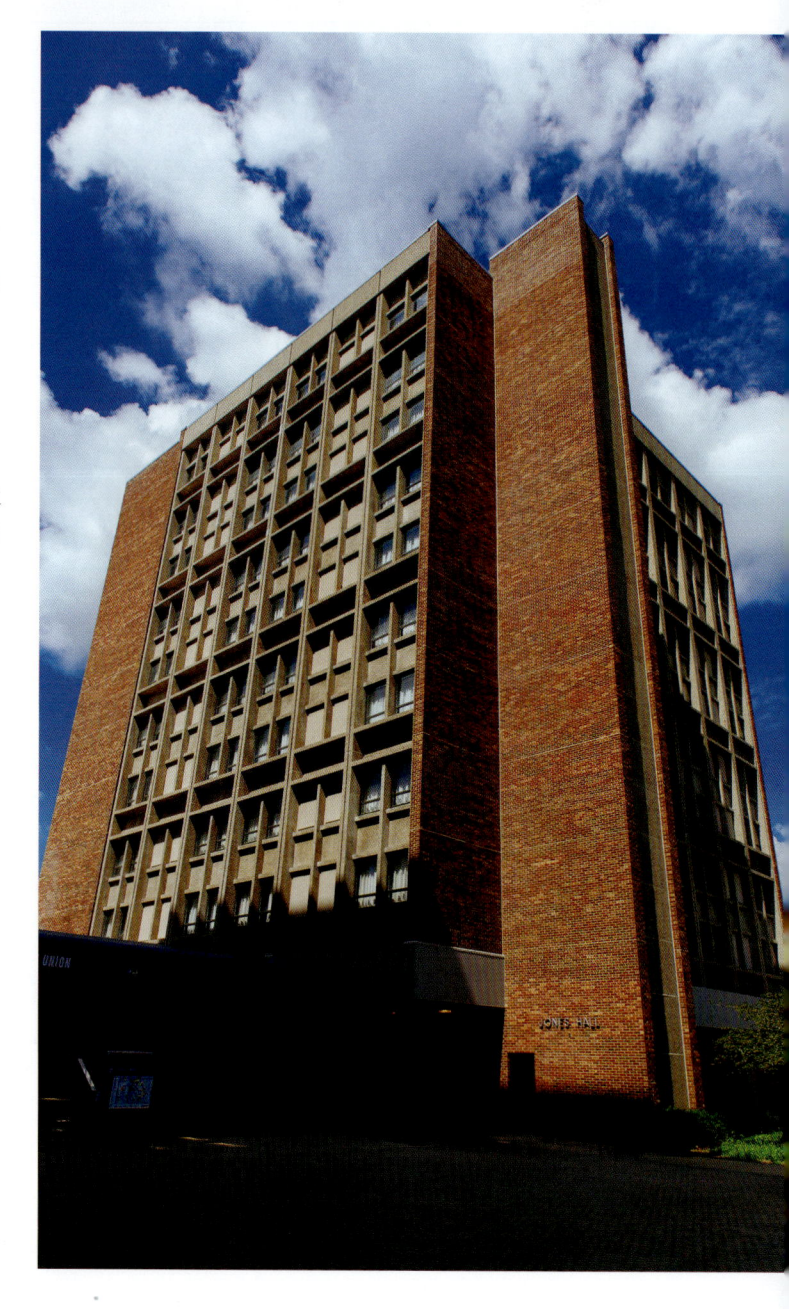

Indiana State University Building a Legacy

Miller was responsible for numerous residence halls. When asked if he liked designing residences, he said he did, but he didn't like the budgets. He stated it was hard to make an interesting facade – something more than a wall of windows. "After all," he stated, "we were not building something to store wheat. So, the question was how to make it interesting without added cost."[36]

The first floor of each building was set back beneath the second floor. This created a shadowed or negative space that played off against the massive brick walls that framed the corners of the structures. The principle entrances are located within this shadowed area. Large steel piers encased in concrete surmounted by a concrete band provide the supportive base from which the structures rise. This feature reflects earlier buildings in New York, particularly the Lever Brothers Building designed by Gordon Bunshaft (1952), and the Seagram Building by Mies van der Rohe and Philip Johnson (1958). Both buildings are elevated with main entries contained within a recessed area that was a continuation of the plaza in front. The building reflects Miller's interest in the International Style: an interesting simple box with some articulation of the structure externally. The grid-like pattern and geometricizing of the walls is also an International Style feature.

Exterior walls were pre-cast panels each with a window. Between the windows and demarcating the floors are alternating square and rectangular panels. The horizontal panels dividing the floors project slightly, creating a play of light and shade – an effect Miller appreciated and used elsewhere, such as Statesman Towers. Originally, Hines and Jones were to be men's residences. Behavioral research done in Buford Hall and Sycamore Towers showed male students preferred smaller lounges, hence the small lounges on the first floor, while the lower level contained large recreational areas, also preferred by men. Miller uses some of these design features in the Statesman Towers.[37] ∎

Hines Renovation
President Moore

Architect: David R. Snapp & Associates, Inc.

Contractors: DI, Inc. (General Construction); Williams Plumbing and Heating (Plumbing and Heating); Crown Electric (Electrical)

Date: 1998-99

Cost: $5.22 million[38]

The renovation of Hines Hall involved the transformation of a typical 400-bed dormitory into a residence hall with private baths. Interior finishes were updated, and insulation and HVAC were improved. Concrete panels replaced the windows in rooms converted into bathrooms.

Jones Remodel
President Benjamin

Architect: RATIO Architects

Date: 2001-02

Cost: $5.52 million[39]

On December 2, 1999, the Indiana Commission for Higher Education approved a $7 million renovation plan for Jones Hall. The renovation work, developed by RATIO Architects, included combining three separate rooms into two, with a semi-private bathroom and walk-in closets in the center. Concrete panels replacing windows were installed in the newly created bathrooms. No major changes were made to the exteriors of the building. The renovation reflected the changes in student expectations about campus living arrangements. Preparation for the renovation began under President Moore and was completed during Benjamin's presidency.

Ewing Miller Associates, Inc. was approved by the State Budget Agency to serve as the architectural firm to design the Boiler Plant project.[40] In 1967, the state approved the issuance of bonds totaling $550,000 to purchase a new 200,000-pound boiler, and $120,000 for additional items necessary to put the boiler in operation. The estimated total cost at that time was $2.5 million.[41]

Ewing Miller presented schematic plans for the Boiler Plant to the Board in October 1968. Miller, who introduced new methods of design and construction in other campus buildings, proposed using Corten steel (sometimes written Cor-Ten) on the exterior of the structure.[42] The first use of Corten for architectural applications was the John Deere World Headquarters (1964) in Moline, Illinois, designed by Eero Saarinen – an influence Miller recognized. Miller continued to keep abreast of new developments in architectural design and construction and was quick to introduce new design ideas on campus.

Corten steel is a group of steel alloys developed to eliminate the need for painting and forms a stable rust-like appearance if exposed to the weather for several years. In essence, Corten was noted for its ability to rust aesthetically. The layer protecting the surface regenerates as it weathers. ISU received an award from the American Institute of Steel Construction in recognition of the "outstanding architectural steel construction work done on the Boiler Plant."[43]

Miller commented there were two key factors that influenced the design. First, the building had to be vertical in order to fit the site. Second was the question of how to make this industrial project compatible with the campus architecture. Corten provided a lighter-weight skin and made an industrial statement, but Miller thought it fit better with the campus than would a tall masonry tower. The Corten was slightly molded, making it somewhat sculptural and interesting in the absence of windows. Miller stated that the surface would age, become darker and appear to diminish the scale of the plant. This would be true for the brick color used in most campus buildings. He began the design from an engineering perspective that influenced the project.[44]

Bids for the construction of the foundations were received in April 1969, and the contract was awarded to Shelton Hannig, Inc. for $138,688.[45] The contract for general construction was awarded to F. A. Wilhelm Construction Company, Inc. for $578,340.[46] ■

Boiler Plant

Architect: Ewing Miller Associates, Inc.[47]

Contractors: Shelton Hannig, Inc. and F. A. Wilhelm Construction, Inc.

Date: 1967-72

Cost: Approx. $2.5 million

Location: 528 North Eighth Street

Razed: 2002-03

Boiler Improvements
President Landini

Contractor: Bailey/Hanning, Inc.

In mid-1975, President Landini was authorized by the Board to request approval and financing from the various agencies of government and the Governor to proceed with the installation of oil-burning equipment in boiler 5. Also initiated was breeching to provide a pathway for particulate from boilers 2 and 3 to the inlet side of boiler 5. This made it possible to burn a greater variety of fuels at lower cost. It also reduced sulfur dioxide emissions in order to meet Environmental Protection Agency requirements.

Bids were received in June 1976. The contract was awarded to 2M Corporation for $159,500. The budget for additional conversion and installation of fuel oil tanks was approved July 17, 1979.

In 1987, additional work was required to complete retrofitting on boiler 5. The entire project totaled $3 million.

(For information regarding the new power plant, see President Moore chapter.)

Demolition of the Boiler Plant
President Benjamin

Contractor: CDI

Project Managers: Steve Culp and Bryan Duncan

Date: 2002-03

Cost: $1.2 million

College of Nursing

Seeing this four-story building from design to completion was fraught with difficulties. The initial design was for a 44,000 square-foot building costing $1.3 million. A Federal grant was approved for $1 million, so, to reduce cost, Miller redesigned the building.[48] However, owing to a delay in construction, building costs increased to $1.8 million – an unacceptable amount. A third plan was rapidly developed for a minimal 33,000 square-foot building costing $1.3 million that was approved by the Trustees in July 1969.[49]

The final design contained classrooms on the first floor, and the second floor was devoted to laboratories, demonstration rooms, nursing stations, study carrels, and student lockers. The third and fourth floors contained faculty offices, seminar and conference rooms, and research areas.

The building was a simple brick structure with a small amount of limestone trim. The building had to be faced with brick rather than a more expensive material that Miller preferred, such as limestone or pre-cast concrete with aggregate. Miller stated the building was "simply conceived" and could accommodate expansion at a future time.[50]

The low bid was for $1.14 million. The exterior continued to be a topic of concern. In December, Miller stated there were two problems with designing the building – a small building site and limited budget. Apparently, precast concrete was still his preference, but the cost was an additional $50,000. The decision was made to use brick facing and split windows for an additional $4,200.[51]

The building was completed by March 1971 and was ready for inspection by the Department of Health, Education, and Welfare. The Trustees toured the building in April 1971.[52]

Architect: Ewing Miller Associates, Inc.

Contractors: Mid Republic Construction, Inc. (General Construction); Healy Mechanical Contractors (Mechanical); and B-A, Inc., (Electrical Construction)[53]

Date: 1968-71

Cost: $1.14 million[54]

Area: 40,083 GSF; 21,655 ASF

Location: 749 Chestnut Street

Chapter 7 President Rankin

Statesman Towers

Architect: Ewing Miller and Associates, Inc.[55]

Contractors: F. A. Wilhelm Construction Company, Inc. (General Construction); Freitag-Weinhardt Company Inc., (Plumbing, Heating and Ventilation); Sanborn Electric Company (Electrical)[56]

Date: Dedication: April 17, 1969
Opened: September 1968

Cost: $8.73 million

Area: 318,708 GSF; 153,547 ASF

Location: 800 Sycamore Street

Statesman Towers were constructed in anticipation of continued enrollment growth, such as the campus experienced during the 1960s. Even before completion, however, enrollment began to diminish, and the buildings were repurposed before being razed in 2016.[57] The preliminary planning included four towers much like the Sycamore Towers on the west side of the campus. Ultimately, only two towers were built. These were named for former Vice Presidents: Schuyler Colfax, Charles W. Fairbanks, Thomas A. Hendricks, and Thomas R. Marshall. In an interview, Ewing explained the university did not want to use eminent domain to claim the additional property needed for four towers, so the solution was to put one on top of the other. "The architecture was good, but the circumstances made for a maverick plan."[58]

The Trustees directed the administration to secure approval of the $5.75 million project from the State Budget Agency. At the outset, there was concern about the viability of the project. Miller told the Trustees it would cost an additional $625,000 for air conditioning. Further, he informed them that based upon the current estimates for the Unit 1, without air conditioning, the project would not be self-supporting and that it would require taking unencumbered excess income of all the other residence halls to insure the sale of bonds. He proposed a graduate residence of smaller size would be a more economically sound investment and would serve better the needs of the institution.[59] The Trustees voted to build without air conditioning.[60] Final plans and specifications were approved by the Board in April 1966.[61]

Demand for on-campus housing, combined with the cost of real estate, led to a reduction of the project to two towers.[62] Initially, the towers were intended to house men, but by 1967 the decision was made to make them co-educational residences. The towers had a massive, masculine aesthetic, reflecting the gender of the originally intended residents. Miller stated he intentionally made the buildings "bulky, geometric, masculine, and designed to house men not women."[63] They can be compared with the Sycamore Towers, designed initially for women, which appear lighter, more fluid, and less massive. The use of pre-cast concrete panels provided visual continuity from the earlier residence halls to these towers.

The buildings were 15-stories high. The ground level of each building was originally a central dining facility and kitchen. The number of spaces for students totaled 1,152 for both structures. When the residence halls opened, the second through eighth floors were reserved for male students, and the ninth through 15th floors for women. Each building contained appropriate support offices and lounge areas and was served by four elevators in each building.

When completed, the two towers were the tallest buildings between Chicago and St. Louis. The

Indiana State University Building a Legacy

contemporary design, engineering, and use of precast concrete were impressive. The buildings earned a first place honor award for the architects in 1968 from the Indiana Society of Architects. This was the first time a campus structure was so honored.

With the decline in enrollment during Rankin's presidency, it became apparent the campus had excess housing capacity, a problem further exacerbating the current financial crises and urgent need for additional classrooms and offices for Education and Business.[64] After sequential remodeling, the School of Education moved into the west tower in 1977, and in 1981, the School of Business occupied the east tower.[65]

In 2009, owing to the renovation of the Laboratory School on Eighth and Chestnut Streets, the College of Education vacated the tower and moved to spacious new quarters. In 2012, Business moved to the Federal Building. The Laboratory School renovation and acquisition of the Federal Building were both accomplished during the Benjamin presidency. The Federal Building renovation was completed during Bradley's administration.

The construction of the towers was innovative. Miller described them:

> *They're strongly architectonic [and express the structure] and plasticity of the pre-cast concrete, these are technologically very innovative buildings in the sense that they had a core – a slipped core – of poured concrete that took all the stress of the building. And then the floors and the walls were all pre-cast and were made in a factory and brought here and erected quickly and welded together and tied with a belt around each floor.*[66]

Building with poured and precast concrete was a relatively new method of construction. Miller explained that it was a technique becoming available because of the improved quality of the precast concrete, made possible by using a system called "shock baton." Miller explained that the precast work was done in Chicago, and the parts were all shipped to Terre Haute. The benefit of shock baton was the poured forms contain no air gaps that can occur if the poured concrete is not vibrated sufficiently before it sets up. In Chicago, the forms were poured on a platform that could shake the panels, assuring a very even and dense structural form. Miller attributed using this innovative form of construction to his structural engineer, Homer Howe, the same person who advised on forming the folded plate roof in the Physical Education Building.[67] All of the towers were composed of pre-cast panels, except for the 11th and 12th floors that were formed by concrete poured in place in order to provide a stable base for the upper floors. Similar to Jones and Hines Halls, an alternating square and rectangular pattern divided floors and windows. Unlike Miller's earlier dormitories, there is an absence of brick, and a more plastic handling of the concrete, which served to create a surface defined by the play of light and shadows. Entry was through a single-story glass and concrete pavilion (a subsidiary building attached to the main building).

Miller was strongly influenced by Louis Kahn, one of the twentieth century's leading architects. Miller's adoption of pre-cast concrete elements perhaps draws from Kahn's designs for the Richards Medical Research Laboratories, located on the campus of the University of Pennsylvania in Philadelphia.[68] The building was not constructed employing a hidden steel frame, rather, it has a structure of reinforced concrete and prefabricated concrete elements.

The two Statesman Towers, in a reserved manner, belonged to the architectural movement of the 1960s and 1970s, defined as Brutalist architecture. The term derives from the French word for 'raw,' and was used by the famous French architect, Le Corbusier, to describe a favored building material "shock beton," or raw concrete. It became popular, especially in England. Miller's English interests and knowledge of Paul Rudolph's recent Yale Art and Architecture Building (1958) may well have influenced his experimentation with that style here. The Brutalist style was especially popular on American campuses, and was used for residence halls and fine and performing arts centers. Typical are repeated geometric modular elements that correspond to distinct functional areas of the structure. One might compare the Statesman Towers to the Trellick Tower, London (1966-72). Another relevant example is the J. Edgar Hoover Building in Washington, D.C. Ultimately, Miller was not satisfied with the label "brutalist." He pointed out that the "International Style" that owed much to the relocation of Bauhaus architects from Germany brought an industrialized approach to building. The other modern current was more sculptural and was developed by the Saarinens. Miller saw the dramatic sculptural supports of the towers as different from the Brutalist style. He wrote, "The expression of structure would have to be used to turn the building from enclosure to expressive architecture."[69]

Statesman Towers represents the last major large scale project undertaken by Ewing Miller on the ISU campus. His professional career at ISU spanned two presidencies and included 27 buildings. He is to be credited with being one of the early pioneers to incorporate behavioral research into residence hall design, and he was one of the first to introduce to the campus a more current or modern style of building design. His contributions to architecture and architectural theory were recognized by the American Institute of Architects Indiana, who awarded him with the Gold Medal Award, its highest award.[70] ∎

West Tower Renovation

President Landini

Architect: Daggett, Naegelle, & Associates

Contractors: Garmong Construction Company (General Construction); Sycamore Engineering (Mechanical and Electrical)[71]

Date: 1977 (West Tower converted into School of Education)

Cost: $1.04 million[72]

M & E Engineering Service, Inc. presented plans for the renovation of this tower into an academic facility. The Department of Housing and Urban Development approved the conversion plans, and the Trustees voted approval and authorized advertising for bids.[73] Bids totaled $815,765.[74] The Commission for Higher Education and State Budget Committee approved an additional $280,000 to complete the project.[75] When completed, approximately 140 School of Education faculty moved into the renovated facility.

East Tower Renovation

President Landini

Architects: M & E Engineering Services with Fleck & Hickey, Inc.[76]

Contractors: Garmong Construction Company; Sycamore Engineering, Inc.[77]

Date: 1981 (East Tower converted into School of Business)

Cost: $890,266[78]

President Landini informed the Board that in the special session of the summer of 1978, ISU was appropriated $600,000 to be applied to the conversion of the East Tower for use by the College of Business.[79] This appropriation anticipated the sale of the Conference Center (old Deming Hotel) to the Bethesda Corporation, and the Housing Authority of Terre Haute.

Plans for vacating the towers and moving the Colleges of Education and Business to new facilities matured during Benjamin's presidency.[80] A workable financial plan was developed. Initially, plans were considered for moving both colleges into the former Lab School, in part because of budget limitations. Finally, an agreement was reached with the state whereby the Lab School would be remodeled for Education, and the Federal Building, given to ISU with some federal support to begin renovations, would be the new home of the College of Business. In September 2001, Schmidt and Associates won a competitive bid to develop designs for the Colleges of Education and Business.

The College of Education vacated the West Tower in 2009 and moved to the newly renovated University Hall. The College of Business relocated to the Federal Building in 2012. The decision to move the Colleges of Business and Education to other facilities was determined by both inherent difficulties with the buildings, and the need for ISU to reduce square footage, a factor monitored by the state. Both buildings, originally built as residence halls, never satisfactorily served as classrooms and offices.[81] They were not energy-efficient. Combined, there were 1,200 single glass pane windows. Cooling was provided by over 500 individual air conditioners. Floor to ceiling heights made remodeling and installing central air conditioning impossible. There was a shortage of power, and the bathrooms did not meet OSHA-ADA guidelines for accessibility.

While thought had been given to repurpose and renovate the structures, it was clear to all that costs were prohibitive. The State Budget Committee approved their demolition on May 29, 2013, and planning for their removal occurred during 2015.

The Statesman Towers were not popular with students, and Miller's ongoing study of student behavior and architectural design led him and the campus to abandon high-rise residence halls in favor of low-rise apartment-style housing found in the Lincoln Quadrangles and, more recently, the Reeve Residence Halls. In an interview, Miller said, "If we had more Lincoln Quadrangles … we probably wouldn't have done the Lincoln Towers (sic. Statesman Towers), although architecturally I think they were one of our better, stronger, building forms …"[82] ∎

Statesman Towers Razed
President Bradley

Architect: Schmidt Associates

Contractor: Renascent Inc.

Razed: 2015

Cost: $1.74 million[83]

The Trustees voted to authorize President Bradley to request from the Commission for Higher Education, the State Budget Committee, and the Governor, the authority to expend up to $4 million for the demolition of the towers.[84] Fortunately, the final cost was significantly less than estimated.

Chapter 7 President Rankin

Nursing Clinic Facilities

Architect: Ewing Miller Associates, Inc.[85]

Contractors: F. A. Wilhelm Construction Co.; Freitag-Weinhart, Inc.; Sycamore Engineering & Electrical Construction Co.

Date: 1969[86]

Cost: $550,000

Area: 18,800 GSF

Location: 1433 North 6 ½ Street

In December 1966, the Trustees were addressed by Dean Dorothy McMullan, who indicated there was an urgent need to have clinical education facilities near Union Hospital. Dr. Wayne A. Crockett suggested the facilities be incorporated into the new hospital addition, but to accommodate this would present a delay of half a year. The decision was reached to build a separate building for clinicals.[87] The Board appointed Ewing Miller's firm to prepare plans and specifications for the facility.[88] Schematic plans, apparently already prepared by Miller, were presented at the same meeting.

President Rankin and Vice President and Treasurer Moulton met with Governor Branigin and the State Budget Committee to request permission to seek federal funds for building the facility. It was reported in the minutes that the "Governor demonstrated a most understanding attitude toward Indiana State University but also expressed concern about future directions in higher education in Indiana."[89] The Trustees visited the newly constructed facility on October 24, 1969.[90]

Final inspection of the facility was conducted by Mr. Samuel Curiale, U.S. Public Health Service, Department of Health, Education, and Welfare. With the understanding that the contractors would correct minor deficiencies, the Trustees formally accepted the building.[91] It was constructed of reinforced concrete, with exterior walls made of precast concrete and brick with precast concrete trim.

Lincoln Quadrangle

Lincoln Quadrangle complex was named in honor of President Abraham Lincoln.[92] Six three- and four-story buildings were planned as co-ed residences that could accommodate up to 805 residents. A one-story building was constructed to house dining and the kitchen. The entire complex underwent renovation beginning with the south section in 2001. The buildings had been plagued with leakage problems. Renovation concentrated on the roof, windows, and stairwell. The uniform scale and design of the buildings suggest a cohesiveness not found on campuses where architects work in diverse styles to express their individuality. In contrast to the high-rise towers, the arrangement of the buildings making up the complex tied in with the brick vernacular used elsewhere on campus and created a sense of community and security for the students living there.

Where to put the buildings challenged the university. Ewing Miller presented plans for the first building. The second building would replicate the same plan and use the same materials with the exception of the kitchen units. Miller proposed locating the buildings east of the Laboratory School, but the Trustees expressed concerns that the university did not own the property, and the need to build was urgent. After visiting the site, the Board delayed action on approving North Residence Hall #1A until a more suitable site could be located. The availability of less expensive land on the north side of campus would allow for the creation of a cluster of low-rise apartment-style residences. The buildings have exteriors of face brick masonry with precast concrete trim. The masonry walls are load bearing.[93]

Ewing Miller studied the interrelationship between his building design and experience of the students. He explained that students who lived in Statesman Towers did not appreciate the restrictive rules limiting male-female student interaction. He stated, "And girls wanted to live with the boys and it was a revolution, I know it was very upsetting to Alan Rankin … and probably brought about his resignation as much as

Lincoln Quadrangle

Architect: Ewing Miller Associates, Inc.

Contractors: Repp and Mundt, Inc. (General Construction); Freitag-Weinhardt, Inc., (Plumbing and HVAC); The Sanborn Electric Company (Electrical); Mrs. Sally Rowland (Interior Designer)

Date: Lincoln North Quad completed: 1969
Lincoln South Quad completed: 1970[94]

Cost: $6.6 million (Unit 1)[95]

Area: North: 81,202 GSF; 50,584 ASF

South: 79,242 GSF; 49,524 ASF

Location: 650 North Sixth Street

President Landini
The dining facilities were remodeled according to designs by architect Susan M. Allen and equipment design by G. V. Aikman.[96] The total cost was $550,000.

In 1989-90, it was necessary to address structural issues, water penetration, plumbing remodeling, and add an elevator for a total cost of $2.2 million.

President Benjamin
Major remodeling was done involving replacing windows, resurfacing roofs, and modifying stairwells.

President Bradley
Two phases of air conditioning replacement were completed.

anything. They were tired of what was called a 'local parentis' (sic)." He went on, "If we had more Lincoln Quadrangles or had noticed how strong this trend was in our research, we probably wouldn't have done … Statesman Towers, although architecturally I think they were one of the better, stronger, building forms that we did."[97]

Miller reflected further on the transition from high-rise to apartment-style housing, "… when it came to designing the Lincoln Quadrangle, we said we think you'd better give up doing any more high-rise and give an alternate form of living. And those apartments remained fully occupied during the great rebellion of everybody moving away from campus."[98]

Miller continued, "But it got a most interesting award one time as being one of the most humane buildings that had been designed. It has a scale. And there was a security angle there, too, that was very good because you can … you enter all of those off-interior courts, and that was a concern that came up in the '60s. You know, how you prevent people from rioting through. It's funny how these things that we don't think about now … how really difficult that period was of '68 through '72 where we were trying to adapt buildings with big glass windows to this phenomena that we hadn't thought about …"[99]

The Board of Trustees authorized the administration to submit a loan application to the federal Department of Housing and Urban Development for $2 million for the second Lincoln Quad unit. The Trustees noted that nearly 1,400 students were currently residing in overcrowded facilities, and there was an urgent need to expand housing on campus. Unit #2 was to accommodate 805 students. ■

Memorial Stadium (the four-cornered track)

Original Stadium

Architect: Shourds-Stoner Company

Date: Groundbreaking: January 30, 1924
Dedication: May 4, 1925[100]

Location: 3300 Wabash Avenue

Phase Two

Architects: Ewing, Miller and Miller Associates, Inc. with Sverdrup and Parcel (St. Louis, Mo.) as consultants

Contractors: Glenroy Construction Company Inc.; Fred G. Christman (Plumbing); AAA Electric of Terre Haute Inc.[101]

Date: 1969-70

Cost: Approx. $2 million

Memorial Stadium was home to the Terre Haute Phillies and Terre Haute "Tots" baseball teams. Built of Bedford limestone, the stadium was originally designed to be a baseball field for Terre Haute baseball teams, and commemorate causalities from World War I.[102]

A special meeting of the Trustees was called for

October 8, 1966. At that meeting, the Board approved a lease agreement with the City of Terre Haute and Vigo County, whereby ISU would rent the stadium and golf course property from the city and county for 99 years, at an annual rate of $10 per year, until October 31, 2016.[103]

In 1969, the university submitted an increased expenditure request to the Indiana General Assembly to expend $2 million for the Stadium development. To help recover costs, the Trustees employed Sverdrup & Parcel, Architects and Engineers, to revise the earlier plan and increase seating from 11,700 to 15,000.[104]

Bids for the stadium renovation were received November 5, 1969, and awards made totaling $1.18 million.[105] The award for site development went to Shelton Hannig, Inc. in June 1971.[106]

The stadium was remodeled at two different times. The first was in 1967. Remodeling consisted of adding bleachers on the north side of the field, re-orienting the playing field, and installing Astro-turf. ISU was the first university/college to have an Astro-turf field.[107] The new grass must have benefited the Sycamores, who beat Eastern Illinois 41-6 in their first game on the new surface.

Phase Two included the demolition of the horseshoe shaped grandstand, installation of concrete stands, the addition of press boxes in the upper section of the stands, and the addition of dressing rooms on the west-end of the field. The $2 million project increased the stadium capacity to 20,500. Of the original structure, only the Memorial Arch remained.[108] It was refurbished to serve as the new entrance to the stadium.

The arch recalls triumphal arches dating back to Roman times. Points of comparison are the Arch of Titus (82 ACE), the Arch of Constantine (312-315 ACE) in Rome, and more recently, the Wellington Arch in London (1826-30). Essentially, a triumphal arch was composed of two massive piers carrying an archway. Triumphal arches were erected, usually by the Roman Senate, to celebrate the victories of the returning emperors. Typically, they were three-arched structures with a raised central arch, flanked on either side by somewhat smaller arches. Those at Memorial Stadium are much smaller in proportion to the Roman prototypes. The classical language is continued in the coffered vault of the central arch, with a pronounced classical cornice and diminutive attic story. Roman

Memorial Stadium Updates

President Benjamin

Project: Turf Replacement
Contractor: Wabash Valley Asphalt
Date: 2001-02
Cost: $642,538[109]

Project: The Indiana Mile
Date: Dedication: December 16, 2004

President Bradley

Project: Locker Room Renovations
Contractor: CDI
Project Managers: Steve Culp, Scott Tillman
Date: 2009-10
Cost: $749,978[110]

Project: Press Box Renovation
Contractor: Garmong
Project Manager: Scott Tillman
Date: 2009-10
Cost: $82,059[111]

Project: Artificial Turf
Date: 2009[112]
Cost: $896,768
(includes turf for baseball field)

The artificial turf for football and women's soccer was replaced and extended.

triumphal arches, by contrast, had vast sculptural programs commemorating the bravery of the emperor and his armies.

In 2004, the City of Terre Haute constructed a one-mile walking trail known as the "Indiana Mile" on the west side of the stadium. The trail, costing $109,000, was planned to be an important addition to the historic National Road.[113] Dr. Marion Jackson (ISU), the city, and TREES, Inc. planted 101 native trees along the mile-long recreational trail. This project reflected the increased collaboration between ISU, the City of Terre Haute, and community organizations.[114] ∎

Driver and Traffic Safety Instructional Demonstration Center

Architect: Ewing H. Miller

Contractors: Kuykendall Construction (General Construction); Sycamore Engineering (Mechanical); AAA Electric of Terre Haute (Electrical); Wabash Valley Asphalt Co. Inc. of Terre Haute (Asphalt)

Date: Dedication: June 18, 1970

Cost: $260,000[115]

Location: Vigo County Fairgrounds

Preliminary plans for the Driver and Traffic Safety Instructional Demonstration Center were presented by Ewing Miller to the Trustees in early 1969. The center was to be located at the Vigo County Fairgrounds. A $215,564 grant was received to build and equip the Center, however, funding proved inadequate to realize the entire complex.[116]

The Driver and Traffic Safety Instructional Demonstration Center was the first of its kind to be built on a university campus. The center consisted of two primary elements: a 500-foot-long oval track that could be arranged to simulate various driving conditions, and a building that housed classrooms, administrative offices, traffic simulation equipment, and study areas. The center served beginning drivers, as well as drivers preparing for licensure to drive commercial and postal vehicles.[117]

African American Cultural Center

President Rankin

Acquired: 1970

Location: 551 North Ninth Street

The former location of the African-American Cultural Center (AACC) was 551 North Ninth Street in the old Union Depot, where the Recreation East Track is located today.[118] The depot was purchased in 1970 during the Rankin Presidency and opened as the Center in 1973.[119]

During President Moore's administration, the Center was moved to its current facility, purchased in 1992 from the United Mine Workers. Following the move, the Union Depot was razed.

The current facility was constructed in 1950 and has 5,396 assignable square feet of space. It houses the offices and resources for programs relevant to African-American culture.

Relocation of the African American Cultural Center
President Moore

Move to the United Mine Workers Building

Architect: Samuel Hannaford

Contractor: Jared Construction Company

Date: Acquired: 1992[120]

Cost: $115,000 Purchase; $215,415 Renovations[121]

Area: 8,200 GSF; 5,396 ASF

Location: 301 North Eighth Street

On a motion by Tim O'Neill, seconded by Dr. Charlotte Zietlow, the Board approved the expenditure of $215,415 for renovation of the facility. The Board believed the move would better integrate the Center into campus and would allow for the demolition of the old Depot.[122] This move no doubt reflects President Moore's interest in diversifying the campus, and initiating programs that broadened participation of minorities in the life of the university.

The Center was home to several murals. Some were first installed in the original center and were moved to the current building, while others were created specifically for the current space.

One of the earliest works is "Man Child in the Promised Land" by Phillips Lindsey Mason in 1968.[123] The work owes to a book by the same title written by Claude Brown in 1965, which treats the hardships of boyhood living amid chaos in Harlem in the 1940s and 1950s. The target on the young boy's shirt is poignant. The painting is a large work with a strong trompe l'oeil effect. The cutoff Pepsi sign to the side, and general cropping of the painting, suggests a photographically inspired image.

Another work now in the Permanent Collection is a Malcolm X portrait by an artist signed as Block (identified as Steve Britt). Several murals from the original building were completed by Tony Shelby in 1976 and are now located in the current Center. Interestingly, Shelby was a high school student when he completed the work. ■

"Manchild in the Promised Land," Phillips Lindsey Mason, 1968

African American Cultural Center Rededication
President Bradley

Rededicated as the Charles E. Brown African-American Cultural Center

Date: April 21, 2012

Charles W. Brown was one of the campus leaders who devoted much of his career (30 years) to serving African-American and minority students, and Center programming. Bradley remarked, "Mr. Brown's accomplishments and impact have created a lasting legacy. This will ensure that this tribute will outlast the current structure housing the center."

Chapter 7 President Rankin

Cunningham Memorial Library

Architects: Archonics Corporation, Ewing Miller and Associates[124]

Contractors: Repp and Mundt, Inc. (General Construction); Prox and Burget Company (Plumbing and HVAC); The Sanborn Electric Company (Electrical); Dial Access Learning System[125]

Consultants: Keyes Dewitt Metcalf, Librarian Emeritus of Harvard University

Interior Design: Jane Miles, Inc.

Cost: $6.5 million

Date: Groundbreaking: January 15, 1971
Ribbon Cutting: January 11, 1973
Dedication: March 8, 1974

Area: 172,356 GSF; 134,172 ASF

Location: 510 North 6 ½ Street

Cunningham Memorial Library is a five-storied building named in honor of Arthur C. Cunningham, who was the first librarian for ISNS.[126] His dedication to the school was so sincere that he gave his house for the land upon which the Normal Library was built in 1909.

The increased enrollment on campus made the space available for students in Normal Library untenable. President Rankin noted that only four percent of the student population could use Normal Library at a time, and the campus needed a facility that could accommodate up to 25 percent of the student body, as well as new shelf space.[127]

Two consultants, Dr. Cecil Byrd and Dr. Raymond Miller, prepared a study of current and long-range needs. They presented their report to the Trustees in December 1965. National standards recommended a campus library should be able to accommodate 20-25 percent of the student body at any one time. The situation was so dire, President Rankin reported to the Board that the ground floor of Holmstedt Hall would be used temporarily to house the reserve book collection and seat about 140 students.[128] When completed, the architect said the library would hold 750,000 volumes and have seating for 2,000 students.

Ewing Miller took great pride in the design of Cunningham Memorial Library. In his interview with Jane Hazledine, he stated, "But I think that probably the library is the best building that we did, frankly."[129] Miller was pleased with the abstract formal properties of the design. "It's a formalist building. It has a classic simplicity and it really deserves fronting on a park."[130]

Miller also recommended the site for the new library. He pointed out the block between Center Street and Sixth Street south of the railroad and recommended that this centrally located space be identified as the best location. This was north of the Science Building and Holmstedt Hall, facing Center Street. He recommended Center Street be made a pedestrian way.[131]

Cunningham Library southeast view

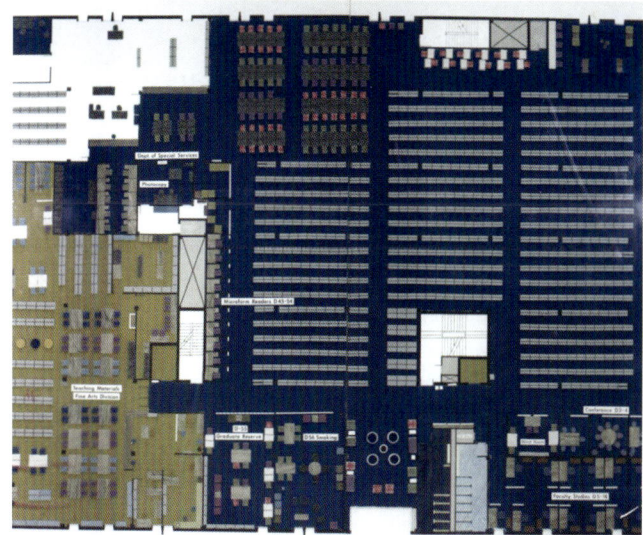

Cunningham Library second floor plan

"The true university of these days is a collection of books." – Thomas Carlyle[132]

Miller continued to experiment with new forms and concepts of design. Just as Statesman Towers made use of pre-cast concrete and "beton brut," and the Physical Education Building was surmounted by a folded concrete slab roof, Cunningham Library was also an innovative design that made use of new technologies in building. The exterior panels and windows comprising the facade could be removed and repositioned. For Miller, planning for the library's future required the building be designed with maximum flexibility.[133] The interior could be completely gutted and, as it was reconstituted, the facade panels could be reinstalled in response to the new interior design. Miller recognized no one could know exactly how a library might

Cunningham Library Rare Books Air Conditioning

President Landini

Architect: R. E. Dimond & Assoc.

Contractor: Sycamore Engineering

Cost: $202,000

Cunningham Library is home to two very important special collections. The first is the Cordell Collection of Dictionaries. It is the finest collection of dictionaries in the world and encompasses almost 10,000 volumes. The collection began in 1969 when Warren N. Cordell, an alumnus, donated 453 early-English dictionaries. Cordell died in 1980 but his wife, Suzanne, continued her interest in the collection.

The collection grew from 453 early-English dictionaries to 3,913 volumes. Additional editions were purchased with funds from the National Endowment for the Humanities, bringing the total to approximately 5,400 volumes. The earlier gifts were displayed in glass cases on shelving in the lobby and storage vault, but rapidly overflowed the available space. In 1985-86, a renovation program adding air conditioning and climate control was undertaken to house the complete world-famous collection.

The second major collection is the Debs Collection, consisting of pamphlets, letters, telegrams, manuscripts, scrapbooks, and other important artifacts concerning Terre Haute native Eugene V. Debs.[134]

Chapter 7 President Rankin

Warren and Suzanne Cordell

function 15 or 20 years into the future. He said, "… they didn't know where libraries were going or whether we were coming into the zippy-zooty age of all entirely electronic retrieval of information …"[135]

Miller received a letter from consultant Dr. Keyes Metcalf commending the planning. He wrote, "Taken as a whole … the series of drawings gives the finest preparation that I have ever seen of spatial relationships and the problems that have to be faced in connection with them. You have my hearty congratulations."[136]

Miller stated there were two elements of the library project that were innovative. The first was the use of moveable panels on the exterior. The second was the covered walkway that runs south from the library on the east side. Miller's original design would have continued the covered walkway from Cunningham to the "old campus" to the south. The walkway would provide safety for students during times of inclement weather and would serve to unify the campus. Reluctance to close streets precluded completion of the pedestrian walkway. "You think sometimes that you are

Cunningham Library coffee shop

Cunningham Library Updates

President Moore

Project: HVAC System and Lighting Upgrade

Contractors: Springhill Heating; AAA Electric Company

Date: 1993-94

Cost: $1.2 million

President Benjamin

Project: Installation of coffee shop

Contractor: GL Hair

Date: 2003-04

Cost: $56,465

President Bradley

Project: Commuter Lounge in Cunningham Library

Date: May 2009

Razed: 2002-03

Interior with original stained-glass panels from Normal Library

doing the right thing but it doesn't pan out in the long run."[137]

The building is five stories (with two below grade), with 230 feet frontage on 6 ½ Street. It measured more than three times the size of the old Normal Library and could accommodate about 2,000 users at any given moment. It was made of precast concrete with precast concrete trim.

A library moving company from Bloomington was hired to move the more than 750,000 books and other items to the new building. Students assisted with the move, which was carefully and skillfully planned by Fred Hanes, Dean of Libraries. ■

Jamison Hall

Date: Acquired: June 19, 1971
Dedication: September 18, 1971
Cost: $41,500

Area: 9,384 GSF
Location: 912 Chestnut Street

Jamison Hall was originally the Family Service Association Building and later housed the Department of Anthropology. Dean Turney and the School of Education faculty recommended to President Rankin that the building be named in honor of Dr. Olis G. Jamison, Principal of the Indiana State University Laboratory School (1928-38) and Chairman of the Department of Education (1946-60).[138] It was a functional brick-clad two-story structure with pronounced moldings surrounding two windows on either end of the facade that were larger than pairs of windows flanking the central doorway. The building had a simple cornice that separated the bottom from the top floor.

President Moore

Razed: 1997

The building was razed and the area turned into parking east of the Ballyhoo.

Chapter 7 President Rankin

Hulman Civic-University Center
(Hulman Center)

Architects: Sverdrup and Parcel, St. Louis; Ewing Miller Associates[139]

Contractors: Hickey Construction Co., Inc., (General Construction); Freitag-Weinhardt, Inc., (Mechanical); The Sanborn Electric Co., (Electrical)[140]

Interior Design: Jane Miles, Inc.

Date: Groundbreaking: December 17, 1971[141]
Opened: December 14, 1973

Cost: $10 million estimated[142]

Area: 174,011 GSF; 115,549 ASF

Location: 200 North Eighth Street

Renamed: Hulman Center, October 27, 1973[143]

Rankin launched the "Excellence in New Dimensions" development campaign with a goal of raising the funds from the private sector for this structure. The first phase of the campaign was a proposed union of the ISU Foundation and the community to create the University Civic Auditorium. It was reported to the Trustees in 1962 that the Hulman Foundation inquired about the university's interest in a proposed Civic Auditorium and contributed $2.5 million for the project. The estimate for the project was $8 million. The community was to raise $1.5 million, the private sector $4 million, and the balance to come from the campaign. Raising these funds proved more difficult than expected.

In early 1969, the firm of Sverdrup & Parcel and Associates, Inc., Consulting Engineers was asked to develop a feasibility study for a proposed multipurpose building.[144] This same firm also advised on the renovation of Memorial Stadium. At a special meeting of the Board in August 1969, President Rankin announced a pledged gift of $2.5 million from an anonymous donor.[145] According to the approved feasibility plans, the projected cost for the Arena would be approximately $8 million. He proposed the university commit to raise $1 million to add to the gift and finance the remainder with the sale of revenue bonds. The Trustees approved his four-point plan which included engaging Ewing Miller Associates and Sverdrup & Parcel and Associates, Inc., in the project.[146]

In the spring of 1970, more details about the proposed building were shared with the Trustees. The architects-planners proposed an unconventional building. The 80-foot high building, it was stated, would have large exterior columns. These were not included in final plans. The building was to be constructed of concrete, glass, and metal paneling. The material used for the exterior was changed to a Fluropon finish that was considered more permanent and rust resistant. The playing floor was to be surfaced with Tartan. It was decided the major entrance would be on the west side of the building with an entry also on Cherry Street off a plaza.

To construct the building and provide access, it would be necessary to close Eighth and Mulberry Streets. The Masonic Temple Association and 2,046 Terre Haute citizens filed remonstrances opposing the vacation of public streets. The Terre Haute Board of Public Works and Safety met on Janaury 12, 1971 and voted unanimously to close the streets in order for the project to continue. The call for bids went out immediately and were to be received by February 24, 1971.[147]

The Masonic Temple Association continued to challenge earlier decisions that granted ISU and the city permission to make street closures necessary for erecting the Center. In April, President Rankin reported Judge Gallagher in Vermillion County declined to support the efforts of the Masons to block the closure of Eighth Street. Both Rankin and Board

Hulman Center Updates
President Moore

Project: Several interior projects including the Fly Loft, Outer concourse area and water heaters.

Contractors: Beck, Inc. (Fly Loft); Concourse (ASI, Whitehouse, and Garmong); Springhill Plumbing and Heating (Water Heaters).

Date: 1994-95

Cost: 485,809.00

Project: Installation of Daktronics Scoreboard

Contractor: CDI, Inc.

Cost: $504,000 (Terre Haute First National Bank paid for the scoreboard.)

Project: Locker Room Renovation

Contractor: Hannig Construction

Date: 1996-97

Cost: $453,536

President McCutchan were adamant in stating it was the intention of the university to build the Center.[148]

The bids received presented another set of problems. The construction bid of $7.91 million was within a manageable range, but the electrical and mechanical bids exceeded estimates. The State Examiner recommended rejecting the bids and re-advertising. The Trustees were given optional steps for further cost reduction by the Project Architects but the preferred option would raise the cost to $12 million. The State Budget Director believed approvals could be gained to increase the project cost by $4 million if the university increased its bonding by $2 million and raised the other $2 million from non-university sources. President Rankin advised the Board the efforts would be made to continue to raise funds while working with the architects to reduce costs further.[149]

By the following month, May, the road closure issue was not settled and the Trustees decided to reject all bids and ask the architects to design a slightly smaller facility that still served the functions contained in the original plan.[150] The initial plan sat on eight acres and provided arena seating for 12,000 and banquet seating for 1,200 to 1,400 people. The plan also provided movable dividers enabling the arena to be reduced for stage events for 3,000 to 8,400 people.

The architects returned twice between May and June with revised plans. The Building Committee and architects were present at a press conference scheduled for June 4 to respond to questions regarding the status of the project and to "reactivate" a flagging fund drive. The new plans showed a building reduced in size seating 10,000 instead of 12,000. The smaller footprint meant the closing of 8th Street was no longer an issue. The height of the building was reduced from 80 feet to 72 feet. Bid specifications were expected to be completed by October, construction underway by December 1971, and be opened for use by December 1973.[151] Another hurdle was crossed when the State Budget Agency approved the total cost of $10 million.[152]

Bids for the Civic Center were advertised in October with a due date in November. The Trustees formally approved the plans and specifications in October. Bids were received in November and contracts totaling $6.54 million were let.

Student fees had to be raised by $2 per semester hour (on average $24 to $30 per semester for a full time student) because of reduced enrollment and the need to provide $545,000 debt service annually to finance the Center.[153] They were again raised in November of the same year.[154]

During the excavation of the site, it was discovered that the Interurban tracks were under the building site. In further digging, an oil well was uncovered. Remediation and capping required an additional expenditure of approximately $43,000.[155] ∎

Chapter 7 President Rankin

Bill Wolfe, "The Legend-Larry Bird," bronze, 2013

Hulman Center Updates
President Benjamin

Project: New Scoreboard

Contractors: NRK (Lighting); Sign Group; Springhill Plumbing and Heating

Date: 2000-02

Cost: $1.04 million; $711,942 Theatrical Rigging

Contractor: First Team

Cost: $294,000

Several improvements were made to the Center. These included new blue seats for the lower concourse, an up-to-date electronic scoreboard, and a "theatre wedge" contributed by the Hulman George family. In 2001-02, new lighting, signs, and repair work were completed. In addition, ADA seating was installed, the exterior painted, a new basketball floor installed, and theatrical lighting (in association with the "wedge") and steam line replacement.[156]

Presidents Bradley and Curtis

Architect: Ratio

Contractor: Hannig Construction Co., Inc.

Date: 2018-20

Cost: $37.5 million state appropriation

Area: 80,000 ASF

The Commission for Higher Education approved ISU's plan to proceed with Hulman renovations and recommended approval to the State Budget Committee. The General Assembly had appropriated $37.5 million in 2015 for the renovation of Hulman Center. No doubt, a favorable decision was premised upon the potential economic development value of the project positively affecting the Wabash Valley. The university planned to use the $37.5 million state appropriation, raise $1 million in gifts, use cash reserves totaling $4.7 million, and fund the balance through indebtedness. The decision was made to adopt a phased approach beginning with renovation and adding the conference center at some future date when a viable plan is in place.

Phase 1 renovation will update obsolete systems that date to 1973. This includes replacement of electrical and mechanical systems and resurfacing the exterior where the metal panel cladding has failed. Safety and fire protection systems will be upgraded. The inadequate loading dock and single elevator currently serving the entire building will be upgraded.

Indiana State University Building a Legacy

Student Health Center[157]

Architect: Ewing Miller and Associates[158]

Contractors: Glenroy Construction Company, Inc.; Freitage-Weinhardt, Inc.; The Sanborn Electric Company[159]

Date: Dedication: June 17, 1972

Cost: $2.11 million

Location: 530 North Fifth Street

Area: 54,475 GSF; 33,892 ASF

Owing to enrollment growth, the need for a student health facility was critical. The previous student health clinic, located in what is today Gillum Hall, had two wards with ten beds each and saw on average 250 to 300 students each day.[160]

The site for the Student Health Center, originally approved by the Trustees, was located between Fifth and Sixth Streets facing Chestnut. The entire building as planned would require the removal of East and West Knisely and the Mary Stewart Buildings – used to house faculty offices. Because offices were in short supply, it was decided to leave the buildings and move the proposed location of the Health Center. Ewing Miller proposed the building site be moved west to the corner of Fifth and Chestnut Streets, facing Fifth Street.[161] The change of location required the building plans to be modified. Mr. David Field, representing Ewing Miller Associates, presented preliminary plans showing the building being shortened by 24 feet with a third story added.[162] The psychiatric area was moved to the third floor.

The Governor did not accept the Miller plans.[163] He returned the request for project approval, "asking that the building be scaled down."[164] Miller responded to the Board, stating the building was comparable in cost to recently constructed buildings elsewhere. He suggested eliminating the pre-cast concrete panels (which he used often in his buildings), which could save $10,000, or they could remove the third floor. The Board asked the administration to meet with Governor Branigin and ask him to reconsider. In January, Ewing Miller and Associates, Inc. was appointed as architects for the project. Miller had presented preliminary plans the previous September.[165] The State Budget Committee, in response, asked that the architects appear before the committee in the near future.[166] A new proposal for the Health Center was sent to the Governor and State Budget Committee in March 1969.[167] In essence, the university's inability to gain the approval of Governor Branigin caused the project to be suspended in 1966 and renewed much later in August 1969. The Board noted the fact that the cost of the center had increased between $200,000 and $300,000 since the project was first initiated.[168]

Chapter 7 President Rankin

Success came in April 1969 when the Governor and State Budget Agency approved the request to construct the facility. The cost was estimated at $2.11 million, with the basement and third floor left mostly unfinished, with room for 38 patient beds on the second floor, and a small kitchen. Miller again proposed using precast concrete.[169] Bids were received and opened on March 31.[170] The bids were close to the estimate and totaled $2.01 million.

Following its completion, the Student Health Services program located in the Administration Building (now Gillum Hall) was moved to the new facility. The move provided much needed additional space in the Administration Building. ∎

Student Health Center Third Floor Completion
President Landini

Architect: Walter Scholer and Associates, Inc.

Contractors: Majors & Sons, Inc.; Harrah Plumbing & Heating Company, Inc.; Potter Engineering & Construction Company, Inc.[171]

Date: July 1982

Cost: $551,946[172]

The third floor of the Student Health Center was not finished, owing to budget restrictions when the original structure was built. The Trustees approved the new plan, calling for the installation of two electron microscopes, laboratories, and an area to be used by the Department of Life Sciences and the Center for Medical Technology. Bids came in higher than budgeted. Landini was authorized to secure an additional $250,000 from state officials.[173]

Student Health Center Updates
President Moore

Project: Third floor remodel for Athletic Training

Contractor: Springhill Plumbing and Heating

Date: 1999

Cost: $53,850

President Bradley

Project 1: Renovation

Architect: MMS A/E, Inc.

Project Managers: Steve Culp and Bryan Duncan

Contractors: Hannig (first floor Athletic Training, Physical Therapy Labs); CDI, Inc. (Wellness and Applied Medicine 2nd and 3rd floors); UAP Area CDI

Date: 2009-11

Cost: $1 million

These renovations constituted the completion of the Sports Therapy and Union Health Care portion of the building. It encompassed transforming offices into patient rooms, a nurse's station, a waiting area, and laboratory space. The second phase created the new physical therapy facility.[174]

Project 2: Creation of Physical Therapy Labs

Contractor: Hannig

Date: 2012-13

Cost: $384,127[175]

Project 3: Occupational Therapy/Physical Therapy 3rd Floor Renovations

Contractor: Hannig

Date: 2013-14

Cost: $520,750[176]

Link Building (Rankin Hall)

Architect: Ewing Miller Associates, Inc.

Contractor: Repp and Mundt, Inc.[177]

Date: Dedication: 1972

Cost: $2.28 million

Area: 37,337 GSF; 22,147 ASF

Location: 210 North Seventh Street

The Link Building is first mentioned in a report presented by representatives of Interior Space Design, Inc. of Chicago. Hired to advise on the expansion of Tirey Union facilities, they recommended the construction of a "link building" between the Union and the recently acquired Elks Lodge to the south.[178] That recommendation was accepted, and the Link Building, as it was originally called, was added to the east side of the campus to connect the Elks building that had been purchased by the college and the Student Union building (now Tirey Hall).[179]

Miller conceived of the building as a gateway onto the campus quadrangle off Seventh Street. At the time, Seventh Street defined the eastern border of the campus south of Chestnut, so defining a principle entrance at this point was directionally important. The renovations in Tirey Hall, which functioned as the student union, were designed to move large eating spaces and the grill underground south of the union. This provided the opportunity to create the gateway and put a building on top for offices and meeting rooms. More recently, the below ground area has been used to house campus computing equipment.

The Link Building is a three-story office building that originally provided office space for Student Union staff,

Howard Kalish, "Chorus of Trumpets," stainless steel, aluminum, tinted urethane, 2011

Chapter 7 President Rankin

Link Building Updates

President Landini

Architects: Scholer Corporation; Interior Design by Ratio Interiors

Contractor: CDI, Inc.

Date: Remodeled: 1992

Cost: $1.16 million

President Landini oversaw major renovations, including new surfaces, lighting, fire suppression, and mechanical equipment and elevators.

The entire complex comprised of Rankin, Tirey, and Parsons Hall were formally named "University Pavilion" in March 1992.[180]

President Moore

The building was renamed in honor of President Rankin on January 28, 1993 (Founders Day). President Rankin was honored to have the building named for him and quipped he was glad the "honor wasn't posthumous."

President Bradley

Contractor: Garmong

Project Managers: Steve Culp and Bryan Duncan

Date: 2011

Cost: $1.83 million[181]

This project involved the installation of a new green (environmentally friendly) roof, a sign of ISU's ongoing commitment to energy conservation.

activities, and students. Miller described the material used for the exterior of the Link Building and how it reflected the impact on building costs. Much of the campus, until his time, was made of face brick and limestone for bases and trim. The next development in building was the use of pre-cast concrete. Miller described how they used limestone as an aggregate in making the pre-cast so it appeared like limestone. The Link Building, however, is made of limestone slabs. Miller stated, "The economy changed, and pre-cast became more expensive, and they learned … how to really cut limestone very thin (to) reduce the weight."[182] Miller also stated the use of limestone helped connect this new structure to Tirey Hall and the Elks building.[183]

The Link Building is noteworthy for its circular form that provides maximum floor area for minimum cost and narrow slotted windows. Miller stated the circular form "gave a lightness to the building, particularly with the walkway underneath …" Ewing Miller must have been particularly sensitive to the way this building joined the old Elks Club and Tirey Memorial, because Warren Miller (Ewing's uncle) and Ralph Yeager had designed Tirey Hall and Matthew Miller the Elks Building. Miller discussed the design issues further. He noted this was a complex site because there was a problem of scale linking the quad with the tall churches on the east side of Seventh Street. The building also needed to respect the neoclassical style of the Elks building and Fairbanks Library. He noted the campus was crisscrossed by streets, and he wanted to create a substantial entry to the campus that opened onto the quiet of the quadrangle. The streetscape was not going to change, so, "he needed to do something different." The round structure was intended to define a different and memorable spatial experience. As an architect, he also appreciated the challenges a round building presented, pointing to the Hirschhorn Museum (1969) in Washington, D.C. Its placement, and the subtlety of its curved surfaces, made it a strong statement, and as he described it, "a more intimate piece of work."[184]

Today, the building houses administrative offices. ∎

Mary Stewart Building

Date: Purchased: October 15, 1963

Cost: $45,000

Location: 410 North Sixth Street

The Mary Stewart Building was acquired when on-campus housing was at a premium. A purchase agreement was reached in August for $45,000. Vice President Moulton informed the Trustees that approximately $30,000 in repairs was being made to have the facility ready for the arrival of residents in the Cuban Refuge Family Project.

Over time it housed 110 graduate assistants, the Upward Bound Program, the Social Science Education Center, and office and laboratory space. The building was destroyed by fire on January 5, 1971. Following the fire, rather than rebuild the apartments, the administration proposed applying the insurance settlement of $234,213 to remodel old residences, provide offices for those displaced, purchase portable classrooms, air condition the Fine Arts Building, and an assortment of other improvements.

One might assume Fine Arts was selected in order to maintain a climate controlled environment for instruments and art objects, but the decision was, in fact, made because it was considered more economical than air conditioning Dreiser or Parsons Hall. In December, the Board revised its plans. Estimates for air conditioning all three buildings totaled $869,000. The Board recommended the sale of bonds and receipt of fees to finance the projects.

Art Annex

Date: Acquired: 1972

Area: 13,800 GSF; 12,732 ASF

Location: 537 North Fourth Street

Creating art is sometimes thought of as a quiet and solitary activity, but it also requires large working areas, heavy equipment, and air quality control. To meet some of these requirements, the Annex was acquired in 1972. It formerly served as a food warehouse. Today it provides studio/classroom space for 3-D design, ceramics, and sculpture.

Chapter 7 References

1. U.S. Decennial Census.
2. See: http:utimes.pitt.edu/?p=4851 for an article published March 18, 1999 in the University Times (Feature, Volume 31, Issue 14) written shortly after Rankin's death. A graduate program in International Relations was developed during his presidency at ISU but was not approved by the Indiana Commission for Higher Education.
3. The Pittsburgh Symphony Orchestra gave their performance on the evening of April 13, 1966.
4. "In the 1920s, only 1 in 5 Americans graduated from high school. By the mid-1960s, however, nearly 3 out of 4 students finished high school, and about half of these students went on to college." See: http:www.lessonsite.com/archivepages/historyof the world/lesson31/p.
5. Rankin reported to the Trustees that a gas canister had been tossed into the entrance of the ROTC and Financial Aid Offices and groups of students protested military recruiters on campus. Trustee Minutes, February 19, 1972, C, p. 226 and May 20, 1972 VC, p. 316.
6. This site is now occupied by the John T. Myers Technology Center. The building was named "Alumni Center" by the Trustees. Trustee Minutes, June 17, 1966, XIII, p. 285.
7. Trustee Minutes, May 18, 1974, C, p. 384.
8. Trustee Minutes, April 20, 1974, K, p. 340.
9. Budget woes were not new. President Emens of Ball State remarked in 1965 that the General Assembly had decided that "… the taxpayer can't afford to build classroom buildings, but the students can." Glenn White, The Ball State Story, p. 118.
10. Trustee Minutes, May 26, 1973, C, p. 308.
11. Trustee Minutes, November 23, 1974, E, p. 115.
12. Trustee Minutes, March 16, 1974, C, p. 293.
13. Trustee Minutes, April 20, 1974, K, pp. 340-341. This is essentially a statement of bankruptcy that allows the institution to take whatever measures necessary to regain solvency, including the termination of tenured faculty. The Trustees expressed concern with respect to the reduction of faculty and passed an amendment stating it was the intention of the Board to endeavor to avoid terminations.
14. For example, the closing of the Statesman Towers and Sandison food service led to student protests.
15. Trustee Minutes, June 16, 1973, I, p. 383.
16. The University of Southern Indiana became autonomous in 1985.
17. Ibid, February 16, G, pp. 269-270.
18. The number of associate (two-year) degree programs preparing graduates for post-degree employment grew significantly. For example, in April 1974, an associate degree in secretarial science was approved by the Commission for Higher Education and in May, 1975, an associate degree in real estate was introduced. Trustee Minutes, October 19, 1974, C, p. 88 and April 26, 1975, I, p. 288. Ironically, the Commission for Higher Education during the Moore and Benjamin administrations urged ISU to give up its two-year programs because they were unnecessarily duplicative of Ivy Tech programs that students could take more economically.
19. Trustee Minutes, October 21, 1972, G.
20. During Rankin's presidency, the university created the "Freshman Opportunity Program" for students who had not performed well in high school but wanted to attend college. It was stated this was "… in keeping with the university's historic function of increasing an individual student's opportunities for worthwhile achievement rather than restricting or limiting admissions." Between 1966 and 1970, 1,950 students were admitted into this program. In essence, ISU was continuing to follow an open admissions policy, which did affect its reputation.
21. Trustee Minutes, October 21, 1972, G, p. 108. President Rankin also reported to the Board that he was not provided a copy of the second volume, delineating a plan for future growth prior to its release by the Commission for Higher Education.
22. Rankin stated in his Five Year Report (1970) that more than half of residence halls had been added in the past five years. Enrollment for 1969-70 was 13,319.
23. The celebration of the opening must have been eclipsed when, on March 17, there was a major train derailment between Fifth and Sixth Streets near Tippecanoe that led to the spillage of vinyl chloride, which is both toxic and explosive. Trustee Minutes, April 20, 1974, D, p. 337.
24. In 2016 dollars, the building would cost about $45 million, assuming an inflation rate of about four percent per year. Ground breaking for the Center was held on December 17, 1971 and it opened on December 14, 1973.
25. The first Symposium of Contemporary American Music at ISU, with support from the Rockefeller Foundation, was held May 8-11, 1967. See: http://www.2.indstate.edu/music/cmf/history/history.html.
26. Trustee Minutes, February 17, 1973, p. 233 and Exhibit B., Sect. 1. The site was located on the east side of North Third Street between Mulberry and Eagle Streets. At Landini's first meeting with the Board, the Trustees approved a lease agreement for

Indiana State University Building a Legacy

27. Trustee Minutes, September 19, 1969.
28. Trustee Minutes, April 20, 1974, A, p. 334.
29. Ibid.
30. Repp and Mundt, Inc. was founded in 1948 in Columbus, Indiana.
31. Trustee Minutes, April 2, 1965, Exhibit A.
32. In his inaugural speech, President Hines had advocated for changing the name of Indiana State Normal School to Indiana State Teachers College.
33. Miller stated in an interview with Michael Flowers in 2015, "… there were supposed to be four that were done just like Sandison and Gillum … we changed that because of our research." Flowers, p. 51. The name of the building identified as Gillum was transferred to the former Administration Building, allowing the former residence hall to be renovated and renamed Hulman Memorial Student Union.
34. Flowers, p. 47.
35. Flowers, p. 51.
36. Miller Interview, June 27, 2018.
37. Miller, E. (1968) "Put a behavioral scientist on the dormitory design team." College and University Business 44, February, 68.
38. Indiana State University Facilities Management Completed Projects, June 30, 1999, p. 25.
39. Indiana State University Physical Plant Building Projects: 2001-02, n.p.
40. Trustee Minutes, November 18, 1966, XVI: A.
41. Trustee Minutes, July 19, 1968, V: B.
42. Trustee Minutes, October 19, 1968, IV.
43. Trustee Minutes, March 17, 1973, D.
44. Interview with Ewing Miller, June 27, 2018.
45. Trustee Minutes, April 17, 1969, Exhibit A.
46. Trustee Minutes, July 18, 1969, Sec. II: A. The Department of Health, Education, and Welfare and the Office of Education approved a grant of $702,550 for construction. Trustee Minutes, March 21, 1969, Sec. II: B.
47. Ewing Miller Associates, Inc. was appointed to prepare plans and specifications for the project. Trustee Minutes, May 27, 1966, VIII: A. Trustees approved schematic plans and use of Corten steel. Trustee Minutes, September 20, 1968, IV.
48. Plans were being developed and the decision had been made to locate the building behind the Walden Apartments on the south side of Chestnut Street, opposite the Laboratory School. Nursing was currently located in Holmstedt Hall.
49. Trustee Minutes, July 18, 1969, I. Ewing Miller explained the building was simply conceived and could be expanded.
50. Trustee Minutes, April 17, 1969, Item I.
51. Trustee Minutes, December 12, 1969, Item I.
52. Trustee Minutes, March 20, 1971, Sec. C, and April 17, 1971, Sec. C.
53. Mid Republic Construction, Inc. (General Construction, $630,227); Healy Mechanical Contractors (Mechanical, $341,100); and B-A, Inc., (Electrical Construction, $168,700). Trustee Minutes, October 24, 1969, Sec. II: A.
54. The Trustees gave authorization to submit a request to the State Budget Agency and Governor for approval to apply for a $1 million federal grant to assist with construction cost. Trustee Minutes, June 16, 1967, IX: C. Ewing Miller Associates, Inc. was appointed the architecture firm for the project pending approval of the Governor. President Rankin announced a grant of $1 million from the Department of Health, Education, and Welfare Public Health Services. Trustee Minutes, December 20, 1968, Sec. II: A.
55. The decision to contract the architectural firm of Ewing Miller Associates, Inc. to design Unit No. 1 was made in October 1965. Trustee Minutes, October 2, 1965, IX: 3. Preliminary plans for the then named East Residence Hall unit 1 were presented to and approved by the Trustees February 4, 1966. Trustee Minutes, February 4, 1966, Item VI. The Board authorized the administration to make application to the Department of Housing and Urban Development for a loan of $2.6 million to supplement a bond issue for $4.31 million. Trustee Minutes, February 4, 1966, Exhibit B. Final plans were approved in April. Trustee Minutes, April 22, 1966, IX: A.
56. F. A. Wilhelm Construction Company, Inc. (General Construction, $5.15 million); Freitag-Weinhardt Company Inc., (Plumbing, Heating, and Ventilation, $1.72 million); Sanborn Electric Company, (Electrical, $726,000). Trustee Minutes, July 15, 1966, VII: B.
57. For example, enrollment in the spring term 1973 dropped by 851 students. Trustee Minutes, February 17, 1973, C. Rankin stated enrollment figures for next year did not look encouraging.
58. Interview with Ewing Miller, June 27, 2018.
59. Trustee Minutes, February 19, 1966, XV: B.
60. Ibid.
61. Trustee Minutes, April 22, 1966, X: A. The Trustees officially accepted the completed building (East Tower) at their September 1968 meeting. Trustee Minutes, September 20, 1968, V: B.
62. Enrollment in campus housing continued to drop, forcing the Board to repeatedly increase room rates in order to cover increased construction costs, bond interest, and the loss of room revenue. Trustee Minutes, March 20, 1971, D.
63. Flowers, p. 58.
64. During the presidencies of Holmstedt and Rankin, 15 residence halls had been constructed. The unoccupied towers presented another problem. ISU, of all public universities in Indiana, had the highest assignable square feet compared to Indiana University for example. The excess square footage proved an obstacle to obtaining funds for other academic and service buildings. The suggestion of remodeling the Towers for academic use was underway in 1975 when a request was made to the State Budget Agency for $500,000 to begin renovation. Trustee Minutes, June 14, 1975, F: 3.
65. Renovation of the west tower was designed by Dagget, Naegelle, & Associates in 1976. The eastern tower was renovated in 1981.
66. Hazledine, p. 34.
67. Flowers, pp. 150-151.
68. Miller acknowledged the influence of Louis Kahn while at the University of Pennsylvania. He described Kahn as "… one of the great American geniuses in the contemporary movement." Hazledine, p. 21. Miller related an interesting story. Having graduated, he was hired by an architectural firm that specialized in the archaizing Beaux-Arts style buildings for $35 a week. He wanted to work for Kahn and asked Kahn if he could pay him the same amount. Kahn responded, "No-to work with me you pay me $35 per week." Miller Interview, June 27, 2018.
69. Email to the author from Ewing Miller, July 30, 2018.
70. "2013 AIA Indiana Service Award Winners."
71. Garmong Construction Company (General Construction, $273,065); Sycamore Engineering (Mechanical and Electrical, $542,700).
72. The State Budget Agency approved $500,000 for remodeling the tower to house the School of Education. President Landini was authorized to engage M & E Engineering to provide engineering services for this project as well as air conditioning for Reeve Hall and the School of Technology. Trustee Minutes, June 14, 1975, F: 3. Changes in Construction Codes and additional changes requested by the School of Education increased costs to exceed the $500,000 estimate. Trustee Minutes, October 24, 1975, M. The university received approval for an additional $430,000. Trustee Minutes, June 4, 1976, J: 1.
73. Trustee Minutes, June 4, 1976, J: 2.
74. Trustee Minutes, July 9, 1976, pp. 113-14.
75. Trustee Minutes, July 1, 1977, H.
76. Trustee Minutes, November 9, 1978, H.

77 Ibid, July 17, 1979, I.

78 Indiana State University Facilities Management Completed Projects, 1979-80, p. 55.

79 Ibid, July 7, 1978, F.

80 One of President Benjamin's goals was to move some of the college population across Cherry Street in order to provide an economic stimulus for the city.

81 In October 1974, Trustee Minutes show the Board was considering several options for the Towers. A Chicago firm had studied using them for commercial use and a hotel. M & E Engineering Service, Inc., conducted a study to determine if the towers could be used for elderly housing and the State Budget Committee had been asked by the administration to approve conversion to academic facilities. Trustee Minutes, October 19, 1974, E. A capital funds requests for $1.8 million for the conversion was submitted.

82 Flowers, p. 142.

83 Funding came from residence hall and university facility reserve funds. Trustee Minutes, February 22, 2013, 5r.

84 Trustee Minutes, February 22, 2013, 5r.

85 The Ewing Miller Associates firm was appointed to prepare plans and specifications for construction in January 1967. Trustee Minutes, January 5, 1967, VI: A.

86 Approval was given by the Trustees for the university to make application for a federal grant for constructing this facility. Trustee Minutes, March 17, 1967, XII.

87 Trustee Minutes, December 16, 1966, XXI, p. 418 and January 5, 1967, VI: A, p 417.

88 Trustee Minutes, January 5, 1967, VI.

89 Trustee Minutes, February 17, 1967, XXV: 3.

90 Trustee Minutes, October 24, 1969, H, p. 130.

91 Trustee Minutes, November 21, 1969, B.

92 It was President Rankin who proposed the name "Lincoln Quadrangles." It was decided, since two buildings were involved, to name them Lincoln North & Lincoln South. Trustee Minutes, December 20, 1968, Sec. 1, K, p. 190.

93 By 1986, when a survey of the buildings was conducted by Perkins and Will, it was found that the precast concrete spandrels were cracked and near failure. On the interior, all of the concrete block walls that run perpendicular to the exterior walls were cracked and the bond between the walls was broken.

94 Lincoln Quadrangles Unit No. 1 was formally accepted by the Trustees in November 1969. Trustee Minutes, November 21, 1969, C.

95 Trustee Minutes, September 20, 1968, Exhibit H. The university would sell a bond issue for $4.6 million, having secured a Federal grant for $2 million.

96 Approval of Allen and Aikman. Trustee Minutes, May 6, 1988, M.

97 Flowers, p. 142.

98 Ewing H. Miller, interview by Jane Hazledine, Terre Haute, Indiana, April 13, 1981, p. 36, transcript, Vigo County Oral History Project in Local History Books Online: Oral Histories, Vigo County Public Library.

99 Hazledine, interview, p. 37. The building was formally accepted by the Board in November 1969. Trustee Minutes, November 21, 1969, C.

100 The Shourds-Stoner Company was also responsible for the John T. Beasley Building (Citizens Gas and Fuel Company, Terre Haute Gas Corporation).

101 Trustee Minutes, November 21, 1969, Sec. II: A.

102 Bronze plaques bearing the names of the 6,780 casualties were attached to the arch.

103 Trustee Minutes, September 9, 1966, p. 367.

104 Trustee Minutes, November 15, 1968, Section II: C, p. 174. The architect and consultants reported on the second stage of planning in September 1969. The plan provided for 20,500 seats and preservation of the Memorial Arch that will serve as the principle entrance into the stadium. Trustee Minutes, September 19, 1969, L.

105 Trustee Minutes, November 21, 1969, Section II: A, p. 190.

106 Trustee Minutes, June 19, 1971, A, p. 479.

107 New Astro-Turf was installed and striped by Monsanto Co. in 1977-78 at a cost of $250,580. Physical Plant Projects Fiscal Year 1977-78, p. 79. The turf was replaced by Al Pro in 1988-89 at a cost of $381,000. Astro-turf (now called AstroPlay) was installed again in time for the 2001 season at a cost of approximately $700,000 The original turf was not installed correctly according to Andi Myers, Indiana State University Athletic Director. Reported by Mark Bennett, Terre Haute Tribune Star, August 3, 2001, p. B 1 and 5.

108 Trustee Minutes, June 16, 1967, XVIII, p. 550. The Board appointed Sverdrup & Parcel and Associates, Inc., as consultants for the Stadium rehabilitation and to prepare for the installation of Astroturf. It also approved the demolition plan and financing for the demolition work.

109 Indiana State University Facilities Management Completed Projects, June 30, 2002, p. 13.

110 Department of Facilities Management Annual Report 2009-10, pp. III-I.

111 Ibid.

112 Approved by the Trustees. Trustee Minutes, February 27, 2009, p. 13. Funding was to come from auxiliary reserves.

113 Peter Ciancone, "Trail to include 'Disco Ernie' memorial," Tribune Star, September 18, 2004, p. A4.

114 See letter from Greg Ruark, Superintendent of Parks and Recreation, to Kevin Runion, Associate Vice President for Facilities Management.

115 The U.S. Department of Transportation National Highway Bureau provided funding of $215,564, matched with funds from the Indiana Department of Traffic Safety.

116 Trustee Minutes, February 21, 1969, K. An additional $87,000 would be required to pay for the classroom and the planned garage would have to postpone.

117 See: http://library.indstate.edu/archives/exhibits/architecture/Driving andTrafficSafetyCenter.htm.

118 The architect for the Union Depot was Samuel Hannaford from Cincinnati.

119 Representatives of black students met with President Rankin in May 1972. The students expressed their concern that the university was not moving expeditiously to complete the Center. Rankin explained this was a complicated matter because the university was renovating property it did not own, but he stated all contracts had been let and furniture ordered; and he expected it would be finished during the summer of 1972, University Archives Box 4848.

120 Trustee Minutes, June 5, 1992, C: 2.

121 Ibid, October 21, 1994, Sec. I, K.

122 Trustee Minutes, October 21, 1994, Sec. 1, p. 8.

123 Mason was born in St Louis, MO in 1939 and studied at UC Berkeley. An African American, he painted figures studies and street genre. Edan Hughes, "Artists in California," 1786-1940.

124 The architectural firm Archonics (Ewing Miller and Associates) was appointed by the Trustees at their June 16, 1967 meeting. The State Budget Agency approved this appointment on June 26, 1967, but construction was delayed pending approval of additional bonding authority by the Indiana General Assembly. The estimated cost was $6.5 million. The Trustees approved final plans in July 1970. Trustee Minutes, July 24, 1970, F. Trustee Minutes, November 21, 1969, Item D, p. 156.

125 Trustee Minutes, December 18, 1970, Sec. II: A, p. 185.

126 Cunningham served as the university's first librarian from 1890-1928. Library holdings increased from 5,300 volumes to over 100,000 during his tenure. The Trustees approved the dedication to Arthur Cunningham at their June 1965 meeting. Trustee Minutes, June 18, 1965, XXI: B. Cunningham gave his house for the land on which Normal Hall is located.

127 Alan Rankin, President's Report:1965-70, p. 13.

128 Trustee Minutes, December 18, 1965, XII, p. 151.

129 Hazledine, p. 38.

130 Miller interview, p. 39.

131 Trustee Minutes, November 15, 1968, Sec. 1, G.

132 These were the opening words spoken by Dr. Keyes Metcalf at the dedication of the Library.

133 Mr. Robert Miller, project director, stated, "The building must be flexible. Technology is developing so rapidly that it is difficult to know where we are going or what will be needed within a few years." Trustee Minutes, November 15, 1968, Sec. 1, G.

134 Eugene Victor Debs (November 5, 1855 – October 20, 1926) was an American socialist, political activist, and trade unionist. He was five times the candidate of the Socialist Party of America for President of the United States.

135 Hazledine, p. 38.

136 Trustee Minutes, November 21, 1969, Sec. I, I.

137 Flowers, p. 153.

138 Trustee Minutes, September 18, 1971, F, p. 55.

139 Sverdrup & Parcel was a civil engineering company formed in 1928 in St. Louis by Sverdrup and his college engineering professor Parcel. The company's specialty was bridges. The firm built the I-35W bridge in Minneapolis that collapsed in 2007. Miller decided early in the process that his firm would leave the project.

140 Trustee Minutes, November 13, 1971, G. Hickey Construction Co., Inc., (General Construction, $3.94 million); Freitag-Weinhardt, Inc., (Mechanical, $1.85 million); The Sanborn Electric Co., (Electrical, $749,285).

141 Rankin stated to the Board that he "wished to report for the record that the groundbreaking ceremonies … were held on December 19, 1971. This was a notable occasion following many complications and delays in the undertaking." Trustee Minutes, December 18, 1971, C.

142 American Standard Seating Co., was awarded the contract for seating. $416,081, Trustee Minutes, February 19, 1972, D.

143 The Trustees approved naming the facility in honor of the principle benefactors, Mr. and Mrs. Anton Hulman Jr. To avoid confusion, the extant Hulman Center (former Deming Hotel) at 6th and Cherry Streets would be renamed the Continuing Education Center. Trustee Minutes, October 27, 1973, K.

144 Trustee Minutes, February 21, 1969, F.

145 This proved to be a gift from the Hulman family.

146 Trustee Minutes, August 6, 1969. Special Meeting of the Board.

147 Ibid. January 16, 1971, E.

148 Ibid. April 17, 1971, I.

149 Ibid. March 20, 1972, G.

150 Ibid. May 15, 1971, K.

151 Ibid. June 19, 1971, Sec. I, Exhibit G.

152 Ibid. July 16, 1971, O: 2.

153 Ibid. October 23, 1971, E.

154 Ibid. November 17, 1973, J.

155 Ibid. June 17, 1972, B.

156 A gift from Mr. Tony George helped defray a portion of the cost of the theater wedge.

157 The name of the building has been changed numerous times: Student Health and Counseling Services Center, Student Health Center, Student Services Building, and Sycamore Center for Wellness and Applied Medicine among the several.

158 The architectural firm was appointed at the July 17, 1964 Trustee Meeting. Trustee Minutes, July 17, 1964, X. The State Budget Agency, however, deferred action on the approval until additional information had been provided. Trustee Minutes, November 18, 1966, VIII. Chronology: Ewing Miller Associates, Inc. requested the Trustees make a final decision about the proposed location of the building. The Board voted to place it north of Chestnut Street between Fifth and Sixth Streets. Trustee Minutes, September 1, 1965, XXIII. On February 19, 1966, a decision was made to move the proposed building site to Fifth and Chestnut with the building facing Fifth Street.

159 Trustee Minutes, April 3, 1970, Section II: A, 1.

160 Alan Rankin, President's Report: 1965-70, p. 10.

161 Trustee Minutes, February 19, 1966, XIII.

162 Ibid. September 9, 1966, XV.

163 Governor Branigin and the State Budget Agency had earlier "deferred action on the approval of the architects." Trustee Minutes, September 18, 1966, XVI. According to one source, Trustee David Day was appointed to the Board by the Governor and his role, it has been suggested, was to contain the cost of buildings at the college.

164 Trustee Minutes, December 16, 1966, XXII.

165 September 19, 1969.

166 Trustee Minutes, March 17, 1967, XIII.

167 The Board authorized the administration to request approval from state offices. Trustee Minutes, February 21, 1969, Section II: G. The proposal included engaging Ewing Miller Associates for architectural services.

168 Trustee Minutes, March 21, 1969, 1.

169 Ibid. September 19, 1969, J.

170 Ibid. April 3, 1970, Sec. II: A.

171 Annual Report of the Physical Plant 1982-83, p. 44.

172 Trustee Minutes, November 5, 1982, G.

173 Ibid, July 23, 1982, J.

174 Information provided by Mr. Steve Culp, Construction Project Leader, ISU Facilities Management.

175 Indiana State University Facilities Management 2012-13 Annual Report, June 30, 2013, n.p.

176 Indiana State University Facilities Management 2013-14 Annual Report, June 30, 2014, III-1.

177 The firm of Repp and Mundt. Inc. was founded in 1948 in Columbus, Indiana and was responsible for constructing nearly half of the buildings there designed by some of the world's outstanding architects. Link Building construction costs are combined with renovations done in the Tirey Memorial Union designed to connect Tirey with the Elks Club that has been transformed into a student activity center after its acquisition.

178 Trustee Minutes, July 18, 1969, K, p. 13. The Board voted to approve the plan and seek state authorization to move forward. Trustee Minutes, September 19, 1969, N. p. 36. Ewing Miller's firm was brought into the project at this time.

179 The Elks Club had been designed by Matthew Miller and the Union Building by Warren Miller and Matt Yeager. According to Ewing Miller, "… we connected these two with a building that serves as a gateway and lets people sort of funnel underneath. Jane C. Hazledine, Interview with Ewing H. Miller, April 13, 1981, p. 5.

180 Trustee Minutes, March 6, 1992, Sec. 1, K, p. 8.

181 Indiana State University Facilties Management 2011-12 Annual Report, June 30, 2012.

182 Hazledine, p. 41.

183 ISU Archives Box 7929, Folder: Rankin Hall.

184 Interview with Ewing Miller, June 27, 2018.

Chapter 7 President Rankin

CHAPTER 8

8TH PRESIDENT
RICHARD GEORGE LANDINI
(1975-1992)

May 15, 1975
Richard George Landini became the eighth President of ISU.

1976
Landini inaugurated Donaghy Day.

June 30, 1979
The new theater opened.

July 23, 1984
The women's P. E. Building was destroyed by fire.

1979
ISU acquired the Emmeline Fairbanks Library.
The men's basketball team was runner-up in NCAA Division 1.

1984
Oakley Plaza was completed.

1985
The sycamore leaf logo was adopted.

1986
Sasaki Associates completed the Campus Master Plan that guided campus development for over a decade.

Indiana State University Building a Legacy

Born: June 4, 1929

Died: October 24, 2004

Wives: Phyllis Elaine Lesnick Landini (married 1953-92)

Barbara Lee Schokley (married 1996-2004)

Education:
Bachelor's Degree
University of Miami, Florida
Literature

Master's Degree
University of Miami, Florida
Literature

Ph.D. Degree
University of Florida
American Literature

Positions held at Indiana State University: President, President Emeritus, and Professor

July 15, 1988
The groundbreaking ceremony was held for Root Hall.

September 14, 1989
The groundbreaking ceremony was held for Dede Plaza.

1992
The Central Chilled Water Plant was under construction.

April 19, 1988
Dedication of the northern addition to the HPER Building took place.

July 19, 1989
The groundbreaking ceremony was held to begin construction of the HMSU.

February 2, 1990
Architects were appointed to design the Musical Recital Hall (Landini Center for Performing and Fine Arts).

May 9, 1992
The University Lab School was closed.

June 5, 1992
The United Mine Workers Building was acquired to become the African-American Cultural Center.

Chapter 8 President Landini

President Landini was a man of many words, sometimes requiring a dictionary to understand. He savored the English language. He was born in Pittsburgh, Pennsylvania, the son of George R. and Alice (Hoy) Landini, on June 4, 1929. He attended Rice High School in Harlem and earned his bachelor's and master's degrees in literature at the University of Miami (Florida) and later, a Ph.D. in American literature from the University of Florida. He was a member of the Arizona State faculty from 1959 to 1970. From 1968-70, he served as assistant to the president. From 1970-75, he was the Academic Vice President at the University of Montana. He became president-elect on February 4, 1975 and took office May 15, 1975.[1] He had the third longest presidency in Indiana State University's history. Nearing retirement, and with plans made for their future with travel and family, his wife Phyllis was diagnosed with adrenal cancer and died 95 days later (March 25, 1992). He married a second time to Barbara Lee Schokley. He retired from the presidency August 1, 1992.

President Landini inherited a university that had grown significantly during the Holmstedt and early years of the Rankin presidencies, but by the time he took office, enrollment had declined significantly. In the 1960s, there were expectations of enrollment of about 25,000 students, but by 1975 there were fewer than 6,000 students in residence on campus, and the university had difficulty paying off bond indebtedness. Indeed, President Rankin had to shift funds from academics to pay for housing. The four units of the Statesman Towers had been vacant since 1972. The end of the Vietnam military draft contributed to the decline. The Indiana Commission for Higher Education, as well as legislators, knew ISU was overbuilt in terms of gross square feet – a factor monitored by the Commission for Higher Education and Legislature. Between 1973 and 1982, the university had no authorization to undertake any significant construction projects. The last major buildings were the Cunningham Library (1972) and Hulman Center (1973). However, from 1986 onward, a number of buildings were constructed during his administration. These included the Animal Research Center, sports complex, Hulman Memorial Student Union, Food Court, Dede Plaza, Root Hall, a new Parsons Hall, and the Computer Center, as well as the remodeling of several buildings, including the Home Economics Building, Dreiser, and Holmstedt Halls. The building formerly called the Tirey Memorial Union Annex was also renovated and renamed Rankin Hall.

Landini stated he found the campus buildings and setting architecturally and aesthetically unattractive.[2] He was also confronted immediately with three problems of great importance that all reflected a campus at risk and under duress. First, in the face of declining enrollment and shortfalls in tuition and fees, the Board adopted a staffing formula in 1974 that was intended to identify overstaffed departments and direct reductions in faculty (over 80 percent were tenured) and staff. This had created a serious morale problem on campus and signaled to state legislators the university was in trouble. Landini did not support this approach to remedying staffing problems.

> **"I take especial pride and satisfaction in the certain knowledge that we ... changed what had to be changed. We held fast to our perdurable values and principles. We nurtured and developed all that makes our beloved institution the ... wonderful university it is."** – President Richard Landini

Second, the university had received a very critical site visit evaluation report from its accrediting agency, the North Central Association, that suggested it was in danger of losing its accreditation. The report delineated a series of "weighty negative or uncertain factors in the overall university;" internal factors that had contributed to what it described as "institutional malaise."[3] Landini convinced the Association to grant a five-year continuing accreditation (the normal period is ten years). In June 1980, he reported to the Trustees that the Evaluation Team, making its campus visit in April 1980, had made a very positive recommendation to the Office Headquarters – continuing accreditation for ten years for all undergraduate programs.[4]

Third, the American Association of University Professors had censured the university in 1972. The censure owed to an instance in 1968 when an untenured instructor in English teaching on symbols

New Theater[5]

Architect: Walter Scholer and Associates, Inc.[6]

Contractors: Mach Van Houtin (General Construction); AAA Electric (Electrical); Freitag-Weinhardt (Mechanical); Strand Century (Stage Lighting)[7]

Date: 1977-78

Cost: $693,339[8]

Area: 12,971 GSF; 7,994 ASF

Location: 536 North Seventh Street

The New Theater was formerly the Bowman Garage. The Trustees approved the name "The New Theater" noting the theater productions were often experimental and in the avant garde.[9]

Because of its favorable location on Seventh Street, with easy access to parking and its capacious unobstructed interior space of 13,000 square feet, a study was undertaken by Hannig & Associates, Inc. to determine if, indeed, it would be cost-effective for the university to remodel the building into a theater. The analysis suggested it was suitable and could provide a savings of about $140,000 rather than beginning anew.[10] The theater faculty also believed the building would provide adequate space for a theater and support functions.

The General Assembly, Special Session, appropriated funds to renovate the garage. The allocation was $600,000, including a $150,000 dimmer control.

With the approval of funding, the university hired Walter Scholer and Associates, Inc., of Lafayette, Indiana to design the transformation from garage to theater. This firm had an outstanding record of theater design work elsewhere in the state, including the Center Loeb Theater at Purdue, the Emens Auditorium and Ball State Theater at Ball State University, and the Experimental Theater at Wabash College.[11]

The New Theater opened on June 30, 1979, with a production of O'Neill's "Ah Wilderness," a popular staple of community repertory.[12]

---

demonstrated a point by burning a small American flag. He was dismissed by President Rankin. This received negative press around the state. By 1975, when Landini arrived, the issue had not been resolved. He was successful, however, when he wrote a letter of assurance to the organization indicating his support for following American Association of University Professors (AAUP) procedures for termination.[13]

A perennial issue for ISU was image. The ongoing decline in enrollment in the mid-1980s was attributed to a decline in high school graduates, the general appearance of the campus, and the caliber of students attending ISU. At the October 1985 meeting of the Trustees, Vice President Dr. Richard Clokey, Professor of History and former Vice President for Academic Affairs, addressed ways the university planned to respond. The response comprised multiple approaches. One was the need for a detailed master plan for the campus that would clarify mission and priorities, helping to map a direction for the future. Another was enrollment management.

Chapter 8 President Landini

With diminishing enrollment, the emphasis would shift from a growth paradigm to maintenance of an enrollment of 11,000 to 12,000 students. Trustee Anthis raised an important question at this meeting. He asked what the impact was of attracting marginal students to attend ISU. Vice President Clokey responded that ISU had a long tradition as an open admission institution, but a new procedure was in place to provide more remediation in English and Mathematics. Remediation would be required of all students who graduated in the "lower one half of their graduating class …"[14] Trustee Breeden then questioned if this approach would improve the image of the campus qualitatively.[15] He stated the university had an image problem across the state, and that greater attention needed to be given to the secondary schools.

Landini is credited with a major achievement that would profoundly impact future campus planning. The university had engaged in negotiations with the goal of purchasing the former Pennsylvania Railroad right-of-way that bisected the campus. In March 1979, the state appropriated funds for the purchase of this property. Acquisition was essential to the physical integrity of the campus.[16]

Landini oversaw the development of a $55 million Master Plan for the campus developed by Sasaki Associates, Inc.[17] In 1985, Landini discussed plans for the 1987-89 biennium budget requests. Until that time, the university had not put forward or been successful in proposing large capital projects. President Landini suggested to Vice President Hilt that continuing down that path would be ruinous for the campus and would not meet the needs of faculty and students.[18] He suggested a major planning initiative be undertaken that would outline the developmental phases of the campus from that period until the end of the century. He requested an extension to provide time to revise the capital projects section of the proposal. After nearly a year of focused analysis and synthesis, the Campus Master Plan was approved, and a plan of action was put in motion that would extend into the foreseeable future.[19]

The plan was significant for the future of campus development. Until the mid-1970s, the university had focused its efforts on acquiring new buildings and resources to accommodate enrollment growth. Landini inherited a campus that had excess capacity in residence halls and was riddled with derelict vacant residencies, and the university had previously purchased commercial and private houses and apartments that had been converted into classrooms and offices. These proved to be unsuited to their intended purpose and expensive to maintain. The Master Plan developed during his presidency emphasized three principles: consolidate, improve facilities, and raze sub-standard buildings.

The plan contained six major features:
1. More city streets needed to be closed.
2. Vehicular traffic should be moved away from the center and out to the periphery of the campus.
3. Emphasis would be given to classroom and office building.
4. Demolition of inadequate "temporary" structures that were intended to be "temporary".
5. Revision of service traffic routes.
6. A comprehensive design for plazas, walkways, and landscaping (to include hundreds of indigenous Indiana trees).

The Trustees adopted and endorsed these goals and objectives that addressed several major issues:
- Campus distribution of activities and functions
- Campus environment – greensward
- Building programs – including location for new structures and demolition of inadequate or unadaptable facilities
- Lighting – street and sidewalk[20]

Landini witnessed growing interest in Indiana State University Evansville (ISUE) and, among some legislators, in separating from ISU and its control by its Trustees. Clearly, Governor Orr was supportive of these efforts. A Board of Incorporators was formed with John Pruis, former President of Ball State, as chairman. The target date for independence was set for July 1, 1985.[21]

The closing of streets running through the campus occupied the attention of many of the presidents. Landini was not an exception. He discussed with the Trustees the desire to close portions of Sixth Street and Chestnut. Selling the plan to the community was obligatory. To substantiate the need, an exhaustive traffic survey was conducted by Professor B. K. Barton. Good data can be persuasive. Landini stated, "It is the intention to assure the public at large, the cultural, economic, and political leadership, that the closing of Sixth and Chestnut Streets will not be detrimental to the City …"[22]

There were many physical changes to the campus during Landini's presidency. A landscaped park, or mall-like area, east of Cunningham Library was added in 1979. In 1980, a new entrance to the campus at Third Street and Chestnut was completed.[23] Predictably, there was dissent "… among that small group of faculty and staff nay-sayers who stand opposed to almost every proposal for institutional enhancement …"[24] Approval by the Board and General Assembly of this $55 million campus plan represented a new chapter in the development of the campus, and led to the completion of the School of Technology, Oakley Plaza, sports arena, Root Hall, University Pavilion, the new Parsons Hall, Dede Plaza, and the Hulman Memorial Student Union. In keeping with his interest in improving the campus, Landini initiated Donaghy Day, a day for cleaning and planting on the campus.

Landini recognized early on an image problem evidenced in the architecture of the campus. Pressed, he would argue that investment in books and research equipment should take precedence over building. (Landini liked to say he did not have an "edifice complex.") At the same time, he also compared building success to academic growth. "It is my hope … that the real success of my administration is in the strengthening and expansion of academic programs, buildings and monuments, plazas and greenswards … contribute handsomely to the personality of a campus. But it is the range and depth of curriculum, the value of scholarship and research and artistic production, the quality and pertinence of classroom teaching, and the future … of graduates that sustain and renew the character of a university."[25] For Landini, the appearance of the campus was a metaphor for its quality.[26] There were those who argued against new buildings and landscaping, believing the money could be better spent on salaries, departmental budgets, and student aid. The fact of the matter was that distinct budget lines could only be used for intended purposes. If money was appropriated to build a new facility on campus, those funds could not be redirected. Landini referred to the complaints as "mischievous piffle."

President Landini led the university through a successful North Central accreditation review that was an acknowledgement of his leadership, as well as the progress made by the faculty and administration, during the past ten years. In 1985, ISU's branch campus in Evansville became the University of Southern Indiana, and the sycamore leaf was adopted as the official university logo.

Later in his tenure, after lengthy study, Landini made the decision to close the Laboratory School located in the building erected during the presidencies of Hines and Tirey. The Laboratory School had provided classes for grades one through 12 and served as a site for students to practice teaching. The decision was based upon several issues with the school as it had evolved. He had seen the school become a maverick enterprise not responsible to the Vigo County School Superintendent or School of Education. The School District was unwilling to increase its support for the Laboratory School. That meant the university was paying for renovations and utilities and was not reimbursed at the same rate as other schools in the Vigo County School Corporation. Landini, always the scholar, saw little substantial research emanating from the school. The State Board of Education had put the Laboratory School on probation and the financial agreement with the School Corporation was ending.

In 1991, the new Dean of the school, Dr. Gail Huffman-Joley, proposed closing grades seven-nine (the high school was already closed), and the creation of a Center for 21st Century Teachers Education. This plan was approved by the School of Education Congress and the University Faculty Senate. The Trustees, disturbed by the backlash to the planned closing of grade levels, voted to close the school entirely and rejected the proposal for the new Professional Development Center. The decision affected about 31 tenured and tenure-track faculty.

Landini found that his counsel had been rejected and was reprimanded by the Trustees for not forewarning them adequately of the intensity of faculty reaction to the closing, and for not forcefully advocating for the development of the 21st Century Center.[27]

A point of pride for the university and President

Donaghy Day

Landini was the 1979 men's basketball team, which was runner-up in the final game of the NCAA Division I Championship. Also, Kurt Thomas and the men's gymnastics team won the NCAA National Championship. In 1984, Bruce Baumgartner won an Olympic gold medal in wrestling. Men's athletic teams joined the Missouri Valley Conference, to which it still belongs today, and ISU was a founding member of the Gateway Collegiate Athletic Conference for women's sports.

Landini was an academic. He supported efforts to bring several national honor societies to the campus. Among them were Phi Kappa Phi, Sigma Xi, and the Mortarboard. During his tenure, the Master of Public Administration, and nearly 40 undergraduate and graduate degree programs, were added. Included in this number were a Master's in Nursing and Doctor of Psychology degree.

President Landini concluded his book, "Owls and Sycamores," with the following reflection, which seemed a fitting conclusion to his professional life: "A university worth its salt ... doesn't change its essence ... as a result of presidential leadership. A university worthy of respect is defined by the vigor, vitality, and intellectual defiance of its faculty, by the fidelity and dedication of its trustees, staff, and administration, by the hopes and idealism of it students, by the pride and respect in which it is held by its graduates."[28]

President Landini died October 24, 2004 and was interred alongside his first wife, Phyllis, in Highland Lawn Cemetery, Terre Haute. ■

Emeline Fairbanks Memorial Library

Architects: William H. Floyd and Charles E. Scott
Contractor: Modern Construction Company[29]
Date: Cornerstone Laid: August 10, 1904
Dedication: April 29, 1906
Formal Opening: August 11, 1906

Acquired by ISU: 1979
Cost: $65,000
Area: 17,760 GSF; 13,292 ASF
Location: 220 North Seventh Street

Emeline Fairbanks Memorial Library Renovation

President Landini

Architects: James Associates Architects and Engineers, Inc.[30]

Contractors: Shelton Hannig, Inc. (General Construction); Freitag-Weinhardt (Mechanical); AAA Electric Co., (Electrical)[31]

Date: Building donated to ISU: 1979
Renovation: 1982-83

Open House to view renovation: January 22, 1984

The Vigo County Public Library Board of Trustees authorized the transfer of the Emeline Fairbanks Library to ISU in June 1978.[32] The building was converted into classrooms and studios for the Department of Art. The building was renamed Fairbanks Hall on January 22, 1984.

The university requested bonding authority of $1.18 million for renovation of the space to accommodate several art disciplines, such as photography, printmaking, painting, and drawing.[33] Bids exceeded the bonding authority chiefly because the state Fire Marshall required the installation of a sprinkler system in part of the building. President Landini returned to Indianapolis to request an additional $260,000 from the Academic Building Facilities Fee Fund. Additional funds amounting to $19,554 were requested by the subcontractor, Unique Art Glass Co., to cover the cost of labor and materials to repair the stained-glass dome.[34]

Fairbanks Memorial Library was offered to the city in a February 2, 1903 letter addressed to the Mayor and Common Council by the late Crawford Fairbanks in memory of his mother. After a suitable site was found, Mr. Fairbanks selected architects (W. H. Floyd and C. E. Scott), and a contract was awarded to Modern Construction Company. Work was completed in April 1906 and the library was formally opened on August 11, 1906.

Fairbanks is a splendid example of Beaux Arts classicism.[35] The use of finely-cut ashlar Indiana limestone, balconies on the main entrance, a triangular pediment, heavy ornamentation, pronounced dentils, and paired columns all reflect Beaux Arts influence. The main floor of Fairbanks is faced with smooth limestone ashlar. Quoins articulate every corner. The classically inspired entablature contains foliated medallions and a large projecting cornice. The windows on the sides and front are subdivided by small Ionic columns and a stained-glass transom. The windows are framed by fluted pilasters with foliated capitals. A unique Beaux Arts feature was the inclusion of Tiffany ornamental leaded glass windows.

The facade is divided into three parts. The central portion clearly takes the form of a stylized Roman temple. There are six fluted columns with composite capitals. The two corners have paired columns. The tympanum (triangular space above supported by the columns) is enriched with curvilinear foliation with beast heads and an open book theme with the motto: "The wit and wisdom of the ages welcomes you."

The entrance is on the main floor, and the doorway is framed by fluted pilasters and classically inspired entablature and pediment. The stained glass found in the window transoms is picked up in the dome, which stands above a central space beyond the entry. The dome features portraits of historically important figures.[36] ■

Chapter 8 President Landini

Emeline Fairbanks Memorial Library Dome Renovation

President Benjamin

Date: 2003

Cost: Approx. $25,000

One of the conditions the university agreed to with the transfer of the library was that the dome be kept in satisfactory condition.[37] By this time, the stained-glass dome needed restoration. The dome was restored and illuminated in a project sponsored by President Benjamin and realized by Mr. Kevin Runion, Associate Vice President for Facilities Management. The restoration involved building a new walkway above the dome to make it easier to clean and replace bulbs. The earlier florescent lights installed when the original skylights were replaced with eight metal halide lights with reflectors to provide brighter and more even illumination.[38]

The restoration work earned ISU the Heritage Award, presented by Terre Haute Landmarks, in recognition of the importance of this restoration to the city.[39] One of the conditions that came with the gift of Fairbanks Library was that the dome would be available to the public. The restoration made good on that promise.[40]

Emeline Fairbanks Library Exterior and Interior Renovations

President Bradley

Contractor: Garmong & Son, Inc.

Project Managers: Scott Tillman and Bryan Duncan

Date: 2008-17

Cost: $186,900[41]

Ceramic tile floors were refurbished, there was work done to the HVAC, plaster was repaired, and snow and ice melt equipment was installed in the roof.

Indiana State University Building a Legacy

Oakley Plaza

Architects: Kevin L. Runion[42]; McGuire and Shook Associates (Landscape)

Date: 1984

Cost: $294,700[43]

Location: Northwest Corner of Seventh and Cherry Streets

The Oakley Plaza was built on the site of a former parking lot.[44] It was made possible by a gift of $150,000 from the Oakley Foundation (Easton "Bud" Perry, treasurer and a director of the foundation). Perry was optimistic the plaza would be an asset to the campus and community.

Runion is a landscape architect from Ball State. He was formerly with McGuire Architects. His specialty was landscape design. Trees and grasses are important elements of his design vocabulary, and here in his design for the plaza he included a variety of trees, including Red Oak, Crab Apple, Honey Locust, and Linden. Over the gravel of the former parking lot, a beautiful lawn was laid down, creating a park-like setting. This plaza was designed to be a gateway connecting the campus with downtown Terre Haute. It represents one of the first formal steps to shape the built environment to encourage community and university interaction. The central seating area, according to Runion, was surrounded by Honey Locust trees that provided shade and modulated the light. The enclosing berms acted as sound buffers.[45]

Chapter 8 President Landini

Physical Plant Department and Central Stores

Acquired by ISU Foundation: March 30, 1984

Cost: $2.02 million[46]

Area: 58,726 GSF; 56,500 ASF

Location: 952 Sycamore Street

The Physical Plant department and Central Stores were located in several old buildings scattered about the campus. None of these structures were designed for their current use. Acquisition of this building from Tri-Industries contributed to enhanced efficiency.

ISU received an appropriation of $1.33 million in the 1985-86 and 1986-87 Biennial Budget. This building was owned by Vern Hux and was purchased by the ISU Foundation. In Landini's Report to the Trustees in June 1985, he informed the Board that the Foundation had purchased the property March 30, 1984, and ISU would lease it from them.[47] The 1985 General Assembly appropriated sufficient funds to purchase the building ($1.08 million) and renovate it ($250,000).

A variety of offices are housed in this and adjacent buildings. They include Purchasing, Shipping and Receiving, Central Stores, Fleet Maintenance and Parking, Environmental Health and Safety, and Facilities Administrative offices. ■

Root Hall

Architects: The Odle Group[48] (Odle McGuire and Shook Architects, Inc.)

Contractors: Jungclaus-Campbell Construction Co., Inc. (General Construction); Williams Plumbing and Heating, Inc. (Mechanical); Steele-Bearde Co., Inc. (Electrical)[49]

Date: Groundbreaking: July 15, 1988
Dedication: November 3, 1989

Cost: $8.8 million ($1.5 million gift from Root family)[50]

Area: 94,620 GSF; 64,250 ASF

Location: 424 North Seventh Street

This building was named after Chapman Shaw and Susan Spear Root in recognition of their financial support for the University Master Plan.[51] The recently adopted Master Plan identified eight buildings that should be demolished. Root Hall represents an important first step in the implementation of the Plan, replacing three obsolete buildings that were razed.

Root Hall utilizes the campus' standard building vocabulary of brick with limestone trim. It is surmounted by a metal sloped roof. It was originally designed to house the Departments of English, Foreign Languages, Humanities, Mathematics and Computer Science, Philosophy, and Psychology and provide offices for approximately 115 faculty, 32 support staff,

Indiana State University Building a Legacy

and 40 graduate assistants. The interior of the building was designed to be a metal frame construction with steel studs and drywall partitions that would allow modification of the floor plan in the future.

The Olde Group (David Blanton, Project Architect) presented a schematic design to the Trustees on February 6, 1987. With the Board's approval, Landini submitted the design to the Commission for Higher Education.[52] The Special Session meeting of the General Assembly on April 30, 1987 approved bonding for $8.8 million.

President Landini announced that the Pulitzer Prize winning author, Toni Morrison, would make presentations on campus as part of the dedication celebration. ■

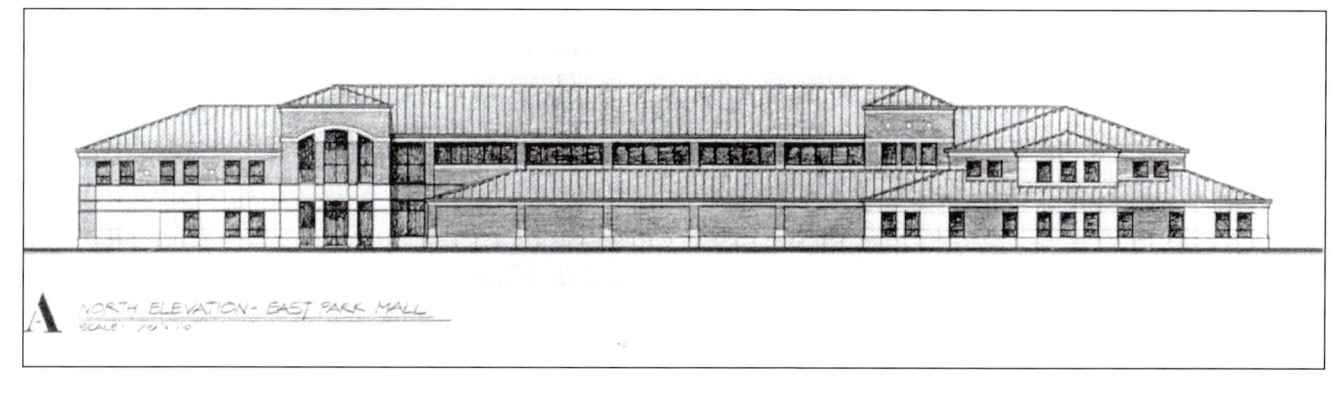

Chapter 8 President Landini

Hulman Memorial Student Union (Formerly Gillum Hall)

Architects: William Browne, RATIO Architects[53]; HDG Architects, Inc.; Hellmuth, Obata & Kassabaum, Inc.; and Fink, Roberts, & Petrie, Inc.[54]

Contractors: CDI and Hannig Construction Co.; Jungclaus-Campbell Co. (General Construction); Crown Electric, Inc.; Steele-Beard Electric Co. (Electrical and Mechanical); Harrah Plumbing and Heating Co., Inc.; and Williams Plumbing and Heating (Plumbing and HVAC)

Developer: Cornerstone Companies, Inc.

Construction Manager: Geupel DeMars, Inc.

Date: Groundbreaking: July 19, 1989
Dedication: October 16, 1991

Cost: $13 million

$2 million from the Mary Fendrich Hulman Charitable Trust

$1 million for Dede Activity Center and $600,000 for Dede Plaza from Edmund and Mary Dede

$8.65 million Bonding Authorization[55]

Area: 98,303 GSF; 66,112 ASF

Location: 550 Chestnut Street

Another manifestation of the 1986 Master Plan was the addition of the new Student Union and Plaza. The former Student Union in Tirey Hall had simply become too small to serve the student population and too impractical and expensive to remodel and accommodate all the amenities students desired. The renovation of the nine-story Gillum Hall and transformation of it into Hulman Memorial Student Union was made possible by a generous gift from Anton Hulman Jr. and Mary Fendrich Hulman.[56] The renovated building was designed to accommodate a variety of student activities, student support services, and organizations. In addition to the transformation of the former student residence hall, student activity rooms

Indiana State University Building a Legacy

Food Court after renovation

were added on the ground floor with a gift from the Dedes (Page 192). These included Dede I which was converted from cafeteria and dining rooms and two large meeting rooms, (Dede II & III) a ballroom, lounge, game room and Le Club fitness center.[57] The food court was a mall-like construction measuring 50,000 sq. ft. The "commons" area provided space for numerous retail and food enterprises and the University Bookstore. The entire complex, except the ninth floor, provided space for formal and informal student gatherings and activities. The

University Suite is located on the ninth floor and contains furniture from the Hulman and George families, stained-glass, a fireplace, and stair railings from the former Elks Club building.

The location of the union and plaza reflect the gradual enlargement of the campus northward. The former student union in Tirey faced the quad and was further away from most of the housing development on campus. The new union sits on the crossroads of the campus and places it in the mainstream of the residential corridor between Fifth and Sixth Streets. It was designed to play a more important role in student life. The thought was that the union would add activities for students and would reduce the number of students leaving on weekends. ■

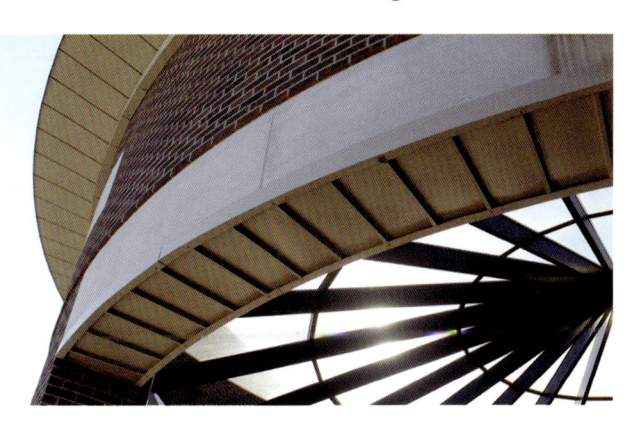

Chapter 8 President Landini

Dede Plaza and Activity Center

Architect: RATIO Architects

Contractors: Geupel DeMars, Inc. (Construction manager)

Date: Groundbreaking: September 14, 1989[58]

Cost: $1.7 million

Location: Sixth and Chestnut Streets

The Dede Plaza and Dede Activity Center were made possible through a gift of $1.7 million from Edmund and Mary Dede. Mr. Dede was the head of Dede Investments. The projects represented an important step in the realization of the new 1986 Master Plan, which recognized the old historic center of campus defined by Tirey and Tilson had shifted to the north.

Public spaces can be as important to one's experience of the campus life as its buildings. The addition of Dede Plaza to the newly-opened Hulman Memorial Student Union contributed to changes in the circulation plan. The Plaza was located at the campus "crossroads" and was conceived to be a gathering place for the entire campus community. Dede Plaza has, as its centerpiece, a 48-foot in diameter fountain.[59] The Plaza is also circular and is the terminal point of walkways from the east, west, and south – a mini-crossroad of Indiana State University. The flat fountain was designed to be converted into a temporary stage surrounded by steps that created amphitheater seating. The fountain, with its vigorous jets of water, provided a cool respite during the summer months, and an improvised play place for neighborhood children who were thrilled with the gushing water. With landscaping and the introduction of the northwest to southeast brick walkway visually tying the historical quad to this new center, Dede Plaza became the focal point of campus life.

The Dede gift also funded the Dede Activity Center, including the renovation of Dede I (formerly the kitchen for Gillum, Sandison, Hines, and Jones residence halls), and the addition of Dede II and III, including a formal lounge (now with art exhibits), a ballroom, fitness center, and game room.

A plaque honoring the Dedes was placed in the main entrance to the Hulman Memorial Student Union. ∎

Future site of Dede Plaza, Sixth and Chestnut, 1964

Indiana State University Building a Legacy

Renovation of Dede Plaza and Fountain

President Bradley

Architect: RATIO Architects

Contractor: ST Construction

Date: 2013-14

Cost: $1.45 million[60]

In December 2013, the Trustees approved plans for the renovation of Dede Plaza.[61] When the plaza was originally built, the fountain and outdoor seating became one of the favorite gathering places for students. The planned renovations did not diminish the attraction of the site.

Renovations included remodeling the fountain, new pavers and sidewalks, upgrading existing seating and adding new terrace seating and additional landscaping.

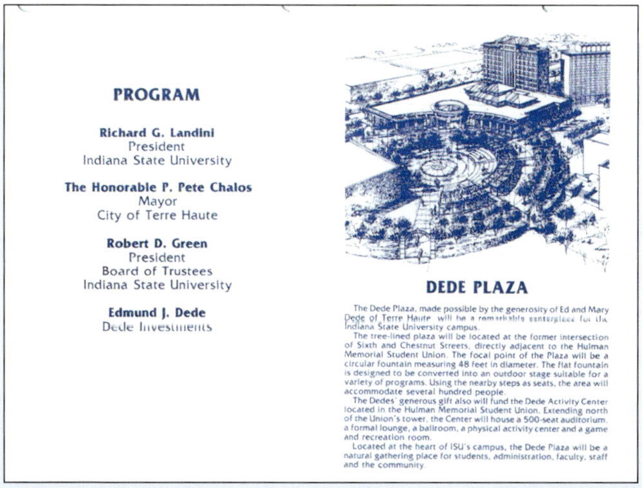

Chapter 8 President Landini

Dede I Renovation

President Benjamin

Project: First Renovation

Architect: Snapp & Associates

Date: 2004

The color scheme was changed to ISU colors, the entry was redefined, and five official seals of the university reflecting the history of the campus were installed. The goal was to create a sense of history in the space often used for special events and presentations to potential students and their families.

Additional Projects

Project 1: Upgrade Air Conditioning in Commons

Contractor: Springhill Plumbing and Heating

Date: 2007-08

Cost: $586,941

Project 2: Created Commuter Lounge

Project Manager: Scott Tillman

Contractor: Garmong

Date: 2008

Cost: $64,000

Sycamore Banquet Center

President Bradley

Architect: RATIO Architects

Contractor: CDI

Project Manager: Steve Culp

Date: 2011-12

Cost: $3.69 million

Indiana State University Building a Legacy

Waste Management and Recycling Center

Date: 1991

Area: 5,483 GSF; 5,000 ASF

Location: 449 North Ninth Street

Recycling began slowly on campus when, in 1990-91, custodians began collecting aluminum cans. Goals were articulated that included reducing material going to landfills and realizing savings by reducing tipping fees and fuel consumption. The effort was soon expanded to include glass.

An initial challenge was where to locate the recycling facility. It was first placed in a very small area behind the custodial building. The university purchased the Turner Coach Garage in the fall of 1990 and recycling was relocated there in early 1991. With a larger facility and more accessible drop-off area, the Center began to collect cardboard, plastics, paper, and eventually scrap metal and some electronics.

In the first year, the Center recycled 90,207 pounds of waste that earlier would have been sent to a landfill. The rest, as they say, is history. Recycling (and sustainability) became campus-wide concerns. The larger community was also encouraged to make use of the new facility. By 2008-09, 1,423 tons of materials were recycled. By contrast, 467 tons went to landfill in 2008-09, compared to 2,368 tons in 1989-90. For the years 2013-14, the Center processed 2,008,068 pounds collected in the drive-through and from across campus.

The Center received the 2010 Governor's Award for Environmental Excellence and was awarded the Best of the Best Award in 2011 for being the most environmentally friendly business of the year.[62]

Barbara Lawrence (pictured below) served as Director of Custodial Services, Waste Management, and Training Services at ISU. She retired after 35 years of service. Her advocacy for recycling contributed to the drive-through at the recycling center being known as "Barb's Way."

John T. Beasley Building
(Citizens Gas and Fuel Company)[63]

Architect: Dalton G. Shourds[64]

Contractors: William Caton & Son; O. A. Toelle; Hartmann Co. Inc.; Pugh Brothers; and Dreiman Brothers

Design Associate: R. H. Bean[65]

Date: Opening Celebration: September 18-19, 1925
Acquired: August 6, 1991

Location: 632 Cherry Street

Area: Approx. 31,850 sq. ft.

Chapter 8 President Landini

The Beasley Building opened for business in 1925 with high amounts of praise. One commentator wrote that it rivaled the best bank buildings both for its exterior, as well as the high quality of its interior finish, including spacious interior rooms, terrazzo floors, and one of the fastest elevators in Terre Haute.

The building was a three-story block reflecting the continuing influence of a Chicago commercial style. Designers drew from the Beaux Arts repertoire with neo-classical elements that were toned down, appearing more refined. What distinguished the Beasley Building from other contemporary buildings in this style was the use of speckled semi-gloss ivory terra cotta for the entire facade, and portions of the east and west sides. One may recall the work of Chicago architect, William Le Baron Jenney, who rebuilt Old Main after the fire of 1888 and used terra cotta ornamentation.[66] The facade contained gargoyles that later could be found on Reeve Hall. ■

Beasley Building Razed
President Moore
Contractor: H&H Trucking
Cost: $93,625[67]

Central Chilled Water Plant
Contractors: Sycamore Engineering; CDI, Inc.; Burton
Date: 1992
Cost: $6 million[68]
Area: 11,634 GSF; 144 ASF
Location: 945 Chestnut Street

Typically, buildings that are part of the campus infrastructure receive less attention than new student housing or laboratory buildings, but they are essential to the operation of the campus. Their chief advocate is most often the leadership in facilities management. This project gestated during two presidencies, beginning with President Landini in 1984 and concluding with additions during the President Moore period.

This project was expensive. However, on November 12, 1991 Public Service Company of Indiana (PSI) Energy announced a gift of $165,000 "energy-efficiency" incentive money to help defray the cost.[69] Estimates at the time suggested ISU would accrue over $250,000 a year in energy savings with the new plant. A Memorandum of Understanding between PSI and ISU reads that the new plant will replace 2,338 tons of existing outdated electric cooling equipment, as well as provide 1,958 tons of ice banks charged during off-peak hours. Chilled water was distributed to the buildings using newly renovated campus tunnels.

Not only was increased efficiency important, but the new plant would consolidate air conditioning for 19 buildings with capacity to serve future needs. Air conditioning was added gradually to campus buildings in a piecemeal manner, building by building to enhance efficiency. An example of that inefficiency could be seen in Statesman Towers, which relied on over 500 window air conditioners for climate control.

New buildings were used as teaching props. During construction, Professor Joe Huber would take his students, who were working on a class chiller project, to the construction site so they could observe the design and installation process. ■

Cooling Tower Upgrade
President Moore
Date: 1995
Cost: $150,000

Parsons Hall (Central Computing and Administrative Services Building)

Architect: Walter Scholer & Associates, Inc.[70]

Contractors: CDI; Harrah Plumbing and Heating; AAA Electric Co.

Date: 1992-93

Cost: $7.81 million Pavilion[71]

Area: 45,115 GSF; 23,766 ASF

Location: 200 North Seventh Street

House Bill 1530 passed in Special Session on May 9, 1989 granting ISU bonding authorization for $7.8 million for a new Central Computing and Administrative Services Building. This building represented the third phase of implementing the 1986 Campus Master Plan.

The new Center (Parsons Hall) was built on the site of the former Terre Haute Elks Lodge. That building was vacated shortly after commencement in the spring of 1990 and was scheduled for demolition during the summer of that year.[72] Fortunately, elements from the building were safeguarded and installed on the ninth floor of the Hulman Memorial Student Union. Among other things, this included stained glass, metal and wooden banisters, and light fixtures. The project was prompted by a $7.8 million bonding authority from the state to remove the Lodge and replace it with a Central Computing and Administrative Services Building. It was designed to attach to the Link Building, which then gave access to Rankin and Tirey Halls.

During discussion of the proposed building, Trustee Breeden raised an interesting point. He asked if the university had guiding principles on architectural style. He suggested the use of common materials and consistent design were important considerations and these principles should govern architects as they plan future projects. Landini said the principles would be drafted in the near future.[73] The Trustees appeared to have been comfortable with the Scholer firm because it had recently completed two major computer facilities at Purdue and Ball State Universities. One must wonder if some Trustees were dissatisfied with Miller's modernist designs for the Statesman Towers and Cunningham Library that clearly diverged from the more prevalent standard brick and limestone buildings. ■

University Pavilion
Three buildings, Rankin, Tirey, and Parsons Halls, were formally named the "University Pavilion" in March 1992.[74]

Chapter 8 President Landini

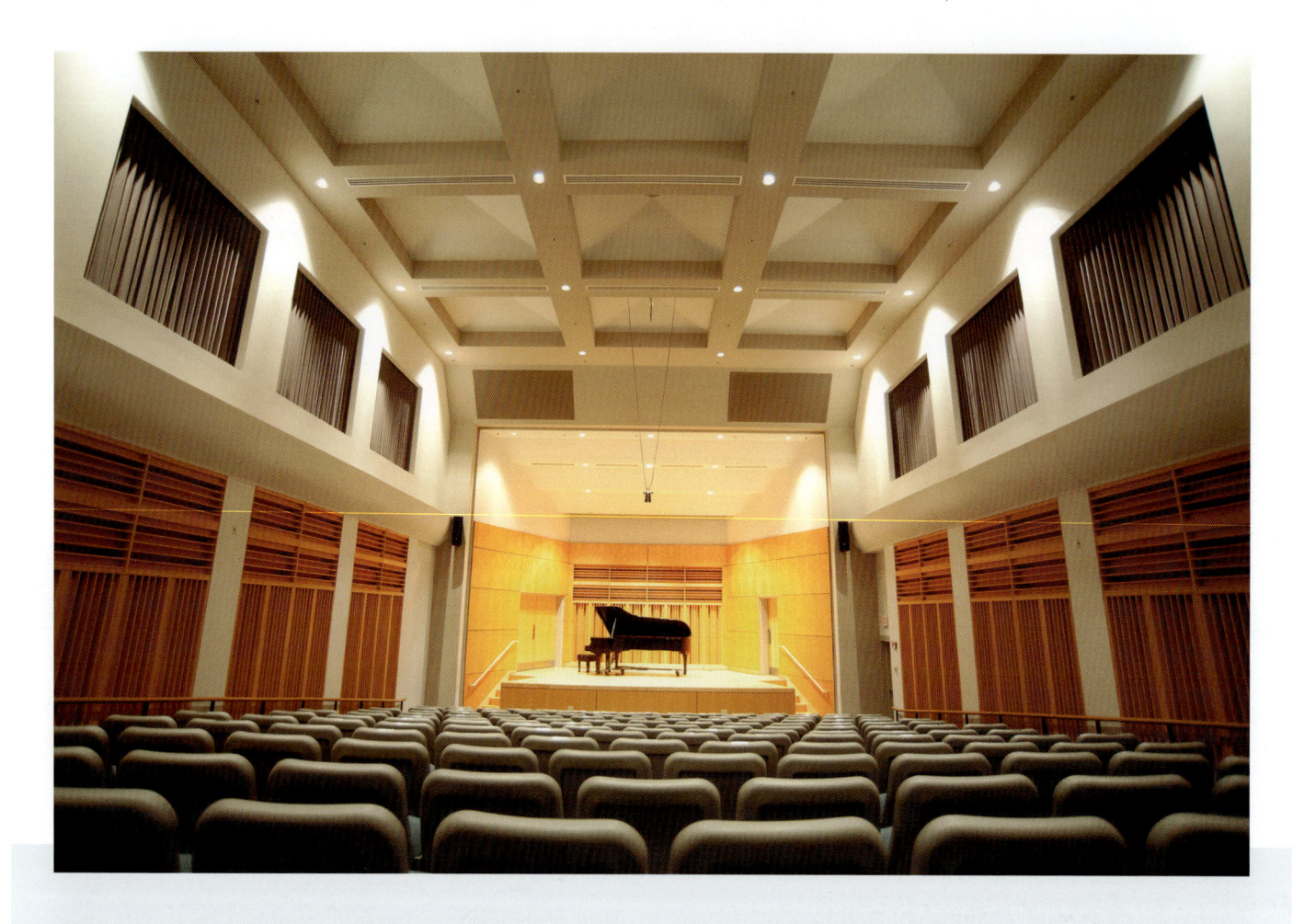

Music Recital Hall – Center for Performing and Fine Arts

Presidents Landini and Moore

Architect: Schmidt and Associates[75] with The Mathes Group (Consultant Architect)[76]

Contractors: Hanning Construction, Inc. (General Construction); SMC, Inc., (Mechanical); NRK (Electrical)[77]

Engineers: The Mathes Group; Yerges Acoustics; R. E. Dimond and Associates, Inc.; Lynch, Harrison, & Brumleve (Structural); Mussett, Nichols & Associates (Mechanical, Electrical, and Plumbing)

Date: Groundbreaking: October 21, 1994
Dedication: October 8, 1997[78]

Cost: $7.02 million[79]

Area: 41,604 GSF

Location: 300 North Seventh Street

The Center for Performing and Fine Arts (CPFA) was built upon the site formerly occupied by the "Gymnasium" built in 1928, which later became the Women's Physical Education Building in 1962. This facility was destroyed by fire and razed in July 1984. In August 1990, the university submitted a proposal for a "Music Recital Hall Addition," with an estimated cost of $5.7 million.[81] The idea of renovating the Parson's era Science Hall in which music had some of its programs was discussed, but ultimately discouraged, as the Commission for Higher Education agreed it made more sense to build a new facility.

The 1991 General Assembly approved bonding authorization of $5.7 million for construction of the

Groundbreaking with Presidents Landini and Moore.

Music Recital Hall addition.[80] It was constructed to provide an acoustically tunable 175-seat performance hall, studios, and offices for half of the music faculty, the music chair, and rehearsal spaces for choirs, orchestras, small ensembles, etc. The hall has an acoustical wall system arranged to diffuse sound evenly. A unique aspect of the music rehearsal space is that it is a "room within a room." The exterior reflects the standard stylistic vocabulary of ISU buildings: brick, limestone, and glass. The new building is connected to Fine Arts by a tunnel.

Arriving at this final design was an arduous process. The original planning centered on the idea that music would be in the new building, and the Turman Art Gallery in the Fine Arts Building would be enlarged and equipped with a new HVAC system. Schmidt recognized that the site for the new building was at a crisscross of student paths through the campus, and that this presented an opportunity to introduce students to both art and music, as well as provide a site for casual interaction. The first three plans kept the departments separate and the Turman Gallery remained in the old Fine Arts Building.

Schmidt introduced the fourth option supported by Robert Cowden, chair of music, which is the structure we see today. The new plan left the Turman Gallery in the original Fine Arts Building, and a new University Gallery would be located on the main floor of the building opposite the Recital Hall. The University Fine Art Gallery is a 5,000 sq. ft. space accessible from the rotunda lobby and directly across from the rehearsal hall. It has 300 running feet of flexible exhibit walls. There is also a video gallery adjoining the main gallery space.

Landini Center-West Facade
President Bradley
Date: 2012

Richard G. Landini Center for Performing Arts

The Trustees approved renaming the Center for Performing and Fine Arts the Richard G. Landini Center for the Performing Arts in August 2011.[82] Since Landini was the originator of Donaghy Day, the renaming ceremony was appropriately held on Donaghy Day in April 2012.

Chapter 8 President Landini

University Art Gallery doors by Jack Gates

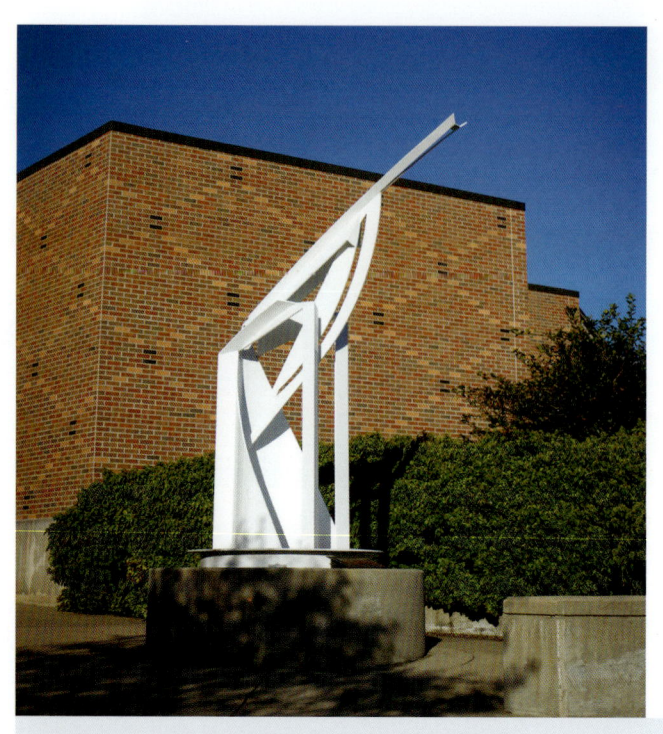

Marcia Woods, "Salute," painted steel, 1998

design that prevents sound transfer to adjacent areas.

The Gallery doors, titled "Hard-Edge Takes a Ride," were designed by art faculty member Jack Gates, and were created from 12 varieties of hardwoods. The location of the Recital Hall across from the University Gallery allows audiences from one event to cross the hall to another and students to experience both music and art in their daily peregrinations through campus.[83]

Events leading up to the actual construction of this facility were not auspicious. While the building had been approved by the Trustees and was included in the 1991-93 Capital Improvement Budget Request (August 1, 1990), a worsening state budget required that the building be put on hold for the 1991-93 biennium.[84] President Moore reported to the Trustees on July 16, 1993 that the budget proposed by the Indiana Commission on Higher Education and the State Budget Agency recommended no capital projects for the 1993-95 biennium. This impacted the Center for Performing Arts, as well as the planned Advanced Technology Center. Fortunately, on October 6, 1994, the State Budget Committee approved $5.7 million in bonding authority, which enabled the project to commence. To illustrate the impact of the delay, the Indiana General Assembly approved the budget of $5.67 million. When contracts were finally let, the estimated cost had risen $1.5 million. Final contract costs came to a total $6.78 million.[85]

University Art Gallery

Indiana State University Building a Legacy

Technology A Building (New Technology Building)

President Landini submitted a Biennium Budget request for $9 million for construction of a new School of Technology building. The State Budget Agency recommended limiting funding to $1.1 million for repairs and rehabilitation of older buildings. In response, Landini sent a letter with an alternate list of requests to the State Budget Director in which he proposed remodeling parts of the 1915 Vocational School and a portion of the 1919 Parson's era Science Hall (also referred to as the Business Building) on the quad and construction of a scaled-down two-story structure adjacent to the Vocational School Building. The revised request was for $6.25 million.[86]

The General Assembly appropriated $1.35 million and approved bonding authorization for $4.73 million for the two-story addition and the proposed remodeling.[87]

Chapter 8 President Landini

Technology A Building

Architect: Walter Scholer and Associates

Contractors: P. R. Duke Construction Co., Inc. (General Construction); Freitag-Weinhardt, Inc. (Mechanical and Electrical)[88]

Date: Bids received: January 9, 1981

Cost: $3.94 million

Area: 51,962 GSF; 36,403 ASF

Location: 101 North Sixth Street

Completed plans and specifications suitable for bidding were presented to the Trustees and approved.[89] The design was for a two-story brick structure with a basement to house mechanical and electrical equipment. It was to be located on a parking lot immediately south of the main Technology Building (Vocational School). The first floor was planned to house the Automotive Technology Programs together with a laboratory and outdoor courtyard for use by the Construction Technology Department.

The second floor would house several laboratories, including Manufacturing Technology, Drafting, and Plastics and Packaging. While this represented significant expansion, the Aerospace department, three drafting laboratories, and two department chairpersons would still be housed across campus in the old Business Building located on the Quad and three chairpersons and the remainder of the faculty would reside in the original Vocational School Building.[90]

Renovation Technology A Phases I and II

President Bradley

Phase I

Contractor: CDI

Project Managers: Scott Tillman and Bryan Duncan

Date: 2011-12

Cost: $323,849

Buildout Interior Design studio, corridor, and rest room

Phase II

Contractor: Garmong

Project Managers: Scott Tillman and Bryan Duncan

Date: 2012-13

Cost: $603,110

Develop office suite, lounge and classroom

Indiana State University Building a Legacy

Advanced Technology Center (Myers Technology Center)

Presidents Landini and Moore

Architect: InterDesign Group

Consulting Architect: Ellerbe Becket

Contractors: Verkler Inc. (General Construction); NRK, Inc. (Electrical)

Date: Groundbreaking: April 19, 1996
Dedication: September 18, 1998

Cost: $17.13 million

Location: 650 Cherry Street

Size: 110,016 GSF; 74,500 ASF

The School of Technology was established in 1967 and was comprised of five major technology fields of study: Manufacturing and Construction, Industrial and Mechanical, Aerospace, Electronics and Computer, and Industrial Technology Education. Technology 'A' was opened to classes in 1982 and provided 36,403 ASF for labs and office space. A report prepared in advance of making a request for a new advanced technology building outlined needs. Critical was the fact that the School of Technology had grown significantly in enrollment, and faculty was housed in three different buildings, the most recent being the 1982 Technology 'A' Building. Technology 'B' was located in the Vocational School constructed in 1915. The third building was the old classroom building built in 1919. The latter two buildings were woefully inadequate to support modern teaching and research. Further, the majority of faculty and departmental offices were actually in the old classroom building because the funds for building Technology 'A' had not been adequate to move to the newer facility. In 1989, Dean Clois Kicklighter began building the case for a new state-of-the-art facility.

In June 1990, Representative John Myers was able to secure $4.84 million to cover a portion of the cost of a new technology center. President Landini indicated ISU was committed to fund the balance. Planning for the Myers Technology Center continued in 1991 when the Board of Trustees, at its October 25, 1991 meeting, approved President Landini's recommendation to hire the InterDesign Group to begin planning for the Center. The location of the Center directly to the east of Technology 'A' would require the demolition of Alumni Hall (Marathon Oil Building), the Old Technology Building, and the Print Shop. Locating the building on this site served to orient the building toward the new quadrangle as well as create a more unified presence on Cherry Street.

Similar to the daunting experience of seeing the Center for Performing and Fine Arts to fruition, the Myers Technology Center (formerly named the Advanced Technology Center) was a perilous and Byzantine process. The same state-level budget concerns that stalled the Center for Performing Arts also delayed this project. However, because the Center for Performing and Fine Arts had been advanced prior to the Advanced Technology Center, its approval was delayed until the 1995-97 biennium, six years after the nearly $5 million commitment of federal funds to help cover the building costs. Myers was credited with helping safe-guard the funds through the period of delays. President Moore wrote Congressman Myers in July 1993 explaining that while the project would be delayed because no bonding authority had been forthcoming, ISU was continuing to make preparations to raze the Gas Company Building that stood in the area for the new Center.

The Center was included in the ISU budget request for the 1993-95 biennium. The Center was to accommodate new needs in technology and technology transfer and address the needs of students, industry, and economic development of the state. By 1994, the General Assembly authorized funding the Center ($13.5 million) of the $18 million cost.[91]

The four-story (including lower level and penthouse levels) Center was designed to include 30 laboratories/classrooms and offices serving six departments, a 100-seat multimedia presentation room, and a distance-learning classroom. The interior of the building contained walls of glass that enabled passersby to see teaching and research underway. Specialized areas included a Beech King Air B200 flight simulator, weather laboratory, and packaging technology laboratory. This comprehensive instructional facility enabled programs that were housed in three separate facilities to be unified and benefit from increased interactivity. The new Center would connect physically and programmatically to Technology A via a second level skywalk. In essence, the building helped create a unified school.

The new Center has a dramatic 3-story sky lit atrium around which the laboratories are dispersed on each floor. Increased areas of glass serve to help define principle entries into the building. This was the first building in which key-cards were used for entry to the buildings and rooms. In this building, as would later occur in the New Power Plant (2000-01), the focus was on making the building a learning opportunity. Viewing panels in each lab enable viewers to see the work done in the various labs, as well as access to the working of the building itself. The building rests on a traditional brick and limestone base while masonry on the second and third floors bracket higher tech. systems and materials.

The building was dedicated in honor of U.S. Representative John T. Myers who served Indiana's 7th district. It was the realization of Landini's and Moore's strategic visions to create facilities to house disciplines that would help ISU address the state needs and assure pathways to employment for graduates that served to secure funding for this impressive building. ■

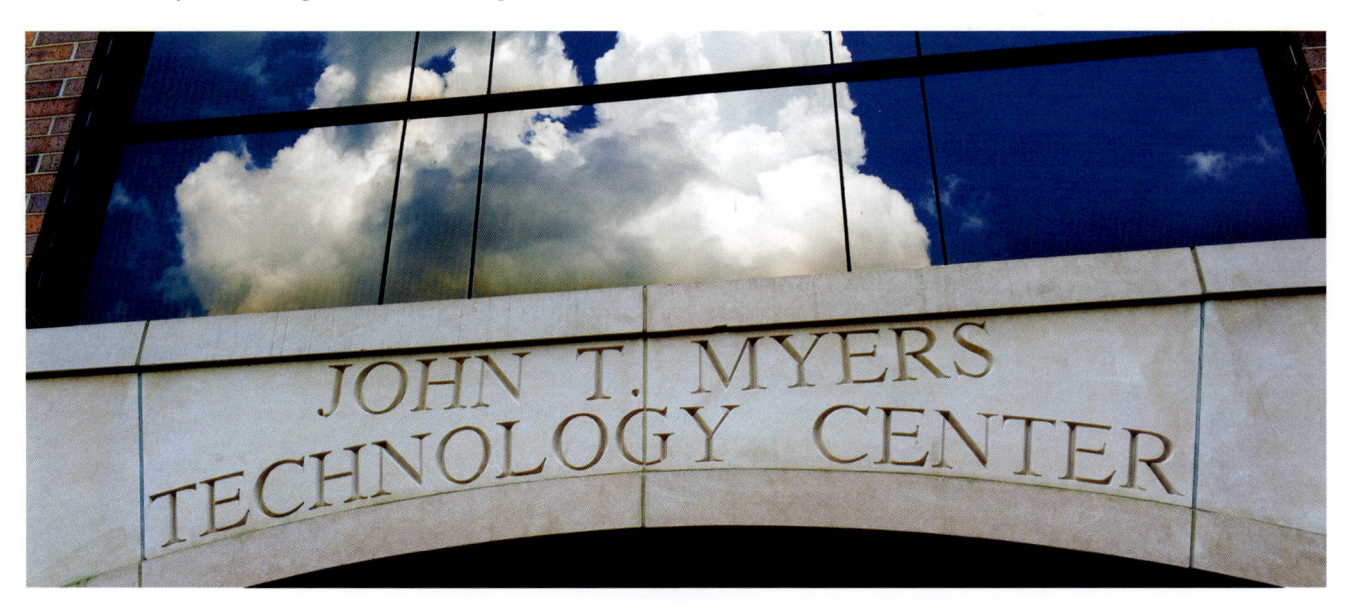

Myers Technology atrium

Myers Technology classroom

Myers Technology south facade

Chapter 8 References

1. The Trustees recommended Landini be named the new president to be effective on or before May 15, 1975. Trustee Minutes, January 25, 1975, p. 250. The letter of offer from James T. Morris, President, Indiana State University Board of Trustees, was sent to Landini on April 18, 1975. For the letter, see Trustee Minutes, April 26, 1975, p. 341. During his tenure as President, he suffered a myocardial infarction September 18, 1988 and on January 18, 1989, a perforation of the duodenum. The author acknowledges John Newton for his review of this chapter.

2. Richard G. Landini, Owls and Sycamores: The Life and Times of Indiana State University and Its President. Terre Haute, Indiana: Indiana State University Press, 1999. (Hereafter "Owls and Sycamores"). By 1978, the established value of the campus was placed at $142.22 million. This included 18 academic buildings, the Cunningham Library, eight administrative and student services buildings, 12 residence halls for unmarried students, and residence halls for married students.

3. Owls and Sycamores, p. 49.

4. Ibid, June 24, 1980, p. 458.

5. The name was officially adopted in 1984. Trustee Minutes, December 7, 1984, Sec. 1: L.

6. Walter Scholer, founder, was born May 8, 1890 in Portland, Indiana. He was one of 13 children. He moved to Indianapolis at 18. He died January 29, 1972. Firm appointed. Trustee Minutes, September 9, 1977, Sec.1: G.

7. Trustee Minutes, May 12, 1978, Sec. 1: E. Mach Van Houtin (General Construction, $341,037); AAA Electric (Electrical, $86,894); Freitag-Weinhardt (Mechanical, $164,755); Strand Century (Stage Lighting, $69,761).

8. Includes running utilities to Theater and new roof installation. Physical Plant Projects Fiscal Year 1977-78, p. 79. The estimate was $600,000 for remodeling. Trustee Minutes, June 3, 1977, Sec. 1: P.

9. Trustee Minutes, December 5, 1984, p. 10.

10. Trustee Minutes, November 5, 1976, pp. 205-208.

11. Trustee Minutes, September 9, 1977, p. 74.

12. Ibid, July 17, 1979, Sec.1: D.

13. Ibid, pp. 54-55.

14. Trustee Minutes, October 18, 1985, Sec. 1: C.

15. Ibid.

16. Trustee Minutes, March 30, 1979, pp. 393-394.

17. The Trustees approved a contract with Sasaki for $95,000. The contract listed five areas to be studied. (1) Land Use/Program definition; (2) Campus Design; (3) Pedestrian Circulation; (4) Vehicular Circulation; (5) Utilities. Trustee Minutes, February 7, 1986, Sec. 1: O.

18. Mr. Donald Hilt was Vice President of Business Affairs and Treasurer (1982-89).

19. The Campus Master Plan, prepared by Sasaki Associates, Inc., was approved by the Trustees June 20, 1986. Trustee Minutes, June 20, 1986, Sec. 1: S, October 30, 1987, M, p. 11.

20. Indiana State University Capital Improvement Budget Request 1987-89, pp. 2-3.

21. Trustee Minutes, May 11, 1984, Sec. 1: C, p. 270.

22. Ibid, December 13, 1979, Sec. 1: C, p. 172.

23 Ibid, February 1, 1980, Sec. 1: C, p. 209.

24 Owls and Sycamores, p. 77. Landini referred to this as "mischievous piffle."

25 Owls and Sycamores, pp. 69-70.

26 Ibid, p. 75.

27 Owls and Sycamores, pp. 181-188. With a change in Trustee membership and the benefit of a clearer proposal, President Moore, his successor, was able to secure the approval of the Board for the proposed Center.

28 Ibid, p. 281.

29 Modern Construction Company was founded by Noah D. Brill. Brill moved to Terre Haute in 1890. After working as a general contractor in the A. Fromme construction business, he resigned and aided in the formation of Modern Construction, becoming President in 1905. His firm is known for constructing many buildings in Terre Haute, among them were People's Brewery, Walden Flats, Elks Lodge, county jail, Union Hospital, and Fairbanks Library. See C. C. Oakey, Greater Terre Haute and Vigo County – Closing the First Century's History of City and County, 1908, Chicago and New York, The Lewis Publishing Company, p. 632.

See also Irene Roberts McDonough, History of the Public Library in Vigo County 1816-1975, Terre Haute: Vigo County Public Library, 1977.

30 James Associates was appointed by the Trustees. Trustee Minutes, July 31, 1981, p. 7.

31 Shelton Hannig, Inc. (General Contractor, $688,362); Freitag-Weinhardt (Mechanical, $408,232); AAA Electric Co., (Electrical, $138,513)

32 Trustee Minutes, June 2, 1978, p. 423.

33 Ibid, June 5, 1981, pp. 397-398.

34 Ibid. July 15, 1983, Sec. II: C, p. 17.

35 The term Beaux Arts derives from Les beaux arts (the fine arts) and is associated with the Ecole des Beaux-Arts in Paris. It was an eclectic style that relied heavily on Greek and Roman architectural styles mingled with Renaissance elements. It became popular in the United States after the 1893 Chicago Colombian Exhibition and waned before the Great Depression when it was seen as too ostentatious. Some of the characteristics include stone construction, balconies, balustrades, paired columns, triangular pediments, symmetrical facade, heavy decoration, and grand stairways.

36 The historical figures in the dome by the Unique Art Glass Co. include: Thomas Edison, Daniel Voorhees, William Shakespeare, Rosa Bonheur, Lew Wallace, Thomas Jefferson, Abraham Lincoln, Ulysses Grant, Harriet Beecher Stowe, H. W. Longfellow, R. W. Thompson, Mark Twain, Ludwig Beethoven, Victor Hugo, Washington Irving, and James Whitcomb Riley. Most unusual was the inclusion of Rosa Bonheur, the most famous, and perhaps infamous, woman artist of 19th century France. She died in 1899.

37 Trustee Minutes, June 2, 1978, p. 423.

38 Information provided by Mr. Jim Jensen, Director of Operations and Maintenance.

39 The award was presented August 6, 2003 by Andrew Connor, President of Terre Haute Landmarks.

40 See also: Irene Roberts McDonough, History of the Public Library in Vigo County, 1816-1975, Terre Haute: Vigo County Public Library, 1977 and Norman Bluebaum, "Meetings Planned to discuss library's fate," The Indiana Statesman, June 30, 1977, p. 2.

41 Indiana State University Facilities Management 2011-12 Annual Report, June 30, 2012.

42 Kevin Runion went on to have a distinguished career at Indiana State University. In 2010, he was named "Individual of the Year" by the Indiana Forest Council in recognition of his volunteer work for TREES, Inc., the National Road Association, the Holly Arboretum, Art Spaces, landscape design for the Vigo County Court House, "101 Trees of Indiana," and Centennial Park.

43 Physical Plant Projects Fiscal Year 1983-84, p. 44.

44 Prior to the parking lot, this was the site of the Rose Dispensary, a gift from Chauncey Rose. It was razed in 1972.

45 Descriptive information from Kevin Runion in an email to the author August 6, 2018.

46 This was the estimated amount in the Indiana State University Capital Improvement Budget Request:1985-87, Attachment A, p. 1.

47 Trustee Minutes, June 7, 1985, p. 7.

48 Odle was founded in 1916 in Indianapolis by Wilbur Shook and William McGuire. In 1971, a new firm, the Odle Group, was formed in Bloomington, Indiana. In 1989, The Odle Group merged with McGuire and Shook (now OMS). One of their recent projects included renovation and an addition to the Law School Library on the Bloomington campus of Indiana University. See: http:/www.omscorp.net/profile/history.

Trustees approved the appointment contract December 5, 1986.

49 Trustee Minutes, July 15, 1988, Sec. 1: K, pp. 13-14. Jungclaus-Campbell Construction Co. Inc. (General Construction, $4.19 million); Williams Plumbing and Heating, Inc. (Mechanical, $1.33 million); Steele-Bearde Co. Inc. (Electrical, $803,816).

50 The State Budget Committee approved bonding authority of $8.8 million, September 24, 1987. Trustee Minutes, October 30, 1987, p. 10.

51 Ibid, March 3, 1989 Sec. 1: I, p. 6.

52 Trustee Minutes, February 6, 1987, Sec.1, C: I.

53 The Trustees voted to allot $90,000 to hire an architect to develop preliminary plans. Trustee Minutes, June 20, 1986, p. 7. In July, the Trustees approved a budget request to the state for $13,114,000 and bonding authority for $8.65 million. Trustee Minutes, July 18, 1986, Sec. 1, p. 13.

54 HDG was approved by the Trustees in October 1987. Trustee Minutes, October 30, 1987, Sect. I: L, p. 10.

55 Ibid, October 13, 1989, Sect. I, p. 8. In the list of projects managed by Facilities Management, the cost was listed at $8.9 million.

56 Financial assistance was provided by a major gift from the Mary Fendrich Hulman Charitable Trust. Trustee Minutes, July 15, 1988, Sec. 1: J, p. 13. A plaque honoring Anton and Mary Fendrich Hulman Jr. was installed in HMSU in 1991.

57 A $1.7 million gift from Edmund and Mary Dede was used for the creation of Dede Plaza and the Dede meeting rooms and student activities spaces in the Union complex.

58 Terre Haute Mayor Chalos attended the groundbreaking ceremony and spoke briefly. Mr. Dede remarked that this was the first time he had ever agreed with everything the Mayor said. Indiana Statesman, September 15, 1989, p. 8. Trustee Minutes, July 19, 1989, Sec. 1: R, p. 13.

59 The fountain bears comparison to the Margery Enes Smith Fountain "Soaring Waters" at Purdue University, which is 30-feet in diameter with jets of water shooting toward the center from the periphery surrounded by seats and benches. Another comparison is with the Arboretum Park fountain at State College, Pennsylvania.

60 Estimated cost. Funding came from gifts and interest income.

61 Trustee Minutes, December 13, 2013, 1: 5, p. 32.

62 Information from Barbara Lawrence, Annual Report Facilities Management Fiscal Year 1990-91, pp. 66-70. The Recycling Center featured "Escrap Super Saturdays," resulting in the collection of 1.5 million pounds of electronic waste not sent to landfills.

63. See: Historic American Building Survey-John T. Beasley Building, National Park Service, Philadelphia, PA., n.d. Beasley was a prominent attorney in Terre Haute. A few of the offices he held included: President of Citizen Gas and Fuel and General Fuel Corporation and Director of the First National Bank and several railroad companies. He died in 1936 at the age of 75 and was buried in Roselawn Memorial Park.

64. Shourds was a local architect working in the Midwest during the first half of the 20th century. His office was in Terre Haute in the Tribune Building. He served as a member of the Board of Directors of the national Boys Club Federation. Two other structures by him are especially noteworthy: the Concannon School in West Terre Haute (opened September 1922) and the arch at Memorial Stadium. See: www://cdn.loc.gov/master/pnp/habshaer/in/in0300/in0349/data/in0349data.pdf.

65. Bean presents another Chicago connection. He was a graduate of the University of Illinois in architecture and a registered architect in Illinois. In addition to managing the Shrouds-Stoner architectural office in Chicago, he had responsibility for special building projects. The drawings for this building indicate his responsibility.

66. William Le Baron Jenney (1832-1907), Chicago architect credited with creating the earliest high-rise buildings.

67. Completed Projects, '93-'94 Facilities Management Department, Indiana State University, June 30, 1994, p. 102.

68. Indiana State University Facilities Management Department Project Update Fiscal Year '92-'93, p. 124.

69. Laura Phillips, "ISU receives $165,000 for chiller," Indiana Statesman, Vol. 98. No. 31, November 13, 1991, p. 1.

70. Scholer and Associates was approved by the Trustees in May 1988. Trustee Minutes, May 6, 1988, I, p. 7.

71. This included the construction of the central computing and administrative services facility, as well as a renovation of the previous student union in Tirey with an addition of 36,000 square feet.

72. Trustee Minutes, July 20, 1990 Sec. 1: D, p. 3.

73. Ibid. June 23, 1989, Sec. I: J.

74. Ibid. March 6, 1992, Sect. I: K, p. 8.

75. Ibid. February 2, 1990, Sect. 1: H, p. 9.

76. The Mathes Group was headquartered in New Orleans. The architect selection committee recommended Schmidt and Associates (with the Mathes Group) in a memorandum dated January 1, 1990.

77. Bid Tabulation Form. Bid Date May 12, 1995. Trustee Minutes, June 16, 1995, Sec. I, Attachment, pp. 11-12. Hanning Construction, Inc. (General Construction, $4.67 million); SMC, Inc., (Mechanical, $1.33 million); NRK (Electrical, $786,269)

78. This date coincided purposefully with the internationally acclaimed Contemporary Music Festival that began with President Rankin.

79. Physical Plant Projects, 1996-97.

80. Trustee Minutes, July 19, 1991, Sec. I: P, p. 14.

81. Indiana State University Capital Improvement Budget Request, 1991-93, "New Construction," p. 1.

82. Trustee Minutes, August 30, 2011, p. 7.

83. Interview with Wayne Schmidt, April 3, 2018.

84. Letter from Jean S. Blackwell, State Budget Director, to Dennis C. Graham, ISU Vice President for Business Affairs and Treasurer, stated the budget constraints (projected for 1993) might put the project at risk.

85. Bids for the project were received and opened May 12, 1995.

86. Letter to Dr. John Huie, Director, State Budget Agency, dated January 19, 1979. Trustee Minutes, August 24, 1978, Schedule A.

87. Trustee Minutes, May 11, 1979, Sec. 1: G.

88. Ibid. January 9, 1981, Sec.1: J. P. R. Duke Construction Co., Inc. (General Construction, $2.43 million); Freitag-Weinhardt, Inc. (Mechanical and Electrical, $1.5 million).

89. Ibid. June 24, 1980, Sec. 1: J.

90. Ibid. March 7, 1980, Sec. 1: C.

91. President Moore, Annual Report, 1994-95, p. 10.

CHAPTER 9

9TH PRESIDENT
JOHN WILLIAM MOORE
(1992-2000)

July 1, 1992
John William Moore became the 9th President of ISU.

Condit House became the Office of the President.

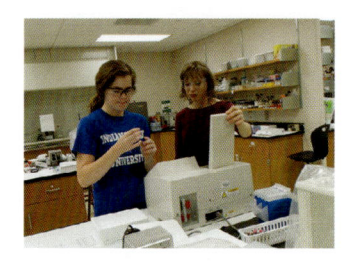

December 3, 1993
Science Building renovations began.

July 14, 1995
Oakley Place and the signature monument were completed.

January 28, 1993
The former Link Building was renamed for President Rankin.

October 21, 1994
Trustees authorized expending $500,000 to renovate the former United Mineworkers Building for use by the African-American Cultural Center.

December 6, 1995
Sycamore Sam was introduced at a basketball game.

Indiana State University Building a Legacy

Born: August 1, 1939

Wife: Nancy Ann Baumann Moore (married 1968-present)

Education:
Bachelor's Degree
Rutgers University

Master's Degree
Indiana University

Ed.D. Degree
Pennsylvania State University

Positions held at Indiana State University: President (1992-2000), President Emeritus, and Trustee Professor

April 19, 1996
The groundbreaking ceremony took place for the Advanced Technology Center (later the John Myers Technology Center).

December 8, 1997
The Center for Performing and Fine Arts was dedicated (renamed the Richard George Landini Center for Performing and Fine Arts).

October 21, 1999
The Central Heating Plant groundbreaking and dedication were held on October 4, 2001.

August 25, 1997
The Class of 2001 was the first to "march through the arch."

September 18, 1998
Dedication of the John T. Myers Technology Center took place.

1999
The first female athletic director was hired (Andrea Myers).

2000
The North Central Association awarded continuing accreditation for 10 years.

Chapter 9 President Moore

Dr. John Moore, President Emeritus, began his presidency at Indiana State University in August of 1992. He received his B.S. from Rutgers University, an M.S. from Indiana University, and an Ed.D. from Pennsylvania State University. He had a rich and varied career prior to coming to Indiana State University (ISU), having served as Vice President at the University of Vermont and Old Dominion University, and as President at the University of California-Stanislaus. He held a leadership role in the American Association of State Colleges and Universities (AASCU) and authored two books, one on presidential succession and a second on servant leadership in teaching. Servant leadership was one of the distinguishing aspects of his administrative style while at ISU.[1]

President Moore followed the eighth President, Dr. Richard G. Landini, whose tenure was the third longest in ISU history. While Landini's agenda for ISU was more internally and academically focused, (to be the "Harvard on the Wabash," or an elite liberal arts college), Moore's vision for ISU was for it to become a recognized "Progressive Public University." The progressive public university was to engage the community and be transformative by stimulating social change, economic growth, technological progress, and broadening educational opportunity, especially for underserved populations. This vision helped guide the renovation and addition of specific buildings on campus.

On assuming the office of President, Moore's early aspirations for ISU were to:
- Enhance the academic image of the campus
- Stabilize and increase enrollment
- Improve undergraduate residential experience
- Expand doctoral programs
- Foster a more inclusive campus
- Strengthen the Foundation
- Increase partnerships across the state in education, health care, the arts, and government
- Strengthen the men's basketball program
- Improve the appearance of the campus and functionality of the buildings[2]

Enhancing the university's academic reputation while at the same time stabilizing, or better, increasing enrollment, was a perennial problem. Moore was keen on enhancing access for a more diverse group of students. An analysis of the incoming freshman class of 1992 shows some noteworthy facts that indicate the degree of preparation of these students. The mean SAT verbal score nationally was 500. ISU students had a mean of 392. The median math score nationally was 501, and for ISU students, 436. Close to 65 percent of the freshman who entered ISU had a high school grade point average of C or lower.[3] During the Landini and Moore presidencies, an extensive number of remedial classes were offered. Moore was able to obtain funding for a First Year Experience Program from the Lilly Endowment to assist students' transition from high school to college and enhance student retention.[4]

During Moore's administration, and continuing into the next century, a profound transformation was underway nationally, and in Indiana, in the higher

President John Moore originated the Student Academic Services Center for Teaching and Learning, the President's Scholars Program, and the Lilly-supported First-Year Experience Program – intended to help under-prepared students make the transition from high school and two-year associates programs to college.

education landscape. External drivers included changing demographics, new societal expectations of the academy, increasing calls from government and the public for greater efficiency and accountability, declining resources with increased competition for a portion of the state budget allocated for higher education, and the entry of new providers of higher education that included community colleges (formerly technical schools) and online providers. In his 1995 convocation speech, "A Call to Compete," he stated, "We ... must recognize that we are engaged in vigorous competition for students, resources, and public support."

State appropriations for higher education were marked by uncertainty. While there was a noticeable decline in appropriations during the 1990s and 2000s, attributable to changing priorities at the state level (social programs, prisons and schools were the chief competitors), budget shortfalls occurred with some regularity. For example, the State Budget Agency called for a 2.6 percent decrease in appropriations during the 1993-95 biennium. ISU's budget was slated for a 2.1 percent cut.

Indiana State University Building a Legacy

With fixed costs such as utilities and energy rising, the additional cut further exacerbated the dire budget situation. Moore pointed out to the Trustees that the "… State Budget Agency proposals represent a significant shift in public policy resulting in a larger portion of the cost of public higher education being transferred from the State to the student."[5] Offsetting the reduction required reallocation of the current budget and a six percent increase in student fees.[6]

Moore recognized the threat posed by the worsening budgetary outlook and used his bully pulpit to encourage incessantly rapid change at ISU.[7] Moore's vision for making ISU more responsive was to focus on five strategies: access, student success, affordability, distinctiveness, and stewardship. Student fees and state appropriations were directly linked to enrollment, and the Indiana Commission for Higher Education made enrollment growth one of its major initiatives during this time. Unfortunately, enrollment was on a downward trajectory at ISU.

Driven by the necessity to enroll and retain students, Moore initiated many new services aimed to help students succeed. He originated the Student Academic Services Center for Teaching and Learning, the President's Scholars Program, and the Lilly-supported First-Year Experience Program – the latter was intended to help under-prepared students make the transition from high school and two-year associates programs to college. Other initiatives aimed to improve students' chances of success were the creation of the reading and math centers, the Student Ombudsman Program, and the Course Transformation Academy.

Moore was intent upon access and collaboration with other higher education providers in the state in order to position ISU as an institution of choice for students who began their post-secondary education at technical schools or two-year colleges. The establishment of DegreeLink, in cooperation with Vincennes College and the Ivy Tech statewide system, was one such strategic step. DegreeLink was intended to assist with admission and credit transfer to ISU. Other examples of collaborative programs included the BA/MD degree program with Indiana University and the Ph.D. degree in Technology Management offered through a consortium of universities across the U.S. Moore also served as President of the ISU Foundation, and during his tenure, with the contributions of Vice Presidents Dr. Dale McKee and Dr. Robert Quatroche, he increased the endowment to $40 million and secured, at the time, the largest donor gift in ISU history ($5 million) to establish the Gongaware Center for Insurance and Risk Management.[8] With the leadership of Dr. Robert Thompson (College of Business), ISU mounted its first major marketing campaign and introduced a university magazine intended to communicate more broadly the accomplishments on campus that better served Hoosiers across the state.

Moore was committed to providing greater opportunities for women and minorities. During his tenure he appointed Marilyn Schultz as Vice President (ISU's first female Vice President), Andi Myers as Athletic Director (the first female Athletic Director for ISU and second in the Missouri Valley Conference), Sherman Dillard as the men's basketball coach (first African-American men's basketball coach at ISU), and created a Commission for Ethnic Diversity that reported directly to him. The renovation of the African-American Student Center demonstrated the firmness of his commitment to enhancing diversity on the campus.

Moore commented in a recent letter that his initial impressions of ISU "were a mixture of favorable and unfavorable images. The physical appearance of the campus and the location of Terre Haute on the western side of the state I thought to be strategic liabilities."[9] He immediately added that these "impressions were mitigated by the promise described in the master plan initiated by President Landini, Vice President Dennis Graham (1986), and Mr. Kevin Runion (former Associate Vice President for Facilities Management)." He concluded by stating he was "committed to making the enhancement of the campus a priority" during his tenure as President.[10]

The Master Plan Moore inherited was the Master Plan for the campus that was approved by the Trustees in June 1986. One of the initiatives of the new 1994 Strategic Plan was implementation of Phase II of the earlier plan. This plan had five guiding principles that served to shape university development into the next century. These were:

1. Facilitate and enhance the academic mission (maintain academic core and add new buildings to meet programmatic needs)
2. Improve the quality of campus life by moving traffic to perimeter, emphasizing pedestrian linkages, and meeting state and federal regulations concerning safety and access
3. Enhance utilization efficiency and raze outdated buildings
4. Enhance students' residential life experiences
5. Enhance campus aesthetics and ambiance

Moore believed addressing the appearance of the campus was a critical factor in successfully recruiting students. Buildings remodeled or built new in his administration further reflected his chief concerns for student success, enhancing access to new technology disciplines and computers, expanding programs meeting social needs (nursing, for example), and supporting diversity. While some buildings were new

Left: Music Recital Hall
Right: Advanced Technology Center

additions to the campus, others disappeared because they were considered obsolete and economically not viable for renovation. Razed were the Terre Haute Gas Building (1993-94), Alumni Hall (1995-96), Old Technology (1997), Jamison Hall (September 1997), Reeve Hall (October 1997), Classroom Building (June 1999), and other smaller properties.

Progress was slow in adding much-needed new buildings on campus because the state budget was inadequate. For example, the decline in state resources in 1992-93 meant building the Music Recital Hall (Center for Performing and Fine Arts or CPFA) and the Advanced Technology Center (John T. Myers Technology Center or ATC) were postponed. The Center for Performing Arts had previously been approved for funding by the legislature in the 1991-93 Biennium, but the funds were not released. Moore could report good news to the Trustees in July 1995, stating the Commission for Higher Education had acted favorably on the Rhoads Hall renovation, Science Building renovation, construction of the Music Recital Hall (CPFA) and Advanced Technology Center (ATC).[11]

There was always a sense of nervousness surrounding capital requests because it was a labyrinthine process accompanied by unanticipated obstacles; for example, budget shortfalls. The Commission for Higher Education represented the initial hurdle followed by legislative budget committees and, even with final approval, the budgeted funds (which were based upon projected revenues) might be withheld until future budget years. This presented then, as well as now, its own set of problems because delayed construction meant increased costs, an especially difficult problem during inflationary times as it falls to the individual campus to find those extra dollars or reduce the scope of the project. In the case of the Advanced Technology Center, federal funds of nearly $5 million had already been secured. Not breaking ground as promised had the potential to put those funds at risk.

In 1994, ground was broken for the $7 million Music Recital Hall (CPFA), and in August 1995, the State Budget Committee approved funding $13.5 million for construction of the $18 million Advanced Technology Center.[12] Renovation funds were also appropriated for the Science Building. The Signature Piece supported by the Oakley Foundation was completed at the corner of Third and Cherry Streets.

Another first during Moore's administration was the introduction of the new mascot, Sycamore Sam, at a basketball game on December 6, 1995. Arriving at a final solution demonstrated how adeptly Moore handled crises. In this instance, the student body had voted for a caricature of a squirrel as the university's mascot. Moore selected some creative individuals to study this unacceptable creature. The result was a blue and white fox-looking animal, "a furry woodland creature," named Sycamore Sam.[13]

Moore's experience in higher education, especially his leadership role in the AASCU, meant that he was well-informed about the pace and nature of changes in higher education affecting campuses like ISU – schools

Continued on pg 217 >>

Sycamore Sam

Indiana State University Building a Legacy

Signature Monument (Oakley Place)

Architect: Steve Arnold, MMS and Associates[14]

Contractors: Jeff Bell Construction and Excavation; Construction Technology Association; Apex Masonry

Date: 1997

Cost: $541,885[15]

Area: 120,000 GSF

Location: 101 North Third at Cherry Street

The ISU "Signature" Monument is located at Third Street (Highway 41) and Cherry Street on the site of the former ISU Federal Credit Union and Marathon Oil station on the southwestern corner of campus.[16] It is an 18-foot-high semicircular brick and limestone structure that marks an important step in realizing Master Plan Phase II. The idea for the monument may owe to a similar project on the University of California, Stanislaus campus where Moore had been President.[17] It is also visible to travelers on Highway 41 and makes ISU a destination.

Inscribed on a frieze on the inside of the structure are the institutional name changes and dates that are part of ISU's history. A replica of the university seal is located in a granite medallion set in the floor. In earlier plans, there was a suggestion for 12 piers and a statue. The piers were maintained but were reduced in number and moved to the inside of the semicircle where they were designed to display plaques honoring important figures from ISU's history. The semicircular form of this structure echoes the curvilinear entry to the Hulman Memorial Student Union and respects the axial organization of the campus developed in the master plan prepared by Sasaki and Associates.

Hulman Memorial Student Union

Chapter 9 President Moore

The Board of Trustees approved the plans and budget at the regular meeting on June 14, 1996. Cost for the project was significantly defrayed by a generous gift of $150,000 from the Oakley Foundation. In 1997, during President Moore's administration, the custom began to have the incoming class of students proceed from the convocation in the Hulman Center, go west on Cherry Street to the monument, and then "march through the arch" stepping on the university seal, cheered on by Sycamore Sam, cheerleaders, the marching band, the President, and other administrators. The class of 2001 was the first to walk through the arch on August 25, 1997. The monument has taken on an important symbolic role as students take a transitional step through the "doors" of the monument, walk across the university seal, and enter the Sycamore family. ∎

Signature Monument (Oakley Place)
Inscribed on a frieze on the inside of this structure are the institutional name changes and dates that are part of Indiana State University's history.

Indiana State University Building a Legacy

Central Heating Plant (Power Plant)

Architect/Engineer: Stanley Consultants, Inc.[18]

Contractors: CDI (General Construction); Sycamore Engineering (Electrical); Freitag-Weinhardt Inc. (Mechanical)

Date: Groundbreaking: October 21, 1999

Dedication: October 4, 2001

Cost: $25.09 million

Area: 44,603 GSF; 5,019 ASF

Location: 625 Seventh Street

The Central Heating Plant, a much-needed upgrade to the campus, replaced an earlier coal-fired plant that was designed by Ewing Miller dating to 1968. Thirteen years in the making, the plant was born out of necessity as the original had exceeded its 30-year life span. Built during a time when energy conservation and pollution control were not major considerations, the old plant incorporated steam tunnels that distributed heat and hot water across campus both inefficiently and inadequately. In August 1997, Stanley Consultants assessed the plant and determined it was beyond rehabilitation. They suggested it be replaced by a natural gas/oil-powered plant. The financial costs for keeping the current system in operation were estimated at nearly $2 million a year by the end of the century, not to mention the safety and pollution issues surrounding the old plant.

President Moore faced difficulties in advocating for a natural gas/oil-fired plant. Fifteen plant options were evaluated that ranged from repairing the existing facility, replacing individual components, or replacing the entire facility. One of the selling points for the new plant was that it would be designed as a teaching model and could be studied for its mechanical properties. Consequently, the design incorporated color coded piping systems and observation areas that enabled students to understand the workings of the plant. The building also served as a prompt to discuss environmental issues. It was estimated the new plant would reduce emissions by approximately 1.4 million pounds annually and also reduce chemical effluents produced in the water treatment process.

On June 27, 1997, The Board of Trustees authorized the administration to spend $1.2 million for planning and engineering. The Power Plant replacement was included in the ISU 1997-99 Capital Request Budget.[19] An additional $11 million for steam tunnels would be necessary for distribution of steam and hot water. Construction began under President Moore with a groundbreaking on October 21, 1999, and the plant came on-line early in President Benjamin's office. The dedication was held on October 4, 2001.

The design for the new power plant reduced the area required for its operation from 69,719 to 32,200 gross square feet. Stylistically, the exterior of the building reflects materials used in other areas of the campus and includes brick, limestone, and glazing in dark bronze panels. Steel framing was used for the superstructure. The Plant was constructed with four gas/oil-fired boilers that could supply 150,000 lbs/hr with the largest boiler out of service.[20]

The building has a classical/Italian Renaissance quality in terms of its measured proportions. The three-story clock tower, reminiscent of Italian campaniles (bell-towers), is not only an attractive decorative element, but it serves to conceal 85-foot high smokestacks. This feature led the Midwest Construction Magazine to name the building "Project of the Year."

The Power Plant has won national recognition and received numerous awards, including the "Grand Conceptor Award for Engineering Excellence" by the Consulting Engineers Council of Iowa, the National Recognition Award, Engineering Excellence Awards Competition, American Council of Engineering Companies, the Build Indiana Award, Certificate of Excellence in Utility Projects, State of Indiana and Outstanding Concrete Achievement Award from the Indiana Ready Mix Concrete Association. ■

> **Central Heating (Power Plant)**
> *The three-story clock tower, reminiscent of Italian campaniles (bell-towers), is not only an attractive decorative addition, but it is functional, serving to conceal 85-foot high smokestacks. This feature led the Midwest Construction Magazine to name the building "Project of the Year."*

Indiana State University Building a Legacy

<< Continued from pg 212

whose origins were as teacher preparatory schools and who now faced new challenges to demonstrate their viability and necessity, and not be overshadowed by state land grant and major research institutions, such as Purdue and Indiana University. He played a major role in mapping a new direction for ISU in the 21st century.

Dr. Moore resigned the presidency in the summer of 2000 but continued briefly to teach and direct doctoral theses in the Education Leadership Program in the College of Education. Based upon his presidential experiences gained in leadership roles at several institutions, he has published on the topic of presidential transition and played a leadership role for the AASCU in directing sessions for new presidents and those transitioning out of the position.

Indiana State University honored President Moore by naming the Welcome Center in his honor.[21] Former President Bradley remarked, "Your commitment to enhancing the student experience, building leadership, embracing diversity, utilizing technology, and improving access to higher education opportunities is unparalleled."

As of publishing, Moore resides in Florida with his wife Nancy Ann Baumann Moore.

Left: John W. Moore Welcome Center
Right: President Moore at ribbon-cutting

Chapter 9 References

1. See: Robert K. Greenleaf, The Power of Servant Leadership, San Francisco: Berett-Koehler, 1998.

2. Letter to author, August 2012, p. 2.

3. Freshman Profile, Fall 1992 presented at the Trustee meeting September 14, 1992. During the Landini period, deficiencies were made up through remedial courses.

4. This program, entitled the Summer Transition Program, was coupled with the ISU Summer Reading Program. Remedial courses represent an institutional cost and the influx of under-prepared students combined with excessive numbers of associate degree programs diminished the institution's reputation in the minds of some.

5. Trustee Minutes, February 3, 1993, Sec. I, p. 4. He continued, "This has important social implications for the Hoosier state." See also Vice President Schultz's further discussion of the anticipated budget shortfalls for the 1993-95 biennium. Trustee Minutes, July 16, 2003, Sec. 1: L., p. 9.

6. Trustee Minutes, February 5, 1993, Sec. 1: C., p. 4.

7. Moore listed his impatience at the pace of change in his June 1999 "Annual Self-Assessment."

    "... at times, impatient with such things as: slow pace of institutional change," p. 2.

8. The gift was announced in June 1998 and presented by Moore to the Trustees at the July meeting of the Board.

9. John Moore, Letter to author, p. 1.

10. John Moore, Letter to author, p. 2.

11. Trustee Minutes, July 14, 1995, Sec. I, p. 4.

12. Ibid, September 1, 1995, Sec. 1, p. 3.

13. This story was recounted by Vice President for Student Affairs, Paul Edgerton, at the dedication. See: http://www2.indstate.edu/news/news.php?newsid=3240.

14. Gulara Design provided the plans for lighting.

15. Does not include the architect's and other fees.

16. The address of the Marathon Property was 101 Cherry.

    The Marathon headquarters in Ohio rejected ISU's offer of $140,000 for the property and obtained their own appraisal for $200,000 in contrast to a local appraisal for $100,000. A local attorney offered $220,000. ISU filed condemnation proceedings.

17. A letter with photographs was sent in February 1995 from Carl Coffey, Sr. Director of Facilities Management and Planning at Stanislaus to Kevin Runion, Assistant Vice President for Facilities at ISU that describes a "Corner Plaza Project" that bears comparison.

18. The Indiana General Assembly approved expenditure and bidding authority for $16.6 million. Stanley Consultants, Inc. was engaged. Trustee Minutes, June 18, 1998, Sec. IV, p. 7.

19. The estimated cost was $28 million. Indiana State University Capital Improvement Budget Request 1997-99, Schedule A.

20. Peak load historically was 125,000 lbs/hr.

21. The Center was the former Home Economics Building built during the Holmstedt presidency.

CHAPTER 10

10TH PRESIDENT
LLOYD WILLIAM BENJAMIN III
(2000-2008)

2000
The Utility Tunnel Renovation was completed.

October 4, 2001
The Central Power Plant became operative.

2002
The Percent for Art program was introduced, setting aside one percent of building cost for purchasing art.

The Lily Endowment awarded $20 million for the creation of the Networks Financial Services Institute.

2003-05
Stalker Hall was renovated and the Van Alstine and de Boer Lichtveld artworks were acquired.

October 21, 2005
The Michael Simmons Student Activity Center was dedicated.

2005
The Center for Public Service and Community Engagement was initiated.

Indiana State University Building a Legacy

Born: September 2, 1944

Wife: Dr. Wieke van der Weijden (married 1971-present)

Education:
Bachelor's Degree
A. B. Emory University
History of Art

Ph.D. Degree
The University of North Carolina-Chapel Hill
History of Art

Positions held at Indiana State University: President (2000-08), President Emeritus, and Trustee Professor

2005-08
The Arts Corridor was completed, from Cherry to Tippecanoe on Seventh Street.

2006
The Cherry Street Multimodal Transportation Facility underway was initiated with the city of Terre Haute.

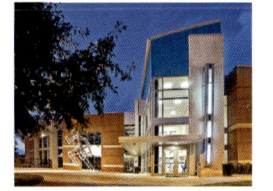

2007
The Athletic Training Facility was created in the Arena.

The Community Garden began.

July 19, 2007
The Student Recreation Center groundbreaking ceremony was held.

2007-08
Renovation of the Federal Building (the Scott College of Business) began.

Renovation of the Laboratory School (University Hall) to house the College of Education began.

The "laptop initiative" began.

Chapter 10 President Benjamin

A useful introduction to Benjamin's agenda as the tenth President of Indiana State University (ISU) would be the interview Martin Blank (former editor of Indiana State University's STATE Magazine) conducted shortly after Benjamin arrived on campus. Regarding upcoming challenges and opportunities, he stated, "they include innovative use of technology in teaching and learning; increasing diversity; reviewing academic curriculum and programs; the identification and promotion of centers of excellence; increasing educational access through distance education; seeking additional partnerships and collaborative relationships with business and industry, health care agencies, K-12 schools, and the arts; and raising the profile of ISU's programs and faculty."[1] Not mentioned, but included, were increasing enrollment, diversifying income streams, stabilizing the budget, enhancing ISU's reputation, and raising external support. The utility of these goals was to focus the campus and provide a means to measure success.

increased communication with legislators and alumni, diversifying resources through increased private giving, and enhancing the online presence of the campus.

A new vision statement was adopted in 2004 that captured how ISU was to become a preeminent public university. Goals included integration of teaching and research, and inspiring students to create and apply knowledge through experiential learning opportunities. A new brand slogan was adopted, "More. From day one," that captured the energy and efforts of the campus to create an engaging and challenging learning environment.

Second, the university needed a clearly articulated aspirational goal. In the Annual Report for 2001-02 entitled "Progress Toward Pre-Eminence," Benjamin stated his vision was to make ISU one of the best comprehensive universities in the Midwest, and an institution of choice for high-achieving students. The goal encompassed the creation of a distinctive learning environment, programs of eminence, and a

> **"At the center is our dedication to being a student-centered preeminent university recognized for our distinctive learning environment, programs of eminence, and a commitment to community engagement."** – Dr. Lloyd W. Benjamin

In 2004, President Benjamin, together with Mr. Greg Goode (Executive Director for External Relations), met with state senator Luke Kinley in Noblesville, whose observations underscored the importance of addressing institutional reputation. The senator asked, "Lloyd, what does Indiana State do? I know you train teachers, but what else do you do down there?" ISU needed a recognized, distinctive identity.

The question of reputation was persistent, going back to the early years of the school. Conservative adherence to the early stated mission of Indiana State Normal School (ISNS), to focus only on preparing teachers for lower grades, and reluctance to modernize mission and develop college-level undergraduate and graduate degree programs (as rapidly as had other universities) colored perceptions of the school. A new strategic plan for the university, "Path to Pre-Eminence," was developed and approved by the Trustees in 2003.[2]

To address the issue of perception, the university first needed to redefine its mission, develop high-profile areas of excellence, and strategically market itself across the state to potential students, alumni, and government officials. Implementation steps included

commitment to community engagement and economic development.[3]

Within three years, ISU was recognized by the Princeton Review as one of the best universities in the Midwest. In 2006, the Review cited the university for its "private school feel," and in addition, in 2007, the Review's publication, America's Best Value Colleges, named ISU one of the nation's "best value" undergraduate institutions.[4]

Managing enrollment was a challenge for every President. Benjamin's vision for ISU was that it become an institution of choice for Hoosiers. It was apparent in 2002 that more students were selecting the school. Total enrollment for Fall 2001 was 11,321 – the highest it had been since 1995. There were unanticipated developments sanctioned by the Indiana Commission for Higher Education that challenged ISU and directly impacted enrollment. Ivy Tech became the community college system of Indiana. Vincennes University, which was 40 miles away, became a four-year university and began to offer off-campus classes in what had been ISU territory.[5]

The regional campuses of Indiana University (IU) and Purdue were allowed to build residence halls and offer graduate-level courses. Finally, the population growth in the ISU catchment area grew more slowly than other areas of the state. Higher education had become extremely competitive. It was imperative that ISU remodel its residential facilities, which resulted in enrollment growth during the Benjamin and Bradley years.

Another issue that needed to be addressed was admission standards and student graduation rates. During the Landini period, students graduating in the lower quarter of their high school class were admitted to ISU with conditions. Open admission did not enhance the institution's reputation. Second, poorly prepared students failed to graduate. Typically, ISU would lose nearly a third of the entering class in the first year. To counter this, admission standards were raised.

In the emerging framework for higher education under development by the Indiana Commission for Higher Education, ISU, to maintain its place with Purdue, IU, and Ball State University, should admit only students who had completed the Core 40 and have academic honors credit. In 2000, fewer than 50 percent of incoming freshmen had met these requirements, and the SAT scores and grade point averages were equal to or lower than IU regional campuses, as well as the University of Southern Indiana. The absence of a strong reputation hindered growth in the enrollment of high-achieving students.

To address this, steps were taken to restructure Admissions and Financial Aid, the position of Vice President for Enrollment Management was created, a new admissions center was created, and a new marketing campaign was developed. Dual enrollment with Ivy Tech helped more associate degree students transfer to ISU seamlessly.[6] Graduate enrollment by 2005 was the highest in ISU history, and despite the adverse effect the attack on the World Trade Towers in New York had on international enrollment country-wide, ISU's international enrollment continued to grow. During the period of 2000 through 2008, graduate enrollment grew by 37 percent, while undergraduate enrollment declined slightly, owing in large measure to circumstances beyond the university's control.

To attract more high-achieving students, a new program began in 2007 that granted each new high school graduate with a grade of 'B' or better, and who had earned an Indiana Core 40 diploma, a new business-grade laptop computer. In the first year, over 700 students received a computer. By 2017, 1,539 laptops and iPads were distributed.[7] In 2007, ISU became the first public university in Indiana to require all first-year students to have notebook computers.

During this time, elevated admission standards caused a slight temporary dip in freshman enrollment, offset in part by increased graduate enrollment. An important outcome was increased graduation rates.

The subject of transfer and commuting students also needed attention. Students who did not live on campus and had responsibilities off-campus were at risk of dropping out. The needs of this population, and understanding of impediments to their continuing, had not been systematically assessed. A generous anonymous gift was given to the university to analyze the problem and put programs in place to assist these students with completing their degrees. This resulted in the creation of a commuting student lounge in the Student Union, with technology that provided a place to study and refresh between classes, as well as incentivizing financial assistance opportunities.

National studies calculated expected six-year graduation rates for institutions across the country. While ISU's population included a proportionally higher percentage of at-risk students, the university's graduation rate at that time exceeded the predicted rate by five percent each year – a result attributable to the hard work of faculty and staff.

The quest for pre-eminence is seen to best advantage in the Networks Financial Services Initiative. In 2002, challenged by the Lilly Endowment, Inc., faculty from the School of Business, together with national representatives from the financial services industry, were challenged to explore ways the School of Business could build on current strengths to serve students, the state, and the financial industry. This resulted in the creation of "Networks." Networks was designed to provide a platform for the development of market-based, innovative approaches for dealing with emerging issues in the financial services industry. The Lilly Endowment provided a $20 million gift – the largest gift in ISU history – to fund this new and challenging initiative.

One of the principle benefactors were outstanding students who were named "Network Scholars" and were provided a four-year $20,000 scholarship, an internship, international travel, and leadership development opportunities. Including the Lilly Endowment gift, the ISU Foundation raised more than $27.1 million in 2002 – the greatest single fundraising year ever at ISU.

President Benjamin created the first Center for Public Service and Community Engagement and appointed its first director. During Bradley's presidency, the director position became a Vice President of the new Division of University Engagement, suggesting how the activities of the Center and its role in the community had grown.[8]

The university joined the national American Humanics Program, which offered a certificate and academic minor for students interested in service-learning and leadership in not-for-profit organizations after graduation. In 2005-06, ISU was listed in President George W. Bush's President's Higher Education Honor Roll for Community Service. Additionally, ISU was selected as one of only 62 institutions in the country to receive the new Carnegie Classification for Community Engagement in the areas of curriculum and community partnerships. Community engagement became pervasive, demonstrated by 5,400 ISU students involved in community-related activities by the 2007-08 academic year.

Strengthening faculty research was another goal of the new ISU mission, "Fulfilling the Promise-The Path to Pre-Eminence." With the assistance of a four-year commitment of $3.5 million from the Lilly Endowment, Inc. to stop the Indiana "brain-drain," President Benjamin, with Provost Maynard, developed the "Promising Scholars" program. Supporting research benefited faculty, as well as the state. In its first year, 16 faculty members were awarded $15,000 each to support their research programs.

President Benjamin saw the physical design of the campus as a way to make the university more cohesive, stimulating, and aesthetically pleasing. Owing to the leadership of Mr. Kevin Runion, Associate Vice President for Facilities Management, attention to the design and appearance of the campus brought recognition. The Professional Ground Management Society and Landscape Magazine presented the Green Star Award to ISU in recognition of its ground maintenance and landscaping accomplishments, selecting ISU as number one in the country.

President Benjamin was strongly committed to expanding ISU's engagement abroad. He believed it was professionally important for students to experience international travel, and for faculty to develop international research partnerships. In 2001, a delegation visited Liaoning University in China to reaffirm and broaden the 1995 inter-institutional exchange agreement. Later, an alumni association was begun in Thailand. ISU signed a collaboration agreement in 2002 with the University Hassan II-Mohammedia in Morocco, making ISU the first American university to sign an exchange agreement with a Moroccan university.

In addition to offering programs in Morocco to develop higher education leadership, ISU was one of two universities to be invited to attend and present in the first International President's Conference on University Design. This conference was sponsored by China's Sichuan University and the government of Sichuan Province. Benjamin, with Dr. Gaston Fernandez (Director of International Programs at ISU), presented a paper on the role of higher education in regional economic development.[9]

By 2006, ISU had established international partnerships with 24 universities worldwide. In recognition of his service to higher education in Morocco, President Benjamin (the first American and third person ever) was presented an honorary doctorate by the University of Hassan II in Mohammedia, and was invited by the Fulbright Commission to represent the U.S. as a keynote speaker in Berlin at the conference on International Dialogue on Education.[10]

A problem first discussed in the North Central Association's accreditation evaluation, conducted during President Landini's administration, was too many academic majors offered to too few students. This observation was repeated during President Moore's time, with further comment by the Indiana Commission for Higher Education, stating there was a critical need to conduct serious program review, the point being that undersubscribed programs should be cut in order to redirect resources to higher priorities.[11] A comprehensive study of programs was undertaken, and the results shared with the Commission.

Another persistent problem was the fact that ISU received the highest appropriation of state funds per FTE (full-time equivalent student) of all other campuses, save one. This was of concern to some state legislators, who did not know the history of why this was so, and preferred savings garnered from a reduction in ISU's appropriation to be spread among other campuses. The origin of the problem is found in the history of the university's efforts to keep tuition low and serve as many students as possible, many of whom were the first generation to attend college. The threat of "equalization of appropriations" meant ISU could experience a reduction in state support, adversely impacting the campus. Thus, steps to intervene, such as program reviews, were critical. Ultimately, ISU did lose approximately 10 percent of its annual state support – a cut that had to be absorbed by the campus within a two-year period.

Despite occasional tensions, ISU/Terre Haute relations had many positive aspects. For example, the creation of family housing (Maehling Terrace) was part of the city's urban development plans. Benjamin considered the decision to acquire the Federal Building on Cherry Street to become the home of the College of Business an important step in the economic development of downtown. The creation of the $13.4 million Cherry Street Multi-Modal Transportation Facility is a most tangible sign of the growing 'town and gown' partnership.

Senator Evan Bayh, who helped ISU with acquiring the Federal Building, was also instrumental in securing funds for building the new Transportation Facility. He said, "The way in which the city of Terre Haute, Indiana State University, and the local businesses are joining together to make the Cherry Street Facility a reality was impressive. I also want to recognize the broader efforts underway to revitalize downtown." First Lady of ISU, Dr. Wieke Benjamin, initiated the Sycamore Showcase program, bringing together university and community leaders to learn about important topics.

To stimulate economic development, ISU created the Center for Business Support and Economic Innovation – a component of the Terre Haute Innovation Alliance. Benjamin named Chris Pfaff to become ISU's official liaison for Business Support Services and Economic Development.

President Benjamin took pride in adding new buildings and renovating others to house students and programs. By 2008, he noted that the ISU urban campus was undergoing one of the most significant transformations in its history, with nearly $130 million in construction projects completed or underway. A major program was the acquisition and demolition of derelict properties north and east of the campus. In one year alone, 42 properties were demolished. These vacant properties were fenced and planted with trees.[12]

A major interest of President Benjamin and Dr. Wieke Benjamin was the integration of art into the built environment on campus.[13] The president initiated a Percent for Art program that dedicated one percent of the cost for new buildings and renovated structures to be devoted to the acquisition of art. That interest extended to architectural preservation and included such projects as the restoration of Sycamore Theater, renovation of Stalker Hall and University Hall (School of Education), restoration of the dome in Fairbanks Hall, and adapting the Federal Building to meet the needs of the College of Business. A committee was established to discuss the renovation of Normal Hall, but action had to be postponed.

In order to maintain traditions, a building of special importance was created – the Michael Simmons Student Activity Center – which was a facility to house the Sycamore Tricycle Derby and the Tandem Race.[14]

Benjamin believed that the role of the President needed to be externally focused in order to advance the university by developing fruitful relations with members of state and federal government, strengthening alumni relations, and raising external funds. The internal building campaign was maintained while safeguarding university reserve funds. Finally, in January 2006, Benjamin led the Foundation to develop the first ever comprehensive campaign for ISU, titled "March On!"

President Benjamin resigned the presidency effective June 30, 2008 after eight years of service. He continues to teach art history and conduct research on the history of ISU architecture and site-specific design in The Netherlands. ■

Utility Tunnel Renovation

Date: 2000

Cost: $11 million

Area: 8,000 GSF

While not visible to those walking the campus, underfoot is a network of tunnels large enough to walk through that serve as the major arteries for the campus. Electronic connections, telecommunications, chilled water, steam heat, and other utilities wind their way through this essential subterranean maze.

Michael Simmons with Debbie and Tom Bareford

Michael Simmons Student Activity Center and Recreation East

Phase I

Contractor: Hannig Construction

Project Manager: Bryan Duncan

Date: 2000-01

Cost: $725,259

Included a new track, fencing, and lighting.

Phase II

Contractors: MS and Jungclaus-Campbell Co., Inc.

Architects: Scott Tillman and MMS A/E Inc.[15]

Date: Dedication: October 21, 2005

Cost: $937,555

Area: 3,000 GSF; 1,600 ASF

Location: 539 North Ninth Street

The Michael Simmons Activity Center was created.

Michael Simmons was one who truly bled Blue. He completed his undergraduate work at ISU in life sciences. He was the co-founder of the Sycamore Tricycle Derby, first held on the Quad during Homecoming weekend in October 1963, together with life-long friends Tom and Debbie Bareford. The trike race is one of the oldest homecoming traditions in the country.

Early in his presidency, Benjamin met with Michael, and it became immediately apparent that the trike race held special meaning for him. He believed it would be

Indiana State University Building a Legacy

helpful to students to have a facility where trikes could be kept in shape for racing, and a facility with seating that allowed the homecoming crowds to see the race from a better vantage point.

The university prepared sketches for the facility and worked with Simmons to achieve a design that met his expectations. Simmons made a generous gift to have the facility built in time for the dedication during Homecoming 2005. Simmons liked to tinker, and he built a motorized trike for President Benjamin to ride around the track to celebrate the event.

The interior consists of the 50-seat Susan M. Bareford Memorial Classroom, a multi-purpose room, alumni lounge, viewing level, restrooms, and storage, while the exterior provides outdoor seating for viewing events on the race track and athletic field, a porte cochere, and walk of fame.

Using the Percent for Art program, Patrick Titzer was commissioned to develop a design appropriate for the building. Titzer designed three different bicycle wheels in metal that were placed in rounded openings on three walls of the building. It was a very successful solution, appropriate to the building and trike/tandem races held every year.[16]

Michael Simmons died February 7, 2017. His student-oriented philanthropy was expressed again when a foundation fund was established to support the Trike Race tradition and experiential learning opportunities for student teams.[17] ∎

Early race on the Quad

Chapter 10 President Benjamin

Landsbaum Center

Architect: BSA Design[18]

Contractors: Hannig Construction Co., Inc. (General Construction); Sycamore Engineering (Electrical and Mechanical); Swiderski Electronics

Date: 2002-03

Dedication: September 26, 2003

Cost: $5.7 million[19]

Area: 34,170 GSF; 20,835 ASF

Location: 1433 North 6 ½ Street

Renamed: Landsbaum Center for Health Education[20]

The Landsbaum Center for Medical Education represents a collaboration of the Indiana University School of Medicine-Terre Haute, the ISU College of Nursing, Health and Human Services students, and resident-physicians from Union Hospital's Family Medicine Residency Program. The joint program serves the academic needs of nursing students and second-year medical students specializing in rural and family practice medicine. Located within the building is the Richard G. Lugar Center for Rural Health, the West Central Indiana Area Health Education Center, and teaching facilities for students in the various programs.

The building is a two-story structure adjacent to the Family Medicine Center on the Union Hospital Campus. The facility contains examination rooms, classrooms, and a 150-seat auditorium/lecture hall. Focusing on rural health care, the new facility provides improved health care services in those areas. It brings under one roof the ISU continuing education program for nurses, the Terre Haute Center for Medical Education Mini-Medical School program, free immunization clinics, and low-cost child and adult health clinics.

Funding came from various sources. In 1999, the state legislature provided $2.5 million to the Indiana University School of Medicine-Terre Haute. The Center for Rural Health was awarded $2.5 million from the U.S. Health Resources and Services Administration. ISU contributed $1.5 million that derived from the sale of the earlier School of Nursing Clinical facility. The estate of Terre Haute businessperson Morris Landsbaum contributed approximately $3 million for construction and equipment. ■

Arts Corridor

Contractor: S. T. Construction

Project Designers/Managers: Bryan Duncan and Kevin Runion

Date: 2003-04

Cost: $338,329[21]

Location: Seventh Street from Cherry Street to Tippecanoe

The planning and labor that went into developing the Arts Corridor cannot be overestimated. Running from Cherry Street through the campus to Tippecanoe, its character owes to aesthetic considerations such as the light fixtures and the landscape design for the central median, luxuriant with a variety of plants and flowers.[22] The Corridor links ISU to downtown arts amenities, such as the Swope Museum and Art Spaces sculptures, and it makes a statement that you have arrived in a special place. The Corridor takes on the appearance of a grand boulevard one might find in a European city, such as Paris.

Completing this segment of the Arts Corridor project required removal of street parking along Seventh Street, yielding sufficient width to insert an eight-foot median with plantings, ornamental lighting, and bicycle lanes.

The second major element was the creation of a 250-space parking lot on the site of the recently razed power plant.

The third element was to add a pull-off loop in front of the New Theater to provide a safe place to unload passengers. The north entry to the campus had not received the same attention as the south entries, so the formal treatment of the street makes for a more impressive entry onto the campus.

One of the practical benefits of the design is to encourage "traffic calming." The median, punctuated with bollards, alerts drivers to crosswalks, which is important as Seventh Street has considerable student foot traffic.

The Arts Corridor makes a formal statement about the interconnectedness of ISU, the city of Terre Haute, and the arts.

Terre Haute Federal Building and Post Office

Architect: Original design by Miller and Yeager

Project Architect: James A. Wetmore

Date: 1934
Acquired: 2005

Cost: $450,000

Area: 84,390 GSF; 55,730 ASF

Location: Sixth and Cherry Streets

The original Post Office and Federal Building was built near the National Highway and Crossroads of America intersection.[23] Funding was provided through the Roosevelt Public Work Project program. It is a rectangular, three-story structure that covers the southwest corner of Seventh and Cherry Streets. The building is an outstanding example of the Art Deco style. The exterior is dressed limestone veneer over an I-beam frame. The symmetrical façade has entry doors in large bays at the extreme east and west ends of the building. The façade is divided into 11 narrow two-story bays defined by fluted piers. The bays are identical and contain narrow windows with metal grillwork. The attic has horizontal banding with decorative carvings over the doorways. The amount of ornamental metalwork, limestone detailing, millwork, door hardware, interior finish, and light fixtures is exceptional.

The designing firm, Miller and Yeager, completed other major landmark buildings in the city including the Terre Haute City Hall, Zorah Shrine, and Woodrow Wilson Junior High School, with which it might be compared.[24] The project architect was James A. Wetmore (1863-1940), however, this is misleading. Wetmore was a lawyer and administrator who oversaw a staff of about 1,700 architects and draftsmen who designed around 2,000 government buildings, including post offices and courthouses.[25]

The magnificent courtroom is decorated with a mural depicting the signing of the Magna Carta.[26] It was painted as a triptych (a work in three parts) by Frederic Webb Ross in New York during the period 1934-35. It was shipped to the Federal Building and assembled by Public Works employees, who were supported by a wooden scaffold during assembly. ∎

Renovation Phase I

Architects: Schmidt and Associates and Architura. Architura functioned as the project representative for the General Services Administration (GSA).

Date: Phase I Construction began: October 2005
GSA and Federal Government gave ownership to ISU:

November 2008

Cost: $6.5 million funded by the General Services Administration (Federal Building Manager)[27]

Area: 90,000 GSF; 63,000 ASF

A series of important steps preceded the beginning of renovation of the Federal Building. In September 2001, Schmidt and Associates won a competitive bid to begin the design process for both the Colleges of Education and Business. In December 2002, Senator Evan Bayh and ISU announced negotiations were underway for the transfer of the Federal Building to ISU. A year later, an agreement was concluded with the United States Postal Service, the General Services Administration (GSA), and ISU that addressed next steps. In May 2004, ISU and the GSA entered into discussions regarding the scope of work for Phase I construction, which would be directed and paid for by the GSA.

President Benjamin, together with Greg Goode, secured the Federal Building for ISU.[28] The pathway to the goal was Byzantine, but with the help of Senator Evan Bayh, the GSA and U.S. Postal Service agreed to the ceding of the property.[29] The Indiana Commission for Higher Education had approved the plan to develop the College of Business in this location after it was decided that the Laboratory School would become the College of Education, and that ISU would raise funds to match state and federal funds.

President Benjamin was committed to the preservation of the Federal Building, which was one of the major remaining downtown structures of architectural importance. Further, as a champion of community engagement, it was his ambition to bring the campus closer to downtown, and by crossing Cherry Street, improve the local economy and neighboring businesses by introducing a sizeable student and faculty population adjacent to Wabash and Seventh Streets.

In 2005, the GSA contracted with Architura to handle Phase I rehabilitation of the post office, and to assist ISU with the conversion of the structure into the College of Business.[30] At the same time, ISU, the GSA, and Schmidt and Associates, began preparing for the Phase II renovation.[31] The principle architect for the GSA was Michael Conly. Renovation needed to be handled in stages in order to allow the USPS to continue to operate in the building. Architura also did extensive renovation in the public areas of the building, including the lobby and interior corridors. Care was taken to restore the historic colors, ceilings, marbled walls, and light fixtures. The first $6 million of restoration work was funded and completed by the GSA.[32] Renovation plans included maintaining the façade without changes and adding a new entry at the south to connect the college with downtown businesses. ■

Continued Renovation
President Bradley

Architect: Schmidt Associates (Project Manager)

Contractors: Shiel Sexton (General Contruction); A. A. Huber & Sons (Mechanical); Hef Services, Inc. (Electrical)

Project Managers: Steve Culp and Bryan Duncan

Date: Dedication and Grand Opening: September 7, 2012

Cost: $14.31 million[33]

Renamed: Scott College of Business[34]

The remaining balance for completing the restoration (Phase III) was $14.31 million[35] When completed, the building would have 11 classrooms; offices for 50 administration, faculty, and staff; and a capacity of approximately 600 students.

There were several significant aspects to the renovation. An entry was created on the south side (the city side) of the building that reflected the design elements of the original building. The new lighting (manufactured in St. Louis) followed the shape of the original lighting. There is transparency in the building. Simulating the stock exchange in New York, the trading room is visible through glass walls to observers in the hallway. There is an interpenetration of workspaces and informal gathering areas. Existing corridors were retained and are noteworthy for their detail, arched plaster ceilings, decorative painting, marble wainscot, and decorative light fixturres – all of which remained intact.

During President Bradley's administration, the third phase of the renovation was completed, and the College of Business was renamed the Scott College of Business. The American Institute of Architects honored the building restoration with its Merit Award for Preservation, Adaptive Reuse, and Renovation (see also Normal Hall). It noted the "successful marriage of history and modern technology in integrating all of the new systems and technology within a historic fabric ..." As Schmidt noted in a recent interview, the architect responsible for renovation needs to "listen to the building," meaning he sees and understands the original architect's vision expressed through shapes, spaces, and materials, and attempts to connect his plans seamlessly, yet distinctively, with the original.[36]

The Federal Building is on the National Register of Historic Places. This meant the architects had to design within the existing structure. A significant issue was the energy inefficiency of the building. Insulation was added to the roof and energy efficient windows were added on the west corridor. A point of honor was to have the renovated building receive Leadership in Energy and Environmental Design (LEED) silver certification from the U.S. Green Building Council.

The Building was honored with the presentation of the 2013 Heritage Award in the category "Design-Public Sector Project." ∎

Hospitality House (Mullen)

Contractors: Nehf Construction; Harrah Plumbing and Heating; Sycamore Engineering

Project Managers: Scott Tillman and Steve Culp

Date: 2006

Cost: $200,000[37]

Location: 936 North Seventh Street

The Hospitality House was acquired from Congregational minister Rev. Don Mullen. Obtaining this house continued the process of acquiring properties north of the campus for renovation or demolition. These properties were an eyesore and made a negative impression on prospective students and their families. During the 2007-08 period, 40 properties were purchased, and houses removed.

President Benjamin believed the purchase of this specific house was important for several reasons. The house was architecturally significant with arts and crafts elements throughout. The renovation work was sensitively done with respect for the period style. Second, prior to the development of a downtown hotel, there was no place close to campus for resident visiting faculty to live. Third, in cooperation with the Terre Haute Symphony, the home provided a place for guest musicians to stay where they could rehearse at their leisure.

Seventh and Cherry Gateway

Architect: RATIO Architects, Inc.

Contractor: CDI, Inc.

Project Manager: Rochelle Gardner

Date: 2007-09

Cost: $596,184

The design was developed to enhance the entry to the campus at Seventh and Cherry Streets. Seventh Street is the "Arts Corridor," and the entry serves both to connect the ISU portion of the Arts Corridor to downtown, while also providing a subtle demarcation announcing the campus. A plaza, named the National Road Plaza, was designed immediately to the west of the new Multimodal Transportation facility.

The gateway is comprised of brick piers and walls, with special attention given to the design of the concrete pavers laid in a herringbone pattern at the intersection. The brick work of the piers and walls matches the campus standard, and the various elements have cut limestone caps. A pull-off was designed on the east side of the street, and a campus wayfinding and information center was introduced to assist campus visitors.

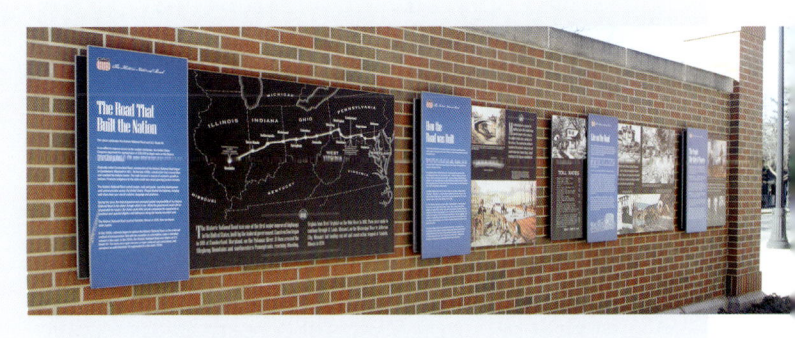

Based on Benjamin's research on Dutch public art, he proposed the design incorporate elements that remind one of the historical importance of the National Road. This historic highway, stretching across the country, was interpreted in the paving pattern and materials and was illuminated with a fiber optic line. A replica of a historic mile marker was installed. Bronze markers are set in the pavement at significant points along the highway, denoting, among other sites, Terre Haute, Vandalia, and San Francisco. A plaque was presented to President Benjamin and his wife in recognition of their support for the arts in Terre Haute. The plaque is included in the National Road Plaza.[38]

Chapter 10 President Benjamin

Cherry Street Multimodal Transportation Facility

Architects: Sanders and Associates; Rich and Associates

Contractor: Hannig Construction Co., Inc.

Date: 2006-10

Dedication: September 10, 2010

Cost: $13.3 million[39]

Location: 750 Cherry Street

Convenient parking is always of concern to university faculty, staff, and students, as well as local businesses and their patrons. Fortunately, collaboration between the university and the City of Terre Haute, aided by the support provided by Senator Bayh, led to the erection of this multimodal transportation facility (so-called because federal funds would not be made available solely for a parking deck).

The idea of building a parking facility on this site had been discussed as early as 1999, when a group of downtown businesses and ISU representatives formed a not-for-profit organization to study the possibility of building a garage. The group recognized the project would take time and funding to be realized. The Federal Transit Administration approved the current plans on September 5, 2005.

This multimodal transportation facility is located at the corner of Cherry and Seventh Streets. It is an L-shaped plan that combines five levels of parking, elevators and open steel stairs. The first floor provides offices and storage, as well as a climate-controlled waiting area for users of city, campus, and interstate bus service. The exterior finish of the structure relates to other brick and limestone trim buildings on campus.

President Benjamin stated one reason for his support of this collaborative project with the city was seeing university students walking more than a mile in bitter winter cold to reach the Greyhound Bus station. This

Indiana State University Building a Legacy

structure makes downtown the center of mass transit. Another reason for supporting the facility was to make parking available for patrons attending events in the Hulman Center and Tilson Auditorium, used by the Terre Haute Symphony for its performance season. The new parking facility would also provide needed parking for the College of Business move into the Federal Building.

This facility was honored for "Outstanding Contributions in the Area of Design-Public Sector," April 10, 2008, by Downtown Terre Haute Inc. ■

President Bradley

The Trustees approved the university purchase of the non-transit portion of the facility from the city in February 2011. In December 2011, the Trustees authorized the sale of $4 million in parking system revenue bonds to support the university's $4.85 million purchase. This purchase made it possible for the city to fund other downtown development projects, and it provided more parking in response to the opening of the Scott College of Business.

Community Garden

Date: 2007
Area: (Building) 1,696 GSF; 1,187 ASF
Location: 219 North Eleventh Street

As part of President Benjamin's emphasis on community engagement, he proposed that some of the lots north of the campus, where houses had been removed and now sat vacant, could be made a productive space. By converting the space into a community garden, families could raise their own produce and introduce their children to gardening. The importance of giving children gardening experience can be traced back to late 18th and 19th century Germany with the educator Friedrich Froebel (1782-1852). Froebel believed the proper education of children should involve cognitive development, but also self-directed play, singing, dancing, and gardening—hence the term kindergarten. By 2013, the Community Garden had about 80 gardeners.

President Bradley

Contractor: White's Creative Landscaping
Date: April 28, 2013
Location: Eleventh and Chestnut Streets

In April 2013, students and faculty, along with local gardeners, convened outside the office of the Institute for Community Sustainability on the grounds of the garden. Their purpose was to build a 1,700-square-foot deck mostly made from recycled materials. The roof was designed to hold water for irrigation. The covered deck would accommodate 40 people throughout all weather conditions. Funding for the deck, and seven solar greenhouses, was provided by the Lilly Endowment.

Chapter 10 President Benjamin

Student Recreation Center

Architect: Hastings and Chivetta Architects, Inc.[40]
Contractor: Hannig Construction
Project Manager: Steve Culp
Date: Groundbreaking: July 19, 2007

Cost: $21.8 million[41]
Area: 109,450 GSF; 80,000 ASF
Location: 231 North Sixth Street

The need to continue growing enrollment was a high priority for President Benjamin. Making a campus attractive for students required far more amenities than it did previously, when dormitories with gang showers and multiple occupants to a room were standard. Across the country, campuses began to vie with one another in something akin to an arms race. Students expected different housing arrangements that more closely reflected home-life. More privacy, better technology, and first-rate recreational facilities became the norm. For decades, ISU had built student residence halls that maximized capacity with an eye to economizing whenever possible; designing residences with common bathrooms and no air conditioning.

Because of effective master planning and carefully designed landscaping, the campus had become more visually appealing to prospective students. At the same time, however, ISU had an inventory of aged residences that did not meet parent and student expectations. The campus also lacked an attractive recreational facility that had become a necessity in the lives of students, much like a library. Aside from Dede Plaza and Union dining facilities, there was not a place for students to meet, exercise, and engage in various sports. Without it, ISU lacked one of the central components necessary to thwart the weekend flight from campus. President Benjamin said the project to

Hastings and Chivetta conceptual rendering

Indiana State University Building a Legacy

build this center grew out of a review of amenities for students and was part of a broader initiative to increase and retain enrollment, and address the importance of fitness and student well-being.

The Student Recreation Center opened in 2009 and represented the completion of the project that began in 2005, with trustee approval of the design architects and concept.[42] Gaining state approval to build the structure was a labyrinthine and trying experience. Prior to the opening of the new facility, the basement of the old Arena provided the only workout space in an area aptly known as the "dungeon." It was a dark, cramped space enclosed by a chain-link fence and barbed wire. It contained weight lifting equipment kept in a wire cage. The facility also contained a pool (that did not meet NCAA competition standards). A second pool with restricted hours was located in the lower level of Tirey (the former Student Union Building, and a long distance from student housing).

The building finally being approved was due to the work of many.[43] The Student Government Association, led by Hobart Scales, worked to have a referendum passed by the student body that would provide the support and funding necessary to pay for the facility from student fees. Vice President for Student Affairs, Tom Ramey, worked closely with the student government in developing the referendum and generating support within the student body. President Benjamin arranged for Scales to attend and make a presentation for the facility at a meeting of the Commission for Higher Education. Scales made it clear to the Commission this was a project approved by the student body, and that the student body had agreed to impose a fee on itself to cover the cost. Benjamin added that the new facility would attract students, enhance student health, and that it supported Governor Mitch Daniels, INShape Indiana Initiative.

When President Benjamin presented the project to the Commission for Higher Education, the Commission pointed out that the project was not in the proper sequence for review of projects. Benjamin explained to the Commission that we considered it inappropriate to seek state approvals without first having the support of the student body. When the student resolution was approved, the project was nine months past the deadline for new capital projects. Benjamin pointed out that waiting until the date for submitting 2007-08 capital budget requests would delay the project until at least the fall of 2007. Owing to the increase in costs during that period, the building would cost an additional $1 million.[44] Representative Clyde Kersey insisted the Commission take it out of order. His insistence, the fact that the project would be self-funded by students, and the work done by legislative liaison Greg Goode, gained the necessary approval to proceed. Miraculously, the General Assembly approved the project in a non-budget year (2006). Kersey recounted that at one point in the process, the Center was stripped out of the state Senate bill after the House had already approved it. Final state approval was received February 14, 2007.

Another hurdle was the Commission's insistence that the project be scaled down to lower the cost. One effect of delaying approval, however, was to increase the price of construction, which then required design modifications to keep the project within approved limits.

The new Center cost $21.8 million. Initial plans called for a slightly more elaborate structure. These

Chapter 10 President Benjamin

were rejected by the state with the recommendation that costs be kept below $200/sq. ft., and that the university consider building a post building, akin to a facility at Southern Indiana University. That suggestion was rejected. Modification of the original design required a whittling down process to keep the project within the approved budget. It was an arduous task led by Vice Presidents Tom Ramey, Gregg Floyd (Vice President of Business and Finance), and Kevin Runion, Associate Vice President for Facilities Management, and his staff. Revised plans necessitated using more brick rather than limestone on the exterior, lowering the ceiling height in the gym, downgrading some finishes and furnishings, and deleting the "lazy river" feature in the pool area – something the students regretted losing. Through everyone's efforts, the campus was able to overcome the Commission's reservations regarding cost. Following approval to proceed, funding was not immediately available, which added an additional $20,000 a month of extra expense.

On the exterior, the building shared features found in other campus buildings, including scale, brick, and limestone. The building fits comfortably among adjacent structures, yet by design, is distinctive. The Center had two major entrances. One faces toward the campus to the south, and the second provides entry from the north-side student parking area. From either entry, and advancing along the central corridor, all of the activities located in different areas can be seen.

The new Center added significantly to the fitness and athletic facilities on campus. Major recreational areas include a three-court gymnasium surmounted by an elevated track, a multi-activity court, fitness center, spinning area, and climbing wall. There is a sun deck on the south side with a sand-filled volleyball court and well-equipped aquatic center, replete with sauna, steam-room, wet classroom, and lap and leisure pool. Directly off the lobby is a lounge, and snack and juice bar. The remainder is devoted to various offices, storage, a training room, and an assessment suite.

Indiana State University Building a Legacy

Since its opening, the Student Recreation Center has become the center of student life on campus. Today, tours for prospective students and their families often begin or conclude in the Center. It's persuasive and makes a strong statement about the quality of student life on the ISU campus, and has served to play a critical role in increasing and sustaining enrollment.[45]

The Center was awarded an NIRSA Outstanding Sports Facilities Award in 2011.[46] John Lentz, ISU's Director of Recreational Sports, noted the Student Recreation Center has changed the culture of the ISU campus.

Mr. A. J. Patton, former Student Government President succeeding Hobart Scales, stated, "This is a transitional period for the university … with a new parking facility, renovated University Hall, Federal Building, and Student Recreation Center, we are helping the university evolve into one of the elite universities of the Midwest." Another anonymous student stated,

"We have gone from the dungeon basement in the Athletic Arena to the Taj Mahal."[47] ■

Dedication

President Bradley

Date: July 10, 2009

President Bradley referred to the facility as "transformative." Research done in 2010 showed that freshmen who used the Center during their first year on campus were more likely to return for their sophomore year. It also showed that those who used the facility more frequently were more likely to re-enroll the following year. John Lentz, Director of Recreational Sports, stated, "The Recreation Center is an opportunity for students to experience not only physical fitness and exercise programs, but also to connect with other students. The data shows the Center is doing what is was intended to do."[48]

In accordance with the Percent for Art program begun by President Benjamin, a sculpture, entitled "Runner" by Douglas Kornfeld, was installed on the south wall of the building. It is a silhouette of a runner rendered in stainless steel and is a perfect image to identify the building. The selection was made by the Art Spaces Site Selection and Acquisition Committee.[49]

Douglas Kornfeld, "Runner," stainless steel, 2009

Chapter 10 President Benjamin

Chapter 10 References

1. Martin Blank, "Looking Ahead," STATE Magazine, Winter 2001, pp. 8-13. "… our goal as a community of learners is to … focus upon ways we can positively impact student learning and integrate it into everything we do as a university." Report of the President Indiana State University 2001-02, p. 1. Blank also wrote a six-page interview covering the first four years of Benjamin's presidency. Martin Blank, "Looking Ahead," STATE Magazine, Spring 2005, pp. 8-13. Portrait by Australian artist Paul Newton.

2. The plan had five goals: enhance the intellectual capital of Indiana, enhance the education of students, contribute to the development of new knowledge with a focus on external engagement, develop a regional and national reputation for engaging students in experiential learning, and sustain enrollment growth.

3. The campus committee, led by President emeritus John Moore, was asked to engage in developing criteria for creating Sycamore Centers of Excellence. These would be programs that could enhance the state, regional, and national awareness of ISU.

4. Only 150 colleges out of more than 3,000 universities and colleges were selected. ISU was one of 67 universities to receive the new Carnegie Classification for Community Engagement.

5. Governor Kernan announced the role change for Vincennes on October 5, 2004.

6. Dr. Kevin Snider, Executive Assistant to the President, assumed the role of Admissions Director and implemented significant changes in admissions and financial aid prior to the arrival of Dr. John Beacon in July 2007.

7. This total includes not only freshmen (1,233) but also transfer (140) and international (five) students meeting the criteria. Approximately an 80 percent increase in 'B' or better students.

8. See: http://www2.indstate.edu/news/news.php?newsid=4313.

9. In 2006, Benjamin was appointed to the executive committee of the North American Council of the International Association of University Presidents.

10. The conference was held in October 2007.

11. The North Central Association recommended the university reduce its academic offerings in 1980, 1990, and 2000. A faculty-led study undertaken in the fall of 2005 found that 90 percent of ISU's students were enrolled in 50 percent of the programs offered. It also found that 400 undergraduate course sections had fewer than ten students. In a letter, Governor Mitch Daniels praised the "… bold move (that) will undoubtedly free up dollars to be re-invested in programs that are in demand and growing …"

12. Indiana State University Facilities Management Completed Projects, June 30, 2008, pp. 12-13.

13. Dr. Wieke Benjamin was appointed President of the Indiana Coalition for the Arts Foundation for 2007-08. She was also a co-founder of Art Spaces and created Sycamore Showcase, a series of periodic presentations for community leaders showcasing ISU activities. To date, 18 unique site-specific public sculptures have been introduced in Terre Haute with several on the ISU campus.

14. Michael Simmons was a 1964 graduate, and together with Debbie and Tom Bareford, founded the Trike race originally run in the quad.

15. MSI Construction (Clinton, Indiana) was paid $695,737.

16. The art budget was $7,542.

17. See: https://www.indstate.edu/university-engagement/community-engagement/awards-and-funding/funding-5

18. Trustee Minutes, May 25, 2001, Sec. 1: K, p. 8. Trustees approved this contract.

19. Indiana State University Facilities Management Projects Completed Fiscal Year '02-03, June 30, 2003, p. 14.

20. Ibid. Trustees approved the name of the facility.

21. $110,695 expended in 2003-04 and $227,634 in 2004-05. Indiana State University Facilities Management Department Completed Projects Fiscal Year '03-'04 and '04-'05, project numbers 1 and 6.

22. The light fixture design is modified Camden Arm with Gothic script on North Yorkshire posts.

23. U.S. Highway 41 was a major north-south route and became part of the Federal highway system In 1926. It intersected U.S. Highway 40 known as the "Old National Road." The site has a historical marker. See: https://www.in.gov/history/markers/374.htm.

24. The firm was founded in 1925 by Ewing Miller and Ralph Oscar Yeager. Art Deco (Arts Décoratifs) originated with the Exposition Internationale des Arts Décoratifs et Industriels Modernes (Paris in 1925). It's sometimes also referred to as the "style moderne" movement in architecture and the decorative arts flourishing in Western Europe and the United States during the 1920s and 30s.

25. Lee, Antoinette J. Architects to the Nation: The Rise and Decline of the Supervising Architect's Office. New York: Oxford University Press, 2000, pp. 222-224, 258.

26. Contrary to the date in the painting, King John signed the Magna Carta on June 15, 1215 and not 1214. This was a Public Works Art Project funded by the U.S. Treasury.

27. Public Law 106-554, Appendix D, Chapter 12 (114 Stat.2763A-211), the U.S. Congress appropriated $2.07 million for renovation and redeveloping portions of the Post Office. It was reported to the Trustees in 2003 that the Senate had appropriated $6.5 million for both the Federal Building and Cherry Street Multimodal Transportation facility. Trustee Minutes, October 24, 2003.

28. Initial preservation efforts were led by Congressman Ed Pease, and subsequently by Senator Evan Bayh.

29. Ed Rynne was the facilitating lead for the USPS during the transfer of the building to ISU.

30. Phase I consisted of upgrading elevators; repairing and cleaning marble and terrazzo; repairing light fixtures, paint, and window glazing; and exterior stone repair and cleaning.

31. Phase II renovation included a new south addition; utility connection to campus; a new roof; new ADA restrooms; a new mechanical room; and new IT, mechanical, electrical, and plumbing equipment.

32. HUD Funding of $273,071 was applied to Phase II.

33. On September 8, 2010, The State Budget Committee authorized the university to proceed with plans for transforming the Federal Building into the Scott College of Business. Earlier, the state General Assembly approved expending $20 million – $10 million from bonding fee replacement and $10 million from private funds. Trustee Minutes, December 18, 2009, p. 32.

34. The Donald W. Scott College of Business honors the long-time owner of the former Sycamore Agency in Terre Haute, now Old National Insurance. The Trustees approved naming the College on October 23, 2009. See: http://www2.indstate.edu/news/news.php?newsid=1991.

35. By December 2010, the estimated amount was $19 million, with $9 million from bonding and $10 million private funds. Trustee Minutes, December 17, 2010, p. 26.

36. Interview with Wayne Schmidt, April 3, 2018.

37. Indiana State University Facilities Management Department Completed Projects Fiscal Year '07-'08, June 30, 2008, p. 13, no. 45.

38. The plaque reads: In recognition of the contributions of Drs. Lloyd W. Benjamin III and Wieke van der Weijden Benjamin to advance and promote the arts for the Terre Haute Community and Indiana State University, presented May 2, 2008. Arts Illiana, Art Spaces Wabash Valley Outdoor Sculpture Collection, City of Terre Haute, Community Theater of Terre Haute, Downtown Terre Haute, Inc., The Sheldon Swope Art Museum, Inc., and Terre Haute Symphony Orchestra Association.

39 Federal support of $8.9 million and city support up to $4.9 million. This was the largest federal earmark in ISU history. Senator Bayh was particularly helpful in securing this support. The somewhat awkward name reflects federal transportation officials requiring that the building serve as more than a parking deck and one transportation system. The project required approval by the City Council. The Council, with a five-two vote, approved the funding measure. Council members Ryan Cummins and George Azar voted against the project. Austin Arceo, "Council Oks funding for new facility downtown," Tribune-Star, July 14, 2006. A critical cash flow necessitated ISU make an advance parking purchase payment of $1 million. Mr. Gregg Floyd, Vice President of Business Affairs, negotiated this arrangement and stated additional funds could be made available if needed. Initial bids for the project exceeded the budget, which required the city to rework the project to bring it more in line with estimates. Sue Loughlin, "ISU to pay $1 million for city parking spaces," Tribune Star, September 23, 2006, p. A3.

40 Hastings and Chivetta was formed in 1960 with headquarters in St. Louis, Missouri. The firm had done similar projects at Duke, Kent State, Univeristy of Nebraska, and Georgia Tech.

41 The Lilly Endowment initiated a program to match gifts to higher education institutions, matching gifts of $10,000 or more at 125 percent. Responding to that opportunity, gifts were made by Jim Wittenauer, Don Mighell, the Hulman and George families, and Beverly Spear (honoring her son and husband). No state funds were used in the construction. Private contributions totaled $6.5 million with the balance paid from student fees.

42 Trustees approved the project in June 2005.

43 The Wabash Journal of Business (February 2007) noted ISU had received approval on April 14, 2007 for the Center.

44 Construction costs had increased significantly owing to increased oil costs, inflation, and paucity of construction materials caused by hurricane Katrina's devastation.

45 A study found that 78 percent of students who used the Recreation Center 31 or more times continued to be enrolled, while nearly 50 percent of the 217 freshmen who never used the Center did not reenroll.

See: http://www2.indstate.edu/news/news.php?newsid=2523.

46 NIRSA is an acronym for National Intramural Recreational Sports Association.

47 See: http://www2.indstate.edu/news/news.php?newsid=2710.

48 Indiana State University Newsroom, November 8, 2010.

49 Contract for the Runner was made February 11, 2009.

CHAPTER 11

11TH PRESIDENT
DANIEL JOSEPH BRADLEY
(2008-2018)

April 16, 2010
Bayh College of Education dedication took place

2011-12
The Sycamore Towers Dining Room was remodeled.

2014
Reeve Hall was constructed.

2010-11
Pickerl Hall was renovated.

September 7, 2012
Federal Hall dedication took place.

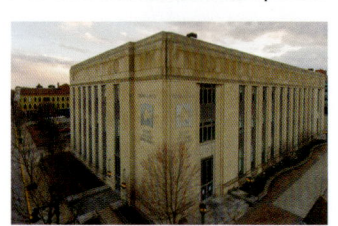

Indiana State University Building a Legacy

Born: August 3, 1949

Wife: Cheri Bradley (married 1981-present)

Education:
Bachelor's Degrees
Montana College of Mineral Science and Technology
Petroleum Engineering

Michigan State
Biochemistry

Master's Degree
University of Tulsa
Petroleum Engineering

Ph.D. Degree
Michigan State University
Physical Chemistry

Positions held at Indiana State University: President (2008-18), President Emeritus, and Trustee Professor

2015
Gibson Track and Field was built.

2018
The Hulman Center renovation began.

2015-16
The Normal Hall Renovation took place.

December 15, 2017
The ribbon cutting was held for the College of Health-Human Services.

Chapter 11 President Bradley

President Bradley earned his bachelor's degree in petroleum engineering from Montana College of Mineral Science and Technology, and a bachelor's degree in biochemistry from Michigan State. He earned a master's degree in petroleum engineering from the University of Tulsa, and his doctorate in physical chemistry from Michigan State University. He was a postdoctoral researcher in the Chemistry Department at the University of California, Berkley prior to joining the faculty at Montana Tech of the University of Montana.

Prior to becoming Indiana State University's (ISU) 11th President, Bradley served as President of Fairmont State University (Fairmont, West Virginia). Bradley began his presidency at ISU on July 31, 2008. He and his wife Cheri made the decision to live in the Condit House, which was remodeled for them. Both President Bradley and Cheri were active participants in student life and campus activities, and Condit House provided ready access to the campus. Cheri was known for interacting frequently with students, even operating a lemonade

as part-time students. Retention had been an ongoing issue. The Indiana Commission for Higher Education adopted a new funding strategy, and important criteria in the formula are retention and graduation rates. The plan to grow enrollment and emphasize intake over output (graduates) began to negatively impact the state's appropriation of operating funds.[2] During Bradley's presidency, considerable new resources were directed toward programs to help students attain success.

The freshman class of 2017 showed a significant increase of Illinois students (66 percent) coming to ISU owing, in part, to the economic difficulties in the state. International student enrollment declined sharply (20 percent), reflecting current political trends.

Two goals constituting a portion of ISU's mission were reaffirmed by President Bradley. These were to encourage experiential learning in all majors, and second, commit to enhancing engagement with the community.[3] President Bradley's "Pathway" goal was to advance hands-on learning opportunities. By 2016, 100 percent of all academic programs required

> **"Indeed, as we review our past, we can feel the strong connection to our present and to our future. These core values have been with us since our beginning and are most certainly the cornerstone of our future."** – President Daniel Bradley

stand giving free drinks and cookies to students. She also devoted time to helping female faculty development.

President Bradley's top priority in coming to ISU was to increase the enrollment. This was one of six major goals identified in the strategic planning process that would guide the institution. The other goals were to advance experiential learning, enhance community engagement, strengthen and leverage program of promise, diversify revenue sources, and attract and retain quality faculty and staff.[1]

The realization of the plan drove the development of new degree programs in fields meeting state needs, such as health care and engineering. The plan also had a major goal of upgrading student housing. Both initiatives stimulated student interest in attending ISU.

During Bradley's administration, enrollment grew to 13,771 students in the fall of 2017. Minority enrollment grew from about 13 percent in 2008 to 26 percent by 2014. ISU has had a tradition of accepting students who have challenges, either in their academic preparation, or financially, that required them to work or continue

an experiential learning component. The Center for Student Research and Creativity included hundreds of students working on various projects.

The second goal around engagement involved students, faculty, and staff in performing projects that promote economic, social, and cultural well-being. This did not go unnoticed. Washington Monthly ranked ISU number one in the nation for two years in the subcategory of community service. For over a decade, ISU has been included on the President's Higher Education Honor Roll for Community Service.[4] In 2015, Bradley created a new Division of University Engagement, noting ISU's national recognition for its commitment to community engagement and experiential learning. He noted several major markers of its successes among them: $4.5 million from the Lilly Endowment to build job readiness; $3 million for Fulfilling the Promise in 2004, of which nearly $1 million was devoted to engagement and experiential learning; 11 years of AmeriCorps funding, totaling over $1 million; continuing recognition by the U.S. President's Higher Education Honor Roll for Community Service; Washington Monthly magazine's listing as number one among 280 national colleges and universities for community service.

In December 2009, President Bradley introduced a new campus master plan to the Trustees. It was ambitious and visionary. It included expansion of the Health and Human Services Building, continued renovation of the Federal Building, and renovation of the old Normal Library. This was proposed to be the site of a new Center for Student Success. The plan included partnering with a local firm to create additional student housing, which would be necessary if the goal of a 15 percent increase in students would be realized within the five-year period.

A series of special task forces was formed to study and make recommendations on a variety of issues important to the university. The Task Force on Affordability Subcommittee's Recommendations on Housing and Dining highlighted the urgent need to address antiquated student housing, which was a barrier to enrollment growth. The report stated:

> *"The university's ability to offer affordable and attractive campus housing alongside convenient and efficient dining units ... is critical to our university's mission, the quality of the educational experience we offer, and our ability to compete effectively for enrollment with peer institutions."*

The report continues:

> *"The last totally new housing building project was begun 40 years ago."*

And, the call to action.

> *"In an effort to match what our competition is offering ... plans are now underway for five construction/ renovation projects on the ISU campus, all to be completed over the next 10 years, with total projected cost estimates to range between $100 and $113 million. These projects are expected to consume the majority of housing reserves that have been amassed over the past several years."*[5]

Bradley aggressively addressed the housing and dining issue. He proposed continued renovation of the current stock of student housing that had not yet been renovated. Many of these buildings dated from the 1960s and no longer met the expectations of students. In rapid order, student housing was renovated, beginning with Sandison in 2009, Pickerl in 2010, and Erickson in 2012. Renovation was completed in four Sycamore Towers, the Lincoln Quad was updated, and new housing was built adjacent to the Lincoln complex. Bradley stated in February 2012 that the housing and dining reserves would be diminished "over the next few years," and that annual debt service would rise from $2 million annually to over $8 million.

President Bradley was a supporter of the Riverscape development plan (an idea first advanced in a study prepared by Ewing Miller in the early 1960s) and proposed ISU cross Third Street to the west and relocate the track and field facilities there. Bradley remarked that this was an achievable plan that will "improve ISU and have a positive impact on downtown Terre Haute."[6]

The relocation of the track and field facilities across Third Street toward the Wabash included creating a more distinctive entry to the campus at Third and Chestnut Streets. An important step in realizing this plan was taken with the acquisition of the former Pillsbury/ICON property on One Sycamore Street. In December 2009, the University Foundation purchased a 16-acre tract that extends from First Street to the Wabash River and transferred the property to the university.

President Bradley faced budgetary problems that seem to beset every president, caused by decreasing state support. For a couple of decades, legislatures across the country were reducing appropriations to higher education, driven by the need to provide additional resources for public schools, prisons, and health-welfare programs. Increasingly, higher education had come to be seen as a personal benefit rather than societal good. This resulted in student tuition and fees increasing annually. Vice President McKee stated the university had reallocated approximately $13 million since July 2010 in order to meet reductions in state funding and fund institutional priorities.[7] McKee noted in 2011 that the proposed 2012 budget was reduced another half of a percent, and that in three years, the state appropriation had been reduced by about 12 percent, representing approximately $9.2 million. McKee noted the latest budget cuts brought the university's state appropriation down to 1996 levels.[8] Bradley managed to lead the institution through these difficult times while continuing to pursue the vision defined in the five-year plan.[9]

Bradley is credited with significant improvements in the university's physical plant (especially in university student housing), and completing the $16 million renovation of Normal Hall, which is the oldest extant building from the Indiana State Normal School days. He also secured funding for several projects, including a major renovation and addition to the Arena Building to house the new College of Health and Human Services ($43 million), Science Building renovations, and the renovation of the Hulman Center. Greg Goode, Executive Director of Government Relations, reported to the Trustees the historical nature of the latest budget session in which $101 million was committed to the College of Health and Human Services and the Hulman Center renovation.[10]

Bradley continued to encourage the development of experiential learning opportunities across the departmental programs, as well as community engagement. ISU had received national recognition in 2006, 2007, and 2008 for these programs. He built on that tradition, earning national recognition for the community-oriented activities of students and faculty. First Lady Cheri Bradley was also committed to strengthening campus and community bonds. One of her noteworthy programs was the creation of a group entitled "Women of ISU." The group met twice annually. In the fall, they presented gifts to women in need, and in the spring, contributed to scholarships for at-risk and nontraditional women.

In 2017, Bradley was named CEO of the Year by the Council for Advancement and Support of Education District V. The award recognizes individuals who have articulated a compelling vision for their institution, led others to embrace it, enhanced the stature of the institution in the community, and provided broad support for advancement efforts. In particular, he was recognized for his successes in growing enrollment, initiating new degree programs in high-demand disciplines (such as health care and engineering), and major improvements on the campus especially renovation projects.

President Bradley announced his retirement on April 26, 2017, effective January 2018. ∎

Satellite Chilled Water Plant

Contractor: Sycamore Engineering
Project Managers: Steve Culp and Bryan Duncan
Date: 2011-12
Cost: $7.01 million[11]
Location: Fifth Street and Tippecanoe Street

The new satellite chiller is located on a former parking lot at Fifth Street and Tippecanoe Street. It connects with a 24-inch waterline to an existing chiller located north of Cunningham Library. It was designed to provide chilled water for air conditioning structures on the west side of campus.[12]

Reeve Hall (New North Residence Hall)

Architect: CSO Architects[13]

Contractors: Hannig (General Construction); Huber and Sons (Plumbing); Crown Electric (Electric and HVAC)

Date: Groundbreaking: November 15, 2012

Dedication: August 27, 2014

Cost: $23.62 million[14]

Location: 550 and 555 Sixth Street

On December 16, 2011, the Trustees authorized President Bradley and the Board Treasurer to obtain state approval for this new housing project to be located on the site of parking lots north of the Hulman Memorial Student Union, and adjacent to Lincoln Quads.[15] The renovation of the latter would reduce the number of beds in the Quads. This new construction provided housing for 352 residents, offsetting the loss due to renovation, and represented the first new housing project on campus since 1960.

The title 'Reeve Hall' was adopted for this new residential complex for women and women's sororities on the north side of campus. The original Reeve Hall was the first residence built on campus for women and it bore the name of Helen Reeve until the building was razed in 1998. Helen Reeve was Women's Residence Hall Director from 1926-47 when she became Dean of Women. This new complex would be the first major residential housing project erected in over 40 years. At their September 2013 meeting, the Trustees approved naming the new residence hall Reeve Hall as a tribute to Ms. Reeve and to preserve the memory of a historic structure (see President Hines).[16]

The concept presented design challenges. How can you design a facility that would allow distinct groups to be housed in the same building, but with each group having its own amenity spaces and unique identity, while also allowing residents to interact and come together as a community? The design solution met that expectation.

These are four-story structures with the exteriors done in the characteristic ISU palette of brick and stone trim. Each building houses four units in which students can select single or double rooms, either with pod-style community bathrooms or in-room private facilities. The complex accommodates the women in eight units with 45 beds each. Each unit has a chapter meeting room, media room, kitchenette, and laundry. These units also have a landscaped outer courtyard area for cookouts and gatherings that tie the community together. ∎

Chapter 11 President Bradley

Riverfront Track and Field (Gibson Track and Field)

Architect: RATIO Architects, Inc.

Contractor: CDI

Date: Groundbreaking: April 2014[17]
Dedication: April 17, 2015

Cost: $4.3 million

Location: 300 and 400 blocks on North First Street

The new Riverfront Track and Field facility is the first new athletic complex built within the previous quarter century. President Bradley recognized Jacquie and Max Gibson for their support of this track and field, as evidenced in construction of the LaVern Gibson course and a significant gift in support of the facility. This new facility will make it a preferred intercollegiate competition venue.[18]

Charlie Williams, President of the Wabash River Development and Beautification Board, stated this was an important step in elevating the way people will view Terre Haute. President Bradley remarked, "Indiana State is proud to serve as a catalyst in helping transform the banks of the Wabash River from an abandoned industrial site into a destination for family-friendly activities."[19]

During Bradley's presidency, the University took significant steps toward increasing the campus footprint in the direction of the Wabash River across U.S. 41. (See pg. 258) This development increased the involvement with Riverscape, a local organization working to reclaim and revitalize areas adjacent to the Wabash River "where family-friendly recreation, passive natural areas and opportunities for education and interpretation about the river ... serve as the catalyst for compatible commercial and residential development." The University also supported the Wabash Valley ArtSpaces' Turn to the River initiative

ICON industrial building, 2014

Riverscape RiverFront Lofts, 2019

to reconnect downtown Terre Haute with the Wabash River through public art and design.

A major achievement of University-led efforts was the redevelopment of the abandoned ICON industrial building, a derelict reminder of Terre Haute's past. ISU purchased the building and led in creating the Wabash River Regional Economic Development Authority to partner with the Indiana Economic Development to propose using tax credits for redeveloping the building. A private developer, CORE Redevelopment, expressed interest in the building that enabled the University, in partnership with Terre Haute Redevelopment Office to transfer ownership of the building for adaptive reuse. The result was RiverFront Lofts, as $26 million project the created 166 apartments along the Wabash. The building represents Terre Haute's future and demonstrates ISU's economic impact through public/private partnerships.

The University envisions the development of a Sycamore Sports District hosting numerous sporting events and the creation of new means for pedestrians to cross highway U.S. 41 safely from the campus to the sports complex. The University recognizes the importance of the River as a natural resource and will continue to support efforts to make it increasingly available to the community.[20] ■

The Artists' Collective, "Solar Sycamore," 2015

Madeline Wiener, "A Reading Place," 2015 Dolomitic Limestone, Reeve Hall.

Chapter 11 References

1. Martin Blank. "Speaking to the Future," Indiana State University Magazine. Summer, 2009. The reader may want to compare these goals with those announced by President Benjamin early in his tenure at ISU that had been reaffirmed by the Trustees in 2008. In 2010, Bradley pledged an additional $5 million would be set aside to strengthen programs of promise and distinction.

2. Bradley "… attributes the decrease to the state's performance funding measures; ISU doesn't fare as well as other state universities in four-year graduation rates." Sue Loughlin, "ISU Operating Budget Didn't Fare as Well," Tribune Star, May 1, 2015, A6. The first year retention rate in 2011 was 58.1 percent.

3. This was a continuation of goals approved by the Trustees during Benjamin's presidency and was considered a distinguishing characteristic of ISU's mission.

4. Libby Roerig, "Success lauded new plan underway," STATE, The Magazine of Indiana State University, Fall-2016, p. 24.

5. Trustee Minutes, February 17, 2012, p. 88.

6. See: http://www2.indstate.edu/news/news.php?newsid=2075.

7. See: http://www2.indstate.edu/news/news.php?newsid=2345.

8. See: http://www2.indstate.edu/news/news.php?newsid=2793.

9. Indiana State University Newsroom, June 17, 2011.

10. Trustee Minutes, August 27, 2015, p. 8.

11. Indiana State University Facilities Management Department Completed Projects Fiscal Year '11-'12, June 30, 2012, No. 028.

12. See: http://www2.indstate.edu/news/news.php?newsid=2269.

13. CSO was formed in 1961 and is located in Indianapolis. The first payment to CSO was in the first quarter of 2012. Trustee Minutes, May 4, 2012, p. 66.

14. Facilities Management Department 2014-15 Annual Report, pp. III-1. The Trustees at their April 2012 meeting authorized the sale of $30 million in bonds to finance the continuing renovation of Erickson Hall and construct this new residence on the north side of the campus. $4 million was to come from housing and dining reserves.

    See: hhtp://www2.indstate.edu/news/news.php?newsid=3294. The original estimate was $24 million but bids came in $5 million over budget. (Trustee Minutes, August 2, 2012, p. 3). The Trustees agreed to spend up to $29 million for the project.

15. See: http://www2.indstate.edu/news/news.php?newsid=2989. Trustee Minutes, December 16, 2011, p. 26. Funds to come from residence hall reserves and bonding not to exceed $24 million.

16. Trustee Minutes, September 6, 2013, p. 15.

17. The Trustees authorized the administration to obtain state approval to spend up to $4.3 million to relocate the Track and Field to One North Street. Trustee Minutes, June 14, 2013, p. 71. Funding was to come from interest income, commissions, and private support.

18. Trustee Minutes, May 2, 2014, p. 51.

19. See: http://www2.indstate.edu/news/news.php?newsid=3952

20. The author acknowledges Greg Goode's contribution to this entry.

DESIGNING A LEGACY: A HISTORY OF CAMPUS MASTER PLANNING
By: Kevin Runion and Bryan Duncan

INTRODUCTION

John R. Reeve and Marion B. Smith (Planning for Master Planning, APPA. 1995) define

> *'Master Planning is an analytical and creative activity that results in a coordinated set of decisions (the plan) about actions to be taken to accomplish stated goals.'*

They further indicate that successful uses for a campus master plan are usually reflected in six areas:

- Serves as a guide for future site development
- Used for scheduling and financial projections
- Used for internal decision making
- Becomes a 'tool' for achieving approval from a variety of authorities
- Becomes a guide for responding to changing needs
- Becomes an aid for facilitating fundraising

Another important aspect of campus master planning is the design of the campus. The term campus in Latin means "field" and was first used in 1774 to define a large field near Nassau Hall at the College of New Jersey. Some of the fondest memories of alumni are walking the campus, playing games on the grass, lying in the sun, or reading under the shade of a tree. A handsomely designed campus can influence prospective students to enroll. Landscape can influence peoples' experience of the campus. It is a three-dimensional design that shapes student perception as they traverse from building to building. It can also serve as a learning environment introducing sustainability, botanical, and ecological issues.

Campus planning activities at the Indiana State Normal School (ISNS) did not commence until almost a century after the original building opened in 1870. The first documented reference to master planning is found in a 1962 study prepared by Educational Research Services Inc. of New York City, followed seven years later by the Ewing Miller 1969 plan.

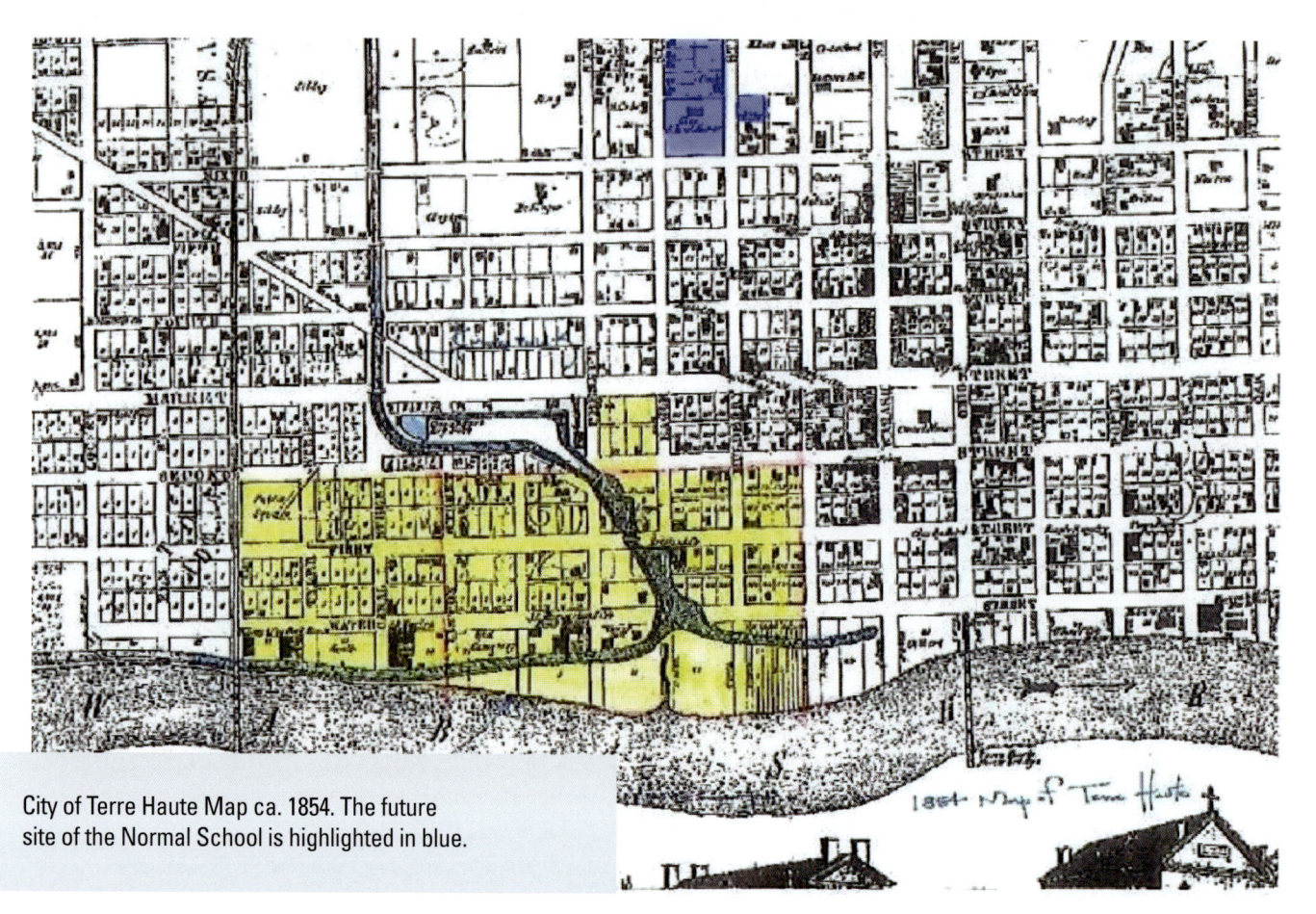

City of Terre Haute Map ca. 1854. The future site of the Normal School is highlighted in blue.

Indiana State University Building a Legacy

Indiana State University (ISU) began as Indiana State Normal School on December 20, 1865 when the Indiana General Assembly adopted House Bill 119, authorizing the formation of a teacher preparatory school. Once adopted, the state advertised for a community's interest in being the site for this new school. An offer of $50,000, land, and a building (the Vigo County Seminary) was made by the Terre Haute community to the State of Indiana, which was accepted, and the future history of the school and Terre Haute became inextricably intertwined.

PRESIDENT WILLIAM JONES (1869-1879)

Master planning was not a major factor in the beginning years of the School. The site for the new ISNS had been previously occupied by the Vigo County Seminary building that was razed in 1867 making way for the new building. This was followed by the erection of the new ISNS, begun in 1867 and opened January 6, 1870 for classes.

The school was hard-pressed for operating funds and could not afford to build a wooden fence to keep the cows out.

The site for the ISNS placed it in the center of Terre Haute. From its origin, what would eventually become Indiana State University was an 'urban campus,' meaning the future growth of the campus would extend it into adjacent neighborhoods and would require thoughtful long-term planning discussions and acquisition of houses and blocks one at a time.

PRESIDENT GEORGE BROWN (1879-1885)

No major improvements were made during Brown's tenure. A telephone was installed but aesthetics were clearly not a concern because the line to the building was attached to an elm tree in the yard.

PRESIDENT WILLIAM PARSONS (1885-1921)

Following the devastating fire of the ISNS building in April of 1888, the Indiana General Assembly authorized its rebuilding. The school was rebuilt on the same site and expanded with the addition of North Hall and the Training School adjacent to the new "Old Main."

Indiana State Normal School, before fire. Taken 1870–1888.

Indiana State Normal School rebuilt, post-fire. Taken 1890–1905.

PRESIDENT LINNAEUS HINES (1921-1933)

Following WWI, and during the Great Depression, the campus grew by 11 buildings, aided by the Public Works Administration and Workers Progress Administration programs that benefited ISNS.

The building of the Laboratory School at Seventh Street and Chestnut Street extended the campus beyond its historical perimeter, a fact not lost on some Hautians (Terre Haute residents) who entered into "much spirited debate" about this transgression.

Other projects from this era included the new Student Union Building (now Tirey Hall) featuring a 1700-seat auditorium (now Tilson Auditorium), the Fine Arts and Commerce Building, and two dormitories (Parsons Hall for men located on Sixth Street and Reeve Hall for women located on Mulberry Street).

Normal Library (1910), built during the Parsons era, along with the Condit House (1860) are the two oldest buildings remaining on the campus.

Master Planning

PRESIDENT RALPH TIREY
(1934-1953)

To accommodate the growth of facilities, one of the greater achievements in early campus master planning for the school was street closures. President Tirey introduced a ten-year improvement plan in 1935, and by 1937, he had succeeded in closing Eagle and Mulberry Streets. This step signaled the beginning of the formation of the historic quad.

Campus development often reflects broader trends in society at large. The increased importance of higher education and teacher training and growth following the Great Depression, fueled by federal government programs to assist with campus construction, stimulated growth on the ISNS campus. Following the end of World War II, GIs supported by the GI Bill returned to college campuses across the country in record numbers. ISU (then Teachers College) experienced record enrollments which, in turn, necessitated new housing and academic buildings.

PRESIDENT RALEIGH HOLMSTEDT
(1953-1965)

1962 Master Plan
In August of 1962, Educational Research Services, Inc., of New York City, presented the findings of a Long-Range Building Program for Indiana State College to President Tirey.

The "flexible" plan was to be used as a working guide for the college as it grew.

The format for the 70-page study showed the master plan divided into:
- Prospective Developments Related to Facilities
- Existing Facilities, Educational and General
- Space Requirements, Educational and General
- Residential and Student Activity Facilities
- Campus Organization and Land Use
- Summary of Requirements

The study, after setting a foundational history of the institution and its mission, provided a cursory condition assessment of 13 academic/service buildings and campus utilities.

The academic and service buildings discussed in the study included: the Administration Building (later to be known as Gillum Hall), the Language and Mathematics Building (later to be known as Dreiser Hall), the Business Education Building (later to be known as the Classroom Building), the Education and Social Studies Building (later to be known as Stalker Hall), the Fine Arts and Commerce Building, the Science Building, the Industrial Education Building (later to be known as the Vocational Building), the Home Economics Building, the Laboratory School, the Women's Physical Education Building, the Men's

Campus in 1927, aerial view

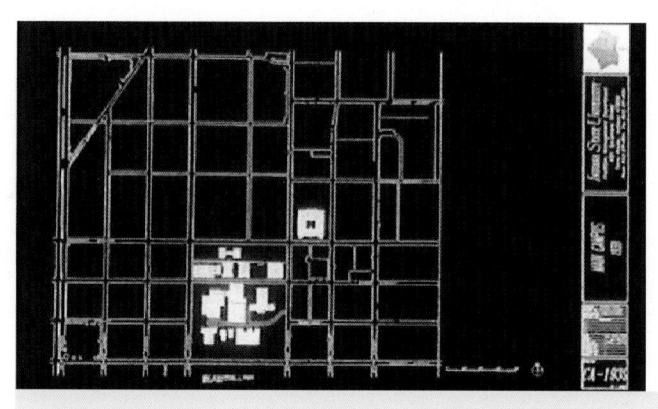

Campus in 1939. Main Building, Normal Hall, and University Hall

Campus in the 1950s.

250

Indiana State University Building a Legacy

Physical Education Building, the Library Building (later to be known as Normal Hall), Condit House, and the Boiler Plant and Utilities Tunnels.

The study also addressed 14 residential facilities, plus student activity venues, including:

Reeve Hall, Burford Hall, Erickson Hall, New Women's Housing Unit #3, Knisley Apartments, Parsons Hall, New Men's Residence Hall Group, Crawford House, Holt Apartments, Scherer Apartments, Scherer House, Parsons Annex, Davis Apartments, Walden Apartments, the Student Union, and the College Bookstore.

In addressing the parking and vehicular traffic aspects of the 1962 campus, and for the future, discussions were already underway to close several city streets crisscrossing the campus, including portions of North Sixth, North Fifth, North Fourth, and Center Streets. This study made the assumption that closing Chestnut Street was not feasible – an assumption that was rectified in the 1986 Sasaki plan (President Richard G. Landini).

An interesting discussion feature in the 1962 plan was the proposal to place Chestnut Street below ground level through campus with buildings and pedestrian walkways built over the road.

Major elements of this plan were variously implemented, but special emphasis was given to the need to acquire additional land to allow for projected student enrollment growth, and to provide for a new health center, student union, and facilities management/power plant structure with accompanying tunnels.

Projected costs for implementation of the entire 1962 Master Plan that included these projects were estimated at $44 million.

Although portions of this plan were well received, most of the 1962 through 1972 master planning concepts and ideas were never implemented.

A comprehensive campus improvement proposal from Scuggs and Hammond was presented in 1964, near the end of Holmstedt's presidency. It addressed planting, pedestrian and vehicular circulation, outdoor study areas, utilities, and best land use suggestions. The proposal was not accepted, and in 1965, Bunch Nurseries and Miller, Miller, and Associates volunteered to serve as consultants to address the same issues.

Campus in the late 1960s

PRESIDENT ALAN RANKIN (1965-1975)

1969 Master Plan

The 1969 Master Plan, begun during the Presidency of Alan Rankin, was the work of a local Terre Haute architectural firm, Ewing Miller Associates Architects, Planners, and Engineers. In January 1969, the University accepted the formal master plan prepared

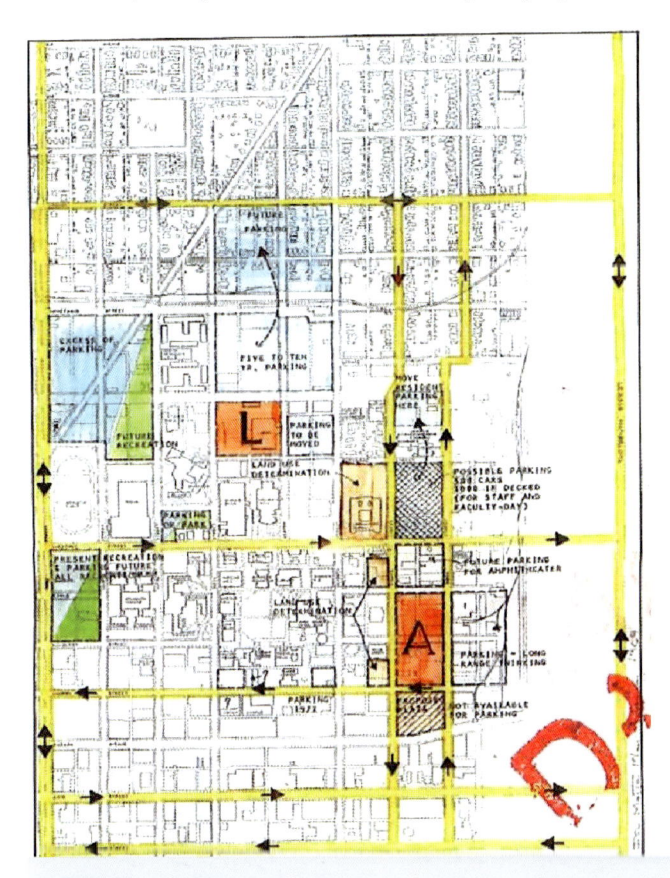

1969 Master Plan, base map

Master Planning

by the Ewing Miller Associates. This plan became the first master plan that addressed campus needs in detail, including: academic facilities, residential facilities, recreation and student service facilities, parking facilities, major vehicular and pedestrian circulation, and existing land use.

Although there is little history on the genesis of this plan, it appears most of the planning efforts were developed by a small group of university administrators along with members of the Miller firm.

At the time, the campus consisted of approximately 35 academic and service buildings and more than a dozen residential life buildings.

The campus boundaries were defined as Cherry Street on the south, Third Street (U.S. 41) on the west, Sycamore Street on the north (with the exception of Lincoln Quad) and Ninth Street on the east.

The plan addressed in detail seven main areas of campus planning:
- Academic Facilities
- Residential Facilities
- Recreation and Student Service Facilities
- Parking Facilities
- Major Vehicular Circulation
- Major Pedestrian Circulation
- Existing Land Use

Existing and Proposed Academic Facilities

The 1969 plan was general in nature but did address where future academic buildings might be located. The plan called for acquiring land to the west of the Home Economics Building (now the John W. Moore Welcome Center), land areas south of the Pickerl/Burford/Erickson complex, which became surface parking in the 1980s, land to the north of Science and Holmstedt Hall, which became the Cunningham Memorial Library (1971-74), and the area to the northeast of Holmstedt Hall which became Root Hall (1988-89).

Finally, a large land mass was identified for future academic needs running from Chestnut Street on the north, Ninth Street on the east, Cherry Street on the south and the alley between Seventh and Eighth Street on the west. The College of Nursing and the Hulman Center, as well as several surface parking lots, were built in this area.

Residential Facilities
By the time the 1969 Master Plan was adopted, most

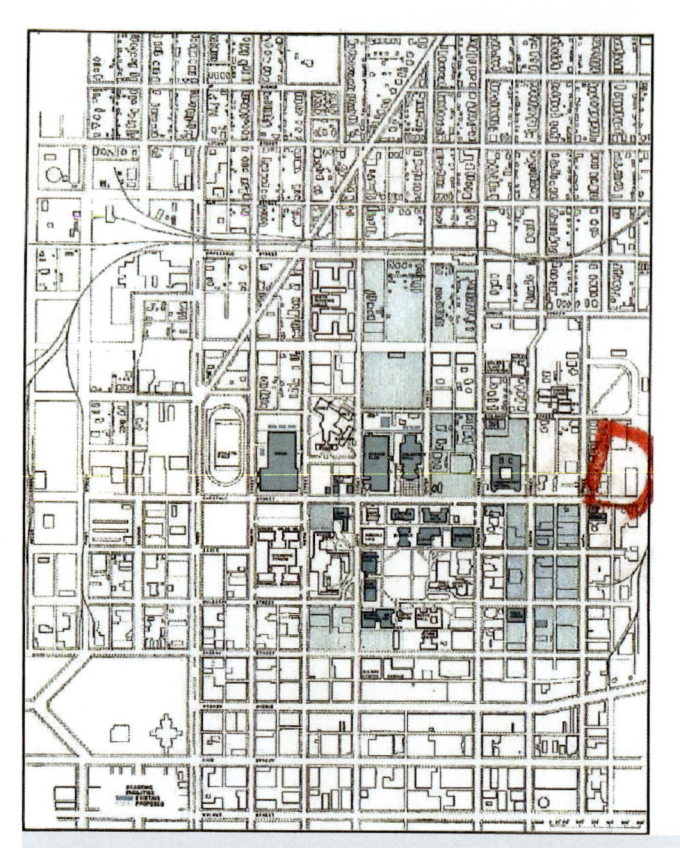

1969 Master Plan, existing and proposed academic facilities

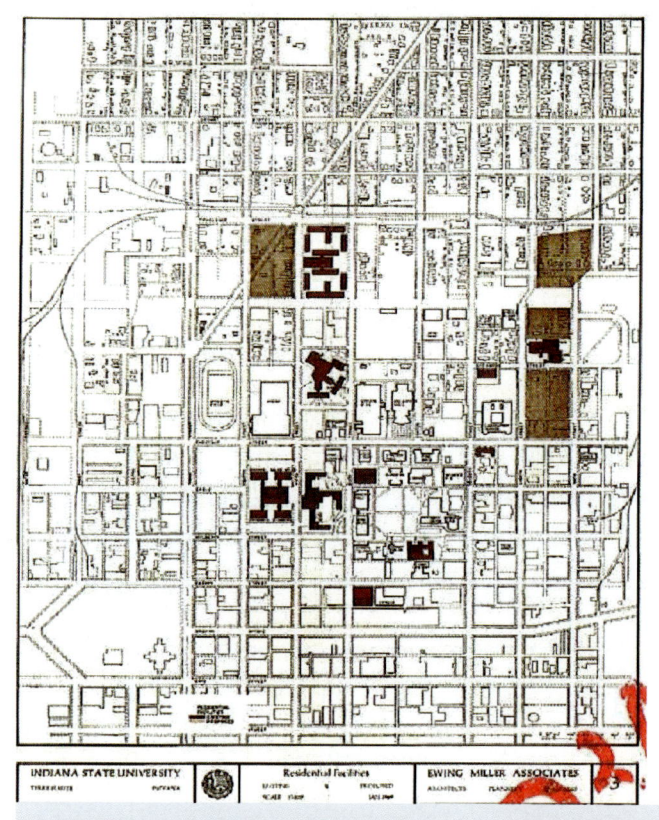

1969 Master Plan, existing and proposed residential facilities

Indiana State University Building a Legacy

residential life housing needs had been met or were in the process of being completed. The plan did identify land areas where future housing might be located, including a large land mass south of Statesman Towers (bounded by Sycamore Street, Chestnut Street, Ninth Street, and Eighth Street), and two land areas to the north of Statesman Towers. Land west of Lincoln Quad (bounded by Tippecanoe Street, Fourth Street, Fifth Street, and Sycamore Street) was recommended for additional housing but was never developed in these areas.

Recreation and Student Service Facilities

With the constraints of its urban location, by 1969, finding adequate space for student recreation was problematic. The plan recommended purchasing land north of the Arena and Science Buildings and west of Lincoln Quad, as well as land south of Wolf Field. Land on the eastern edge of campus between Ninth Street and the railroad at Tenth Street (from Spruce Street to the north and south to Eagle Street) was also recommended to be purchased. In the future, this land was used for softball fields, student housing, Recreation East, and the Michael Simmons Student Activity Center at Ninth and Sycamore Streets.

Parking Facilities

Parking is a perennial problem on a college campus. The 1969 plan recognized this and proposed the university purchase large areas of land north of the railroad tracks from Third Street east to Ninth Street and north to Locust Street (much of this land today is private student housing). This parking area would take up nearly 14 city blocks, running from Third Street on the west to Ninth Street on the east, from the railroad tracks north to Locust Street. The plan was not pursued. Moving parking to the perimeter of the campus, however, remained a common theme in future planning.

Traffic

While the campus expanded one building at a time, amassing properties in sizes large enough to construct university buildings while city streets remained open and functioning was also an issue addressed in the 1986 plan. The 1969 plan did recommend the creation of parallel road improvements either side of the east-west railroad tracks located on the north side of campus, as well as minor recommendations to improve traffic flow on Ninth Street, eliminating a 'z-shaped' intersection at Spruce Street.

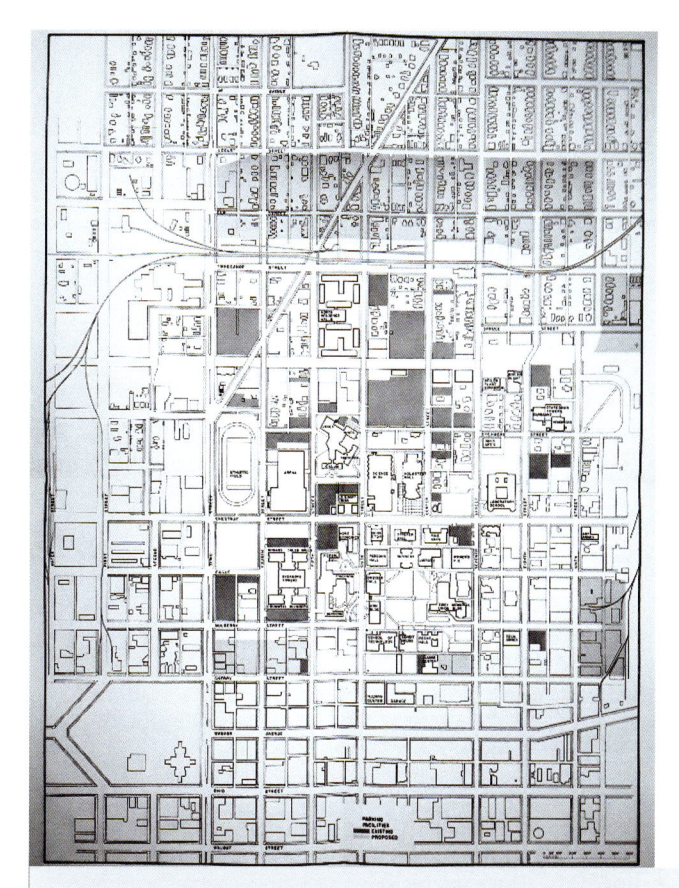

1969 Master Plan, existing and proposed parking facilities

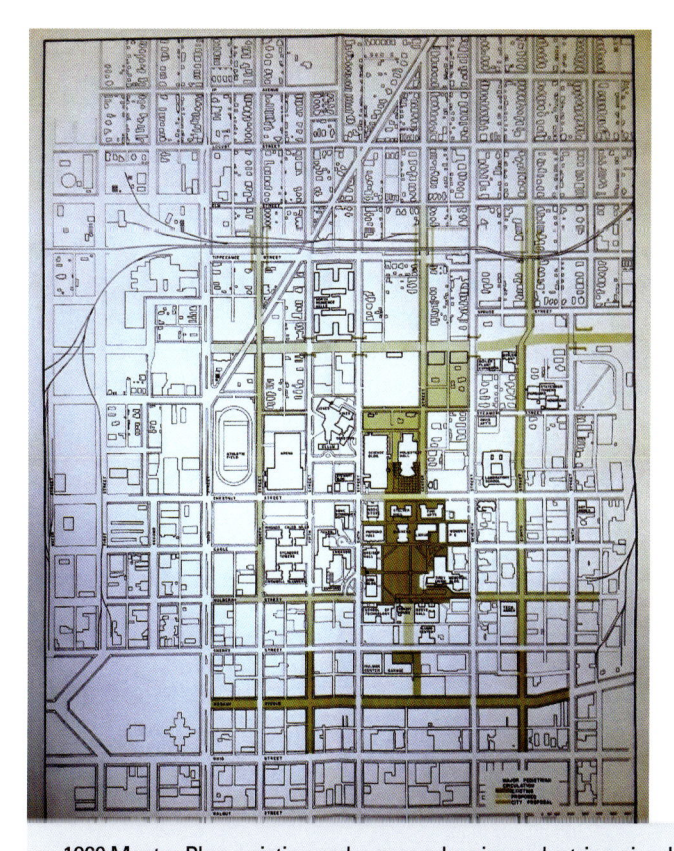

1969 Master Plan, existing and proposed major pedestrian circulation

Master Planning

Major Pedestrian Circulation

Perhaps the most aggressive recommendation for improving pedestrian circulation on campus in 1969 was the desire to build pedestrian bridges over streets to separate vehicles from people – a technique employed in New York City's Central Park by Frederick Law Olmsted. The plan depicted bridges over the railroad tracks running along the campus' north side, as well as bridges on campus' Spruce Street. While these pedestrian bridges were never constructed, the circulation plan did recommend closing several streets to vehicular traffic. Those recommendations included closing Center Street (6 1/2 Street) from Tippecanoe Street south to Chestnut Street and portions of Sycamore Street from Seventh Street west to Fourth Street.

Although historic data regarding the origin of this plan is minimal, it appears these efforts addressed the needs for moving parking to the outer edges of campus, and even north across existing major rail lines. By relocating surface parking to the edges of campus, this move freed up buildable open green space within the heart of campus to serve as in-fill parcels for future campus capital projects.

PRESIDENT RICHARD LANDINI (1975-1992)

Although there was no formal 'master plan' undertaken during 1978, an important event that year did occur that would change the face of the university's campus for decades to come. On October 30, 1978, President Richard Landini addressed a letter to key members of his staff, including then Facilities Director Thomas Dawson. In that letter, Landini outlined his desire to create a 'street study committee' whose charge would be to discuss the pros and cons of closing city streets that crisscrossed the campus (Chestnut Street and Sixth Street).

At the first committee meeting, the following street considerations were discussed:
- Closing streets required the establishment a peripheral traffic movement
- Street closings required a study of current and projected parking needs
- The closing of these streets would alter the landscape and future land use

Landini stated:

> "My own cursory study has uncovered 'paper' on the subject dating back to the 1962-63 year. It is my guess, however, that the subject has been discussed, debated, mentioned now and then, and generally 'thought about' for an even longer period. The university moved north to the southern side of Chestnut in the 30s, and so we can reasonably expect that the Tirey administration had discussed the closing of Chestnut even then."

He continues:

> "It is time to advance deliberately and firmly toward a resolution of the issue. It is my perception that the mutual best interests of the university and of the off-campus community are best served by the closing of both streets to vehicular traffic. It is my conviction that the university will be the stronger – academically, socially, culturally, physically, aesthetically, and in fact in every possible way – by the closing of those two streets."

With this one letter, the charge was given, and historic campus changes would be set in motion, culminating in the creation of the 1986 Sasaki Master Plan.

In December 1978, as a result of Dr. Landini's charge to the street study committee, LANDPLUS WEST, Inc. prepared maps of campus outlining:

- On-street parking (metered and unmetered)
- Surface lot parking
- Potential land acquisition areas
- Designations for potential lots (commuter, dorm, faculty/staff, and visitor)
- Possible sites for new additional parking

1986 Master Plan

For many on campus, when one speaks of "The Master Plan," they are referring to the 1986 Master Plan developed by Sasaki Associates of Watertown, MA. This implemented plan forever changed the landscape of the ISU campus.

There were three major planning objectives developed, including:

1. An extensive analysis conducted by administrators, deans, department chairpersons, staff members, and students
2. An analysis by Sasaki Associates of the information, statistical data, and premises developed by the university
3. Intensive discussions between university and Sasaki representatives to determine planning principles and premises

From these objectives came a planning process to:

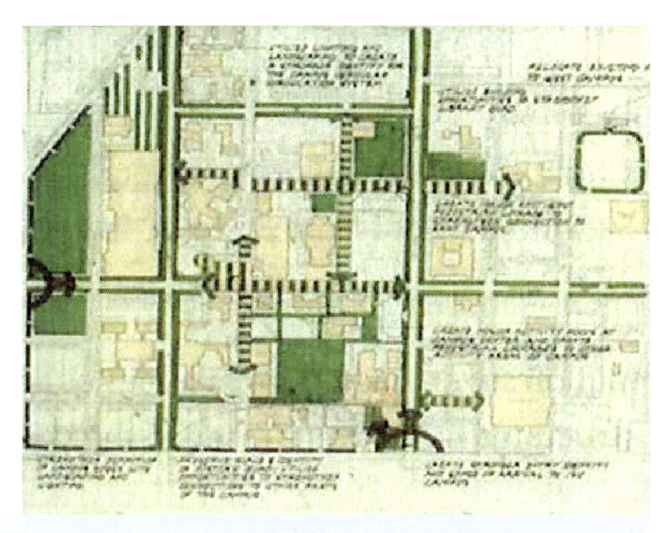

1986 Master Plan, proposed walkways and green spaces

1. Accommodate existing and planned university programs
2. Raze outdated structures located within the boundaries of the campus
3. Identify needed new buildings
4. Improve the campus ambience
5. Create improved patterns of circulation
6. Create a stronger more cohesive campus structure
7. Reduce traffic conflicts between pedestrians and vehicular traffic

A major recommendation of the 1986 plan was to create internal land bank opportunities for future building needs by moving the parking to the perimeter of campus. This single move also began the process of separating vehicular and pedestrian traffic, thus improving safety on campus. This recommendation was accomplished early in the implementation phase of this plan.

Next was recognition that the compact size of the campus was a defining characteristic. The plan graphically pointed out that most buildings and venues could be reached in a five-minute walk. Maintaining compactness and "walkability" governed future development.

Perhaps the most dramatic change to the campus as a result of the 1986 plan was the design of pedestrian walkways uniting the campus supplanting former streets. These brick paver walkways transformed the atomized campus into a unified green pastoral setting. Both Chestnut Street from Seventh to Fifth Streets, and Sycamore Street from Eighth to Fifth Streets, as well as Sixth Street from Cherry to Spruce Streets were vacated and transformed.

Sites for future buildings led to the systematic demolition of seven university buildings and several private businesses located within the campus.

Plans for new buildings included a Classroom Building (Root Hall), an Administrative Building (later satisfied by the construction of New Parsons Hall), and a Music Rehearsal Hall. Recognition that changing foot traffic patterns and dense student housing west and north of the quad meant that Tirey Memorial Student Union was no longer the center of campus life. This resulted in the construction of the Hulman Student Union and Dede Plaza.

Closing streets, razing sub-standard structures, building new structures, and planting nearly 4,000 trees over the next three decades created a unified campus oasis in downtown Terre Haute.

The May 9, 1986 Minutes of the Indiana State University Board of Trustees noted President Landini commented that "... the action (approval of the Sasaki plan) just taken was perhaps the most far reaching and important action taken in certainly the last ten years, and possibly the last 20 years. It is a step of enormous good for ISU and higher education in the State of Indiana."

PRESIDENT JOHN MOORE (1992-2000)

1996 Master Plan
Following ten years of aggressive and successful implementation of the 1986 Master Plan, President John W. Moore and Vice President Dennis Graham asked that the 1986 plan be revisited to determine the status of what had succeeded and what needed attention. The new 1996 plan derived from a 1994 Report of the university's Strategic Plan for the 21st Century.

The result of the 1995-96 planning process showed the need for 14 new facilities and renovation of 19 major buildings.

The detail in this plan showed major needs to be addressed over the period of 1996-2015. Among them were:
- Build a new women's intercollegiate soccer field
- Eliminate Lafayette Avenue through campus
- Construct a new softball complex including a press box and restroom facilities
- Renovate the 1960s Arena/HHP

Master Planning

- Renovate all four towers of Sycamore Towers (Rhoads, Mills, Blumberg, Cromwell)
- Construct a landmark edge to campus to be known as Oakley Place
- Transition Erickson Hall from housing to academic space
- Construct a new, more environmentally friendly steam plant
- Renovate the aging Hulman Center

The 1996 Master Plan established a list of projects, some of which were begun in the Moore era. Others appeared in the 2000, 2009, and 2017 Master Plans.

2000 Master Plan

In February 2000, the university completed a campus-wide strategic plan known as 'Strategic Plan for the 21st Century: A Year 2000 Update.' This plan, subtitled 'Balancing Change & Continuity,' was submitted to President John W. Moore on February 4, 2000. It grew out of a recent self-study for reaccreditation for the North Central Association (accrediting body), and specifically, Initiative #14: Improving Physical Facilities and Assuring an Accessible and Secure Campus.

Under the direction of Vice President Robert Schafer, a planning team of 13 Deans, Directors, and key administrators studied campus planning needs for the near-term (2001-03), the medium-term (2003-05), and the long-term (2005-11). Perhaps one of the more significant developments that came from the adoption of this plan was that priorities for the university's next ten years were established, allowing for input from the campus community, as well as the identification of funding options, and creation of appropriate design time for each project.

Topics covered in the plan included academic/administrative building projects and 11 separate master plans. From this effort came a blueprint for addressing campus physical needs through 2011. This plan, although addressing individual building and campus needs, was most beneficial in creating an atmosphere of planning, data collection, and analysis for plans yet to come.

Much of the planning, coordination, and facilitation of this master plan was developed within the Department of Facilities Management under the direction of Associate Vice President Kevin Runion, utilizing ISU's on-staff architects and engineers.

Academic/Administrative Building Projects

In brief, some of the highlights of this plan included a recognition that capital improvements were needed in several buildings over the ten-year period. Buildings and facilities identified for major renovations were:

- Stalker Hall
- Science Undergraduate Laboratory Spaces
- Holmstedt Hall
- School of Education and/or School of Business (replacement)
- University Hall
- Fine Arts Building
- Arena Building
- Fairbanks Hall
- Science Building (addition for Chemistry)
- Library (addition for long-term storage)

The Strategic Plan contained a subset of plans to address specific areas of need. These included technology, accessibility, recreation, parking, dining services, and auxiliaries.

PRESIDENT LLOYD BENJAMIN III (2000-2008)

"For those of you who are new to Indiana State, it is important that you understand not only are we striving to become nationally known for our distinctive programs, experiential learning, and community engagement, but also for creating a vibrant campus culture of learning and social development. Our Vision 2025 Plan shows how we intend to get there and what we will hold ourselves accountable for along the way …"

With that charge, the Vision 2025 Facilities Master Plan was born.

Early in 2003, the foundation for the plan began to take shape as key planning elements were established. These included:

- Creating interconnected quads and open spaces
- Extending existing linear pedestrian corridors
- Enhancing signature open spaces
- Developing new primary and secondary campus gateways
- Enhancing campus edges
- Enhancing wayfinding systems
- Guiding future building development

- Focusing acquisition opportunities
- Consolidating and improving athletic facilities
- Enhancing areas of university influence
- Providing clarity and ease of vehicular circulation
- Guiding future parking decisions
- Enhancing safe pedestrian circulation and linkages

Foundationally, the Vision 2025 Plan was to build upon the successes of previous plans adopted in 1969, 1986, 1996, and 2000.

Working with design/planning consultant JJR, the university began a process that was three-fold. First, the Discovery Stage required an open and candid dialogue over several days on campus with faculty students, staff, and key administrators. This was followed shortly thereafter with planning the development of the Alternative Campus Futures Stage, where professional consultants took the information they had gathered during the first phase and developed four distinct growth concept plans to share on campus to secure input from the administration, Master Planning Committee, faculty, staff, and students. The Final Facilities Master Plan Stage incorporated graphics and text outlining the history of the developed plan and its guiding principles that was shared with the entire campus community.

Buildings
The planning process identified the desire to create 'clusters' that would further enhance the academic experience.

Clusters identified included the following elements:
- Academic Village
- Athletics and Recreation cluster
- Business/Technology/Technology Transfer/Community Outreach cluster
- Education cluster
- Future Academic facility
- New Health Sciences facility
- Visual and Performing Arts building

Within the master plan for buildings, new construction was detailed including:
- Library (expansion)
- Health Science Center (addition)
- Family and Consumer Science Building
- Art Annex
- Early Childhood Education Center
- Academic Village
- Student Recreation Center
- Indoor Field House with Practice Facilities
- Visitor Center and Student Support Services Center

Additionally, long term the plan indicates a need for the construction of:
- Athletics Hall of Fame
- Private/Public Partnership Development in the university's "areas of influence" to the north and east of campus

Long a desired plan on campus, this Vision 2025 Plan clearly articulated the need to consolidate all athletic venues into a single location, which was identified to be the areas directly east of campus between Tenth and Thirteenth Streets (Eagle Street north to Locust Street). Another option discussed at the time was to move athletic venues across Third Street toward the river.

2005 Master Plan
During the Benjamin presidency, considerable attention was given to the physical limitations of the campus and sub-standard housing that surrounded it, especially to the north and east. These neighborhoods were felt to impact negatively prospective students' and their families' perceptions of the campus, and restricted future growth of the campus.

After much internal discussion, a decision was made to develop a long range plan (2005-25) that would address the surrounding neighborhoods and the current and potential future needs of the university, as well as the desire to consolidate venues for athletics that were scattered on campus as well as miles from campus (Memorial Stadium for football was over two miles east of campus).

In August 2005, the Board of Trustees adopted a policy authorizing the acquisition of properties north of campus to First Avenue (Third Street to Thirteenth Street) and east of campus from Tenth Street to Thirteenth Street. It should be noted that eminent domain was not used in the following years as the university acquired in excess of 300 small individual parcels from 2005 through 2017. Once the properties were acquired, all sub-standard dwellings were removed, and the areas were returned to natural open green space.

The plan was ambitious, showing the creation of two distinct expansion areas to the north from Tippecanoe Street to Locust Street and Third Street to Tenth Street. These "would-be zones" created public-private partnerships for housing and later opportunities for partnering with our neighbor eight blocks to the north, Union Hospital.

There were aspects of this plan that continued to guide the university into the next administration. Mid-way through Benjamin's presidency, however, the focus shifted from eastward expansion to expansion into downtown Terre Haute and the renovation of historically important buildings on and off campus. Prior to July 2008, the Federal Building located on Cherry Street was acquired to become the College of Business (the first university building across Cherry Street in the downtown). Funds were secured to renovate the Laboratory School (University Hall) to serve the College of Education and a $21.8 million Student Recreation Center was begun north of the Library and Lincoln Quad – a development that addressed the decades old problem of inadequate recreation facilities. Property located at 22 North Fifth Street was acquired (also across Cherry Street) that became the Barnes & Noble bookstore and home for the ISU Foundation. Finally, in collaboration with the City of Terre Haute, a multi-modal transportation and parking facility was built to provide increased parking for students and faculty working along the Cherry Street corridor. The Arts Corridor (Seventh Street) was also completed and tied the campus to the downtown arts district. In conjunction with Rose Hulman, a technology transfer center was developed to serve the community and the university provided the salary funding for the Director of the Downtown Terre Haute organization to further cement "town and gown" ties.

The need for developed, defined campus gateways and campus edges were additional key findings in the study, with the recommended development of secondary gateway entrances at Thirteenth Street and Chestnut Street, Locust Street and Seventh Street, and Seventh Street and Cherry Street, as well as the need for improvements to the campus main entrance at Third (U.S. 41) and Chestnut Street. The plan outlined the need to further enhance and create a robust wayfinding system for pedestrians and vehicular traffic.

Many aspects of this plan, as well several transformative building projects underway, were finalized during the Bradley administration. The southward development of the campus that had begun was continued with the development of student housing on Wabash Avenue and Cherry Street.

PRESIDENT DANIEL BRADLEY (2008-2017)

During the fall of 2008, the university retained RATIO Architects to assist in the development of a Campus Master Plan in conjunction with a strategic planning process undertaken with consultation by Stratus-Herry. In December 2009, the Trustees accepted the new plan.

2009 Master Plan

The horizon for this plan was set to be 15 to 20 years. President Bradley explained that the primary components of the plan included: meeting functional needs of academic programs, improving student housing options, serving as a catalyst for redevelopment of Terre Haute, improving wayfinding, supporting redevelopment of the Wabash River riverfront, and creating competitive athletic venues comparable to our peers.

The most transformative element in this plan was to jump across U.S. 41/Third Street. Academically, six projects were identified, some were new and others were a continuation of projects currently underway:

1. Continue renovation of the former Federal Building/U.S. Post Office into the Scott College of Business.
2. Consolidate the College of Nursing with other health related fields on campus into a single new/renovated building to be known as the College of Health and Human Performance.
3. Accelerate improvement in the Science Building, including undergraduate laboratories.
4. Complete the renovation of the former University Lab School into the Bayh College of Education.
5. Renovate the 1910 Normal Hall (former University Library) into a Student Success Center while maintaining the structure's historic significance.
6. Study the need for potentially increasing storage space for library collection items, and dedicate the newly completed Student Recreation Center.

Six residential housing needs were identified.

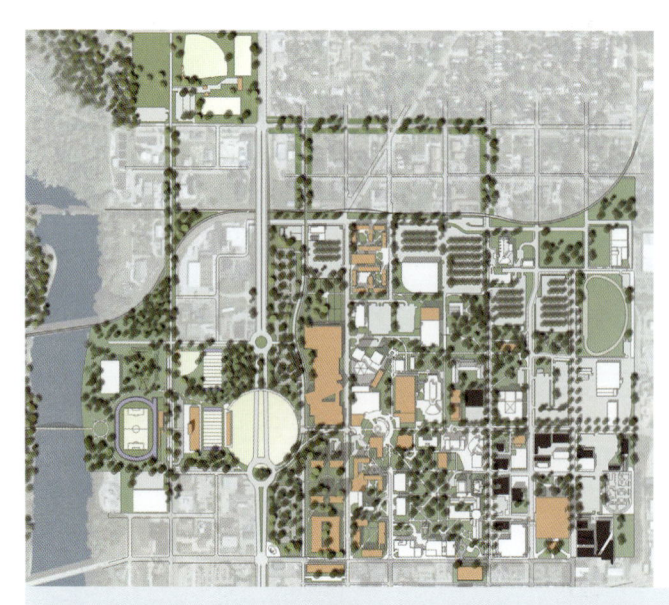

2009 Master Plan, base map

Those included:
1. Creation of a housing complex focused on the "first year experience" (Burford, Erickson, and Pickerl).
2. Develop a true Greek Village for sororities housed on campus.
3. Construct new in-fill housing on campus to allow for the planned increase in student enrollments identified in the university's strategic plan.
4. Plan for complete modernization and updating of the four towers that make up Sycamore Towers on the southwest edge of campus (Rhoads, Mills, Blumberg, and Cromwell).
5. Complete renovations of dining facilities.

Administrative buildings identified for needed attention included the creation of a Welcome Center, new offices for the ISU Foundation, and other administrative needs created by the repurposing of Erickson Hall back in to student housing.

Along with the massive commitment to upgrading residential housing options for students, the second greatest change was in the area of athletics.

The plan addressed the creation and consolidation of the athletics venues to the west of Third Street/U.S. 41 with the construction of a new track and field facility to replace the aged Marks Field, soccer fields, and indoor baseball training facilities. Also addressed was the need to expand the indoor track and field venue located on the north end of the Arena Building, as well as the need to plan for major improvements to the university's basketball venue in Hulman Center.

Just as the 1986 Master Plan tackled the need to reduce traffic conflicts between vehicles and pedestrians by closing several streets, the 2009 Master Plan recommended the closing of Fourth Street through campus, as well as acquiring Chestnut, Fifth, and Sixth Streets to allow for future improvements for these campus circulation arteries.

Finally, following nearly 30 years without significant changes to the campus wayfinding system, a plan was developed to identify not only buildings, but to strengthen the information signage and routes for walking students, staff, and visitors to campus through the addition of 'you are here' signs.

Guiding principles for the planning efforts included:
- Satisfy functional needs of academic programs, while ensuring non-residential facility square footage remains constant
- Offer better student housing options, while ensuring bed capacity does not increase by more than 10 percent
- Provide more practical vehicular and pedestrian circulation systems
- Maintain the compact form of the campus
- Coordinate campus planning with riverfront re-development
- Develop on-campus athletic facilities that are competitive with other venues in the Missouri Valley Conference
- Improve the campus in a manner that responds to contemporary and practical sustainable design practices

Academic/Administrative Facilities
- Federal Building – complete the renovation begun in 2005 to become the Scott College of Business.
- College of Nursing, Health, and Human Services – located in two separate facilities at the time. The proposed renovation of the Arena/HHP facility with the addition of approximately 50,000 ASF would allow for the academic programs surrounding health professions to be housed in one location.
- Student Academic Success Center – consolidation of several student academic functions into a single location would allow the university to serve the academic needs of students in terms of tutoring and counseling. Normal Hall, dedicated in 1910, was identified as the facility that could be used to serve these purposes.
- Science Building – with a long-term planning horizon, the replacement of the roofing system, as well as mechanical and electrical systems in this facility constructed in 1960 and 1969, were identified as critical needs. Additional needs included cosmetic updating of the building's

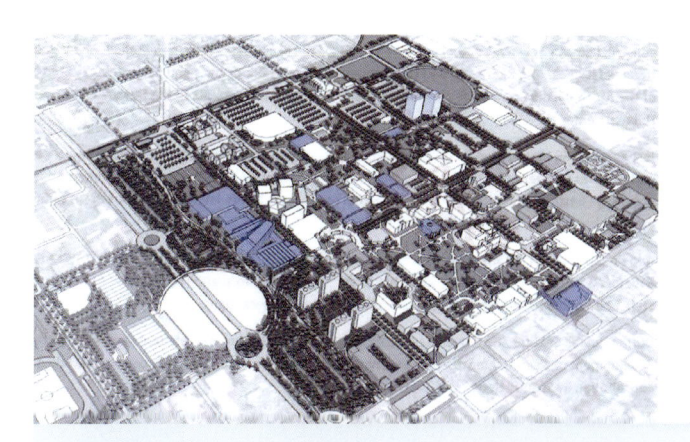

2009 Master Plan, academic facilities highlighted in blue

Master Planning

entire interior. Renovations of approximately 18 laboratory classrooms began in the spring 2010 semester.
- Theater and Art Venues – renovate or replace the existing theater facilities. Create new 2D and 3D studio facilities.
- Repurpose the Student Computing Building to become the Student Career Center.
- Transform the former Family and Consumer Sciences Building into the ISU Welcome Center. Programs housed within the Family and Consumer Sciences department were combined with existing engineering programs in Tech A, improving the interdisciplinary aspects of our students' experiences on campus.

Residential Life
Throughout the campus planning process, it became apparent the need to upgrade student housing to meet the expectations of today's student and their parents was paramount. Most of the university's housing stock was constructed in the 1950s and 60s. Significant upgrades to Hines and Jones Halls had occurred in 1998 and 2000 but were now approaching 20 years of age. Burford Hall, renovated in 2006, serves freshmen, while Sandison Hall was renovated for occupancy in the fall of 2010. Pickerl Hall renovations occurred during 2010-11. All renovations were planned to provide for double rooms with private baths and individual heat and air controls in each room. Further proposed renovations and developments included:
- First Year Housing – In order to offer more market-friendly options to first time students, the Master Plan called for first year housing to be focused on the Hines, Jones, Sandison and Erickson, Burford, Pickerl complexes.
- Lincoln Quad/Greek Housing – Constructed in 1969, this facility had traditionally been a home to several Greek organizations. While routine maintenance has occurred over the years, no major aesthetic upgrades or reconfigurations had taken place. The Greek community had indicated a preference to occupy a distinct Greek Village.
- Sycamore Towers – These towers consist of four 14-story towers constructed in 1964-65. Like Lincoln Quad, no major aesthetic upgrades or reconfigurations of the existing bed capacity had taken place since the original construction. These towers did not have central air or private bathrooms. A major commitment to upgrade one tower each year for four consecutive years was made, with the first being Mills, renovated in 2015, Blumberg in 2016, Cromwell in 2017, and finally, Rhoads Hall in 2018. This also had the effect of reducing bed capacity by approximately one-third.
- Off-Campus Housing – A loss in bed count as a result of reconfiguration of existing layouts and the need for additional beds was addressed by the construction of apartment-style housing units on Wabash Avenue in downtown Terre Haute, known as '500 Wabash,' between Fifth and Sixth Streets.
- Dining Services – The existing dining hall at Sycamore Towers was antiquated and oversized for today's student dining needs. Sodexo expressed an interest in studying other potential sites for relocation of the dining services located in Sycamore Tower.

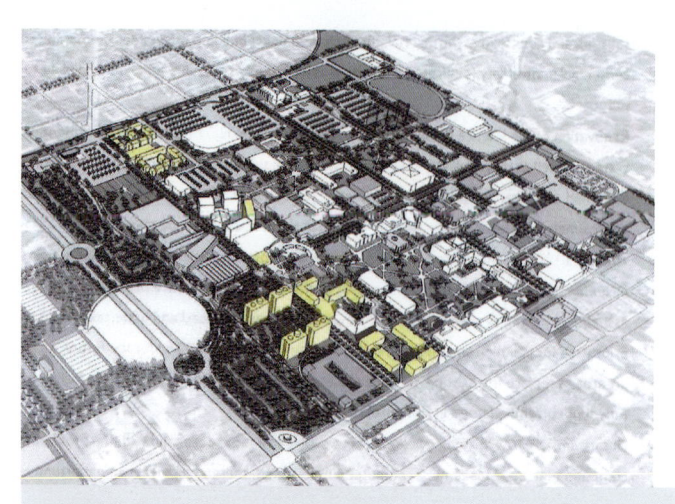

2009 Master Plan, existing/proposed Residential Life facilities

Athletic Facilities
Most of the athletic facilities had not seen significant upgrades in over 40 years. Many of ISU's existing competition venues were ranked at or near the bottom by the Missouri Valley Conference. The under-utilized land west of Third Street/U.S. 41, formerly industrial sites, were identified as appropriate locations for new athletic competition and training facilities. This decision rested on the relative proximity to the existing athletic training facilities located in the College of Nursing, Health, and Human Services Building (former Arena/HHP); the availability of large contiguous tracts of land; and the existence of existing athletic and student recreation areas already sited west of Third Street. One of the guiding principles of the Master Plan was to support the efforts of the Terre Haute community to revitalize the riverfront.
- Track and Field – The current outdoor track and field facility, known as Marks Field needed

extensive repairs to the track surface and its location severely constrained amenities for fans. The Plan proposed to relocate the track and field facility to property west of Third Street, adjacent to the riverfront.
- Indoor Track – The existing indoor track, located in the College of Nursing, Health, and Human Services Building, did not meet the requirements for NCAA sanctioned events. The Plan proposed an expansion of the existing facility to create a quality Division 1 competition and training facility. Work was completed in 2017-18.
- Soccer – To provide operational cost savings, a soccer competition field was proposed to be built in the center of the new track and field facility.
- Softball – Like Marks Field, the existing softball fields were constrained in size and could be negatively impacted by changes to Fourth Street. The Master Plan depicted the eventual relocation of the competition softball fields west of Third Street, or perhaps north, to be adjacent to the baseball complex, allowing for shared resources.
- Basketball – Hulman Center, constructed in the early 1970s, still has much of its original mechanical, electrical, and HVAC systems and exterior skin. The facility needs a major renovation.
- Football – Even with the replacement of the stadium turf and upgrades to locker room facilities at Memorial Stadium, there is a need for more extensive upgrades to this remote campus property. A new stadium was depicted in a prominent location west of Third Street. This facility could be phased in over several years.
- Athletics Administration/Strength and Conditioning Training – Currently Athletics administrative offices and training facilities are located in a portion of the College of Nursing, Health, and Human Services Building. The Campus Land Use Plan suggests a new facility could be located immediately south of the existing CNHHS Building.

Way Finding
- U.S. 41/Third Street Corridor – The portion of the corridor immediately west of the campus was planned to create a major entry point with the creation of a large, circular green space supported by enhanced medians and roundabouts.
- Fourth and Fifth Street Corridors – Several interior streets are proposed to change from one-way to two-way streets. This would include Fourth, Fifth, Eighth, and Ninth Streets. The Plan

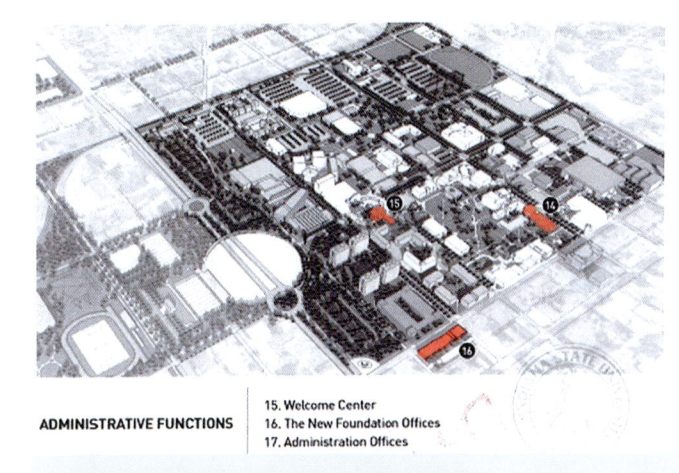

ADMINISTRATIVE FUNCTIONS
15. Welcome Center
16. The New Foundation Offices
17. Administration Offices

Above: Administrative Functions, 2009
Below: Way-finding Signage, 2009

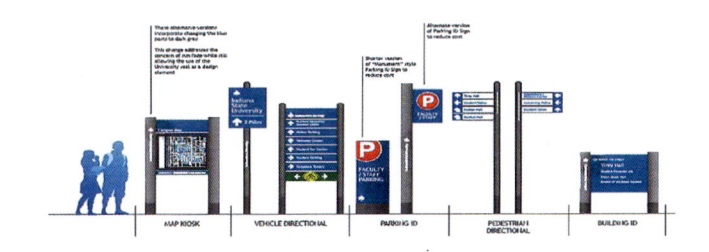

also suggests removing on-street parking from both Fourth and Fifth Streets while adding traffic calming features.
- Cherry Street Corridor – The street is state-owned but early conversations concerning transfer of control are underway between the City of Terre Haute and the state. The Plan suggests Cherry Street also be converted to a two-way street.
- West of U.S. 41/Third Street – As the campus expands recreational and athletic facilities west of Third Street, it will be necessary to improve Eagle, Sycamore, and First Streets to serve the area and provide street parking to satisfy the demands for small- to medium-sized sporting events.

2016 Master Plan
In the fall of 2016, the university instituted a new campus-wide strategic plan – There's More to BLUE.

In its development, assumptions from the 2009 Plan were revisited and modified, including the major areas of the 2009 Plan: Academic /Administrative Facilities, Residential Life, Athletic Facilities, Way Finding, and General Campus Improvements.

Under the Academic Facilities section, renovation focused on the Health and Human Services Building, Fine Arts and Commerce Building, Holmstedt Hall, Dreiser Hall, Root Hall, Fairbanks Hall, New Theater, Library

Master Planning

Services, College of Technology, Gillum Hall, Tirey Hall/Tilson Hall, and the College of Nursing. The Fine Arts and Commerce Building, built and dedicated in the late 1930s, was noted as the facility needing attention first, and a major capital improvement project was requested, funded, and designed in 2018 to address the needs of those departments today. Athletic venues were also marked for improvement, including developing a soccer presence at the Gibson Track and Field site.

The plan proposed addressing the need for an improved 'front door' entrance to campus at U.S. 41/Third Street and Chestnut Street, addressing secondary entrance points to campus by adding signage and landscape elements, and improving access to the riverfront athletic facilities across the heavily traveled Third Street.

CONCLUSION

One of the first planned campuses in the United States was the University of Virginia designed by Thomas Jefferson. He envisioned an "academical village" which, by its very design, was considered a teaching tool intended to elevate aesthetic awareness of faculty and students and instill an appreciation for building in a grand tradition. For Jefferson, the interdependence between academic mission and campus design was essential. Building in a Neoclassical style was, for him, a metaphor for building a sound republic.

This chapter on planning provides insight into the historical context within which the campus evolved, and the ongoing dialogue of planners and dreamers back and forth across the history of this university. Building a Legacy required Designing a Legacy. ∎

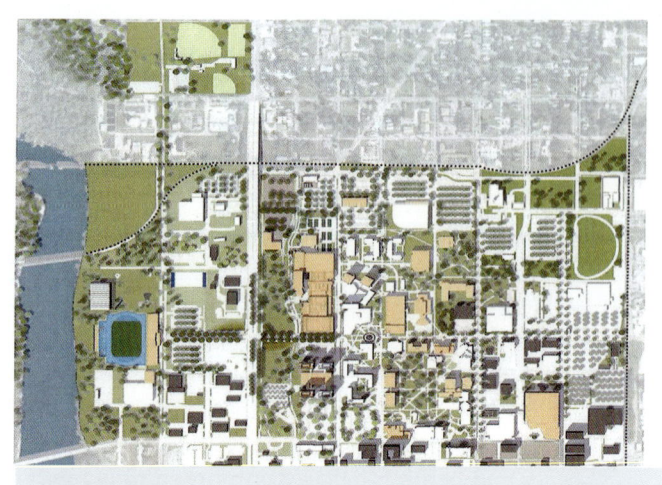

2016 Master Plan, base map

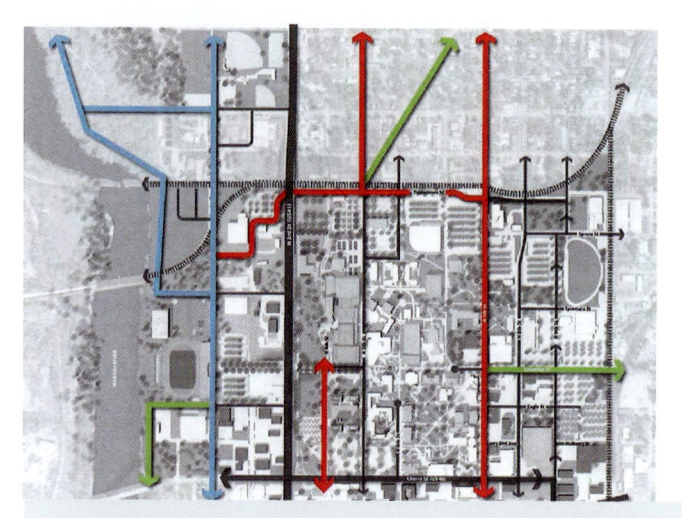

2016 Master Plan, ISU/city alternative transportation plan

TIMELINE

"We shape our buildings; thereafter, they shape us." – Winston Churchill

1865

April 14, 1865
Abraham Lincoln was shot by John Wilkes Booth at Ford's theater and died April 15.

May 9, 1865
The American Civil War ended by Proclamation (Last shot fired: June 22, 1865).

December 20, 1865
The Indiana General Assembly passed House Bill 119 establishing Indiana State Normal School (ISNS). The bill was signed into law by then Governor Oliver P. Morton.

1866

January 9-10, 1866
The first meeting of the Board of Trustees for the ISNS was held in Indianapolis, Indiana at the office of the State Superintendent of Public Instruction. The Trustees consisted of John Ingle Jr. (Evansville), Isaac Kinley (Richmond), Barnabas C. Hobbs (Bloomingdale), William C. Hannah (LaPorte), and State Superintendent of Public Instruction George W. Hoss.

May 15, 1866
A committee from Terre Haute consisting of William R. McKeen, J. H. Barr, and John M. Olcott appeared to make an offer to the Board of $50,000 cash plus real estate valued at $25,000. The plot of land involved was the County Seminary site of Vigo County, east of Sixth Street between Eagle and Mulberry Streets. A building committee was appointed comprised of McKeen (a banker and treasurer of the Board) and Trustees Barnabus C. Hobbs and George W. Hoss.

August 10, 1866
J. A. Vrydagh, from Terre Haute, was chosen as the architect by the ISNS Board to design the Normal School Building (Old Main). At later meetings, the Board decided on an eclectic Gothic style structure with an estimated cost of $100,000.

1867

March 8, 1867
By special act, the Indiana General Assembly awarded $50,000 from the Township Library Fund collections to the Trustees of the ISNS, and then added an additional $79,000 to the construction fund in 1869, for a total of $129,000.

August 10, 1867
The Normal School Board of Trustees and the City of Terre Haute entered into a contract, in which the city agreed to pay "forever" one-half the cost of maintaining the ISNS building and grounds.

August 13, 1867
The cornerstone was laid for the new Indiana State Normal School (Old Main), with the total cost of the building estimated to be $189,000.

1869

PRESIDENT WILLIAM JONES

November 2, 1869
President William Albert Jones was appointed as ISNS's First President and served in this capacity until May 16, 1879.

December 3, 1869
The Board of Trustees concluded that the south entrance of the ISNS building would be designated as the girls' entrance and the north as the boys' entrance.

1870

January 5, 1870
Inauguration ceremonies were held on the second floor of the new building in the large assembly room. Conrad Baker (the Governor of Indiana) and Colonel Richard W. Thompson (Attorney, former U.S. Secretary of the Navy, U.S. House of Representative from the State of Indiana, Indiana State Senator, and former Judge of the 18th Circuit Court for the State of Indiana), delivered the inauguration addresses. State Superintendent Barnabus C. Hobbs presided.

January 6, 1870
The doors to ISNS opened to 21 students. The grounds of the new Normal School were still covered in construction debris and the building, with only two floors ready for use, contained "the most necessary furniture" and a library with only a dictionary and a Bible.

May 17, 1870
Miss Newell (Lady Principal) reported to the Board of Trustees that the boarding facilities for females in the city were insufficient. President Jones, Miss Newell, and the Secretary of the Board were appointed to a Committee on Boarding to study options.

November 17, 1870
The Board of Trustees approved a plan of Music Teaching to be arranged by Professor Paige.

1872

President Jones presented his resignation to the Board of Trustees. The Board then requested that Mr. Jones withdraw his letter stating that it would be an embarrassment to the institution. After a full conference with the Board, Jones withdrew his resignation.

June 25, 1872
The first graduating class of ISNS was comprised of nine students.

1873

August 27, 1873
President Jones reported to the Board of Trustees that he was unable to purchase books for ISNS due to the credit of future appropriations by the State of Indiana. As a result, Chauncey Rose donated $4,000 to the Normal School for the purchase of books for the library. The Rose Library Fund was then established for this purpose.

1874

The Board of Trustees and the Superintendent of the Terre Haute Public Schools entered into a contract known as the Normal Training School Articles of Agreement.

An advanced two-year course was offered to graduates of the regular normal course or equivalently prepared students.

June 25, 1874
Regulations for the management and use of the library were approved. Professor Hodgin was appointed the librarian.

October 17, 1874
A contract was awarded to Crane Breed and Co. (Cincinnati, OH) to furnish a central steam heating apparatus for the ISNS building. The apparatus was to cost $13,355. Prior to the central heat system being installed, the building was heated by coal stoves in individual rooms. The smoke from the stoves and lamps made for a murky and dirty atmosphere.

1875

The Indiana State Legislature appropriated $10,000 to complete the construction of the basement and third floor of the ISNS, as well as purchase much needed equipment for the school.

Historic reports say the school had an inadequate library at this time and students were asked to bring their own textbooks to the school.

1876

September 1876
William Wood Parsons was hired on to the faculty into a position declined by Howard Sandison, who accepted a position to teach Latin in the Terre Haute High School (1875-77). Parsons would become the third President of the school in 1885.

1878

Students requested that a piano be purchased for the school, even though there were no funds available.

October 18, 1878
President Jones submitted yet another resignation to the Board of Trustees. Again, the Board of Trustees did not accept his resignation and, instead, gave him an extended leave of absence in hopes that he would return ready to continue his work.

November 22, 1878
James M. Wilson and Cyrus W. Hodgin were appointed to fulfill the duties of the President of the Faculty in the absence of President Jones.

1879

May 16, 1879
President William Albert Jones stepped down as President.

June 30, 1879
Murray Briggs, the President of the Board of Trustees, was authorized to speak with William Jones about withdrawing his resignation for a third time. In the event Mr. Jones did not withdraw his resignation, Briggs was authorized to offer the position to George Pliny Brown.

PRESIDENT GEORGE BROWN

July 1879
George Pliny Brown became the second President of Indiana Normal School. He served in this role until July 1, 1885.

1880

March 25, 1880
A Committee on Grounds was formed to arrange for grounds improvement by planting trees and seeding grass. The Board of Trustees approved spending $100 for the project.

December 17, 1880
After repeated efforts to rectify the failure of the heating apparatus, the Board of Trustees agreed not to pay Crane Breed and Co. any part of the bill.

1881

March 11, 1881
The Board of Trustees adopted a report from the Committee on Rules, which outlined the ISNS System of Government, the Duties of the President of the Faculty, and the Duties of Teachers.

May 26, 1881
58 trees were planted on the grounds along the sidewalks.

June 17, 1881
Five members (half) of the faculty resigned due to policies implemented by President Brown and the rules the Board had approved on March 11, 1881. They held strongly to President Jones' ideals and were unhappy with the new courses being offered.

July 7, 1881
The Board of Trustees accepted the resignation of the five faculty members. President Brown quickly filled all positions and continued with his changes. Some of the men asked to fill the positions were Howard Sandison, elected to a position in Methods of Primary Teaching, and William Wood Parsons, elected to head both the Department of History and Civil Government and the Department of Grammar and Composition.

November 18, 1881
A course for college graduates was offered in 1881-82.

1882

February 22, 1882
The Committee on Grounds was authorized to spend $100 on improvements.

May 24, 1882
The Board of Trustees approved the addition of a Department of Music.

June 15, 1882
The Board of Trustees approved a $1.00 lab fee for each student in class at the beginning of each term.

September 21, 1882
President Brown approved the purchase of six new dictionaries and 100 song books for the school.

November 24, 1882
The Women's Christian Temperance Union donated to ISNS a "Temperance Library," made up of a large amount of books.

1883

April 19, 1883
The Board of Trustees approved the expenditure of $1,500 for an apparatus in the Department of Science, as well as $500 for professional books to be added to the library.

September 22, 1883
The Board of Trustees authorized an overdraft from the ISNS account for the purchase of a scientific apparatus. This was made necessary by the failure of the Indiana General Assembly (Legislature) to pass an appropriation bill during the last assembly.

1885

The Normal School Advance began publication.

May 1, 1885
President Brown submitted his resignation to the Board of Trustees, which was accepted. His resignation became effective July 1, 1885.

June 11, 1885
Petitions, one from the faculty, one from the alumni association, and one from 164 students, were presented to the Board of Trustees, requesting that Professor William Wood Parsons be elected the President of the school.

PRESIDENT WILLIAM PARSONS

July 1, 1885
President George Pliny Brown stepped down as President, William Wood Parsons became the third President of ISNS.

July 17, 1885
The Secretary of the Board of Trustees was instructed to purchase 30 wooden buckets and 300 feet of hose for fire protection. The topic of building insurance was discussed, but the Board chose not to take any action on insurance, unless the City of Terre Haute agreed to participate equally in covering the cost – something the city had agreed to during the founding days of the school.

1886

April 9, 1886
Professor Howard Sandison was elected as Vice President.

July 1, 1886
Due to increased enrollment in both the high school and ISNS, the Terre Haute High School moved to its new home on South Seventh Street, thus allowing ISNS to expand onto the second floor of the Normal Building.

1887

February 22, 1887
A large group of Indiana state legislators arrived by special train to visit and inspect ISNS. The members visited recitation rooms, made speeches, and were honored at a banquet at the Terre Haute House.

October 14, 1887
The Board of Trustees agreed to insure the building for $50,000 at a cost of $500 for five years. The cost was to be split with the Terre Haute School Board.

November 21, 1887
President Parsons reported that nothing had been done about purchasing insurance for the building.

1888

February 14, 1888
The Secretary of the Board of Trustees was approved to purchase 50 additional buckets for fire protection.

April 9, 1888
A fire aided by strong winds started in the building's attic around 8:40 a.m. Within minutes, 175 training school children and their teachers and faculty were evacuated from the building. The building was a total loss, estimated at over $225,000, with no insurance.

Students, watching their school building go up in flames, began going to the train station to head home. President Parsons reportedly ran to the train station to inform students that classes would be held tomorrow and the ensuing days.

April 10, 1888
Centenary Methodist Church offered the use of its building as a meeting place until the school was rebuilt. Other churches offered the use of their buildings as well until the second story of the new high school could be used. Because of the generosity of the church during this hard time, ISNS repaid the favor in 1901 by allowing Centenary Church to use the ISNS building for their Sunday morning services.

April 17, 1888
1,000 citizens signed a petition and presented it to the Terre Haute City Council, requesting that the council appropriate enough funds to pay for one-half the cost of repairing ISNS.

The Terre Haute City Council was able to appropriate $25,000 in April and $25,000 in July for rebuilding the school.

July 6, 1888
The Common Council of the City of Terre Haute appropriated $25,000 to the Board of ISNS to be used for repairs.

October 11, 1888
The Board of Trustees formed several committees to help in managing the recovery of the school.

1889

January 30, 1889
The Committee of Education and Finance of the General Assembly visited ISNS to check the operation of the school in its temporary quarters and examine the work of rebuilding the school.

February 16, 1889
The Indiana General Assembly appropriated a total of $100,000 during the 1889 session to meet the needs of ISNS. $60,000 of these funds were used to complete the rebuilding of the school after the fire, $13,000 for the construction of the heating plant, etc.

April 11, 1889
The Board of Trustees and the City of Terre Haute insured the ISNS building for $50,000.

September 13, 1889
The Board of Trustees met for the first time in the reconstructed building (Old Main).

1890

July 15, 1890
Arthur Cunningham became the head of the Normal School Library. He was the first librarian appointed to the position and oversaw a book collection of 5,286 volumes.

September 30, 1890
The Library Fund was created with the $1,500 given by the last legislature. The President was authorized to spend $600 for the purchase of books during the school year.

The average number of students enrolled per term increased ten percent to 526 students.

1891

A four-year course of study at ISNS was introduced to replace the three-year course, which had been in the curriculum since 1885.

1892

February 9, 1892
The heating system of the ISNS building was declared inadequate by the Board, after causing so much frustration. At the contractor's expense, a replacement of the system was authorized.

September 9, 1892
Francis Marion Stalker (for whom Stalker Hall would be named) was appointed to the faculty in psychology and methods.

October 31, 1892
The ISNS annual report noted that there was an issue with the chemical lab being in the basement of the building (Old Main) that involved offensive odors and fire hazard. Ultimately, this would support the request for construction of a new building (North Hall) to house the labs.

December 15-16, 1892
The Board of Trustees reviewed plans for the proposed new building (North Hall). After review, the plans of W. H. Floyd and Guy Stone were adopted.

1893

March 6, 1893
The Indiana General Assembly (Legislature) approved $40,000 for a new building (North Hall) to house the library, science classes, and gymnasium. The structure was planned to be built next to the main building (Old Main) on the north side.

June 8, 1893
The Board's dismissal of popular Professor Thompkins precipitated student protests. The Board cancelled commencement exercises for June 30, 1893 and insisted that all members of the class sign formal statements of apology to the Board prior to receiving their degrees.

1894

February 21, 1894
The Board of Trustees approved a resolution stating that no person be admitted to the school who does not intend to teach after they graduate.

Summer 1894
The first six-week summer session took place. Three professors offered courses and divided the $10 tuition. 110 students enrolled. Three years later, these summer sessions became formal classes, a regular part of the academic calendar year, and no tuition was charged.

ISNS athletes introduced baseball, football, and basketball to the school.

William T. Turman was elected Head of the Department of Penmanship and Drawing.

1895

March 8, 1895
The Indiana General Assembly (Legislature) approved a tax that would benefit state schools. Normal School was supported by the tax of 1/20 of one mill levied and collected, approximately $65,000 annually.

April 25, 1895
New admission requirements were put in place in order to limit enrollment.

Fall Term 1895
North Hall, or North Annex, a northwest wing of the main building, opened in the fall. Within its first two years, it housed a library on the first floor, science departments on the second floor, and offices and meeting rooms on the third floor. On a Saturday afternoon, 100 student volunteers helped relocate books from the main building to North Hall. The library had two gyms underneath.

November 1895
The Normal Advance, the first student newspaper, started with its first issue. It was published monthly during the school year for 19 years. In 1915, it was changed to a weekly publication and continued this way until it became the Indiana Statesman in 1929.

The first basketball and football teams were organized, and the Athletic Association was admitted to the Indiana Inter-Collegiate Athletic Association.

1896

April 24, 1896
Booker T. Washington delivered a lecture in the Opera House entitled "Solving the Problem of the Colored Man in the Black Belt of the South."

Fall 1896
The library of the Normal School was estimated to contain over 16,000 books. Acquisition was supported by student fees in the "Library Fund" of the school.

1901

Students were first classified as Freshmen, Sophomores, Juniors, and Seniors.

1902

Fall 1902
A Rural Training School was organized during the summer and opened for the fall term. Known as School #6, at Chamberlain's Crossing, Lost Creek Township, it was located six miles east of Terre Haute on the interurban line between Terre Haute and Brazil.

1903

As the athletic program continued to develop, the first athletics letters were awarded and the first practice field, Parsons Field, was acquired.

1904

August 10, 1904
The cornerstone was laid for Fairbanks Memorial Library, what would become the city library.

1905

Fall 1905
The Training School opened with elementary grades on the first floor and the high school on the upper floors. The building's name was changed in 1936 to Stalker Hall in honor of Francis Marion Stalker. (NOTE: This Stalker Hall, now razed, was located adjacent to Old Main.)

1906

August 12, 1906
Fairbanks Hall, the former City Library, opened and later officially became part of the University in 1979, providing classroom space and a student gallery for the Department of Art.

1907

A high school diploma was now required for admission.

1908

The first bachelor's degree was awarded.

1910

June 21, 1910
Normal Hall Library was opened on the northern edge of the historic quadrangle as the university's library. Architects for the building were J. F. Alexander and Son, and the Contractor was August Ohm. The cost was $155,000.

1914

June 28, 1914
World War I was presumed to have begun when Archduke Franz Ferdinand and his wife were assassinated by Serbian rebels.

1915

December 2, 1915
The Vocational Education Building was accepted by the Board of Trustees. Cost for construction was approximately $130,000.

1917

The Science Building, later known as the Classroom Building, opened, which housed standard classrooms, labs, several photographic darkrooms, and a rooftop greenhouse. The architect was Clarence Martindale and the contractor was W. A. Stoolman. The cost of this building was $132,000. (NOTE: This building was razed in 1998.)

Originally named the Science Building, in 1962 this became the College of Business, and in 1981, the Classroom Building.

June 25, 1917
American armed forces landed in France, signaling America's entrance into the war.

1918

The Board of Trustees purchased a house west of the Emmeline Fairbanks Memorial Library for use as a Student Union. Another house across the street was bought in order to be converted into a cafeteria with seating for over 100 students.

The Eastern Division branch of the campus opened in Muncie, later to become Ball State University (1927).

November 11, 1918
Known as Armistice Day, fighting ended on the 11th day of the 11th month on the 11th hour.

1919

The first homecoming parade was held.

Faculty of the ISNS totaled 39 during the 1919-20 year.

1920

The 50th Anniversary of ISNS marked it as "one of the largest and best of the nation's 300 normal schools."

1921

July 7, 1921
Permission was given to purchase land for Professor Fred Donaghy's experimental farm. This property would later become the Allendale Lodge on April 3, 1939.

The cost of the 8.3-acre property was $2,490. The property would later include four major structures: the Holmstedt Home, the lodge, the 1 1/2 story caretaker's house, and a small detached garage.

The Holmstedt Home would be built in 1966 and would be a single story, wood-frame structure of approximately 1,800 square feet, with a partial basement and an attached garage.

The lodge was an open structure with some small service areas, large fireplace, full basement, and a screened porch, totaling approximately 2,000 square feet.

September 30, 1921
President Parsons stepped down as President.

PRESIDENT LINNAEUS HINES
(Hines also served as the President of Ball State Teachers College from 1921-24.)

October 1, 1921
Linnaeus Neal Hines became the fourth President, serving until 1933.

1924

All Normal School courses were placed on the collegiate level.

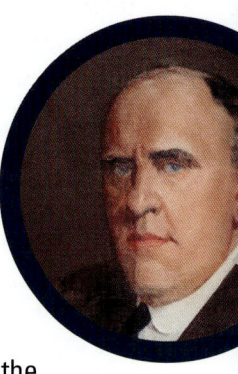

November 19, 1924
The cornerstone of Reeve Hall was laid. The architectural firm for this building was Johnson, Miller, Miller, and Yeager of Terre Haute. (NOTE: This was the first Reeve Hall, razed in 1998. The Reeve Hall name was later transferred to a new residential complex in 2014.)

1925

The first student night was held, which was a forerunner to the Campus Revue.

October 28, 1925
Reeve Hall, located south of the Tirey Student Union Building and east of Condit House, was dedicated. From 1924-59, Reeve Hall served as the only Women's Dormitory on campus. From 1944-46, it was used by the U.S. Navy as barracks for its V-5 and V-12 programs.

1927

The Graduate Division was established.

1928

The first master's degree was awarded.

Enrollment reached 1,452 students.

February 21-22, 1928
The Women's Physical Education Building was dedicated. Architects for the building were Johnson, Miller, Miller, and Yeager of Terre Haute. The building cost $307,623. The building burned to the ground on July 23, 1984.

1929

ISNS was renamed Indiana State Teacher's College (ISTC) by the Indiana General Assembly. Courses were on the collegiate level and a Master's program had earlier been established, so the name change recognized the new status of the school.

Faculty during the 1929-30 year totaled 85 (compared with 39 in 1919-20).

The Indiana Statesman replaced the Normal Advance.

1930

The North Central Association of Secondary Schools and Colleges raised ISTC to the full rank of an accredited college. The American Association of Teacher's Colleges admitted ISTC to the highest rank of Teachers Colleges without conditions, and ISTC was admitted to membership in the American Council on Education.

1932

February 11, 1932
ISTC purchased the Central Christian Church on Mulberry Street for $12,000 with plans to convert it to the college's bookstore.

1933

June 8, 1933
Hines stepped down as President. He was chosen to be the Director of the Extension Division and Placement Bureau, and in 1934 he was placed in charge of the Office of Student Activities and Alumni Secretary.

INTERIM PRESIDENT LEMUEL PITTENGER

August 10, 1933
Lemuel M. Pittenger was named Interim President. He served in this role until January 4, 1934.

Governor McNutt, with the Trustees, directed Pittenger to conduct a thorough survey of ISTC. The survey recommended significant improvements. The report was not binding on the next president.

PRESIDENT RALPH TIREY

December 22, 1933
Ralph Noble Tirey was elected the fifth President. He formally served in this role from March 5, 1934 until June 30, 1953.

1934

September 8, 1934
The cornerstone of the Laboratory School was laid.

1935

The college bookstore moved into the renovated Central Christian Church that was located near the Condit House.

February 4, 1935
President Tirey presented a ten-year improvement plan to the Board of Trustees.

1936

July 14, 1936
Past President Linnaeus N. Hines passed away in Terre Haute.

1937

November 12, 1937
The men's residence hall (Parsons Hall) was dedicated. (NOTE: This building was razed in 1991.)

The Lab School was dedicated. (NOTE: On September 10, 2009, the Lab School was renovated, reopened, and named University Hall - Bayh College of Education.)

1938

April 11, 1938
The ISTC received a WPA labor grant and the Trustees approved spending $36,463 for Tirey's campus improvement project that included the closing of Eagle and Mulberry Streets (north of the Student Union and south of the Student Union). This included landscaping, the addition of sidewalks and access drives, and property acquisition. This plan was an important step in creating a proper collegiate setting.

1939

June 19, 1939
Plans were completed for the Allendale Lodge that President Tirey wanted built, with the help of the National Youth Administration. The projected cost was $12,000. The Board of Trustees authorized the expenditure of $3,500 in college funds and utilized the labor of college students under the direction of a Physical Plant carpenter. The lodge was used for many college gatherings until it was sold to the neighboring Carmelite Monastery in 1997.

1940

March 15-17, 1940
Both the Student Union Building and the Fine Arts Building were dedicated. Special guests for the event included First Lady Eleanor Roosevelt and world-renowned opera singer Rose Bampton. Architects for the buildings were Miller and Yeager, and cost for construction of both buildings was listed at $794,760.

April 25, 1940
The Board of Trustees approved the naming of the art gallery in the new Fine Arts and Commerce Building as the Turman Art Gallery in honor of Professor William Turman, who served as Chairperson of the Art Department from 1894-1934.

A bachelor's degree was required for a teacher's license in Indiana.

1941

December 7, 1941
The Japanese bombed Pearl Harbor.

December 8, 1941
The United States and Britain declared war on Japan.

1943

June 15, 1943
The Walden Apartments (private property) located at the southeast corner of Chestnut Street and Seventh Street was acquired.

Enrollment decreased to 750 due to World War II.

1944

Navy V-5 and V-12 programs were on campus.

1945

May 7, 1945
Germany surrendered to Western allies.

August 6, 1945
The first atomic bomb dropped on Hiroshima, Japan.

August 9, 1945
The second atomic bomb dropped on Nagasaki, Japan.

August 14, 1945
The Japanese agreed to unconditional surrender.

1947

Enrollment increased to 2,555.

1948

June 13, 1948
Groundbreaking took place for the Communications and Math Building, today known as Dreiser Hall, and

the Administration and Health Building, currently known as Gillum Hall, designed by Ralph O. Yeager. The combined cost was $1.7 million.

1950

February 19, 1950
Demolition began on Old Main, North Hall, and Stalker Hall in the historic quadrangle. A new central coal/oil power plant was soon completed on North Seventh Street near Tippecanoe Street.

April 14, 1950
The Administration and Health Center (Gillum Hall) and the Communications and Mathematics Building (Dreiser Hall) were both dedicated.

June 27, 1950
Americans entered the Korean War.

1952

April 23, 1952
Trustees voted to remove the old Power Plant.

1953

April 7, 1953
The smokestack for the old boiler plant was toppled.

June 27, 1953
A North Korean armistice was reached, with both America and North Korea claiming victory.

The former Training School (1905), renamed Stalker Hall in 1936, was razed.

June 30, 1953
President Tirey stepped down.

November 12, 1953
Trustees accepted the completed new Stalker Hall, constructed as the Education and Social Studies Building. It was located directly west of the Fine Arts and Commerce Building. The architect for this building was Ralph O. Yeager and the cost was approximately $850,000. Originally named the E&S Building (Education and Social Studies Building), the building was renamed in 1966 to honor Francis Marion Stalker, a member of the faculty from 1892-1929.

PRESIDENT WARREN HOLMSTEDT

July 1, 1953
Raleigh Warren Holmstedt became the sixth President of Indiana State University, serving until June 30, 1965.

Enrollment declined to 1,886.

1954

January 6, 1954
Inauguration ceremonies were held for President Holmstedt.

1956

November 9, 1956
The Home Economics Building opened. The original architects of the building were Miller, Vrydagh, and Miller and the cost was $482,950. Later, the building was renamed the Family and Consumer Sciences Building. In 2012, the building was again renamed the John W. Moore Welcome Center, honoring John W. Moore, the ninth President of the University.

1957

April 23, 1957
The firm of Miller, Vrydaugh, and Miller was appointed to develop plans for a new Science Building to eventually be constructed on the northeast corner of Sixth Street and Chestnut Street.

1958

June 23, 1958
The Board of Trustees approved Miller, Vrydagh, and Miller as the architect for the new Physical Education Building today known as the College of Health and Human Performance, located on Chestnut Street between Fourth and Fifth Streets.

December 18, 1958
Trustees approved the plans and specifications for the new Science Building.

1959

October 18, 1959
The new women's residence hall (Burford Hall) was dedicated, the first residence hall constructed in 23

years. Charlotte Burford served as Dean of Women from 1910-46. The architect was Miller, Vrydagh, and Miller and the cost was $1.45 million. This initiated a residence hall building program which included both women's and men's dorms.

1960

The Sparkettes Corp was formed. (The Sparkettes features students who perform on the Dance Team at football and basketball games.)

The School of Education was founded.

September 14, 1960
The Board of Trustees approved plans from Miller, Vrydagh, and Miller for the new bookstore, to be located at the southeast corner of Sixth Street and Chestnut Street.

1961

A School of Graduate Studies was established.

Enrollment reached 5,313.

April 25, 1961
The Science Building was dedicated.

July 1, 1961
The school's name changed to Indiana State College.

1962

The University Bookstore opened at the southeast corner of Sixth Street and Chestnut Street.

The College of Arts and Sciences and School of Nursing were established.

May 25, 1962
Architects Weber and Curry were appointed to develop plans for a Classroom Building (later named Holmstedt Hall).

September 26, 1962
Trustees accepted the completed Erickson Hall.

October 26, 1962
The university acquired the Mary Stewart apartments, located at 410 North Sixth Street.

November 4, 1962
Erickson and Sandison Residence Halls were dedicated.

December 1, 1962
The Men's Physical Education Building (Arena) was dedicated.

1963

The Computer Center was established.

The MBA program began.

January 18, 1963
The Condit House was vested with the university. (NOTE: Helen Condit signed an agreement with ISTC in 1928 stipulating her intent to transfer ownership to ISNS.)

March-April, 1963
Deming Hotel (Deming Center) was acquired by the university.

June 21, 1963
The Board of Trustees approved naming the Student Union Building the "Tirey Memorial Student Union" and the auditorium in Tirey Memorial Student Union was named in honor of Professor Lowell M. Tilson, former Chairperson of the Department of Music (1915-40).

November 3, 1963
Pickerl and Gillum Halls were both dedicated. Gillum Hall was named in honor of Robert Green Gillum, department chair and professor of chemistry for 37 years. Pickerl was named to honor Dorothea Maude Pickerl, an ISNS graduate in 1914.

1964

Enrollment for the fall reached 7,777.

August 7, 1964
The Tonkin Gulf Resolution was passed by Congress, launching a full-scale involvement in Vietnam.

November 1, 1964
Both Blumberg and Cromwell Halls were dedicated. The architecture firm for both buildings was Miller-Miller and Associates.

1965

The School of Health, Physical Education, and Recreation was established.

Ph.D. programs were started, the first degrees were awarded in 1967.

Married Student Housing (Maehling Terrace) was made available. Four units were built between 1964 and 1971.

February 8, 1965
The Indiana Governor signed a bill changing the name from Indiana State Teacher's College to Indiana State University (ISU). This change was hotly debated and protested by other universities within the state, most notably Indiana University.

June 30, 1965
President Holmstedt stepped down.

PRESIDENT ALAN RANKIN

July 1, 1965
Alan Carson Rankin became the seventh President.

The Classroom Building was renamed in honor of President Emeritus Raleigh W. Holmstedt.

Fall 1965
The Evansville branch campus was established.

November 19, 1965
Both Mills Hall (named in honor of Caleb Mills, 'Father of Public Schools in Indiana') and Rhoads Hall (named in honor of legislator Baskin E. Rhoads) were dedicated. The architecture firm for both was Miller-Miller and Associates.

1966

Condit House was remodeled and became the official residence of the President. This is the oldest structure on campus, built in 1860.

January 20, 1966
The Language and Mathematics Building was renamed Dreiser Hall after those departments moved to Holmstedt Hall.

February 24, 1966
Groundbreaking took place for the Science Building (Phase 2) addition. The architecture firm for this project was Miller-Miller and Associates. It was dedicated on April 16, 1969.

July 1, 1966
Holmstedt Hall was dedicated, becoming housing offices and classrooms. It was named in honor of President Raleigh Holmstedt, the sixth President of ISU.

July 1966
The university acquired the Marathon Building on Cherry Street. This became the Alumni Center.

October 8, 1966
ISU acquired a 99-year lease on Terre Haute's Memorial Stadium.

1967

The Outdoor Field Campus (known also as the Brazil Field Campus) was acquired.

The Blue Beret Corps was established.

The Caleb Mills Distinguished Teaching Awards were first presented.

January 5, 1967
Both Jones Hall and Hines Halls were dedicated. The architect for both buildings was Ewing Miller Associates, Inc.

September 16, 1967
Memorial Stadium was dedicated. Phase one of the remodeling program was completed in time for football season. ISU was the first university or college to have an outdoor AstroTurf playing surface.

1968

Trustees approved the Aerospace Technology Program and adopted stronger rules on student discipline.

Total enrollment on the Terre Haute and Evansville campuses was 16,688.

The School of Technology was established.

July 10, 1968
Groundbreaking occurred for the new College of Nursing, located at 749 Chestnut Street. The building was designed by Ewing Miller Associates, Inc.

September 20, 1968
Trustees formally accepted the Statesman Towers, named for U.S. Vice Presidents from Indiana (Colfax, Fairbanks, Hendricks, and Marshall). The architecture firm for the towers was Ewing Miller Associates, Inc.

1969

The Nursing Clinical Education Building adjoining Union Hospital was formally accepted by the Trustees.

Timeline

April 16, 1969
Dedication took place for Phase II of the Science Building. Miller, Miller, and Associates completed this project.

April 17, 1969
The Statesman Towers were dedicated. In his dedicatory address, President Rankin said, "Indiana is often called the Mother of Vice Presidents because of the great number of Indiana statesmen who have been nominated for the office of the Vice President of the United States. It is indeed appropriate and with great pride that our state university, Indiana State University, recognizes and memorializes the public service these four Indiana statesmen rendered to the citizens of our state, our nation, and our world."

November 21, 1969
Unit #1 of the Lincoln Quads was dedicated. Opening in 1969, Lincoln Quadrangles were named in honor of Abraham Lincoln. These co-educational residential units allowed for students to share a suite with common living room spaces. These low rise structures proved more popular than the tall Statesman Towers which, between 1977 and 1981, were converted into academic buildings. The architect for this project was Ewing Miller.

1970

Indiana State University celebrated its centennial anniversary.

Union Station Depot was acquired and became ISU's first African American Cultural Center.

The Tandem Bike Race, Tandemonia, was first held.

June 18, 1970
The Drivers Training Facility at the Vigo County Fairgrounds was dedicated.

September 19, 1970
Memorial Stadium Phase II was dedicated.

1971

January 5, 1971
The Mary Stewart Building was destroyed by fire.

January 15, 1971
Groundbreaking ceremonies took place for the new Cunningham Memorial Library located at Sycamore and North Center Streets (6 ½ Street). The architectural firm for this project was Archonics Corporation with Ewing Miller as President.

September 18, 1971
Jamison Hall on East Chestnut Street at 912 Chestnut Street was acquired and dedicated in honor of Olis Jamison, principal of the Indiana State University Laboratory School. At first this building was known as the Family Welfare Service Building, but it would later become the offices and laboratories for the Department of Anthropology.

December 17, 1971
Groundbreaking for the Hulman Civic Center took place. Architects Sverdrup and Parcel of St. Louis completed this work at an approximate cost of $10 million.

1972

The school acquired Art Annex West, formerly a business known as the Shirley Wholesale Foods Distributors.

The 'Link' Building, later named Rankin Hall in honor of the seventh ISU President, Alan Rankin, was constructed, connecting the Elks Club Building on the south and the Tirey Union on the north along Seventh Street at Larry Bird Street. The architect was Ewing Miller Associates, Inc.

June 17, 1972
Dedication took place for the Student Health and Counseling Center located on 530 North Fifth Street. The $2.3 million building was designed by Ewing Miller Associates, Inc.

1973

December 14, 1973
The Hulman Center was dedicated and opened.

1974

March 8, 1974
Cunningham Memorial Library was dedicated. The architect was Ewing Miller, President of Archonics Corporation, the general contractor was Rupp and Mundt, and the library design consultant was Keyes D. Metcalf, the Librarian Emeritus at Harvard University. This project cost approximately $6.5 million.

1975

April 30, 1975
South Vietnam surrendered, ending the Vietnam War.

May 14, 1975
President Rankin stepped down.

PRESIDENT RICHARD LANDINI

May 15, 1975
Richard George Landini became the eighth President.

1976

President Landini initiated Donaghey Day as the campus clean-up day.

1978

Hilgemier Building, located at 629 Cherry Street, was razed.

1979

The university acquired Emmeline Fairbanks Hall (1906), the former City library, and renovated the structure to become a part of the Art Department. This building housed drawing, painting, photography, and printmaking.

The men's basketball team was runner-up in the NCAA Division 1 Tournament.

June 30, 1979
The New Theater opened with a production of "Ah, Wilderness!" by Eugene O'Neill. The building was formerly Bowman Garage.

1980

Kurt Thomas was recognized as an outstanding world gymnast.

August 29, 1980
The contract was signed for remodeling the old Vocational Building (1915).

1982

ISU was a founding member of the Gateway Conference for women's sports.

1984

The Kiewig property was conveyed by the Nature Conservancy to the university. The property is six miles west of Terre Haute and contains 40 acres of heavily wooded old growth beech-maple dominated forest with a man-made five-acre lake.

Oakley Place was completed, located on the northwest corner of Seventh and Cherry Streets. The architect was Kevin L. Runion for McGuire and Shook Associates.

Bruce Baumgartner won the Olympic gold medal in wrestling.

July 23, 1984
The Women's PE Building was destroyed by fire.

1985

The sycamore leaf logo was adopted.

1986

A campus master plan, prepared by Sasaki Associates Inc., was approved by the Trustees.

December 5, 1986
Trustees contracted with the Odle Group to develop plans for Root Hall.

1987

April 10, 1987
The Indiana General Assembly passed House Bill 1700, which included bonding authorization for a New Student Union Mall project, to be constructed on the campus at ISU, in the amount of $8.65 million.

1988

March 4, 1988
The Board of Trustees began to discuss building a Central Computing and Administrative Services Building, estimated at $5.3 million.

April 19, 1988
The northern addition to the HPER Building was dedicated. Designed and supervised by Walter Scholer & Associates, the cost was $11.61 million.

May 6, 1988
The Board of Trustees gave approval for the appointment of Walter Scholer & Associates as architects for the Central Computing and Administrative Services Building.

June 3, 1988
The Board of Trustees authorized an agreement with University Development Group III (Cornerstone Companies, Inc.) for a campus-oriented retail and food court facility to form a part of a student union complex on the ISU campus.

July 15, 1988
Groundbreaking took place for Root Hall. The Odle Group, Architects and Engineers, were the architects for the project. The cost was $8.8 million.

The Board of Trustees approved the naming of the Student Union Complex, located at Chestnut and Fifth/Sixth Streets, in honor of Anton and Mary Fendrich Hulman.

December 2, 1988
The Board of Trustees approved plans for the renovation of Sandison Hall. This was the first renovation since the residence hall was built in 1962. The cost was $1.11 million.

1989

March 3, 1989
The Board of Trustees officially designated the newly constructed classroom building located at Sycamore Street and Seventh Street as Root Hall, in honor of the Chapman Root family, who financially assisted in the funding for this project.

April 7, 1989
The Office for the Indiana Center for Study of Waste Recycling was housed in Statesman Towers. The Center was created by a bill introduced by Jerome Kearns, promoting the establishment of a Statewide Center for a Waste Recycling Center on ISU's campus.

May 9, 1989
The Indiana General Assembly passed House Bill 1530, which included bonding authorization for a New Central Computing and Administrative Services Building (later to be known as University Pavilion, which included Parsons Hall, Rankin Hall, and Tirey Hall) to be constructed at ISU for $7.8 million.

July 19, 1989
Groundbreaking ceremonies took place, marking the beginning of construction of the food court/mall that would become the new Hulman Memorial Student Union (HMSU). The Hulman and George families gave $2 million for the project, and Edmund and Mary Dede gave a $1.7 million gift to the university for Dede Plaza and meeting rooms in the Dede Activity Center.

July 21, 1989
The Board of Trustees approved the appointment of Schmidt Associates to complete the renovation of Holmstedt Hall, Dreiser Hall, and the Bookstore. The Board also approved the current Administration Building, located on the western side of the historic quad on Sixth Street, to be designated as Gillum Hall, since the previous Gillum Hall was renamed the Hulman Memorial Student Union.

September 14, 1989
The groundbreaking for Dede Plaza took place.

October 13, 1989
The Board of Trustees approved the selection of RATIO Architects, Inc., for the restoration of Normal Hall, although renovations would not occur until 2015, using different plans than developed by arcDesign Architects.

November 3, 1989
The dedication ceremony for Root Hall took place.

1990

The Americans with Disabilities Act (ADA) of 1990 made it a civil rights violation to deny services to the physically challenged.

February 2, 1990
The Board of Trustees approved appointing Schmidt Associates Architects, Inc. as architects for the new Music Recital Hall and the remodeling of both the Fine Arts Building and Gillum Hall.

October 19, 1990
The Board of Trustees authorized seeking the necessary state agency approvals and authority to engage an architectural firm to design Phase II of the renovation of the Sycamore Towers dining hall. The estimated cost of the project was $800,000.

1991

Parson's Hall, the former men's residence hall, was razed.

May 10, 1991
The Board of Trustees authorized securing approval from state authorities to expend $6 million for the Central Chilled Water Plant project.

President Landini submitted a letter to the Trustees indicating his wish to retire from the presidency no later than June 30, 1992.

July 19, 1991
The Board of Trustees authorized the President to secure state authority to expend $5.7 million for the Music Recital addition and related renovations in Fine Arts.

August 1991
ISU received official notice from the Department of Energy for a grant in the amount of $4.81 million toward the construction of an Advanced Technology Center (ATC). Cost of this project was estimated at $17 million, with a total of 110,000 square feet. The old Technology Building, Print Shop, Alumni Hall, and Reeve Hall would all be demolished to make way for the new facility. InterDesign Group was engaged as architects.

October 16, 1991
The HMSU was dedicated.

October 25, 1991
John T. Myers introduced legislation that resulted in $1.5 million being appropriated by the U.S. Congress for planning purposes for sciences facilities. President Landini informed the Board of Trustees that a site had been chosen for the new Advanced Technology Center, where the Terre Haute Gas Company building and Alumni Hall (former Marathon Building) existed. Reeve Hall would eventually be demolished to complete development of the site. The estimated construction start date was 1993. The two entrances for the building, one on Cherry Street and the other on the quad with a central soaring atrium space, were discussed as becoming a link between ISU's campus and downtown Terre Haute.

1992

Construction of the university's Central Chilled Water Plant began, located at 945 Chestnut Street. It was designed by RATIO Architects, Inc. and R. E. Dimond Engineering at a cost of $6 million.

March 6, 1992
The Board of Trustees approved naming the Administrative/Conference Facility as Tirey, Rankin, and Parsons Hall, or collectively the "University Pavilion."

May 1992
The University School (Lab School) officially closed.

June 5, 1992
The United Mine Workers Building, which would become the African American Cultural Center (AACC), was purchased. On April 21, 2012, it was renamed the Charles E. Brown African-American Cultural Center. This structure replaced the former AACC located in the Union Station Depot at 551 North Ninth Street.

June 30, 1992
President Richard G. Landini stepped down.

PRESIDENT JOHN MOORE

July 1, 1992
John William Moore became the ninth President.

Condit House became the location of the President's office.

1993

Ground was broken for the Student Computing Complex (24-hour Computer Lab Building) on the southeast edge of Dede Plaza (231 North Sixth Street). This site was formerly occupied by the campus bookstore. The architect was Schmidt Associates. Eventually this building would be repurposed, during the Administration of President Bradley, to serve as the home for ISU's Career Center.

The Student Computing Complex opened.

The first University Provost, Dr. Richard Wells, was appointed.

January 28, 1993
On this Founders Day in 1993, the former Link Building was rededicated and named in honor of Alan Carson Rankin. The architect was Scholer, the general contractor was CDI, and interior design was completed by RATIO Interiors.

April 13, 1993
The Inauguration took place to formally install Dr. John Moore as the ninth president of ISU.

September 3, 1993
The State Budget Director, Jean Blackwell, informed universities that all capital budget projects were on hold, including the Music Rehearsal Hall and the Advanced Technology Center.

December 3, 1993
The Science Building renovation began. The total cost of the project was projected at $1.75 million, with $1.4 million in financing from an SBA grant, along with a $200,000 PSI energy grant and $155,000 from university plant reserves. The Board also authorized the acquisition of the Marathon Oil Company property.

1994

The groundbreaking ceremony took place for the Music Recital Hall.

Initial development began of a new ISU strategic plan.

October 21, 1994
The Board of Trustees authorized requesting approval from state authorities to expend $500,000 for the renovation of the former United Mine Workers Building for use by the African-American Cultural Center. The project was funded with $215,415 from State Repair and Rehabilitation, and $284,685 from Plant Fund Capital Reserves.

November 10-11, 1994
The Commission for Higher Education approved the 1995-97 capital projects budget plan, which included funding for the ISU Advanced Technology Center. Capital funds requested included $13.6 million for the ATC.

1995

The Center for Teaching and Learning was established.

IQ Magazine was first published.

March 31, 1995
The Board of Trustees authorized the university to engage architects/engineers in connection with the renovation of Rhoads Hall. The estimated price was $3 million and was to be funded through the sale of ISU Housing and Dining System Revenue Bonds.

June 6, 1995
The contract for the Music Rehearsal addition was awarded to Hannig Construction and SMC/NRK. The total award came to $6.78 million.

July 14, 1995
The Board of Trustees dedicated Oakley Place, including the ISU Signature Piece. The architect was Steve Arnold of MMS Architects.

December 6, 1995
Sycamore Sam was introduced for the first time at an ISU men's basketball game.

1996

The university presented plans to renovate Erickson Hall from an out-of-service residence hall to an academic/administrative facility to accommodate the departments currently housed in the old Reeve Hall, including the School of Graduate Studies, Communications, Continuing Education, Credit Outreach/Independent Studies, Conferences and Non-Credit Services, Instructional Services, Social Work, ROTC, Interlink, Environmental Safety, and the Employee Assistance Program. The estimated project cost was $4.9 million.

The university again presented plans to complete a major renovation of the Cromwell Residence Hall. The renovation would include the central core areas of each student floor (baths, lounges, and corridor areas) and a redesign of the seventh floor to include a recreation area, laundry, staff apartment, and guest rooms. Appropriate life safety and ADA issues were to be addressed. The estimated project cost was $2.5 million and was to be funded through the sale of Indiana State University Housing and Dining System Revenue Bonds.

The ISU Magazine began publication.

The President's Medal for outstanding achievement was first presented.

March 8, 1996
Vice President Dennis Graham presented the Campus Master Plan Update. This was a revision of the existing Sasaki Campus Master Plan from 1986, prepared during Landini's presidency.

April 19, 1996
Groundbreaking ceremonies took place for the ATC, later to be known as John Myers Technology Center. Dedication ceremonies took place September 18, 1998.

June 5, 1996
The Indiana State University Facilities Master Plan Phase II was Initiative 13 of the 1994 Report of the University's Strategic Plan for the 21st Century. Phase I was approved in 1986 and was substantially completed in 1994. This new study was commissioned to prepare a University Master Plan Phase II. The new plan proposed the renovation of 19 existing facilities and the construction of 14 new facilities on the main campus.

June 14, 1996
Included among the 1997-99 Capital Budget Request was the replacement of the University Power Plant and repair of the steam/condensate distribution system, estimated at $28 million.

1997

The demolition of Reeve Hall took place.

The DegreeLink degree completion program began.

The Lilly First-Year Experience program began.

The first University Medallion was awarded.

Jamison Hall, former home of the Anthropology Department, located at 912 Chestnut Street, was demolished.

February 27, 1997
The ISU Foundation purchased the Brentlinger Distributing Company, Inc. at 960 Spruce Street, as well as the adjoining real estate, on behalf of ISU for $970,000. This property would later become the home for ISU's Grounds Maintenance Unit. The Indiana General Assembly appropriated $1 million for the purchase and renovation of the Brentlinger property.

May 9, 1997
ISU determined that the Allendale property was no longer essential to the university, since much of the activities that used to take place at the Allendale Lodge now took place in the Hulman Memorial Student Union. The property was sold to the adjacent Carmelite Monastery.

October 8, 1997
The Center for Performing and Fine Arts Center was dedicated. The cost of this building project was $7.25 million.

1998

September 17-18, 1998
Dedication took place for the John T. Myers Technology Center.

1999

The first female Athletic Director (Andrea Myers) was appointed.

The Gongaware Center for Insurance Management opened.

Summer 1999
The Classroom Building; Hamilton Harris; Facilities Management Building #2, #3, and #4; and University Police Building were all demolished.

October 21, 1999
Groundbreaking took place for the university's Central Steam Heating Plant located at 625 North Seventh Street. This gas-fired plant was designed originally by ISU Staff Architect Kevin Runion, with the assistance of Plant Manager John Little and Assistant Plant Manager James Gregg, and then was codified in design by Architect Wes Walker of Stanley Consulting. The cost of this project was $16.86 million.

2000

The North Central Association commended the university for its Self-Study and continued their accreditation for 10 years.

The Recreation East Building was completed.

June 30, 2000
President Moore stepped down as President.

PRESIDENT LLOYD BENJAMIN III

July 1, 2000
Lloyd William Benjamin III became the tenth President.

December 14-15, 2000
The inauguration ceremony for President Benjamin was held.

The Utility Tunnel renovation began.

Timeline

2001

The southern half of Lincoln Quad received a $1.2 million renovation that included new roofs, new energy efficient windows, and refurbished stairwells.

October 4, 2001
The University Utilities Center (Power Plant) became operational. The cost of this project was $17 million.

December 6, 2001
Permission was requested to continue with completion of the north half of Lincoln Quad.

2002

Jones Hall was renovated at a cost of $5.52 million.

Construction began for the Landsbaum Center for Health Education on the campus of Union Hospital. The architect was BSA Design and the cost was $7,600,000.

February 22, 2002
Several dining facilities were identified as needing to be remodeled, including the HMSU Commons ($875,000), Lincoln Quad Dining ($950,000), and Sycamore Towers Dining ($700,000). This was part of a Sodexo dining service proposal.

June 7, 2002
The rehabilitation of University Hall was proposed at an estimated cost of $32 million.

2003

January 16, 2003
Renovations began on Stalker Hall. The Board of Trustees authorized the President to request from state authority to expend up to $4.5 million for the renovation.

September 26, 2003
The Landsbaum Center for Health Education was dedicated.

2003-07
Science Lab Renovations were completed at a cost of $8.9 million.

2004

Fall enrollment reached 11,200.

2004-05
Stalker Hall Renovations were completed at a cost of $5.5 million.

2005

The Michael Simmons Student Activity Center was established at 539 North Ninth Street. Architects for this project were Scott Tillman and MMS A/E Inc. The cost of this project was $937,555.

2005-08
The Arts Corridor on Seventh Street was completed for a cost of $750,000.

2006

Burford Hall was renovated, costing $8.5 million.

2006-08
The Cherry Street Multimodal Transportation Facility was completed in the spring of 2008, costing $13.3 million. The project architects were Sanders and Associates, Rich and Associates, and Hannig Construction.

2007

The Athletics Weight Training Facility was established. This cost $450,000.

The Admissions Welcome Center in Erickson Hall was established. This project cost $188,000.

Mullen House (International House) was remodeled to serve as a guest house for international visitors and guest musicians performing with the Terre Symphony Orchestra. This cost $100,000.

The Community Garden was created at 291 North 11th Street.

Planning and renovations began on the Federal Building (College of Business). The original design was completed by Miller and Yeager. This project was completed in the Spring of 2011. Phase I of this project cost $6 million.

July 19, 2007
Groundbreaking took place for the Student Recreation Center. The architecture firm for this project was Hastings and Chivetta Architects, Inc. The Recreation Center was completed for a total cost of $21.8 million.

November 21, 2007
The Seventh and Cherry Gateway plans were reviewed, and this project was completed in 2009 at a cost of $596,184. The architects were RATIO Architects, Inc. and Contractor CDI, Inc.

2007-08
Major renovations took place to house the College of Education that would leave Statesman Towers (West) completed in the spring of 2008. This project cost $26.88 million.

2008

June 30, 2008
President Benjamin stepped down.

PRESIDENT DANIEL BRADLEY

July 1, 2008
Daniel Joseph Bradley became the 11th President, serving until January 3, 2018.

2009

University Hall (Bayh College of Education) and several significant Condit House renovations were completed.

July 2009
The College of Education/College of Business Towers/Statesmen Towers were closed.

July 10, 2009
The Student Recreation Center was dedicated.

2010

Sandison Hall was renovated.

2011

The Satellite Chilled Water Plant was completed. Additionally, the Family and Consumer Sciences Building (now the John W. Moore Welcome Center) and Pickerl Hall were renovated.

The old bookstore located in the HMSU was remodeled into the Sycamore Banquet Center.

2012

April 20, 2012
The Center for Performing and Fine Arts was rededicated and named the Richard G. Landini Center for Performing and Fine Arts, in honor of the eighth President of the university.

September 7, 2012
The dedication and grand opening took place for the Scott College of Business (former U.S. Post Office/Federal Hall).

2013

Erickson Hall was renovated back to its original use as a residence hall.

Daycare facilities in Maehling Terrace were expanded.

2014

August 27, 2014
The new Reeve Hall was dedicated. It was planned to house special programs such as on-campus sororities.

2015

The Athletics Annex West was acquired and renovated from its original use as a shipping truck facility to an indoor practice facility for baseball and track programs.

Renovations took place on Normal Hall and Mills Hall.

The Statesman Towers complex was demolished.

April 17, 2015
The Gibson Track and Field Complex was dedicated.

2015-17
Blumberg, Rhoads, Mills, and Cromwell Halls were renovated.

2017

December 15, 2017
Ribbon cutting for the $64 million expansion took place, and renovation of the College of Nursing, Health, and Human Services began.

Timeline

2018

January 3, 2018
President Bradley stepped down.

PRESIDENT DEBORAH CURTIS

Deborah Curtis became the 12th President of Indiana State University.

March 29, 2018
Bids were received and opened for a $50 million major renovation of the Hulman Center, which first opened in 1973. The renovation, designed by RATIO Architects, Inc. of Indianapolis and R. E. Dimond Engineering of Indianapolis, included a complete two-year facelift of the venue, including the installation of a new outer building skin, all new mechanical systems, additional vertical circulation through the addition of elevators and escalators, as well as improvements to the 'bowl' and the seating options for the venue.

April 13, 2018
The inauguration ceremony of President Deborah Curtis took place.

April 17, 2018
Bids were received and opened for a major $15 million complete renovation of the Fine Arts and Commerce Building. Originally opened and dedicated in 1940 by then First Lady Eleanor Roosevelt, this WPA project's first major facelift included completely new finishes throughout, new mechanicals, and the addition of a new southern façade to house new stair tower access and elevator access. Renovation design was completed by arcDesign Architects of Indianapolis.

Credit to Kevin Runion for directing completion of and contributing to this timeline.

"We require from buildings two kinds of goodness: first, the doing their practical duty well: then that they be graceful and pleasing in doing it." *- John Ruskin*

GLOSSARY

Arcade: A series of arches supported on columns or piers.

Arch: A curved structural form that spans an opening.

Architrave: The lowest part of a classical entablature that rests on columns with capitals. Also a molded framework around a door or window.

Archivolt: A molding that follows the face or curve of an arch.

Ashlar: Masonry. Finely finished stone of similar size, shape and texture.

Avantcorps: A part of a building that projects beyond the plane of the facade.

Bay: A vertical unit of a building usually defined by the number of doors and windows on each floor.

Belt Course: A horizontal band that protrudes from an exterior wall. Most often the belt course defines the levels of a building and can be made of stone, tile, brick, terra cotta, or shingles.

Berm: A raised barrier separating two areas.

Bollard: A short post used to divert traffic from an area or road.

Bracket: A projecting element that appears to support the eaves or extension of the roof beyond the walls.

Broken Pediment: A pediment in which the cornice is not continued at the top or bottom.

Brutalist Architecture: Developed in the mid to third quarter of the 20th century. The term derives from the French word for "raw." The Swiss-French architect Le Corbusier used béton brut, meaning "raw concrete." The concrete was left unfinished or roughly finished and exposed.

Campanile: Italian for bell tower.

Clerestory: The window (upper) story of a Gothic church or a wall with windows providing light and ventilation.

Coffer: A sunken or depressed panel in a vault, ceiling, or dome.

Colonnade: A line of columns that carry arches or an entablature.

Column: A vertical round support. Columns can come in different shapes and determine various styles of classical architecture. For example, the classical Greek orders were Doric, Ionic, and Corinthian.

Corbel: A structural block with one end embedded in the wall that projects outward to support a cornice, entablature, or other architectural member.

Core 40: The course and credit requirements for earning a high school diploma, as defined by the Indiana State Board of Education.

Cornice: The projecting molding atop of the wall, gable, or pediment or upper portion of an entablature.

Dado: A decorative band usually near the base of a wall.

Diaper: Small patterns, lozenges, or squares, repeated continuously cross a wall.

Double Portico: A projecting two-story porch.

Embrasure: A flared frame surrounding a door or window.

Engaged Column: A column that is not freestanding but is attached to the wall or a pier.

Entablature: Originally, the portion of a classical temple between the columns and the roof.

Foliation: A carved lead-shaped ornamentation.

Fret: A decorative band made up of geometric forms.

Frieze: A decorative band along the top of a wall that was usually sculpted.

Gable: The triangular wall segment at the end of a gabled-roof.

Gargoyle: A water spout in the form of an imaginary figure.

Hood Molding: A large molding over a window also known as dripstone.

Hoosier: a native or inhabitant of Indiana.

International Style: A major architectural movement of the 1920s and 30s characterized by the absence of decorative ornamentation. Typically buildings in this style will show repeated modules, industrial building materials, large areas of glass to stress volume over mass, and flat surfaces. *See: Bauhaus in Dessau, Germany.*

Jacobean: Refers to the renaissance style building and is named after James I.

Jambs: Sides of doors or windows.

Loggia: Like a porch or gallery usually with columns across the front and closed in the back by a wall.

Lunette: A small arched opening often set in a larger vault.

Module: The basic unit of a building.

Molding: A decorative band that can be carved into a surface or applied to it.

Mullion: A vertical element often used to separate windows into different lights or to separate doors.

Neo-classical: A style deriving from ancient art that became popular in the late 18th century and persisted into the 19th. Often used for banks and civic buildings.

Normal School: Formerly, a school or college for the training of teachers.

Oriel: Window corbelled out from the face of a wall by means of projecting stones. For example, a bay window.

Parapet: A low wall or railing along the edge of a roof or a balcony.

Pavilion: Part of a facade given prominence because it projects forward. Especially prominent in French Baroque architecture.

Pediment: Deriving from classical architecture, the triangular roof or gable above the facade of a building or over doors and windows. A segmented pediment has a semi-circular or curvilinear form in place of the triangular form.

Piano Nobile: Means noble level and is the major floor of a large home, most often the floor located one story above the ground level, especially in Italian palazzi.

Pier: A mass of masonry, in contrast to a column, that supports arches.

Pilaster: A shallow pier that projects slightly from the wall.

Plinth: Base for a column or pier.

Porte Cochere: A passageway through a building or screen wall designed to let vehicles pass from the street to an interior courtyard.

Portico: A porch usually with a pedimented roof supported by piers or columns.

Quoins: French term meaning corner. Refers to dressed stone, alternating large and small, at the corners of a masonry building.

Romanesque: Refers to the style of buildings built between roughly 1000 and 1200 that made use of elements drawn from Roman building.

Spandrel: The triangular space between a continuous row of arches or an infill panel below a window frame in a wall.

Spire: A vertical tapering structure built on a roof or tower.

Stringcourse: A narrow ornamental band running horizontally across the façade of a building.

Terrazzo: A material used for walls and floors that can be poured or precast containing chips of various material such as marble, granite, quartz, etc.

Terrecotta: Means "cooked earth." Brownish-red fired clay used for tiles and decoration. It is harder than brick, making it suitable for exterior decorative elements.

Tondo: a circular painting or relief.

INDEX

Administration and Health Building ....(See Gillum Hall)

Advanced Technology Center ....(See Myers Technology Center)

African American Cultural Center 160-161, 179, 208, 276, 279-280

Allendale Lodge 52-53, 270, 272, 281

Alumni Center (Marathon Oil) 118, 145, 204, 275

Arena (Physical Education Building) 93-94, 112-115, 163, 243-244, 258, 273-274

Art Annex 174, 257, 276

Arts Corridor 219, 227, 231, 258, 282

Bayh College of Education .... (See University Hall)

Beasley Building 195-196
(Citizens Gas and Fuel)

Benjamin, President 218-239
5, 41, 62-64, 77, 87-88, 100, 103, 105, 113, 124, 134, 149, 150, 157, 159, 164, 168, 186, 194, 216, 259-261, 283-285

Blumberg Hall .... (See Sycamore Towers)

Boiler Plant ....(See Power Plants)

Bookstore 104-105, 191, 279

Bradley, President 240-247
42, 65, 77, 80, 83, 85, 87, 98, 100, 103, 105, 108, 110, 111, 114-116, 119, 121, 125, 127, 130-134, 155, 157, 159, 161, 164, 168, 170, 172, 186, 193, 194, 199, 202, 230, 233, 237, 258-262, 283-284

Brown, President 20-24
28, 249, 266-267

Burford Hall 92, 95, 99-100, 108, 120, 129, 251, 260, 273, 282

Campus Master Planning 248-262

Center for Performing Arts 58, 179, 198-200,
(Landini Center for   204, 209, 212, 281, 283
Performing and Fine Arts)

Central Chilled Water Plant 179, 196, 279

Central Computing and ....(See Parsons Hall)
Administrative Services Building

Central Heating Plant ....(See Power Plants)

Cherry Street Multimodal 219, 232-233, 282
Transportation Facility

Classroom Building ....(See Holmstedt Hall)

Clinical Psychology Building 147

Colfax, Fairbanks, Hendricks, ... (See Statesman Towers)
Marshall Halls

College Bookstore (Former 59, 251, 271, 274, 278
Central Christian Church)

College of Business ....(See Terra Haute Federal Building and Post Office)

College of Health and Human Services .... (See Arena)

College of Nursing 114, 116, 151, 252, 258-262, 275, 283

Community Garden 219, 233, 282

Condit House 59, 93, 117-119, 134, 147, 208, 242, 249, 251, 271, 274-275, 279, 283

Country Training School.. 35-36

Cromwell Hall .... (See Sycamore Towers)

Cunningham Memorial Library 147, 162-165, 252, 276

Curtis, President 3, 80, 168, 284

Dede Plaza and Activity Center 179-180, 183, 192-194, 234, 255, 278-279

Deming Hotel 122-123, 154, 274
(Former Hulman Center)

Dreiser Hall (Former Language ....71-72, 84-85, 250, and Mathematics Building)   262, 272, 273, 275, 278

288

Indiana State University Building a Legacy

Driver and Traffic Safety 160
Instructional Demonstration Center

Education and Social Studies Building .... (See Stalker Hall)

Erickson Hall 31, 99, 106-108, 120, 251, 256,
259, 274, 280, 282, 283

Fairbanks Memorial Library 184-186, 269-270

Family and Consumer 97-98, 257-260, 273, 283
Science Building

Federal Building (Federal Hall) .... (See Terra Haute
Federal Building
and Post Office)

Fine Arts and Commerce Building 72, 76-80, 249-250,
262, 272-273, 284

Gibson Track and Field .... (See Riverfront Track and Field)

Gillum Hall (Former Administration 82-83, 273
and Health Building)

Gillum Hall (Former Dormitory) 109-111, 126,
169-170, 190, 274

Gillum Hall .... (See Hulman Memorial
Student Union)

Grosjean Counseling Clinic 63

Hines Hall 51, 142, 148-149, 153, 275

Hines, President 48-69
249, 270-272

Holmstedt Hall 30, 123-125, 162, 180, 252,
(Former Classroom Building) 256, 262, 274-275, 278

Holmstedt, President 92-140
41, 44, 53, 56, 58, 79, 82,
85-87, 250-251, 273-275

Home Economics Building   (See Family and Consumer
Science Building)

Hospitality House (Mullens) 231

Hulman Civic Center 143, 147, 166-168, 180,
214, 233, 241, 244, 252,
256, 259, 261, 276, 284

Hulman Memorial Student Union 53, 82, 105, 110-111,
(Former Gillum Hall) 180, 183 190-192, 197,
213, 245, 278, 281

Indiana State Normal School 7-10, 14-18, 22-23,
26, 28-34, 36, 50, 73, 95,
220, 243, 248-249, 264

Jamison Hall 165, 212, 276, 281

John W. Moore Welcome Center..........98, 217, 252, 273, 283

Jones, President 12-19
7, 10, 22-23, 249, 264-266

Jones Hall 148-149, 260, 275, 282

Laboratory School .... (See University Hall)

Landini, President 178-207
41, 44, 58, 62, 74, 76, 79, 81, 83,
85, 86, 98, 105, 109, 111, 113,
119, 122, 124, 134, 145, 147,
150, 154, 157, 163, 170, 172,
211, 251, 254-255, 277-279

Landsbaum Center 226, 282

Language and Mathematics Building ...... (See Dreiser Hall)

Lincoln Quadrangle 155-158, 276

Link Building .... (See Rankin Hall)

Maehling University .... (See University
Terrace Apartments (Family Housing)

Mary Stewart Building 169, 173, 276

Memorial Stadium 8, 147, 158-160, 166,
257, 261, 275, 276

Michael Simmons 218, 223-225
Student Activity Center

Mills Hall .... (See Sycamore Towers)

Moore, President 208-217
44, 53, 56, 76, 80, 83, 103, 105,
107, 119, 120, 131-132, 145, 149,
161, 164, 165, 167, 170, 172, 198,
203, 204, 255-256, 279-281

Index

Music Recital Hall ....(See Center for Performing Arts)

Myers Technology Center 203-205, 209, 212, 279-281
(Advanced Technology Center)

New North Residence Hall ....(See Reeve Hall)

New Technology Building ....(See Technology A Building)

New Theater 178, 181, 227, 260, 262, 277

Normal Hall (Library) 5, 14, 30, 38-42, 55, 223, 230, 241, 243, 250-251, 258-259, 270, 278, 283

North Hall 26, 30, 34-35, 38, 43, 57, 72, 249, 268-269, 273

Nursing Clinic Facilities 156, 226, 276

Oakley Plaza 57, 178, 183, 187

Old Main 31-37, 60, 71, 73, 82, 122, 196, 249, 264, 268-269, 273

Parsons Hall (Residence) 72-74, 95, 119, 172-173, 249, 251, 272

Parsons Hall (Central Computing) 180, 183, 197, 255, 278-279

Parsons, President **26-47**
22-23, 50, 54-55, 57, 73, 106, 249, 265-270

Physical Education Building 51, 57-58, 93-94, 112, 113, 163, 251, 273, 274

Physical Plant Department 73, 188
and Central Stores

Pickerl Hall 94, 120-121, 240, 260, 283

Pittenger, Interim President **51, 67, 271**

Power Plants 34, 71, 85-86, 150, 204, 215-216, 218, 227, 251, 273, 281-282

Rankin Hall 171-173, 180, 276, 278
(Former Link Building)

Rankin, President **142-177**
44, 56, 74, 75, 86, 102, 118, 122, 124, 127, 181, 208, 251-254, 275-277, 279

Reeve Hall 240, 245, 247, 283
(New North Residence Hall)

Reeve Hall 30, 48, 54-57, 59, 61, 73,
(Former Women's Residence Hall)   95, 99, 196, 212, 249, 251, 271, 279-281

Rhoads Hall ....(See Sycamore Towers)

Riverfront Track and Field 241, 246, 262, 283
(Gibson Track and Field)

Root Hall 124, 179-180, 183, 188-189, 252, 255, 262, 277-278

Sandison Hall 109, 121, 260, 278, 283

Satellite Chilled Water Plant 244, 283

Science Building 27, 43, 79, 92, 94, 101-103, 124, 162, 208, 212, 243, 250, 253, 256, 258-259, 270, 273-276, 280,

Science Hall 30, 43-44, 72, 198, 201

Seventh and Cherry Gateway 231, 283

Signature Monument (Oakley Place) 208, 213-214

Stalker Hall (Former Education 36-37, 39, 71-72, 85-88,
& Social Studies Building)   218, 223, 250, 256, 268, 273, 282

Stalker Hall 36-37
(Former Training School)

Statesman Towers 64, 100, 146, 149, 152-155, 157-158, 163, 180, 196-197, 253, 275, 276, 278, 283

Student Computing Center 104-105
(Former Bookstore)

Student Health Center 169-170

Student Recreation Center 219, 234-237, 257-259, 282-283

Student Union Building ....(See Tirey Hall)

Sycamore Towers (Blumberg, Cromwell,
Mills, Rhoads) 93, 100, 127-134, 148-149, 152, 240, 243, 255, 259-260, 275, 278, 282, 283

Technology A Building 201-202, 204
(New Technology Building)

Terra Haute Federal Building and Post Office (Federal Building) 63, 64, 78, 84, 153, 155, 219, 223, 228-230, 233, 237, 243, 258-259, 282

Timeline **264-284**

Tirey Hall (Student Union Building) 72-77, 171, 235, 249, 271-272, 274

Tirey, President **70-91**
31, 34, 37, 40, 51-53, 56, 60, 62, 67, 97, 250, 271-273

Training School 30-31, 35-37, 39, 85, 249, 269, 273

University Family Housing 126, 275, 283
(Maehling University Terrace Apartments)

University Hall (Former Laboratory School) 37, 49, 51, 60-65, 155, 219, 223, 237, 240, 250, 256, 258, 272, 282-283

Utility Tunnel 218, 223, 281

Vigo County Seminary 17, 28, 117, 249

Walden Apartments 58, 81, 251, 272

Waste Management and Recycling Center 195

ART INDEX

De Boer Lichtveld, Frans and Marja *Three Elements* 88

Dunbar, Michael *Arthur's Odyssey* 66

Gates, Jack *Hard-Edge Takes a Ride** 200

Kalish, Howard *A Chorus of Trumpets* 171

Kornfeld, Douglas *Runner* 237

Laska, John *Prometheus* 103

Mason, Phillips *Man Child in the Promised Land* 161

Morrison, Deedee *Our River-Our Future* 114

The Artists' Collective *Solar Sycamore* 247

Titzer, Patrick *Wheels** 225

Van Alstein, John *Via Solaris* 87

Wann, Harry *Dedication to Service* 82

Wiener, Madeline *A Reading Place* 247

Wilson, Gilbert *Murals in University Hall* 66

Woods, Marcia *Salute* 200

Wolfe, Bill *The Legend-Larry Bird* 168

Zebold, Brandon *ISU Sphere* 125

* *Not Illustrated*

PHOTO CREDITS

The author and publisher gratefully acknowledge the owners or custodians of the images contained in this book and permission to reproduce them in this book.

If no other designation is given for multiple images on a page, they all belong to the same source.

Martin's Photo Shop images are listed as **Martin**. These files are accessible at visions.indstate.edu and located in the Archives, Cunningham Library, Indiana State University, Terre Haute, Indiana.

Images in the **Vision and Voices** collection not contained in the Martin's Photo Shop are identified with a **V**.

Images provided by **Indiana State University Archives** are noted as **AR** and can be found at Archives-Historical-Photos-fro/Archive-images.

All other images, unless noted, are accessible from **University Marketing,** Indiana State University, Terre Haute, Indiana and will contain only the page number and the letters **UM**. (Principle photographer Tony Campbell)

Images are listed by chapter and page.

Cover
Left AR; right UM

Table of Contents
p. 1 UM

Foreword
p. 3 UM

The Beginning
p. 8a V; pp. 8cd-9 AR

Chapter 1 Jones
p. 13 UM; pp. 16-17 ARf

Chapter 2 Brown
p. 21 UM

Chapter 3 Parsons
p. 26 AR; p. 27a UM; p. 27b AR; p. 28 AR; p. 30 Martin; p. 31 AR; p. 32 Sycamore 1970, page 11 AR; p. 33 V; p. 34bc Martin; p. 34d AR; pp. 35-36 V; pp. 38-42 UM; p. 43 Martin

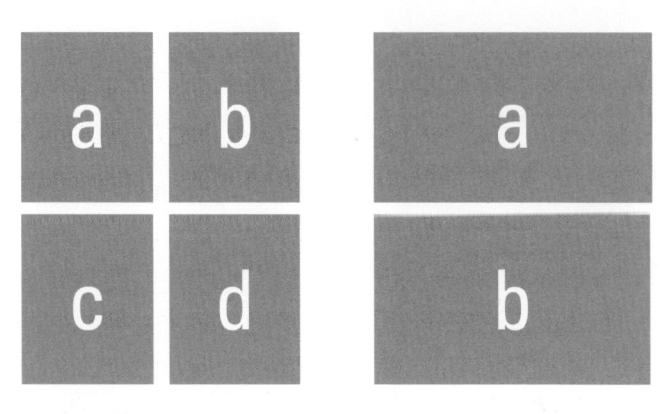

a	b	a
c	d	b

Chapter 4 Hines
p. 48 Martin; p. 49 UM; pp. 52-55 Martin; p. 56 UM; p. 57a, UM; pp. 57b-59 Martin; pp. 60-66 UM

Chapter 5 Tirey
p. 70 (January 1, 1934) V; (September 8, 1934) UM; (March 15-17, 1940) V; (December 7, 1941) Everett Historical/Shutterstock.com; p. 71a UM; p. 71 (May 7, 1945) https://commons.wikimedia.org.wiki/File:News._V.E._Day_BAnQ_P48S1012270.jpg; (June 13,1948) Martin; (February 19, 1950) V (Sycamore, 1950, p. 8); (April 7, 1953) Martin; p. 73 Martin; p. 74 UM; p. 75a Martin; p. 75b V (Sycamore, 1972, p. 153); pp. 76-80 UM; p. 81ab Martin, c AR; p. 82a Martin; p. 82b UM; p. 83 UM; p. 84abd Martin; p. 84c UM; pp. 85-86 Martin; pp. 87- 88 UM

Chapter 6 Holmstedt
p. 92 (November 9, 1956) Martin; (October 18, 1959) Martin; (April 25, 1961) Miller, Vrydagh, Miller; (July 1, 1961) UM; p. 93a UM (1961; 1962; 1963; January 18, 1963; 1964-65) Martin; (December 1, 1962; February 8, 1965) UM; p. 94 Martin; p. 97 Martin; p. 98 UM; p. 99a,b2 UM; p. 99b1 Martin; p. 100 UM; p. 101a UM; p. 101b1,b2 Martin; p. 102-103 UM; p. 104 Martin; p. 105a AR; p. 105b UM; p. 106-108 UM; p. 109a AR; p. 109b UM; p. 110a UM; p. 110b AR; p. 111 UM; p. 112a UM; p. 112b AR; pp. 113-117 UM; p. 118 AR; p. 119 UM; p. 120a AR; pp. 120cd U-121 UM; p. 122 AR; pp. 123-125 UM; p. 126 Martin; pp. 127-128 UM; pp. 130-134 UM

Chapter 7 Rankin
p. 142 Martin; p. 143a UM; (June 1970) UM; (January 15, 1971; December 17, 1971) Martin (April 30, 1975) Keith Tarrier/Shutterstock.com; p. 144 Martin; p. 145 AR; p. 147 UM; p. 148a Martin; p. 148b Ewing Miller Associates, Inc. AR; p. 148c UM; p. 149 UM; p. 150 AR; p. 151 UM; p. 152 Martin; pp. 154-155 UM; p. 156 Martin; pp. 157-159 UM; p. 160 Martin; p.

161ac UM; p. 161b Permanent Collection, Cunningham Library, Indiana State University; p. 162a AR; p. 162b1 Martin; p. 162b2-b3 UM; p. 163a UM; p. 163b Ewing Miller Associates, Inc.; p. 163d UM; p. 164ac UM; p. 164b Watercolor, Cordell Collection, Cunningham Memorial Library, Indiana State University; p. 165ab UM; p. 165c AR; p. 166AR;
p. 167-172 UM; p. 173a AR; p. 173b. Martin; p. 174 UM

Chapter 8 Landini

p. 178 (1976) Martin; (1979; June 30, 1979; 1984; 1985) UM; (July 23, 1984) AR; p. 179 UM; pp. 181; 183-187a UM; p. 187b AR; pp. 188-189b UM; p. 189c The Odle Group; pp. 190-191 UM; p. 192a UM; p. 192b Martin; pp. 193-194 UM; p. 195ab UM; p. 195c www.loc.gov/item/in0349, Historic American Building Survey, Dalton G. Shourds; p. 196 -197 UM; p. 198a UM; p. 198b AR; pp. 199-201a UM; p. 201b Walter Scholer and Associates, Inc.; p. 202 Martin;
pp. 203-205 UM

Chapter 9 Moore

p. 208 UM; p. 209 (April 19, 1996) AR; p. 209; 212-217 UM

Chapter 10 Benjamin

pp. 218-219; 224a UM; p. 224b AR; p. 225a UM; p. 225b AR; pp. 226-234a UM; p. 234b Hastings and Chivetta Architects, Inc.; pp. 235-237 UM

Chapter 11 Bradley

pp. 240-241, 244-246c UM; p. 246d RATIO Architects; p. 247 UM

Master Planning

p. 248 Vigo County Historical Society and Museum; p. 249 AR; p. 250a AR; p. 250b Facilities Management, Indiana State University; p. 250c Martin; p. 251 Martin; pp. 252-254 Ewing Miller Associates, Inc.;
p. 255 Sasaki Associates, Inc.; p. 258, 260-262 RATIO Architects

Timeline

p. 264, 266-267, 270-271, 273, 275, 277, 279, 281, 283-284 UM

Photo Credits